Comparative Programming Languages

Third Edition

Leslie B. Wilson and Robert G. Clark

University of Stirling

Revised and updated by
Robert G. Clark

Addison-Wesley

Harlow, England ● London ● New York ● Reading, Massachusetts ● San Francisco
Toronto ● Don Mills, Ontario ● Sydney ● Tokyo ● Singapore ● Hong Kong ● Seoul
Taipei ● Cape Town ● Madrid ● Mexico City ● Amsterdam ● Paris ● Milan

Pearson Education Limited

Edinburgh Gate

Harlow

Essex CM20 2JE

England

and Associated Companies throughout the world

Visit us on the World Wide Web at:

www.pearsoneduc.com

First published 1988
Second edition 1993
Third edition published 2001

ISBN 0 201 71012 9

British Library Cataloguing-in-Publication Data
A catalogue record for this book is available from the British Library

Library of Congress Cataloging-in-Publication Data

Wilson, Leslie B.
 Comparative programming languages / Leslie B. Wilson, Robert G. Clark.--3rd ed. /
rev. and updated by Robert G. Clark.
     p. cm
 Includes bibliographical references and index.
 ISBN 0-201-71012-9 (softcover)
  1. Programming languages (Electronic computers) I. Clark, Robert G. Clark. (Robert
George), 1944- II. Title.

QA76.7 .W55 2000
005.13--dc21

00-061075

10 9 8 7 6 5 4 3 2
06 05 04 03 02
Typeset by 56 in 10/12 pt Times
Printed in Great Britain by Henry Ling Limited, at the Dorset Press, Dorchester, DT1 1HD

Comparative Programming Languages

INTERNATIONAL COMPUTER SCIENCE SERIES

Consulting Editor: **A D McGettrick** *University of Strathclyde*

To Jenna

Contents

Preface to the third edition

Aims and objectives

In this book we consider the principal programming language concepts and show how they are dealt with in object-oriented languages such as Java and Delphi, in traditional procedural languages such as Pascal, C and Fortran, in hybrid object-oriented or object-based languages such as C++ and Ada 95, in functional languages such as ML and in logic languages like Prolog.

The programming language scene has always been bedevilled by protagonists pushing their favourite language. This often leads to a reluctance to examine rival languages and to a 'love me, love my language' approach. The lack of a scientific approach to languages tends to emphasise the differences between them, even when these are quite minor. Our approach is to find common ground between languages and to identify the underlying principles. Although the top-level organisation of a program written in an object-oriented language is different from that of one written in a procedural language, their underlying principles are the same. Similarly, although the approach of logic languages and functional languages is different from that of procedural and object-oriented languages, there are many areas of similarity, and seeing these helps us to understand the differences better.

This approach is important at the present time when there are major and important controversies as to which way we should be heading. To what extent is it worthwhile developing new versions of the old faithfuls as has happened with Fortran 90 and Object Oriented Cobol? Should we standardise instead on modern object-oriented languages like Java? It is certainly the case that procedural languages have proved themselves extremely resilient and have been given a new lease of life by the incorporation of object-oriented features as has happened with C++, Ada 95 and Object Pascal. What is going to be the future position of functional and logic languages? What effect will new hardware designs and the growth of the Internet have on programming languages? Although it is likely that many of these issues will not be resolved for many years, it is important that they are addressed.

The type of course taught in our department is, we think, fairly typical. It combines both theoretical and practical work and so there is a limit to the amount of material that can be covered. We feel that it is important to get the balance right. A purely theoretical approach usually leaves most computing students unable to fit the theory with their practical experience, while an approach that merely piles one language on top of the other leaves the student ignorant of the common threads in language design.

Changes from the second edition

There have been major developments in programming languages and their use since the second edition was published in 1993 and the changes reflect this. Revisions have been made throughout the book to bring material up to date and as a result of feedback from students at Stirling University. Although object orientation was a major paradigm in 1993, object-oriented languages had not achieved the central position that they enjoy today. Secondly, features to support Graphical User Interfaces (GUIs) have only recently become an integral part of language design. This has meant that topics such as event-driven programming have moved from being advanced to being taught in introductory courses.

Changes include:

- Java joins Pascal and C++ as one of the central languages used in the book,
- the object-oriented approach plays a central role,
- discussion of language support for graphical user interfaces and event-driven programs,
- discussion of scripting languages such as Perl,
- revised discussion of concurrency is centred on Ada 95 tasks and Java threads,
- discussion of Internet programming includes applets, CGI programs and CORBA,
- revised discussion on exceptions with exception handling in Eiffel being replaced by exception handling in Java,
- web site giving course support and executable program examples.

Our aim has been to keep the size of the book within bounds. Therefore, to offset the inclusion of new material, we have significantly reduced or removed coverage of languages which are no longer in widespread use.

The first two editions were written jointly by Leslie Wilson and Robert Clark while the changes to the third edition are solely the work of Robert Clark. He therefore takes full responsibility for any errors that may have been introduced!

Intended audience

Although this book is intended primarily as a student text for a comparative language or language concepts course, we hope that it will also be read by practising computer programmers. It is easy to be overwhelmed by the large number of available programming languages and we hope this book provides some guidance through the programming language jungle.

Students are likely to have been taught either an object-oriented or a procedural language as their first language with the proportion being taught an object-oriented language continuing to increase in the next few years. Hence, while the previous editions assumed proficiency in a structured procedural language such as Pascal, C or Ada, this edition is equally suited to students whose first language is an object-oriented language such as Java, C++ or Delphi and who do not have experience of a procedural language. We have not assumed any prior knowledge of logic or functional languages.

Structure and contents

Many books on comparative programming languages have separate chapters on each of the main languages covered. We have not adopted this approach, but have organised the book so that there are separate chapters on the main language concepts with examples and discussion of how they are dealt with in particular languages. The emphasis is on object-oriented and procedural languages and although a wide range of languages are covered, Java, Pascal, Ada, C and C++ are used in a central role.

Chapter 1   Introduction   This shows how programming languages fit into the software development process and the effect this has had on language design.

Chapter 2   Historical survey   This provides a historical survey so that the development of present languages can be traced.

Chapter 3   Types, values and declarations   This deals with variables, types and declarations. It is shown that many of the differences between languages can be explained in terms of the binding time of their attributes.

Chapter 4   Expressions and statements   This discusses expressions and statements with the emphasis on structured control statements.

Chapter 5   Program structure   This deals with the high-level organisation of object-oriented and procedural languages, including hybrids between the two.

Chapter 6   Procedures, functions and methods   This looks at procedures and methods with particular attention being paid to parameter-passing mechanisms.

Chapter 7   Structured data   This deals with arrays, records and dynamic data structures and how classes can be used to implement abstract data types.

Chapter 8   Inheritance and dynamic binding   The concepts of inheritance and dynamic binding are introduced and explained through examples in Java, C++ and Ada 95.

Chapter 9   Functional languages   This introduces functional languages and describes both the traditional LISP approach, together with its modern dialect Scheme, and the approach taken in newer languages such as FP and ML.

Chapter 10   Logic programming   This deals with logic programming and is mainly concerned with the language Prolog.

Chapter 11   Concurrency and networking   This describes how concurrency is handled in Ada 95 and Java and how these languages deal with inter-process communication and synchronisation. Applets, CGI scripts and distributed programming are then discussed.

Chapter 12   Syntax and semantics   This describes how the syntax of programming languages can be described formally in BNF and outlines two approaches, denotational and axiomatic semantics, for formally describing the semantics of programming language constructs.

Chapter 13   Input, output and GUIs   This describes both traditional text-based input and output and the now standard approach of graphical user interfaces.

Chapter 14   The future   This reviews the present situation and attempts to predict the direction in which language design is likely to go.

Appendix 1   Language summaries   This summarises the features of the principal languages dealt with in the text.

Appendix 2   Language texts   This gives an annotated bibliography for a wide range of programming languages.

Chapters 1–6 introduce the basic concepts and are best read in the given order, while Chapters 7–13 build on earlier material and, as they are largely self-contained, can be taken in any order. Each chapter contains a synopsis, outlining the major topics to be covered, a concise end-of-chapter summary, exercises and an annotated bibliography. Solutions to selected exercises are given at the end of the book.

Finally we should make clear what this book is not. It is not a language reference manual or a text on language implementation. We make no attempt to teach any particular language, but the annotated bibliography at the end of the book gives suggestions for further reading in all the languages covered. It is also not a book on the principles of program construction, although throughout the book we view each language construct from the point of view of whether or not it helps or hinders the construction of readable and reliable programs.

Acknowledgements

We would like to thank colleagues in the Computing Science Department at the University of Stirling, in particular Alan Hamilton, Simon Jones, Sam Nelson, Charles Rattray and Leslie Smith. They have acted as an ideal sounding board and their helpful criticisms of various chapter drafts have prevented us from straying too far into error.

In addition, we would like to thank Kate Brewin of Pearson Education for her help and encouragement.

Robert Clark
Stirling, June 2000

Introduction

This chapter looks at the different stages involved in the development of software and concludes that the main purpose of a programming language is to help in the construction of reliable software. It also discusses how designers have tried to include expressive power, simplicity and orthogonality in their languages whilst noting that pragmatic matters such as implementation and error detection have a significant influence. We also consider the distinction between a language and its development environment.

The basic low-level building blocks used in the construction of a language are considered; that is, the character set, the rules for identifiers and special symbols, and how comments, blanks and layout are handled.

1.1 The diversity of languages

Although over a thousand different programming languages have been designed by various research groups, international committees and computer companies, most of these languages have never been used outside the group which designed them while others, once popular, have been replaced by newer languages. Nevertheless, a large number of languages remain in current use and new languages continue to emerge. This situation can appear very confusing to students who have mastered one language, often Pascal, Delphi, C++ or Java, and perhaps have a reading knowledge of a couple of others. They might well ask: 'Does a lifetime of learning new languages await me?'

Fortunately, the situation is not as bleak as it appears because, although two languages may seem to be superficially very different, they often have many more similarities than differences. Individual languages are not usually built on separate principles; in fact, their differences are often due to quite minor variations in the same principle.

The aim of this book is to consider the principal programming language concepts and to show how they have been dealt with in various languages. We will see that by studying these features and principles we can better understand why languages have been designed in the way they have. Furthermore, when faced with a new language, we can identify where the language differs from those we already know and where it provides the same facilities disguised in a different syntax.

(1.2) The software development process

A computer is a tool that solves problems by means of programs (or **software**) written in a programming language. The development of software is a multi-stage process. First, it is necessary to determine what needs to be done. Unfortunately, initial informal user requirements are usually vague, inconsistent, ambiguous and incomplete. The purpose of **requirements analysis** is to understand and clarify the requirements and often involves resolving the conflicting views of different users.

The next stage is concerned with the production of a document, the **specification**, which defines as accurately as possible the problem to be solved; in other words, it determines what the system is to do. Requirements analysis and specification are the most difficult tasks in software development.

Having defined what the system is to achieve, we then **design** a solution and **implement** the design on a computer. It is only at the implementation stage that a programming language becomes directly involved.

The aim of **validation** and **verification** is to show that the implemented solution does what the users expect and satisfies the original specification. Although there has been a lot of theoretical work on verification, or **program proving**, it is usually still necessary to run the program with carefully chosen test data. But the problem with program testing is that it can only show the *presence* of errors, it can never prove their absence.

The final stage of software development, usually termed **maintenance**, covers two quite distinct activities:

1. The correction of errors that were missed at an earlier stage but have been detected after the program has been in active service.

2. Modification of the program to take account of additions or changes in the users' requirements.

Although a programming language is only explicitly introduced during the implementation stage, it has traditionally influenced the earlier stages of the process. Designers are, for example, often aware of the implementation language to be used and bias their designs to take account of the language's strong points.

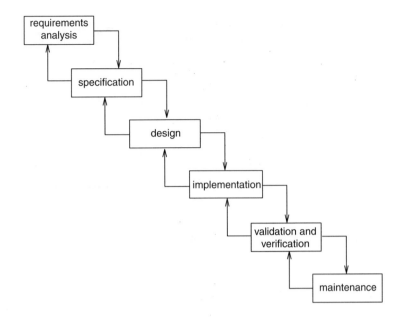

Figure 1.1 The waterfall model of software development.

Development models

It is important to realise that the software development process is iterative, not sequential. Therefore, knowledge gained at any one of the stages outlined can (and should) be used to give feedback to earlier stages. The traditional approach is to treat the different stages in the development process as being self-contained and this has led to the waterfall model of software development shown in Figure 1.1.

However, there has been increasing acceptance of the idea that an **incremental and iterative approach** is much more realistic. Central to this approach is the idea of **risk management**. Every time we make a decision, there is the possibility that we get it wrong. We therefore want to have continual feedback to show up possible errors because the longer an error remains undetected, the more expensive it will be to put right. This led to the spiral model shown in Figure 1.2 (Boehm, 1988). We start at the centre of the spiral and go repeatedly through the different stages as our system is built incrementally.

Many modern languages are object-oriented and this has led to the creation of object-oriented development methods. In other development methods, there is a clear distinction in the techniques used in specification, design and implementation. However, in object-oriented development, a problem can be understood and a solution designed and then implemented using the same framework of a set of communicating objects. The object-oriented development process is therefore well suited to an incremental and iterative approach. At any given stage, different objects can be described at different levels of abstraction. As the iterative development process continues, we incrementally add more detail to the object descriptions.

The need for a notation in which a specification or design can be written down

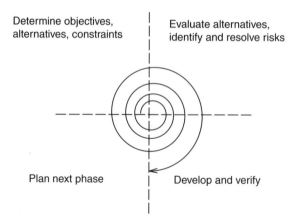

Determine objectives,
alternatives, constraints

Evaluate alternatives,
identify and resolve risks

Plan next phase

Develop and verify

Figure 1.2   Simplified Boehm spiral model.

has led to the development of both **specification** and **program design languages**. Such languages are at a higher level of abstraction and give fewer details than implementation languages. Many specification languages are mathematical in form and are amenable to proof techniques. However, languages of this type are outside the scope of this book and so we only look at what are conventionally considered to be implementation languages, although some **functional languages** have been used as executable specification languages.

Another approach is to use graphical notations to capture the requirements and represent designs. Examples of diagrams that occur in many different development methods are data flow diagrams, entity relationship diagrams, state transition diagrams and message sequence charts. A problem is that each development method can use its own set of diagram notations which, although they are representing much the same thing, can differ in detail. This situation is far from satisfactory as it can suggest differences in the development process that do not really exist. In object-oriented development, a standard notation called the Unified Modeling Language (UML) has been adopted so that different methods now use a common notation (Booch *et al.*, 1998). There are several different kinds of diagram in UML, but the single most important is the class diagram which shows the classes involved in an object system and their associations. An example class diagram is shown in Chapter 8.

The use of a systematic software development process has greatly influenced both language design and how languages are used. For example, Pascal was designed to support the ideas of **structured programming**. The problems of constructing large systems and of program maintenance led to the introduction of language features that allow large systems to be broken down into self-contained **modules**. Packages in Ada and classes in object-oriented languages satisfy that need. It is clear, therefore, that programming languages do not exist in a vacuum; rather, the design of modern languages is a direct response to the needs and problems of the software development process.

1.3 Language design

Most widely used programming languages are **imperative**; examples are Fortran, COBOL, C, C++, Pascal, Ada and Java. A program written in an imperative language achieves its effect by changing the value of variables or the attributes of objects by means of assignment statements. Until quite recently, most widely used imperative languages were **procedural**, that is their organisation was centred around the definition of procedures. Many procedural languages have now been extended to include **object-oriented** features (C by C++, Pascal by Delphi, Ada by Ada 95, COBOL by OOCOBOL, Basic by Visual Basic) while other new purely object-oriented languages such as Eiffel and Java have been designed. Object-oriented programs are organised as a set of objects which communicate with one another through small strictly defined interfaces.

Other approaches to language design include **functional languages** (such as pure Lisp and ML) and **logic languages** (such as Prolog). These alternative approaches are dealt with in Chapters 9 and 10 respectively.

The primary purpose of a programming language is to support the construction of reliable software. Hence, in most modern languages, type checking takes place at compile time, which is a considerable help in catching logical errors before the program is run. It is also important that a language is user friendly so that it is straightforward to design, write, read, test, run, document and modify programs written in that language.

To understand how these objectives may be achieved, the issues of language design can be divided into several broad categories:

- expressive power,
- simplicity and orthogonality,
- implementation,
- error detection and correction,
- correctness and standards.

Expressive power

A programming language with high expressive power enables solutions to be expressed in terms of the problem being solved rather than in terms of the computer on which the solution is to be implemented. Hence, the programmer can concentrate on problem solving. Such a language should provide a convenient notation to describe both algorithms and data structures in addition to supporting the ideas of structured programming and modularisation.

Another aspect of expressive power is the number of types provided together with their associated operations. Instead of providing a large number of built-in types, most modern languages provide facilities, such as the Ada package or the C++ and Java class, for defining new types, called **abstract data types**. Such languages can then provide a wide range of predefined types by means of standard libraries which the programmer can use to build new types for the problem in hand. When a language, together with its standard libraries, does not include a suitable range of types and operations, then the programmer generally has to provide these by declarations, thereby distracting the programmer's attention to the lower level aspects of solving the problem. Often, languages may have high expressive power in some areas, but not in others; for example, Ada has a range of numerical operations that give it expressive power for numerical work, but it is less effective in data processing applications.

Also included under the heading of expressive power is **readability**; that is, the ease with which someone familiar with the language can read and understand programs written by other people. Readability is considerably enhanced by a well-designed comment facility, and good layout and naming conventions. In practice, it should be possible to write programs that can act, to an extent, as their own documentation, thereby making maintenance and extension of the program much easier.

Simplicity and orthogonality

Simplicity implies that a language allows programs to be expressed concisely in a manner that is easily written, understood and read. This objective is often underrated by computer scientists, but is a high priority for non-professional programmers. The success, first of Basic and then of Visual Basic, is an eloquent commentary on the importance that users place on simplicity.

A simple language either avoids complexity or handles it well. Inherent in most simple languages is the avoidance of features that most human programmers find difficult. Simple languages should not allow alternative ways of implementing constructs nor should they produce surprising results from standard applications of their rules. An orthogonal language is one in which any combination of the basic language constructs is allowed and so there are few, if any, restrictions or special cases. Examples of orthogonal languages are Algol 68 and Smalltalk, which were both designed with the aim of keeping the number of basic concepts as small as possible. The idea was that the resulting language would be simple as it would only consist of combinations of features from a small set of basic concepts.

There can, however, be a clash between the ideas of orthogonality and simplicity. For example, Pascal, which is not orthogonal, is simpler to learn and use than Algol 68. Where a new special construct is introduced in Pascal, the same effect is achieved in Algol 68 by the combination of simpler existing constructs. As an example, Pascal separates the notion of the type of a parameter from whether it is a value or a variable parameter. (Details are given in Chapter 6.) Algol 68, on the other hand, combines both pieces of information within the parameter type. Although the Algol 68 approach is elegant and powerful, the more pragmatic approach (Wirth, 1975) taken in the design of Pascal has led to a more understandable language.

What is generally agreed is that the use of constructs should be **consistent**; that is, they should have a similar effect wherever they appear. This is an important design principle for any language although it is obviously of great importance in an orthogonal language which gets its expressive power from a large number of combinations of basic concepts. Whether simplicity or orthogonality is the goal, once the basic constructs are known, their combination should be predictable. This is sometimes called the **law of minimum surprise**. However, again the importance of simplicity should not be underestimated. In Java, the declaration int x; defines x to be an integer variable while the declaration SomeClass x; defines x to be a **reference** to a SomeClass object. We therefore have the same syntax meaning different things. Although this is inconsistent, it can be argued that inventing new syntax to make the distinction clear would have just complicated matters.

Implementation

Execution of a program written in an imperative language, such as Pascal, Ada or C++, normally takes place by translating (compiling) the source program into an equivalent machine code program. This machine code program is then executed. The ease with which a language can be translated and the efficiency of the resulting code can be major factors in a language's success. Large languages, for example, have an inherent disadvantage in this respect because the compiler will, almost inevitably, be large, slow and expensive.

An alternative to compiling a source program is to use an **interpreter**. An interpreter can directly execute a source program, but what is more common is for a source program to be translated into some intermediate form which is then executed by the interpreter. The interpreter can be said to implement a **virtual machine**. Executing a program under the control of an interpreter is much slower than running the equivalent machine code program, but does give much more flexibility at run time. The added flexibility is important in languages whose main purpose is symbolic manipulation rather than numerical calculation. Examples of such languages are the string processing language SNOBOL4, the object-oriented language Smalltalk, the functional language Lisp, the logic language Prolog and the scripting language Perl.

The use of an interpreter also supports an **interactive programming environment** in which programs may be developed incrementally. When developing a Lisp program, for example, a programmer can interact directly with the Lisp interpreter and type in the definition of functions followed by expressions which call these functions. The expressions are immediately executed and the results made available. This allows the early detection, and easy correction, of logical errors. Once the complete program has been developed, it can be compiled so that it will run faster.

Java is an imperative language and so we would expect that it would normally be compiled into machine code. However, that is not the case; Java programs are interpreted. An exciting use of Java is to animate web pages. A person can download a web page which contains a Java applet (a small application) and, using a Java-enabled web browser such as Netscape or Internet Explorer, can run the applet. To achieve this, it must be possible for a Java program to be translated on one computer and to run on a different kind of computer and the easiest way of doing this is to translate Java source programs into code for a **Java virtual machine**. Java-enabled browsers provide interpreters for the Java virtual machine.

Some language designers, notably Wirth the designer of Pascal and Modula-2, have made many of their design decisions on the basis of the ease with which a feature can be compiled and executed efficiently. One of the many advantages of having a close working relationship between the language design and language implementation teams is that the designers can obtain early feedback on constructs that are causing trouble. Often, features that are difficult to translate are also difficult for human programmers to understand. Algol 68 is a prime example of a language that had a lack of success due to the fact that it was designed by a committee who largely ignored implementation considerations, as they felt that such considerations would restrict the ability to produce a powerful language. In contrast, the implementation of C, C++, Pascal and Java went hand in hand with their design and the Ada design team was dominated by language implementers.

However, it is necessary to achieve a proper balance between the introduction of powerful new features and their ease of implementation. ISO Standard Pascal, for example, has features, such as procedures being able to accept array parameters of differing lengths, which were omitted from the original version of the language on the grounds that they were too expensive to implement.

Error detection and correction

It is important that programs are correct and satisfy their original specification. However, demonstrating that this is indeed the case is no easy matter. As most programmers still rely on program testing as a means of showing that a program is error free, a good language should assist in this task. It is therefore sensible for language designers to include features that help in error detection and to omit features that are difficult to check.

Ideally, errors should be found at compile time when they are easier to pinpoint and correct. The later an error is detected in the software development process, the more difficult it is to find and correct without destroying the program structure.

As an example of the importance of language design on error detection, consider the original Fortran method of type declarations where the initial letter of a variable name implicitly determines the type of the variable. Although this method is convenient and greatly reduces the number of declarations required, it is in fact inherently unsound since any misspelling of variable names is not detected at compile time and leads to logical errors.

Conversely, explicit type declarations have the following advantages. Firstly, they provide extra information that enables more checking to be carried out at compile time and, secondly, they act as part of the program documentation.

Correctness and standards

The most exacting requirement of correctness is proving that a program satisfies its original specification. With the major exception of purely functional languages, which are amenable to mathematical reasoning, such proofs of correctness have not, as yet, had a major influence on language design. However, the basic ideas of structured programming do support the notion of proving the correctness of a program, as it is clearly easier to reason about a program with high-level control structures than about one with unrestricted **goto** statements.

To prove that a program is correct, or to reason about the meaning of a program, it is necessary to have a rigorous definition of the meaning of each language construct. (Methods for defining the syntax and semantics of a language are discussed in Chapter 12.) However, although it is not difficult to provide a precise definition of the syntax of a language, it is very difficult, if not impossible, to produce a full semantic definition, and as far as most programmers are concerned it is unreadable anyway.

It is therefore vital in the early stages of a language's development to have an informal description that is understandable by programmers. As in many aspects of computer science, there needs to be a compromise between exactness and informality.

A programming language should also have an official standard definition to which all implementers adhere. Unfortunately, this seldom happens as implementers often omit features that are difficult to implement and add features that they feel will improve the language. As a result, program portability suffers. The exception to this is Ada. An Ada compiler must be validated using a specially constructed suite of test programs before it can be called an Ada compiler. It is interesting that one of the aims of these tests is to rule out supersets as well as subsets of the language. This is an excellent idea and it is hoped that it will become the norm.

1.4 Languages or systems?

An important feature of many modern languages is that they support network programming and the creation of graphical user interfaces (GUIs). These features are often provided through libraries and so we have the question of whether they are part of a language or part of its support environment. The problem is compounded by the fact that GUIs and networking are often highly dependent on the facilities provided by the operating system.

A major advantage of Java is that it provides support for GUIs and network programming in a way that is independent of any particular operating system. Java has an extensive set of standard libraries where the necessary facilities are defined in terms of the Java Virtual Machine. As all Java programs make heavy use of these libraries, they are regarded by Java programmers as an integral part of the language.

Languages such as Visual Basic and Delphi also provide these facilities through an extensive set of libraries, but differ from Java in that they are closely tied to a particular operating system, namely Microsoft Windows. This allows a close and efficient integration between the language and operating system facilities. However, it does do away with one of the major advantages of high-level languages which is that they are machine independent. It also raises the question of when are we talking about a new language and when are we talking about a new implementation of an existing language.

There are many different implementations of C++, each of which provides its own set of libraries for GUIs. It is therefore clear when we are talking about the C++ language and when we are talking about a particular implementation. However, the GUI and networking facilities of Visual Basic and Delphi form such a large part of the system used by their programmers that they can claim to be new languages although they do have Basic and Object Pascal respectively as their core. Moreover, Visual Basic and Delphi both provide extensive visual development environments. One view is therefore that they are not languages, but are system development environments. This lack of a clear distinction between a language and its development environment will continue to increase as support facilities become ever more sophisticated.

An important feature of programs that use graphical user interfaces is that they are **event driven**. They wait for some user event such as the click of a mouse over the representation of a button on the screen, handle that event and then wait for the next user event to occur. This leads to a very different program structure from that provided by traditional programming languages. Writing event driven programs is difficult, but is dealt with in languages such as Java, Visual Basic and Delphi by most of the work being done behind the scenes. This allows the programmer to work at a very high level of abstraction and not worry about implementation details. With earlier languages, event handling had to be explicitly programmed. This is therefore another example of where the distinction between a language and its supporting environment has become blurred.

1.5 The lexical elements

The basic building blocks used in writing programs in a particular language are often known as the **lexical elements**. This covers such items as the character set, the rules for identifiers and operators, the use of keywords or reserved words, how comments are written, and the manner in which blanks and layout are handled.

Character set

The character set can be thought of as containing the basic building blocks of a programming language – letters, digits and special characters such as arithmetic operators and punctuation symbols. Two different approaches were taken when deciding the character set to be used in early languages. One is to choose all the characters deemed necessary. This is the approach taken with APL and Algol 60, but it has the drawback that either special input/output equipment has to be used or changes have to be made to the published language when it is used on a computer.

The other approach is to use only the characters commonly available with current input and output devices. Hence, the character set of early versions of Fortran was restricted by the 64 characters available with punched cards while Pascal initially was constrained by the character set available with the CDC 6000 series computer on which it was first implemented.

Since the early 1970s, most input and output devices have supported internationally accepted character sets such as ASCII (American Standard Code for Information Interchange) and this has been reflected in the character sets of languages. The ASCII character set has 128 characters of which 95 are printable; the remaining characters are special control characters. The printable characters are the upper and lower case letters, digits, punctuation characters, arithmetic operators and three different sets of brackets (), [] and {}. Composite symbols are used to extend the range of symbols available. Commonly used examples are the relational operators <= and >= and the assignment operator := used in the Algol family of languages.

More recently, the **Unicode** character set has been created to give a much larger range of characters. Each Unicode character occupies 16 bits rather than the 8 used with ASCII characters. Java uses the **Unicode** character set.

Identifiers and reserved words

The character set is the collection from which the symbols making up the vocabulary of a programming language are formed. Clearly, a language needs conventions for grouping characters into words so that names (usually known as **identifiers** in computing) can be given to entities such as variables, constants, etc. (Naming conventions are discussed in Chapter 3.)

Some of the words in a programming language are given a special meaning. Examples of this are DO and GOTO in Fortran and **begin**, **end** and **for** in Pascal. Two methods are used for including such words in a language. The method adopted by Fortran is to allow such words to have their special well-defined meaning in certain contexts. The words are then called **keywords**. This method was also adopted by the designers of PL/I since it limited the number of special words that the programmer had to remember – the scientific programmer using PL/I is unlikely to know all the business-oriented keywords, while the business programmer is unlikely to know all the scientific keywords. However, the drawback of this method is that the reader of a program written in a language with keywords has the task of deciding whether a keyword is being used for its special meaning or is an occurrence of an ordinary identifier. Furthermore, when an error occurs due to the inadvertent use of an unknown keyword, it is not always clear when a word has its special meaning, without consulting all the declarations.

The alternative method, used initially by COBOL and adopted by most modern languages, is to restrict the use of such words to their special meaning. The words are then called **reserved words**. The advantage of the reserved word method is best seen in languages like Pascal and C++ where the number of such words is quite small. In COBOL, however, the number of reserved words is much larger – over 300 – and so the programmer has the task of remembering a large number of words that must not be used for such things as variables. As well as reserved words, languages often have **predefined identifiers**. These are ordinary identifiers that have been given an initial definition by the system, but which may be redefined by the programmer. Examples, in Pascal, are the predefined type Integer and the input and output procedures read and write. In languages such as Ada and Java, a large number of identifiers are defined in the standard libraries. Such identifiers can be redefined in programs.

In Algol 60 programs, reserved words are written in a different typeface, either underlined or bold face, depending on the situation. The drawback of this is that many input devices cannot cope with underlined words, so less attractive alternatives, such as writing reserved words in quotes, had to be used. In handwritten versions of programs in Pascal and Ada, for example, reserved words are often underlined so that they stand out while in books they are often printed in boldface. In the version presented to a compiler, however, they are typed in the same way as ordinary identifiers.

Comments

Almost all languages allow comments, thereby making the program more readily understood by the human reader. Such comments are, however, ignored by the compiler. In early languages such as Fortran, which has a fixed format of one statement per line, comments are terminated by the end of a line. In Fortran's case, the comment lines were started by a C in column 1. A similar method is used in other early languages such as COBOL and SNOBOL4.

Algol 60 uses a different method for comments: they begin with the reserved word **comment** and terminate with a semi-colon. However, the problem with this method is that programmers often fail to terminate comments correctly. Consequently, the compiler, interpreting the program exactly, incorporates the next declaration or statement into the comment. Errors caused in this way are difficult to find as the error message, if one is generated, is usually quite unrelated to the actual error.

Most later languages enclose comments in brackets. Pascal, for example, uses either (* and *) or { and } while C uses / * and * / . But this approach still leaves the problem of terminating a comment unresolved. Some compilers alleviate this problem by giving a warning if a statement separator – that is, a semi-colon – occurs within a comment. Ada, in contrast, commences a comment with two hyphens and ends it by the end of a line, so reverting to the methods of the earliest high-level languages. In C++ and Java, the programmer can either use C style comments or start a comment by / / and terminate it by the end of a line.

The problem of failing to properly terminate a comment is largely solved by integrated development environments (IDEs) which automatically colour-code different parts of the program. When a comment is in a different colour, it is obvious when it has not been properly terminated.

Spaces and line termination

Early programming languages varied considerably in the importance they attached to spaces. At one extreme, languages such as Algol 60 (and Fortran within columns 7 to 72 of a line) ignore spaces wherever they occur while, at the other extreme, SNOBOL4 uses spaces as separators and as the primitive operation of concatenating two strings. Most languages, however, use spaces as separators in a manner similar to that of natural language. Several spaces or new lines may also be used wherever a single space is allowed. Spaces in identifiers are normally forbidden, but to aid readability many languages, for example C++ and Ada, include the underscore character so identifiers like current_account and centre_of_gravity can be used. A recent trend is not to use the underscore, even when it is available, but to capitalise inner words as in: currentAccount and centreOfGravity.

The significance of the end of a line also varies according to the language. Early versions of Fortran and COBOL, because they were card oriented, adopted the convention that the end of a line terminated a statement. If the statement could not be contained within one line, a continuation character was required in the following line. Most recent high-level languages use the semi-colon either to separate (Pascal) or to terminate (Ada, C++, Java) statements. This method is often known as **free format** since it means that a new line can be started anywhere that a space may occur in a statement. Fortran 90 includes a free format option in which spaces are significant and in which columns 1 to 6 have no special significance.

Summary

1. Although there are many different programming languages in existence, languages do, in fact, have more similarities than they have differences.

2. The stages in software development are requirements analysis, specification, design, implementation, verification and maintenance. A programming language is not directly involved until the implementation stage.

3. The evolution of systematic software development methods has greatly influenced language design.

4. The primary purpose of a programming language is to support the construction of reliable software.

5. A programming language should be simple, have high expressive power and language constructs that are consistent – that is, they should have a similar effect wherever they appear.

6. It is important to have a proper balance between the introduction of powerful language features and their ease of implementation.

7. Languages should support the detection of as many errors as possible at compile time.

8. A language should have a single official definition to which all implementers adhere.

9. It is often difficult to distinguish between a language and its development environment.

10. The lexical elements of a language cover such items as the character set and the rules for identifiers and special symbols.

11. Fortran and PL/I have keywords while most other languages such as Pascal have reserved words.

Exercises

1.1 An orthogonal language is constructed by combining a small set of basic language constructs. It should therefore be simple to learn and use. Discuss whether that is in fact the case.

1.2 Smalltalk can be regarded as a purer object-oriented language than Java. Does that make it easier to write object-oriented programs in Smalltalk than it is in Java?

1.3 Describe the importance of readability in the creation of reliable software. What are the features of a language that enhance readability and what makes it more difficult?

1.4 How important is it that there is a single standard definition of a language?

1.5 What are the advantages and disadvantages of considering a library to be part of a language definition as opposed to it being considered part of a language implementation?

Bibliography

The approach taken in this book to focus on language concepts and show how these concepts are realised in different programming languages is similar to that adopted by Ghezzi and Jazayeri (1997) and Sebesta (1998). The book by Sethi (1996) also takes this approach, but is more theoretical.

The alternative approach of having separate chapters on the main programming languages has been adopted by MacLennan (1987) and Friedman (1991). Pratt and Zelkowitz (1996), on the other hand, has combined both approaches: the language features are discussed in the first part of the book while the second part is devoted to individual languages. The result is comprehensive, although it leads to a very large text. Both Pratt and MacLennan also contain a large amount of material on language implementation.

Boehm, B.W. (1988). 'A Spiral Model of Software Development and Enhancement'. *Computer*, **21**(5), 61–72.

Booch, G., Rumbaugh, J. and Jacobson, I. (1998). *The Unified Modeling Language User Guide*. Addison-Wesley.

Friedman, L.W. (1991). *Comparative Programming Languages*. Prentice-Hall.

Ghezzi, C. and Jazayeri, M. (1997). *Programming Language Concepts* (Third Edition). John Wiley & Sons.

MacLennan, B.J. (1987). *Principles of Programming Languages* (Second Edition). Holt, Rinehart and Winston.

Pratt, T.W. and Zelkowitz, M. (1996). *Programming Languages: Design and Implementation* (Third Edition). Prentice-Hall.

Sebesta, R. (1998). *Concepts of Programming Languages* (Fourth Edition). Addison-Wesley.

Sethi, R. (1996). *Programming Languages* (Second Edition). Addison-Wesley.

Wirth, N. (1975). 'On the Design of Programming Languages', *IFIP 74*, pp. 386–393, North-Holland.

Historical survey

There are two main reasons for studying the history of programming languages. Firstly, the languages available today are only explicable by examining how they grew up. One has to look at their development to understand why, for example, two of the major languages, Fortran and COBOL, are still in use 40 years after their first appearance. There is in fact a huge inertia in the programming field, which means that once a language has been successful, it is very difficult to supersede it by a newer language. The large investment in established systems ensures the continuing use of old languages.

The second reason for looking at the history of programming languages is to pinpoint some of the errors made in the past and so try to avoid repeating them. A prime example where this was not the case was the early development of microprocessor systems which paralleled that of the early computers in many respects. Unfortunately, many of the same mistakes were repeated because the software designers were unaware of the historical lessons.

This chapter starts its survey from the languages used with the early computers and traces their development to Ada 95, Prolog, C++, ML and Java. While every attempt has been made to be historically accurate, the main purpose of this survey is to give the flavour of programming language development and to try to recapture the feelings of programmers at the time when each new language arrived on the scene.

2.1 Early machines

The birth of programming languages is a matter for some conjecture. Some people might consider that Ada, Countess of Lovelace, was the first programmer because she worked with Charles Babbage on the Analytical Engine. However, such academic speculations are best left to the historians. Likewise, the early work on the machines and languages of the late 1940s is of little interest in the development of high-level programming languages.

The early languages, called **order codes** or **instruction codes**, were in fact very primitive, even in comparison with assemblers. They used numbers, not only for store locations and the special registers (called accumulators) of the central processing unit (CPU), but also for operation codes. Often, there were no mnemonics or floating point, and library routines, which were used for routine calculations and for input and output, were not called, but were inserted in the code. Also, loops, in which the instructions could be changed, were far from the modern **for** loop in ease of operation although their purpose was the same.

Although order codes with mnemonics were used on machines such as the EDSAC I, programming at this level was soon seen to be a considerable drawback in the advance of computers. Machine codes were both hard to learn and difficult to use, which meant that early programs were full of errors and the 'patch' – that is, actually changing the executable code – was the standard method of correction. However, the middle and late 1950s saw a surge in the attempt to improve programming languages on both sides of the Atlantic.

2.2 Fortran

The birth of Fortran

The big breakthrough in the early years was 'The IBM Mathematical FORmula TRANslating system', known then and subsequently as Fortran. This was by no means an isolated development, but depended very much on the previous attempts to raise the level of programming languages. The manual for Fortran I was released in 1956, but it was 1958 before successful compilers were running programs correctly. After this, Fortran took off in a manner that probably surprised even its most ardent advocates.

One of the principal designers of Fortran, Backus, has made it clear that the motivating factor behind the language was not the beauty of programming in a mathematical notation but the economics of programming at that time (Wexelblat, 1981). Programming and debugging costs exceeded running costs and the situation was worsening with the advent of faster computers. The only solution was to design a language for scientific computations that allowed the programmer to use mathematical notation. However, the designers of Fortran felt that this had to be done in a way that produced efficient object code, otherwise practising programmers would reject the language if they could produce a hand-coded version that ran much faster than the compiled Fortran program. Such worries have left their mark on Fortran and considerations of run-time efficiency played a major role in its design, as did the IBM 704 machine and its punched card input.

Since Fortran was designed primarily for scientific calculations, string handling facilities were almost non-existent and the only data structure was the array. Although the array was hedged about with limitations, it did represent a considerable step forward. Other Fortran features that were attractive to its new devotees were:

- Comments.
- Assignment statements that allowed mathematical expressions of some complexity on the 'right-hand' side.
- The simplicity of writing loops with the DO statement.
- Subroutines and functions: the idea of the subroutine and function was not new, but Fortran did improve on them by employing a symbolic notation close to mathematics.
- Formats for input and output: input and output conversions were notoriously difficult on early computers, but Fortran formatting took a lot of the pain away.
- Machine independence: a Fortran program could be run on different machines.

Considering the lack of experience of compiling in the late 1950s, the early Fortran compilers were remarkably good; but even so they were unable to achieve the aim of their designers, which was to produce code that was as efficient as hand-coded versions. Despite this, Fortran became enormously popular in a very short time, the main reasons for its success being:

- It made efficient use of programmers' time.
- It was easy to learn and opened the door to the computer for non-specialist programmers.
- It was supported by IBM, which soon became the most powerful firm in computing; in effect, Fortran and IBM rose together.
- When it was introduced, most applications and users were scientific, and Fortran had the right facilities for such users.
- It simplified several areas of computing in which programming was very tedious; notably, input and output.

A Fortran program

The following program finds the mean of a list of numbers and the number of values that are greater than the mean.

```
C FORTRAN PROGRAM TO FIND MEAN OF N NUMBERS AND
C NUMBER OF VALUES GREATER THAN THE MEAN
         DIMENSION A(99)
         REAL MEAN
         READ(1,5)N
    5    FORMAT(I2)
         READ(1,10)(A(I),I=1,N)
   10    FORMAT(6F10.5)
         SUM=0.0
         DO 15 I=1,N
   15    SUM=SUM+A(I)
         MEAN=SUM/FLOAT(N)
         NUMBER=0
         DO 20 I=1,N
         IF (A(I).LE. MEAN) GOTO 20
         NUMBER=NUMBER+1
   20    CONTINUE
         WRITE(2,25) MEAN,NUMBER
   25    FORMAT(8H MEAN = ,F10.5,5X,20H NUMBER OVER MEAN = ,I5)
         STOP
         END
```

Notes

1. The first two lines are comments.

2. In the third line, the array has to be declared and its size given; in this case 99 elements with subscripts from 1 to 99. (The Algol 60 program later in this section shows the use of an array with variable bounds.)

3. Most Fortran variables are declared implicitly by use. However, MEAN is declared explicitly as REAL because if it was declared implicitly, it would be an INTEGER variable, as its first letter is between I and N.

The development of Fortran

The success of Fortran was not without its problems, the principal one being that programmers were reluctant to use any other language. Thus, Fortran was used in circumstances for which it lacked the relevant language features – for example, for data processing applications and as an interactive language.

Another problem was that there was no standard for Fortran and so slightly different versions were used in the compilers. Hence, a program that ran successfully with one Fortran compiler would more than likely fail when used with a different compiler. The clear need for a standard was underlined by the development of Algol 60 with its more precise definition. Eventually, the American National Standards Institute (ANSI) developed a standard for Fortran in 1966 while Fortran 77 emerged in 1978 and Fortran 90 in 1991.

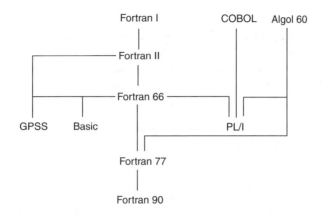

Figure 2.1 Development of Fortran.

Fortran 90 supports many new features: allocation of space for arrays on block entry, records, modules, pointers, etc., but to protect the huge investment in existing Fortran programs, all legal Fortran 77 programs are also legal in Fortran 90. This means that the language is a mixture of old and new features, although some old features are labelled as obsolescent with the intention that their use will wither away so that they can be removed from the next standard. The development of Fortran and associated languages is shown in Figure 2.1.

2.3 Algol

The period of the late 1950s was a very important one in the history of programming languages. Not only did it see the development of Fortran and COBOL but also a third major language – namely, Algol. No other language has had such a profound influence on programming language design and definition as that of Algol.

Algol emerged from a joint committee of European and American programming language experts that was set up with the aim of producing a common language (Wexelblat, 1981). Originally, this language was called IAL (International Algebraic Language) but later it became known as Algol (ALGOrithmic Language). The objectives of the language were stated as follows:

- It should be as close as possible to standard mathematical notation and be readable without too much additional explanation.
- It should be possible to use it for the description of computing processes in publications.
- It should be mechanically translatable into machine code.

The committee's first product, usually known as Algol 58, was never implemented but the criticisms raised did help in the development of a subsequent version, Algol 60. The 'Report on the Algorithmic Language ALGOL 60' (Naur *et al.*, 1960) was a major event in the history of programming languages and the 'Revised Report' (Naur *et al.*, 1963), published three years later, is a classic. It may seem surprising to make such a song and dance about a language that was never in widespread use in the United States. However, its influence has been greater than that of Fortran and no other language has added so much to programming language theory.

The major concepts introduced by Algol 60 were:

- Language definition: a formal language (BNF) was used to define the syntax for the first time, a concept that led naturally to syntax-directed compilers. The semantics, however, proved more difficult and the definitions in English did lead to some ambiguity.

- Algol 60 was structured: it was the original block-structured language and variables were not visible outside the block in which they were declared.

- Arrays could have variable bounds at compile time, although the bounds had to be fixed when the block, in which the array was declared, was entered at run time so that suitable storage could be allocated.

- Algol 60 contained several structured control statements. The **if** statement and **for** statement were considerable advances on similar constructs in Fortran although the Algol 60 control statements were simplified in later Algol-like languages.

- Algol 60 was the first language to introduce recursive procedures. However, there was some argument as to whether the original committee realised the full import of their proposals in this area. Originally, recursion was decried as 'academic' and of little practical utility. But this view was partly caused by the difficulties the early Algol 60 compilers had in implementing the concept. However, there is no doubt now that the ability to use recursion is a very important programming skill and with improved compilers it is not inefficient.

As already indicated, Algol 60 was intended as a reference and publication language as well as a language for writing programs to run on computers. This led to its use by, amongst others, the Association for Computing Machinery (ACM) to communicate algorithms between users. But despite its powerful and improved facilities, Algol 60 was unable to supersede Fortran as the main scientific language. Several reasons have been advanced for this, but it was probably a combination of factors that kept Fortran well ahead, namely:

- Since Algol 60 compilers came out approximately three years after Fortran, the latter was strongly entrenched and programmers were reluctant to change. This was the first (but not last) instance of a new language being unable to supersede an established competitor.

- Since Algol 60 had more features, it was harder to learn.

- Although IBM initially supported Algol 60, they eventually decided that its customers were happy with Fortran and so did not wish to change. The great success of IBM in the 1960s helped to boost Fortran.

- Fortran compilers were simpler and produced more efficient code than Algol 60 compilers.

● Algol 60 had no official input/output (I/O). It was decided to leave this to the individual manufacturers so that they could tailor it to their computers. Although this seemed a reasonable decision, if a semi-official standard I/O had been agreed, then many manufacturers would have used it and a *de facto* standard Algol 60 would have been formulated.

An Algol 60 program

The following Algol 60 program solves the problem of finding the mean of a list of numbers and how many numbers are greater than the mean.

```
begin
    comment this program finds the mean of n numbers
        and the number of values greater than the mean;
    integer n;
    read(n);
    begin
      real array a[1:n];
      integer i, number;
      real sum, mean;
      for i := 1 step 1 until n do
        read (a[i]);
      sum := 0.0;
      for i := 1 step 1 until n do
        sum := sum + a[i];
      mean := sum / n;
      number := 0;
      for i := 1 step 1 until n do
        if a[i] > mean then
          number := number + 1;
      write("MEAN = ", mean, "NUMBER OVER MEAN = ", number)
    end
end
```

Notes

1. Unlike Fortran, the array declarations in Algol 60 could have variable bounds, as the array a has in this program. Variable bounded arrays can only be declared in an inner block and the value of the variable bound must be known before the block is entered at run time.

2. There are no implicit declarations in Algol 60 – all variables must be declared.

Algol W and Algol 68

Algol has had a strong influence on many subsequent languages as is shown diagrammatically in Figure 2.2. The immediate successor to Algol 60 was Algol W (Wirth

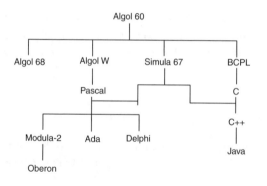

Figure 2.2 The main members of the Algol family.

and Hoare, 1966). In essence, this represented a tidying up of Algol 60 with several important new features. The most important changes and additions were:

- Records and references: they provided data structures other than arrays and allowed linked lists, trees and graphs.
- The **case** statement.
- Changes which separated the **for** and **while** statements and made the **for** statement more restricted and less prone to error.
- Procedure and function parameters could be called by value, result and value-result. The call-by-name method of parameter passing introduced by Algol 60 used the obvious mathematical approach of replacing a formal parameter by the corresponding actual parameter wherever it occurred. However, this method had been found to be inefficient and in some instances it led to unexpected results. Although it was still available in Algol W, it was discouraged.
- Long real and complex data types were introduced to enable double-length and complex arithmetic.
- The bits data type gave low-level processing ability.
- Some string facilities were included, but they were still very primitive.
- Assert statements were allowed and the assertions tested during a program run.

Algol W was indeed a worthy successor to Algol 60 and, although not widely available, it was well liked by its users.

The next Algol-like language was Algol 68, which was produced amid much controversy by the International Federation for Information Processing (IFIP) Algol working party in 1968. Its initial specification was so abstruse that there was some delay in its implementation and simple guides were produced before even partial acceptance of the language was achieved. Although Algol 68 had many virtues, these were rather lost in the controversy about its specification (Bergin and Gibson, 1996).

Consequently, the large claims made for Algol 68 were never achieved. The idea of it being a universal language and ideally suited for data processing applications may have had some validity, but this made little impact on practising programmers.

The better points of Algol 68 were:

- An economy of constructs: the idea was to produce a core language with a small number of powerful constructs. (Note that PL/I, which is discussed in Section 2.5, went the other way by trying to be a comprehensive language.)
- Orthogonality: this was a major design goal of Algol 68. Having determined how a feature worked in one situation, it could be expected to behave in a similar way in any other situation; that is, there were no interactions between constructs when they were combined.

Pascal

Pascal was developed by Niklaus Wirth in the late 1960s and early 1970s building on his earlier work with Algol W. His aims were to produce a language that could be efficiently implemented on most computers and be suitable for teaching programming as a logical and systematic discipline, thus encouraging well-structured and well-organised programs. Although Pascal is a direct descendant of Algol 60, there was a determined effort by Wirth to make his language efficient. He felt that this was the only way to challenge the strong grip Fortran had on programming, particularly in the United States. Thus, Pascal contains certain features for efficiency reasons.

The static array is probably the most controversial feature of Pascal. In most Algol-like languages, the size of an array does not have to be specified until a block is entered at run time. Although this allows for more flexible programming and a more efficient use of storage, it does usually slow down program execution. Pascal adopted the static array, as used in Fortran, where the size is determined at compile time. In addition, the passing of array parameters in procedures also used fixed sized arrays. This was an even more controversial decision because of the restrictions it imposed, particularly on those doing numerical calculations. However, this restriction was removed when the ISO Standard for Pascal was published in 1982 (ISO, 1982).

One of the positive aspects of Pascal is the inclusion of features that encourage well-written and well-structured programs. For example, although **goto** statements are included, they are a restricted and minor feature of the language. Data types are a prominent feature of Pascal and they can be built up from the primitive, unstructured types `Integer`, `Real`, `Boolean`, `Char` and enumeration types. The structured user-defined types include arrays, records, sets and files. In addition, pointer types may be used, usually in conjunction with records, to form linked lists or trees. Strings can be declared and manipulated in Pascal, but the rigid size of the string and the lack of suitable string operations make string handling clumsy.

Pascal became widely used in the late 1970s when many universities adopted it as their initial teaching language for computer science students and by the mid-1980s it had become the dominant teaching language. The reasons for this movement were the need for a language that provided a comprehensive set of data structures and which encouraged good programming style.

Many implementations of Pascal have added modules, leading to incompatible extensions to the language. As well as being a widely used language in its own right, Pascal has been very influential in the design of later programming languages. Wirth's next language was Modula, followed by Modula-2. Both were developed from Pascal and, as the names suggest, the main extension was modules. It also provided a foundation for the design of Ada while Delphi includes an object-oriented Pascal. We return to the topic of modules in Section 2.8.

2.4 Business data processing languages

In the early stages of their development, computers were thought of as instruments for carrying out scientific calculations. However, it was soon realised that computers manipulated symbols and that these symbols did not necessarily have to be in the form of numbers. This realisation led to some consideration of how the computer could be used to help solve the data processing problems inherent in large businesses. One of the major problems that existed in trying to develop a language for this purpose was the lack of a recognised notation – applications of this type were quite different from scientific calculations for which the language of mathematics had for years been the notational basis. One possible language that provided a basis on which to build a notation was the English language; however, on examination, it was found to have too many ambiguities and was unsuited in its natural form to the precision of a computer.

The first business programming language, started in about 1955, was FLOW-MATIC and this led on to the development of COBOL. FLOW-MATIC used English words for operations and data and the data designs were written independently of the manipulation routines. It was planned and implemented only on the UNIVAC 1.

COBOL

COBOL (COmmon Business Oriented Language) was yet another important language developed in the late 1950s. Its development was co-ordinated by a committee consisting mainly of representatives of computer manufacturers in the United States. Although the major influence on the design of COBOL was FLOW-MATIC, other earlier languages, notably Commercial Translator and AIMACO, also had some effect. COBOL was in fact a development from previous languages and ideas rather than a designed language. Its use has been widespread and for many years it was the single most-used programming language in the world. Undoubtedly, the policy of the US Department of Defense (DOD), which was strongly influenced by Grace Hopper, had a considerable effect on the success of COBOL. Apart from being one of the prime protagonists of the early meetings and committees when COBOL was introduced, the Department made it its policy to award contracts only where a COBOL compiler was available, and all computers purchased with Government funds had to have such a compiler. In fact, the DOD made COBOL a *de facto* standard long before 1968 when its standard definition was published.

Since COBOL is essentially a data processing language, it differs significantly from Fortran and Algol, which emerged at about the same time. It places considerable emphasis on data and file processing, while keeping language features necessary for calculations very simple. As the language statements have an English-like syntax, COBOL is verbose. This was a deliberate design feature, its intention being that managers as well as programmers would find the final programs readable. The verbosity does cause some experienced programmers anguish and attempts were made, via systems like Rapidwrite (Humby, 1964), to allow a shorthand version of COBOL to be written by the professional programmer, from which the compiler could produce full COBOL.

While COBOL was never intended as an innovative language – indeed, it has had very little influence on subsequent languages – it did introduce the basic idea of distinguishing between the description of the data, the physical environment in which the computing was to be done and the actual processes performed on the data. Thus, the logical description of the data of the problem could be described independently of the physical characteristics of the media on which it was stored and manipulated; that is, the description is machine independent without being too inefficient. This separation is an important feature of COBOL and represented a major advance in its time.

A COBOL program is divided into four parts:

1. The identification division, which provides commentary and program documentation.

2. The environment division, which contains machine-dependent program specifications. Thus, it specifies the connections between the COBOL program and the external data files.

3. The data division, which gives a logical description of the data.

4. The procedure division, which contains the algorithms necessary to solve the problem.

Not all of the design features of COBOL have proved successful. For example, few programmers consider that the English-like form of the COBOL statement makes the overall program easily comprehensible. The difficulties of readability was compounded by the lack of structured statements, although this has been rectified in later versions.

The development of COBOL

The development of COBOL for use in business data processing paralleled that of Fortran in the scientific community in many respects. However, the proliferation of different dialects of COBOL never happened to the extent that it did with Fortran due to its tightly controlled development. There has been an orderly maintenance and enhancement of the language, something that is not so necessary for a dynamic, new language but is necessary for a language that is intended for wide use in business data processing.

Although the tight control on COBOL has had some good effects – for example, making it effectively a universal language for data processing – it has had the drawback that the language hardly changed in the first 25 years of its active life. Those changes (for example, the 1974 and 1985 Standards) that have come about have been mainly to keep up with major equipment advances, but these have been relatively modest. However, the version of COBOL being developed in the late 1990s does make radical changes as it includes object-oriented features and garbage collection. Object-oriented COBOL is a superset of previous versions, whose programs can therefore run unchanged.

Fourth generation languages

Programming languages are sometimes classified by their generation. Machine codes formed the first generation, autocodes and symbolic assemblers the second generation, while high-level languages such as Fortran, COBOL and Pascal are often referred to as being of the third generation.

A feature that distinguishes third-generation languages from their predecessors is their independence from particular computer hardware. The aim of the fourth generation is to make languages much more problem oriented.

Fourth-generation languages (4GLs) are languages that were developed as a result of the dissatisfaction of business users with large conventional languages like COBOL. These users were often not professional programmers and wished to obtain quick results from data stored in the computer.

Report Program Generator (RPG) was probably the first 4GL and was produced in the 1960s in response to customer requests for a simple language for the generation of reports. The requests were usually from users of small IBM computers who found the COBOL compiler too large and Assembler too difficult to use. RPG has a fixed coding structure with formats for input, conditional switches, calculations and output.

The alternative approach to solving data processing problems is to use software systems that concentrate on a particular application. A large proportion of computer applications involve the use of spreadsheets or databases. Users of these applications typically regard themselves as interacting with a system or package rather using a programming language. However, several authors have looked at how spreadsheets can be used as general-purpose programming languages and the interested reader is referred to a paper by Casimir (1992) which includes an extensive bibliography.

Database systems virtually all use SQL (Structured Query Language) as their underlying language although that may be hidden from their users by a user-friendly graphical user interface. Languages like Java and Delphi include library classes that support calls to SQL commands so that these languages can be used to access databases, including remote access over the Internet.

(2.5) General or multipurpose languages

In the late 1950s and early 1960s, language designers started working on the integration of the data processing ideas which had resulted in COBOL with the principles underlying scientific languages such as Algol and Fortran. The first multipurpose language was JOVIAL (Jules Own Version of the International Algebraic Language), which was developed at System Development Corporation (SDC). The major influence on its design was IAL, i.e. Algol 58. As the language was developed to program a very large real-time system called SAGE, which had previously been written in machine code, the major objective in developing JOVIAL was to produce a language for programming large complex systems. In effect, JOVIAL combined the ability of doing numerical scientific computations with non-trivial data handling, manipulation and storage as well as adequate input/output facilities.

PL/I

In the early 1960s, two categories of programmer were fairly clearly distinguished. On the one hand, there was the scientific programmer, usually using Fortran, whose needs were floating-point arithmetic, arrays, procedures and fast computation, usually via batch job processing. On the other hand, there was the commercial user who merely required decimal arithmetic, but who also required fast and asynchronous input/output, string handling facilities and efficient searching and sorting routines. However, there was also a growing band of special-purpose users who had diverse requirements, such as efficient real-time working, string pattern matching facilities, low-level systems programming and list processing.

IBM was very much in the forefront of progress at this time and saw the opportunity in providing a computer system suitable for a wide range of users. The computer that emerged was the IBM 360. Together with the new hardware, a new programming language was to be developed. It was originally called NPL, but that acronym was later dropped in favour of PL/I (Programming Language I) because of confusion with the National Physical Laboratory at Teddington, UK.

The new programming language was originally designed by a committee of IBM and their users who solicited views from a wide range of people as well as studying the major current languages Fortran, Algol, COBOL and JOVIAL. The guiding principles of the designers were as follows:

- programmers' time is an important asset and should not be wasted,
- there is a unity in programming which the current division between scientific and commercial languages did not reflect.

The designers hoped, therefore, to produce a language that was comprehensive, easy to learn, teach and use, and capable of extension and subsetting. There were to be as few machine dependencies as possible while allowing the programmer to have full access to machine and operating system facilities without resorting to assembly language coding.

To accomplish all these design criteria, a large language was obviously going to be required. However, the designers felt that the programmers need not know all the features of the language to be able to use it efficiently. The result was the crucial and controversial idea at the heart of PL/I – namely, default. Every attribute of a variable, every option and every specification had a default interpretation and this was set to be the one most likely to be required by a programmer who does not know that alternatives exist.

PL/I combined ideas from Fortran, Algol and COBOL. From Fortran, came the parameter passing mechanisms, independently compiled subprograms, formatted input/output and COMMON blocks; from Algol, block structure and structured statements; from COBOL, record input/output, PICTURE type declarations and heterogeneous data structures. There were, however, ideas culled from elsewhere; namely, list-processing concepts, control structures and methods for storage management. One new feature was exception handling by means of ON-conditions.

Before PL/I, language designers had either opted for run-time efficiency at the expense of flexibility (as was done, for example, in Fortran and COBOL) or else had allowed flexibility at the expense of run-time inefficiency (for example, SNOBOL and

Lisp). PL/I, in contrast, attempted to have both run-time efficiency and flexibility, but the penalty it paid was language complexity. It did, by its existence, highlight the problems in trying to design a general-purpose language that tries to satisfy all programmers. Nevertheless, it represents one extreme in design philosophy; that is, providing features for all applications within a fixed framework – what might be called a 'complete' language.

An alternative strategy to PL/I, represented by Algol 68, was to have a small core of language features that could be combined to form more complex structures. The argument of core versus complete languages was much debated in the late 1960s and early 1970s but no worthwhile conclusions were reached. Object-oriented languages, which can have a small core coupled with the ability to extend existing and to define new types, can claim to provide the answer to this problem.

A PL/I program

Here is a PL/I solution to the problem of finding the mean of a list of numbers and the number of values that are greater than the mean:

```
EXAMPLE : PROCEDURE OPTIONS (MAIN);
   /* Program to find the mean of n numbers and the number
      of values greater than the mean */
   GET LIST (N);
   IF N > 0 THEN BEGIN;
     DECLARE MEAN, A(N) DECIMAL FLOAT,
       SUM DEC FLOAT INITIAL(0), NUMBER FIXED INITIAL (0);
     GET LIST (A);
     DO I = 1 TO N;
       SUM = SUM + A(I);
     END;
     MEAN = SUM/N;
     DO I = 1 TO N;
       IF A(I) > MEAN THEN
         NUMBER = NUMBER + 1;
     END;
     PUT LIST ('MEAN=', MEAN, 'NUMBER GREATER THAN MEAN=', NUMBER);
END EXAMPLE;
```

Notes

1. PL/I allows both explicit and implicit declarations which can include initialisation as in the case of SUM and NUMBER above.

2. It allows operations with entire arrays like GET LIST (A).

3. The final END can be used to terminate any inner blocks as well as the outermost block.

The future of general-purpose languages

PL/I suffered from considerable teething problems and, indeed, without the massive backing of IBM, it would probably have died an early death. IBM's support kept it alive but even they could not force users to accept it. At one stage, IBM tried to replace Fortran and COBOL by PL/I, making it the universal language. However, customer resistance was too strong and many people threatened to take their business elsewhere if IBM would not provide Fortran and COBOL compilers. Hence, IBM, being a sound commercial organisation, capitulated. So PL/I had to exist and justify itself in competition with Fortran and COBOL.

The size of PL/I produced large compilers and hence slow compile times, particularly with small machines where the overlaying of code for the compiler was necessary. The availability of larger computer stores and the production of optimising compilers did help to alleviate these problems but, even so, PL/I never replaced either Fortran or COBOL, never mind both. The search for a universal language did not stop with PL/I, although its lack of success considerably dented the hopes of designers.

2.6 Developing programs interactively

Early computers only ran one program at a time, but as computers developed and became more complex, operating systems were designed to use the available facilities – high speed store, backing store, input/output devices – more efficiently. For example, the slowness of the input/output operations in comparison with the speed of the central processor led to **time sharing**, with many remote stations sharing the time of the central computer. Eventually, the remote terminal became the normal tool of the programmer. Changes such as these started in the early 1960s and gradually gathered momentum until by the mid-1970s it was commonplace.

Although programming languages began to adapt to these changing circumstances, the provisions varied widely. Most language compilers are available to programmers at their terminals or workstations in more or less the same way as that for batch processing. Programmers put their programs into a file and then run the appropriate language compiler using the file as the source program. Errors, if there are any, are output to the terminal and, if necessary, placed in a file for reference. The programmer can then modify the original file and re-run the compiler. That is still how programs in most current languages are developed.

Some languages, for example functional and logic languages, are designed so that their programs are normally developed interactively. There have also been attempts to provide procedural programmers with facilities for developing programs interactively. JOSS (Johnniac Open Shop System), developed in the early 1960s at the RAND Corporation, was probably the first interactive language. It demonstrated the value of on-line access to a computer and provided simple calculating facilities, a feature that was particularly useful to non-specialist engineers. QUIKTRAN, which emerged a little later, was the result of an attempt to adapt an existing language, Fortran, for use on a remote terminal: features of Fortran that were unsuitable for an interactive environment were omitted while a number of features that facilitated on-line debugging were added. QUIKTRAN was kept compatible with Fortran so that programs developed and debugged on a terminal could also use the regular Fortran compiler in batch mode.

However, it is the interactive language Basic that has had most impact on programming.

Basic

Basic (Beginner's All Purpose Symbolic Instruction Code) was developed at Dartmouth College by Kemeny and Kurtz in the mid-1960s. Their intention was to produce a language that was very simple for students to learn and one that was easy to translate. The idea was that students could be merely casual users or go on from Basic to more sophisticated and powerful languages, and that a casual programmer who has done nothing for six months can still remember how to program in Basic (JOSS also claims this benefit). As someone described it, it is like learning to ride a bicycle or swim: once learned never forgotten. For many programmers, Basic was like a return to the early autocodes: it could be learnt very quickly and programs written after one or two day's practice. However, it was not without its problems, particularly with large programs.

Like Fortran a decade earlier, the success of Basic surprised its inventors. However, this success was, no doubt, due mainly to the need for a simple high-level language for the new microcomputers of the mid-1970s, and Basic was available, well known and certainly simple. It caught on in a big way.

In addition to the normal statements of a traditional programming language, Basic has a few simple user commands which represent the interactive part of the language. The NEW command is used to create a Basic program, which may be listed by the LIST command, executed by the RUN command and saved by the SAVE command. Any previously saved program can be retrieved for further use by the OLD command. Basic is therefore not just a language, but incorporates sufficient operating system commands to make it complete in itself.

A Basic program

The solution to the problem of finding the mean and the number of values greater than the mean is given here in Basic for comparison:

```
10   REM THIS IS A BASIC PROGRAM FOR FINDING THE MEAN
20   DIM A(99)
30   INPUT N
40   FOR I = 1 TO N
50   INPUT A(I)
60   LET S = S + A(I)
70   NEXT I
80   LET M = S/N
90   LET K = 0
100  FOR I = 1 TO N
110  IF A(I) < M THEN 130
120  LET K = K + 1
```

```
130 NEXT I
140 PRINT "MEAN IS", MEAN
150 PRINT "NUMBER GREATER THAN MEAN IS", K
160 STOP
170 END
```

Note

1. Variables cannot be declared, are single letters and automatically initialise to zero. The variable S does not therefore have to be given an initial value.

Basic continues to be widely used and many dialects have been developed, most of which add more structure to the language. An object-oriented extension to Basic is the underlying language of Visual Basic which is widely used in the production of applications requiring graphical user interfaces on Microsoft Windows systems.

APL

APL (A Programming Language) was originally defined by Iverson as a mathematical language for the concise description of numerical algorithms. In its original form, it contained a large number of operators; in addition to the standard there were exotic ones for operating on arrays. However, when the language was eventually implemented on a computer, several operators were omitted, but it still remained in its programming language form a remarkably 'rich' language.

APL has a large alphabet (52 letters, 10 digits and 52 other characters) and the following unusual characteristics:

- The primitive objects are arrays (lists, tables, or matrices).
- It is an operator-driven language. Although branching operations are possible, they are little used in practice and the power of the language mainly comes from its array operators.
- There is no operator precedence: all statements are parsed from right to left.

APL generally requires a programming technique very different from that used with traditional scientific languages. Indeed, many programmers find the ability to program in a traditional language is more of a hindrance than a help when using APL. To be successful, a programmer needs to envisage what effect different operators, either on their own or in conjunction with other operators, have on arrays. Programs often contain, therefore, a succession of such operators. The designer Iverson recommended beginners to 'play' with the language to get a feel for the effect of the operators, both on their own and in conjunction.

Although there has been a lot of controversy about APL, it nevertheless seems to attract devotees who consider it the only language for the programmer. It has also been suggested that it brings computing and mathematics closer together.

(2.7) Special-purpose languages

Special-purpose, or domain-specific, languages provide two main advantages over general-purpose languages. They can increase productivity because of their higher level of abstraction and they should be attractive to people expert in the application area as they allow them to express their ideas in a notation with which they are familiar. There are many hundreds of application areas and this section only looks at languages that are important either in their own right or because of their influence on the development of other programming languages. Other application areas are discussed by Wile and Ramming (1999).

String manipulation languages

The first effective string manipulation language was COMIT, which provided a means of searching a string pattern and performing transformations when that pattern was found. COMIT was developed at the Massachusetts Institute of Technology (MIT) in the period 1957–61. A more widely used and influential string manipulation language was SNOBOL, which was developed at Bell Laboratories several years after COMIT. The early versions of SNOBOL had several teething troubles and when discussing the language, it is usually SNOBOL4, which came out in 1967, that is considered as the definitive version. These early string manipulation languages were used in areas such as symbolic mathematics, text preparation, and natural language applications.

In SNOBOL4, the basic element is the character string. Although there are operations for joining and separating these character strings, the most fundamental operation in SNOBOL4 is the pattern match. This operation examines a string to see if it possesses a particular substring or other property. If a match is found, then various possibilities, such as replacement, can take place.

There are two types of data structure: ARRAY and TABLE. ARRAY is a collection of data items that need not be of uniform type. The items are indexed by numeric subscripts in the normal way. TABLE, on the other hand, is an associative array with each element indexed by a unique associative value that is not necessarily an integer; for example, it could be a string such as COLOUR ['RED'].

Although SNOBOL4 has had little influence on the major general-purpose languages, whose string handling facilities fall far short of those provided by SNOBOL, the ideas embedded in SNOBOL did have an impact on the designers of text editors. It should be remembered that the more sophisticated operations in SNOBOL, such as pattern matching with replacement, can extend the length of the original string, but that to do this satisfactorily requires dynamic storage allocation.

The successor to SNOBOL4 is Icon whose development started in the late 1970s. Icon looks much more like a conventional imperative language such as C than did SNOBOL4. However, while values in Icon have types, variables do not and can be assigned values of any type. Strings can change in length and most string processing is done using a large number of built-in operations.

A distinctive feature of Icon is that it contains generators and has a goal-directed expression evaluation mechanism. Examples of generators are the expression 1 to 10, which generates the first ten integers, and !s which, when s is a string, generates all the characters in the string and, when s is a structure, generates all the elements in the structure.

List-processing languages

In the early scientific languages (Fortran and Algol), the only data structure was the array. All of its elements were of the same type and, in the case of Fortran, it was of fixed size. Although COBOL had a data structure that allowed elements of different types, in none of these early languages was there scope for altering the basic structure of the array. This is in essence what list-processing accomplishes, usually by having an element divided into an information part and a pointer part. The pointer part can, in the case of a linked list, reference the next element in the list, but in tree structures there are usually at least two pointers. In general, the linkage can be as complex as required by the problem although in languages such as Lisp the pointers are implicit.

The early list-processing languages were developed to show the value of such processing in the programming environment. The first such language was IPL-V, which was developed at the Carnegie Institute of Technology in the period 1957–61. IPL-V was really an assembly level set of commands for doing list processing on a hypothetical machine – the commands were interpreted. The significance of IPL-V was to define the concept of a list and to show how it could be implemented, albeit very crudely. It was used mainly by those programming artificial intelligence problems and it pioneered many of the fundamental concepts of list processing – in particular, the idea of a **free space list** from which storage space for new elements of the list could be obtained and to which storage space could be returned when no longer required.

The other early list-processing language, Lisp, has had a more lasting effect on programming language design. It was developed by John McCarthy at MIT in the late 1950s and he and his co-workers produced a workable language in the early 1960s.

The principal features of Lisp are as follows:

- It performs computations with symbolic expressions rather than numbers. This arose mainly because the designers were particularly interested in applying computing to artificial intelligence problems (game playing, theorem proving, natural language processing).
- It represents symbolic expressions and other information in the form of list structures in computer memory – this idea originated from IPL.
- It uses a small set of constructor and selector operations to create and extract information from lists. These operations are expressed as functions and use the mathematical idea of the composition of functions as a means of constructing more complex functions.
- Control is recursive rather than iterative.
- Data and programs are equivalent forms. Thus, programs can be modified as data and data structures executed as programs.

In addition to these features, Lisp was probably the first language to implement storage management by garbage collection. Lisp as implemented on a computer is somewhat different from the 'pure' Lisp of the original definitions. It does, however, come close to being a **functional language** (as pure Lisp is). A functional language has as its fundamental operation the evaluation of expressions. This is in contrast to the majority of languages (Fortran, Pascal, C++, Java), known as **imperative languages**, which use a sequence of commands to carry out the desired operations. Interest in functional languages increased significantly during the 1980s and their recent development is discussed in Section 2.9.

Lisp has survived as a language despite the death of most list-processing languages and there are several reasons for this. It is an elegant mathematical system, with a simple basic functional structure capable of expressing the ideas of the Lambda calculus. These features, together with the fact that Lisp systems allow programs to be developed interactively, make Lisp well suited to artificial intelligence applications. Finally, the survival of Lisp has been helped by the development of modern dialects such as Scheme, and an agreement on a standard version of the language known as Common Lisp.

The early 1960s saw a rash of list-processing languages: for example, L6, IPL, SLIP, WISP. However, their day was soon over as the general-purpose languages (Algol W, Algol 68, PL/I and Pascal) started to include list processing within the language.

Simulation languages

The simulation of discrete systems was one of the first problems that computers were used to solve. These systems are modelled by a series of state changes that often occur in parallel. Complex interactions could arise between the elements of the system as they compete for restricted system resources. The simulation technique itself follows the system elements through their changes of state gathering quantitative information. This information is then used to predict the properties of the system under hypothetical situations. For example, simulation of a traffic system can predict how the proposed model will perform as traffic densities increase and hopefully show where bottlenecks could occur.

The earliest simulation language to be widely used was GPSS (General-Purpose Simulation System). Although it was first described in 1961, it was somewhat later before the system was available to programmers. In GPSS, the system being simulated is described by a block diagram in which the blocks represent the activities and the lines joining the blocks indicate the logical sequence in which the activities can be executed. When there is a choice of activities, this is represented by several lines leaving a block and the conditions under which this choice is made is stated in the block.

GPSS has often been criticised for the slow execution time of its programs. While not denying the slow run time, which is due mainly to the use of interpretative programming to implement the block diagram, the designers point out that the ease of using GPSS means that the overall time for developing the model and obtaining the final results is shorter than that in many other languages.

In Europe in the early 1960s a group led by Ole-Johan Dahl and Kristan Nygaard at the Norwegian Computer Centre were also designing a simulation language which eventually became known as Simula 67, although this was not the first working version of the language. It was designed for system description and simulation; a system in this case being a collection of independent objects with a common objective. Systems were simulated by examining the life cycle of the elements of the system.

Simula was based on Algol 60 with one very important addition – the class concept. It is possible to declare a class, generate objects of that class, name these objects and form a hierarchical structure of class declarations. Although this concept was only introduced to describe the life cycles of the elements in the discrete simulation, later it was recognised as a general programming tool ideal for describing and designing programs in an abstract way. The basic idea was that the data (or data structure) and the operations performed on it belonged together, and this forms the basis for object-oriented programming and for the implementation of abstract data types.

When viewed objectively, Simula is more like a general-purpose language than a special-purpose simulation language. Indeed, the simulation is usually done by using two supplied classes SIMSET and SIMULATION. It has proved to be particularly useful in concurrent programming. Classes in Simula are based on procedure declarations and the block structure of Algol 60, but free the latter concept from its inherently nested structure by allowing several block instances to co-exist.

The impact of Simula on the design of programming languages is large as it is the original object-oriented language. The class concept has been taken over and used in many later languages, such as C++, Ada, Smalltalk, Eiffel and Java.

Scripting languages

A common task in programming is the need either to analyse a large amount of textual information or to convert it from one format to another. Central to such a task is the ability to perform pattern matching on strings of characters. Often, such a task can be programmed in only a few lines in a language with suitable pattern matching facilities, while it takes considerable programming effort in a traditional language like C. Special pattern matching languages such as *awk* have been developed for this purpose. A more recent language is Perl which combines the power of *awk* with a more conventional syntax based on C.

Both Perl and *awk* were developed for the Unix operating system, but Perl is now widely available on other platforms. Perl has grown into a large language with functions and modules and the ability to support object-oriented programming. A major use of scripting languages like Perl is with the World Wide Web. Often, a Web client and server need to communicate with each other and this is done through what is known as the Common Gateway Interface (CGI). Perl is one of the most popular languages for writing CGI programs. Other scripting languages include Python, Tcl and JavaScript.

Variables in Perl do not have a type, but are classified as scalar (numbers and strings), array or hash and have the prefix $, @ and % respectively. Hash variables are associative arrays and we can write:

```
%month = ("April" => 30, "May" => 31, "June" => 30);
```

To access the value of an element we write $month{"May"} which gives us the scalar value 31. Arrays can be extended and so we can add elements by writing for example:

```
$month{"July"} = 31;
```

Note that we use the prefix $ as each element of %month is a scalar. There are extensive pattern matching facilities which use a notation that will be familiar to those used to Unix editors and utilities. For example, if $st has the value "Hi, there", the statement:

```
$st =~ s/i, /ello/;
```

will replace the string "i, " by "ello" and so $st will now have the value "Hello there". The subsequent statement:

```
$st =~ tr/a − m/A − M/;
```

will transform each lower case character in the range a to m into its upper case counterpart. Hence, $st will now have the value "HELLo tHErE".

Scripting languages are for getting things done quickly and simply. In many ways, they are 'glue languages' used to facilitate communication between programs written in other languages.

2.8 Systems programming languages

In the 1960s there was considerable resistance to the use of a high-level language on the part of programmers who were writing systems programs (such as compilers and operating systems). They argued that the needs of efficiency dictated the use of assembly languages. Gradually, systems programmers moved away (often reluctantly) from low-level programming to high-level languages such as PL/I. However, they still tended to retreat back into low-level code for the 'vital' parts of the system because, basically, the general-purpose languages did not contain the low-level facilities required in systems work. What was really needed was a specialist systems programming language, but unfortunately there seemed to be no agreement on what such a language should contain. Hence, the result was a proliferation of such languages – it almost seemed that you could not be considered an advanced systems programming group if you did not have your own language.

Systems languages is rather a broad term, covering a wide range of applications such as operating systems and real-time systems. Such languages should have facilities for activating several processes simultaneously, synchronising these processes as appropriate and responding to interrupts.

BCPL and Coral 66, introduced during the late 1960s and early 1970s, were the most popular systems languages in the UK, the latter being more widely used because of the support given to it by the UK Ministry of Defence. In the United States, the situation was less clear as several languages (for example, JOVIAL, BLISS, and XPL) were being used. The most widely used systems programming language now is C and its extension C++.

C

Historically, C evolved from BCPL through the language B during the years 1969–73 and was the systems programming language used to implement the Unix operating system. C and the Unix system were developed together at Bell Laboratories by Ritchie and Thompson. Neither BCPL nor B is a typed language. Although C has types, its ancestry and its application area meant that its type checking is rather weak. C has continued to evolve, with some of the main changes being in tightening up its type checking facilities.

Although C was originally tied to the Unix operating system, its use spread in the 1980s so that implementations are now almost universally available. Before C, much systems programming work was carried out in assembly language. It is C that can take most credit for changing that situation. C has remained a relatively small language and the existence of a portable compiler means that it can be implemented relatively easily on a new machine. Work on the ANSI Standard for C started in 1983 and the Report was published in 1989.

The strength of C lies in the fact that it combines the advantages of a high-level language with the facilities and efficiency of an assembly language. The flexibility required by a systems programming language is provided by the lack of full type checking and the ability to perform arithmetic on store addresses and operations on bit patterns. This flexibility, combined with the availability of a wide range of operators that may be freely combined, means that it is possible to write very compact and efficient code. However, the major drawback is that the code is often far from readable and the lack of full type checking means that it is much easier to write erroneous programs in C than in a language like Pascal.

Although it originated as a systems programming language, C can be used as an ordinary high-level language. Its structure is a cross between Algol and Fortran and it has structured control statements, recursion, records and dynamic data structures. It is, however, a language for experienced programmers rather than novices.

An object-oriented extension to C, called C++, was developed by Stroustrup in the early 1980s. The two languages have evolved together to the extent that there is little difference between ANSI C and the C subset of C++. Compilers support both C and C++ so that C is disappearing as a separate language. We discuss C++ in Section 2.9.

A C program

A C program to solve the problem of finding the mean of a list of numbers and how many are greater than the mean is as follows:

```c
main() {
    /* this is the C version of the program to find the
       mean and the number of those greater than the mean */
    float a[100], mean, sum;
    /*the array a has 100 elements - a[0], .. a[99] */
    int n, i, number;
    scanf("%d", &n);
    for(i = 0; i < n; i++)
        scanf("%f", &a[i]);
    sum = 0.0;
    for (i = 0; i < n; i++)
```

```
      sum += a[i];
  mean = sum / n;
  number = 0;
  for(i = 0; i < n; i++) {
    if (a[i] > mean)
      number++;
  }
  printf("MEAN = %f\n", mean);
  printf("NUMBER OVER MEAN = %d\n", number);
}
```

Note

1. The three statements:

```
  i++; i += 1; i = i + 1;
```

all have the same effect although the first two are more efficient as they only need to determine the address of i once.

occam

The language occam was developed as the systems programming language of a particular computer – the transputer. The idea is to build powerful computers from a network of transputers operating in parallel. Communication and synchronisation are therefore central to the design of both the transputer and of the language occam.

Occam is a simple language that has the process as the central concept. What would be subprograms in a conventional language are processes in occam. Processes communicate with one another by sending messages over channels which correspond closely to the hardware links between transputers. The general approach to communication and synchronisation is in fact very similar to that used in Ada. Although occam and transputers generated a lot of interest in the late 1980s, the ever increasing power and decreasing cost of single CPU machines has meant that they have not fulfilled their potential.

2.9 Modules, classes and abstract data types

In the 1970s, there was a growing acceptance of the need for language support so that large programs could be organised as a set of modules that had a small public interface together with a hidden implementation. The need to be able to re-use software and build systems out of existing components had long been the aim of software engineers. Modules are the obvious candidates for being re-usable components.

Modularity has two aspects: one is concerned with **physical** decomposition into separate files while the other is concerned with **logical** decomposition and being able to raise the level of abstraction at which programmers can think about their designs. These two aspects are, of course, compatible.

A problem can be specified as a set of **abstract data types**. That has led to the notion that a module should implement an abstract data type with the representation of the type and the implementation of the operations being hidden. Languages such as CLU and Alphard follow this approach. A related idea is that modules should represent objects which can then be regarded as the implementations of abstract data types. The object-oriented approach comes from the original ideas of Simula and differs from the original work on abstract data types in that there is less emphasis on theory while there is the extra notion of inheritance and dynamic binding. This led to the object-oriented languages such as Smalltalk, C++, Eiffel and Java and to object-oriented development. Languages such as Modula 2 and Ada, on the other hand, concentrate on modules as program structuring devices. Modules in Modula 2 and packages in Ada are often used to define abstract data types, but they are not restricted to that.

Object-oriented programming took off in a big way in the 1980s, and by the late 1990s had become a dominant language paradigm. Originally, a large number of experimental languages were designed, many of which combined object-oriented and functional programming. Although languages such as Ada support the implementation of abstract data types, the full object-oriented approach with classes, inheritance and dynamic binding was seen as being very different from traditional procedural languages. Object-oriented languages such as Smalltalk were regarded as being good at exploratory programming and rapid prototyping, but not for the engineering of industrial-strength products. (The one exception was the implementation of graphical user interfaces.) The language that changed this view was C++ which, by adding object-oriented features to an existing procedural language, opened up object-oriented programming to a large new class of users. Eiffel also had a major influence. It is purely object-oriented, but as its aim is the engineering of large robust systems and its syntax is based on Pascal, it was acceptable to traditional procedural programmers. The position of object-oriented languages has been further enhanced by the success of Java.

We look first at the development of Ada and Modula-2 and then at Smalltalk before looking at four languages (Eiffel, Delphi, C++ and Java) that have been responsible for converting procedural programmers to the object-oriented approach.

Ada

The US Department of Defense (DoD), the largest user of computers in the world, decided to sponsor the development of a new programming language in the mid-1970s. It was dissatisfied with the conglomeration of different languages used in its computer systems and wanted a standard programming language for embedded computer systems. Embedded computer systems are used to control part of a larger system, such as an industrial plant, an aircraft or a hospital life support system. These applications are normally very large, highly complex, contain a high degree of concurrency and change with time. The other important requirement of such systems is high reliability combined with the ability to recover from errors.

The original requirements for this new language were given in a series of documents. At an early stage, it was decided there was no suitable existing language and so an international design competition was organised. This was won by a group from

CII-Honeywell Bull of France headed by Jean Ichbiah. The resulting language was called Ada after Ada, Countess of Lovelace, who worked on Babbage's Analytical Engine and was considered by many to be the first programmer. The Ada language definition was published in 1983.

Although Ada is Pascal based, it is a much larger and more complex language. It not only extends Pascal constructs, but contains features that have no analogue in Pascal. One of the key features of Ada is the package, which is designed for the description of large software components. It can contain type definitions together with operations for manipulating variables of the types. Packages aid information hiding because both the representation of data and the implementation of the operations may be hidden from the user. Ada also has the notion of a library of packages, thereby enabling the programmer to create a system from combinations of existing packages, rather than writing a new program from scratch.

Apart from a broad range of built-in data types, there is a powerful set of data typing mechanisms. Ada is a strongly typed language, there are no loopholes in the type checking. Sequencing, control statements, procedures and functions are similar to those in Pascal, but the parameter-passing mechanisms using **in**, **out** and **in out** correspond to Algol W's value, result, and value-result.

The task facility in Ada is included to permit parallel processing and there is a `Clock` data type to exercise control and allow the programmer to handle real-time applications. Ada also contains an extensive set of features for interrupt and exception handling.

The DoD decreed that there should be no dialects of Ada; all Ada compilers had to implement the language in the Report with no subsets or supersets being allowed. To enforce this, a compiler validation suite of programs has been developed and a compiler has to satisfy this suite before it can be called an Ada compiler.

Ada is a very comprehensive language and the support of the DoD has ensured its prominent place in the programming environment. However, it is large and complex and requires large and complex compilers, which has hindered its widespread adoption. It has not therefore turned out to be as successful as had been hoped and has had difficulty in fighting off competition, first from C and Modula-2 and then from C++.

A revised Ada standard was published in 1995, the main addition being the inclusion of object-oriented features. When the two versions differ in the facilities provided, we will refer specifically to Ada 83 and Ada 95. When there is no difference, we will just refer to Ada.

Modula-2

The language Modula-2 was designed by Wirth in the late 1970s. Modula was Wirth's first attempt to extend Pascal with modules and, while not wholly successful, pointed the way forward. Modula-2 is, in effect, Pascal with the module concept and some multiprogramming facilities added.

As Modula-2 is less complex and much easier to implement than Ada, it was widely adopted as a teaching language. However, the competition of Ada and C++ (and more recently Java) has proved too much and it is no longer widely used.

Smalltalk

Smalltalk emerged out of work by Alan Kay and others to produce a personal computer (the Dynabook) which could be used by non-experts who would communicate with it through a graphical user-friendly interface. The first version of Smalltalk was developed by Xerox at their research centre in Palo Alto in the early 1970s and required powerful graphics workstations. There have been several different versions, the best known being Smalltalk-80.

The approach taken in Smalltalk is to integrate the language fully with its support tools, thus providing a complete programming environment. Indeed, with Smalltalk, it is impossible to say where the language stops and the environment begins. Its supporting environment (pop-up menus, overlapping windows, icons and mouse input) led the way in providing a user-friendly interface for both the expert and non-expert user that is now commonplace. The language in which these graphical user interface concepts were developed is Smalltalk.

Smalltalk developed the class concept of Simula although its philosophy was also very influenced by Lisp. Until the upsurge of interest in object-oriented languages in the 1980s, Smalltalk was **the** object-oriented language. The fundamental concept in Smalltalk is the object; that is, some local data together with a set of procedures that operate on that data. All calculations are performed by sending messages to objects and problems are solved by identifying real-world objects and modelling them by Smalltalk objects. Everything in Smalltalk is an object. Later object-oriented languages such as Eiffel and Java have not gone as far and do not treat classes as objects. Also, unlike Smalltalk, they have static type checking. This makes them less flexible, but perhaps better suited for engineering large products.

Message passing, the support of a sophisticated environment and graphical user interfaces are expensive in terms of computer resources. In the early days of computing, computer time was very expensive compared with people's time. Languages and systems were therefore developed so that they made the best use of machine resources. The Smalltalk philosophy, on the other hand, is that computers are cheap and so systems should be developed to make the best use of people's time. The recent developments in computer design and reduction in computer costs have made this approach attainable.

Eiffel

The language Eiffel was designed by Bertrand Meyer in the 1980s with the aim of providing a language which would support the creation of large robust systems from existing tried and tested components. An important difference from Smalltalk is that, in order to support the creation of reliable software, type checking is performed at compile time.

Eiffel is a purely object-oriented language. With the exception of the simple types `Integer`, `Boolean`, `Char` and `Real`, the type of all objects are defined by class definitions. Objects are always created dynamically and accessed by reference.

Program correctness is a major theme of Eiffel which includes **pre- and post-conditions** to specify the meaning of operations and **class invariants** that must be true for all class instances (objects). A pre-condition must be true when an operation is called while a post-condition is guaranteed to be true when the operation has finished executing. This provides a systematic method for the construction of classes: we first specify the effect of a class as an abstract data type using pre- and post-conditions and class invariants and then implement the class so that it satisfies the specification. Users of the class just need to know about the specification, the implementation remains hidden.

C++

The aim of C++ was to produce an efficient language that added Simula's class facility to C. In any reckoning, it must be credited with having fully achieved that aim. It was developed by Stroustrup at Bell Labs, the home of C. Development began in 1979 with the first version being called *C with Classes*. C++ was released commercially in 1985 and the international standardisation process started in 1989. The ANSI Standard for C++ was accepted in 1998. C++ has had a major impact on the evolution of C.

The C++ class construct builds on the `struct` (record) facility of C by allowing function members in addition to data members. It supports multiple inheritance and dynamic binding is achieved by declaring a member function to be **virtual**. Objects may therefore contain both statically and dynamically bound function members, unlike other object-oriented languages where all function calls are bound dynamically. Generic classes are supported and are called **class templates**. Type checking is stricter in C++ than in C.

By extending a widely used procedural language, C++ provided the bridge which brought object-oriented programming into widespread industrial use. It is not a purely object-oriented language and therefore supports rather than mandates an object-oriented approach. Many programmers use C++ as a better and safer C. They use classes to create abstract data types, but do not make use of object-oriented features such as dynamic binding. As C++ supports both low-level systems programming as well as object-oriented programming, it is a large language which offers alternative ways of achieving the same effect. This can be confusing. Nevertheless, it has become one of the most widely used programming languages and forms the base from which Java was developed.

Delphi

Various object-oriented extensions to Pascal have been developed, with the best known being Object Pascal. Delphi is a development of Object Pascal that provides support for graphical user interfaces, databases and Internet programming. Delphi is not just a language, it is also a Rapid Application Development (RAD) system in which a **visual development environment** supports program creation. For example, instead of writing the code to implement a graphical user interface, the Delphi programmer draws the interface by choosing and positioning predefined graphical components in a window. The required Delphi (i.e. Object Pascal) code is then generated behind the scenes.

The Delphi system is very much oriented towards use on a Microsoft Windows environment and makes direct use of Windows components and system facilities. There are various versions of Delphi, with the main language differences being between

Delphi 1 and Delphi 2. Delphi 2 was the first version to take advantage of Windows 95 and we do not discuss features specific to Delphi 1 in the book. The changes introduced in later versions of Delphi (Delphi 5 is the latest at this time of writing) have mainly concerned additions to the development environment.

As Delphi incorporates an object-oriented extension to Pascal, references to Pascal in the text can also be regarded as references to Delphi. We only mention Delphi explicitly when we are discussing features where it extends Pascal or are discussing its program development environment.

Java

The rapid spread in the use of Java has been phenomenal. It was originally called Oak and design started at Sun Microsystems in 1990–91 as a small language for programming household devices. With the growth of the World Wide Web, the language was re-targeted as the language for the Internet and renamed Java in 1995. The idea of applets (little applications) that could be used to animate web pages was an immediate success. Although it was not designed as a teaching language, in only a few years it has become perhaps the most common initial teaching language in universities. Java is therefore playing a major role in making object-orientation the dominant language paradigm

Why then, has it become so successful in such a short time? One reason is that it is a relatively small language that achieves much of its power through an extensive and comprehensive standard library called the **Java Application Programming Interface** (the Java API). Whereas with most languages the library is an extra, with Java it is a central part of the language. Also, it was developed as a simplification of C++ and so there was a large user base who could quickly learn the language. A major feature of the Java API is a set of library classes which provide a platform independent way of creating graphical user interfaces. In most previous languages creating a graphical user interface is difficult, but in Java it is straightforward.

The advantage of providing facilities through the library is that users can concentrate on the facilities that they need. For example, if they do not need to do network programming, they can ignore that part of the library. Java offers component engineering; the ability to create programs out of predefined components rather than having to construct everything for oneself.

A Java program can be translated on one kind of machine and run on a different kind of machine. To achieve this, a Java program is first translated into an intermediate language called **Java bytecode** so that it can be interpreted by a Java interpreter. Java bytecode can be regarded as the machine language of the **Java Virtual Machine** and the free Java Development Kit (JDK) which implements it can be downloaded over the Internet from Sun. Also, Internet browsers such as Netscape and Internet Explorer are **Java-enabled**, i.e. they contain an implementation of the Java Virtual Machine, and this allows them to run Java applets. A major selling point of Java is that the same program can be run on many different kinds of computer.

As well as the addition of a significant number of extra facilities in each new version of the JDK, there have been significant changes in the standard libraries. The event-handling model changed radically from JDK 1.0 to JDK 1.1 while the Swing classes were introduced in JDK 1.2 as an alternative to the abstract windowing toolkit (AWT) for the production of graphical user interfaces.

Java differs from C++ in that it is a purely object-oriented language. There are no free standing procedures or functions, all operations are members of a class. However, the predefined simple types such as `int`, `char`, `float`, `double` and `boolean` act as ordinary variables as they would in a procedural language.

Several points greatly simplify the use of objects in Java compared with C++:

- There is only one way in which objects can be allocated space and accessed. (All objects are allocated space on the heap and are accessed by reference as in Eiffel.)
- Pointer arithmetic is not allowed.
- There is automatic garbage collection.
- There is only single inheritance while the advantages of multiple inheritance can be achieved using **interfaces**. (An interface is like an abstract class which has no attributes and all of whose operations are abstract.)

(2.10) Functional and logic languages

In a very influential paper, Backus (1978) introduced the language FP and made the case that imperative languages were fundamentally flawed because of their reliance on side-effects. As a purely functional language only involves the evaluation of expressions, it is possible to reason formally about the effect of a functional program and to prove that it meets its specification.

FP is too simple to become an effective programming language, but it generated a lot of interest in the functional paradigm. Two other functional languages developed in the late 1970s and early 1980s are ML and Hope, many of whose features were combined in producing the language Standard ML. An important feature of ML is its type inference system. ML is strongly typed, but the programmer does not have to declare the types of all identifiers as the system can infer what their type must be by scanning the program text and can report on any inconsistencies.

ML is not a purely functional language as I/O is performed using side-effects. Purists argue that, as a functional program should contain no side-effects, even I/O should be performed in a purely functional style. This is achieved in the languages Miranda and Haskell by the use of lazy evaluation.

A description of functional languages is given in Chapter 9.

Prolog

Prolog originated at the University of Marseilles in the early 1970s. Its development, including the writing of compilers, was carried out at Marseilles and in Edinburgh in the mid- and late 1970s. Although Prolog represented the first step towards programming in logic, it is not the complete logic programming language.

Prolog's approach to programming is quite different from that of conventional languages, perhaps because it started as a language for solving artificial intelligence problems. Using the language of logic, a Prolog programmer provides a specification for a problem by giving the known facts together with the relationships between the objects and what relationships are true. Unlike procedural programs, there is very little explicit control of how the problem is to be solved – the solution to the problem is produced by inference from the given facts and rules.

A Prolog program consists of a series of clauses, which are of three basic types.

1. Those declaring facts about objects and their relationships. Such facts are always deemed to be unconditionally true.

2. Those defining rules about objects and their relationships.

3. Those asking questions about objects and their relationships. Such questions ask the program whether some statements are true or false.

A more detailed description of Prolog is given in Chapter 10 together with a simple example showing facts, rules and questions.

Interest in Prolog grew rapidly throughout the 1980s, particularly when Japan announced that Prolog would have an important part to play in their fifth-generation computer initiative.

There has been considerable discussion of the merits of logic programming as opposed to functional programming, particularly as regards the use of Prolog and Lisp programs to solve the same problems. It is doubtful whether such detailed comparisons will result in any definite conclusions. (Those who are interested in such comparisons can read the paper by O'Keefe (1983).) In contrast to Lisp, which is effective when list processing is required, Prolog is best used in searching applications with databases and expert systems.

Prolog is not ideally suited for data processing work and the lack of compound expressions in the language can make some applications very clumsy. Furthermore, a strictly logical approach to programming can often lead to severe inefficiencies at run time. Although Prolog programmers have found ways to avoid some of these difficulties, these methods seem *ad hoc* and represent a move away from the purity of mathematical logic.

(2.11) Conclusions

The 1960s saw the establishment of many programming languages – notably Fortran, Algol, COBOL, PL/I and Basic. These languages consolidated their grip on the market and made it exceedingly difficult for any new language to make a major impact. Fortran, COBOL and Basic are still major languages although they have changed significantly over the years. Of the languages that emerged during the 1970s and early 1980s, three have continued to be important in the 1990s and look well set for the twenty-first century in the form of direct descendants or new versions.

● Pascal, for many years, was the dominant initial teaching language in universities throughout the world. Although that is no longer the case, its extensions such as Delphi are still widely used.

- C became the dominant language for systems programmers and was originally boosted by the importance of the Unix operating system. Along with C++, it is now widely used with other operating systems. Indeed, C++ is now regarded as a general-purpose language rather than just a systems programming language. Java was developed from C++.

- The development of Ada started in the late 1970s, with the final report being published in 1983. The language was revised in 1995.

It is significant that the latest development in all these languages have been in the direction of adding object-oriented facilities.

The 1980s saw a significant increase in interest in logic and functional languages, largely because, as they are at a higher level of abstraction, they are easier to reason about than their imperative counterparts. The main logic language is Prolog which was developed in the 1970s but made little impact until the 1980s. Modern functional languages include Scheme (a dialect of Lisp), ML and Haskell.

The major development in the 1980s and 1990s has been in object-oriented programming which has become the dominant programming paradigm. The main imperative languages have been extended to include object-oriented features. The most widely used object-oriented languages are Smalltalk, Eiffel, C++, Delphi, Ada 95 and Java.

The way computers are used changed radically in the 1990s. Powerful personal computers became cheap and are now commonly to be found in homes. Although graphical user interfaces were developed in the 1970s and were available on Apple machines in the 1980s, it was in the 1990s that they became the normal way for a user to interact with a PC. Similarly, although it was not new, it was in the 1990s that the Internet became all pervasive. As facilities for creating graphical user interfaces and for Internet programming are usually provided by class libraries, these developments contributed to the growing importance of object-oriented languages.

In fact, there is often no clear distinction between a language, its class library and its development environment and we should now perhaps talk about programming systems rather than programming languages. For example, Java programmers regard the Java standard libraries as a central part of the language, Delphi is essentially a set of class libraries and a development environment on top of object-oriented Pascal, while programmers using Visual C++ or Visual Basic regard the development environment and its support tools as central to their programming system. As personal computers become ever more powerful, and therefore able to support more sophisticated tools, the importance of development environments is sure to increase.

Summary

1. High-level languages (often called third-generation languages) developed from the need to make programming easier for the non-specialist programmer and to make languages independent of specific computer hardware.

2. Fortran was the first widely used high-level language. It was immensely successful when it emerged in the late 1950s and is still widely used today in its Fortran 77 and Fortran 90 versions for scientific and engineering applications.

3. Algol 60, which appeared a few years after Fortran, was not as successful in terms of numbers of users, but it had a much greater influence on subsequent languages, such as Pascal and Ada. It introduced many new concepts into programming languages including recursion, block structure, syntax definition and structured statements.

4. COBOL was the first effective high-level language for commercial data processing. It is still a major language and the latest standard includes object-oriented features.

5. PL/I attempted to provide a general multipurpose language by combining many of the features of Fortran, Algol 60 and COBOL. However, it proved to be too large and unwieldy.

6. The use of terminals attached to a central computer led to the introduction of interactive languages in the 1960s, one of which, Basic, has become very popular due to its simplicity and the fact that its interpreter will fit into the memory of small machines.

7. Lisp is oriented towards the manipulation of symbols, rather than numbers, and for three decades has been the dominant language in artificial intelligence.

8. Lisp is a list-processing language and is close to being a functional language. Functional languages are easier to reason about than their imperative counterparts.

9. Pascal became the major teaching language of the 1980s and has had a beneficial influence on programming style.

10. C, and its C++ development, have proved to be the most successful systems programming languages.

11. Ada 95, Java and C++ are the most important of the modern generation of general-purpose imperative languages. They incorporate the current ideas of modularity and information hiding.

12. Object-oriented programming has received increasing attention in recent years. The latest versions of many procedural languages have object-oriented features.

Exercises

Some of the following exercises will require further reading.

2.1 What were the original design goals of Fortran and how far were they realised? What new concepts did Fortran introduce into programming languages and what influence did it have on later languages?

2.2 Algol 60 was less successful than Fortran, but it has had a much greater impact on the design of later languages. Explain this apparent paradox.

2.3 Consider a text editor known to you and compare its string handling facilities with those typically found in programming languages.

2.4 Apart from Lisp, the list-processing languages introduced in the 1960s have disappeared. Lisp is still widely used, particularly in Artificial Intelligence applications. Describe the properties of Lisp that have contributed to its longevity.

2.5 How important in the rise or fall of a new programming language is the availability of efficient compilers for a wide range of computers? What factors affect the provision of suitable compilers?

2.6 Identify Ada facilities that:

(a) are similar to those in Pascal,

(b) extend a Pascal construct,

(c) differ significantly from anything in Pascal.

Choose an example from each group and suggest reasons why the Ada construct was designed as it was.

2.7 James Martin (1985) claims that computer science departments have ignored 4GLs. How far do you think his comments are justified? Are universities ignoring languages which are of fundamental importance?

2.8 Why are object-oriented languages well suited to providing support for graphical user interfaces and Internet programming?

2.9 In what ways has Java simplified C++?

2.10 Discuss how programming in Prolog differs from programming in conventional languages such as Pascal.

Bibliography

The development of programming languages are well covered by the following books and articles. Two good starting points are the article by Wegner (1976) and the paper by Knuth entitled 'Early development of programming languages' (Metroplis *et al.*, 1980), which is excellent on languages up to and including Fortran I. Much more detail is provided in the book by Sammet (1969) which gives all the major, and many minor, languages from the 1950s and 1960s. Two further papers by Sammet (1972, 1981) bring the history of languages up to date.

In a conference in 1978 (Wexelblat, 1981), the designers of the major languages of the 1950s and 1960s were asked to give their view of the language's design and development. The languages covered with the speaker's name in brackets are:

Fortran (J. Backus), Algol (A. Perlis, P. Naur), Lisp (J. McCarthy), COBOL (J. Sammet), APT (D. Ross), JOVIAL (J. Schwartz), GPSS (G. Gordon), Simula (K. Nygaard), JOSS (C. Baker), Basic (T. Kurtz), PL/I (G. Radin), SNOBOL (R. Griswold), APL (K. Iverson).

A second conference in 1993 (Bergin and Gibson, 1996) covered the following languages:

Concurrent Pascal (P. Brinch Hansen), Prolog (A. Colmerauer, P. Roussel), Icon (R. Griswold, M. Griswold), Smalltalk (A. Kay), Algol 68 (C. H. Lindsey), CLU (B. Liskov), Simulation Languages (R. Nance), Forth (E. Rather, D. Colburn, C. Moore), C (D. Ritchie), FORMAC (J. Sammet), Lisp (G. Steele, R. Gabriel), C++ (B. Stroustrup), Ada (W. Whitaker), Pascal (N. Wirth).

The evolution of modern functional languages is described by Hudak (1989).

Backus, J. (1978). 'Can Programming be Liberated from the Von Neumann Style?'. *Comm. ACM*, **21**, 613–641.

Bergin, T.J. and Gibson, R.G. (1996). *History of Programming Languages*. Addison-Wesley.

Casimir, R.J. (1992). 'Real Programmers don't use Spreadsheets'. ACM Sigplan Notices, **27**(6), 10–16.

Hudak, P. (1989). 'Conception, Evolution, and Application of Functional Programming Languages'. *ACM Computing Surveys*, **21**, 359–411.

Humby, E. (1964). 'ICT COBOL Rapidwrite' in *Introduction to System Programming* (P. Wegner, ed.). Academic Press, pp. 166–177.

ISO (1982). *Specification for Computer Programming Language Pascal*. ISO 7185-1982.

Martin, J. (1985). 'Excerpts from: An Information Systems Manifesto'. *Comm. ACM*, **28**, 252–262.

Metroplis, N., Howlett, J. and Rota, G-C. (1980). *A History of Computing in the Twentieth Century*. Academic Press.

Naur, P. *et al.* (eds) (1960). 'Report on the Algorithmic Language ALGOL 60'. *Comm. ACM*, **3**, 299–314.

Naur, P. *et al.* (eds.) (1963). 'Revised Report on the Algorithmic Language ALGOL 60'. *Comm. ACM*, **6**, 1–17.

O'Keefe, R.A. (1983). 'Prolog Compared with Lisp'. *ACM Sigplan Notices*, **18**(5), 46–56.

Sammet, J.E. (1969). *Programming Languages: History and Fundamentals*. Prentice-Hall.

Sammet, J.E. (1972). 'Programming Languages: History and Future'. *Comm. ACM*, **15**, 601–610.

Sammet, J.E. (1981). 'An Overview of High-Level Languages' in *Advances in Computers*, **20**, Academic Press, pp. 199–259.

Wegner, P. (1976). 'Programming Languages – the First 25 years'. *IEEE Transactions on Computers*, **C-25**, 1207–1255.

Wexelblat, R.L. (1981). *History of Programming Languages*. Academic Press.

Wile, D.S. and Ramming, J.C. (1999). 'Introduction to Special Section on Domain-Specific Languages'. *IEEE Trans Software Engineering*, **25**(3), 289–290.

Wirth, N. and Hoare, C.A.R. (1966). 'A Contribution to the Development of ALGOL'. *Comm. ACM*, **9**, 413–431.

Chapter 3

Types, values and declarations

This chapter looks at the declaration of simple variables and constants and at the binding time of their various attributes. Variables can be divided into three groups: simple (scalar) variables, structured variables and reference variables.

An important attribute of a variable is its type. This chapter looks at the numerical types (integer, floating point and complex) as well as the logical type Boolean, the character type, enumeration types and references. In addition, it shows how languages have developed so that a programmer can express a solution in terms of the problem to be solved rather than in terms of the computer being used.

The efficiency and flexibility of a language is largely governed by whether attributes are bound early (for example, at compile time) or whether the binding is delayed until run time. This chapter distinguishes between static and dynamic scope and between the scope (name-declaration binding) and the lifetime (declaration-reference binding) of a variable.

3.1 Names

A program may be regarded as the specification of a series of operations that are to be performed on data items. Languages vary as to the types of item that are allowed, the operations that can be applied to them and the method of controlling the sequencing of those operations. (Operations are dealt with in Chapter 4.)

The type of a data item determines its allowed values together with the set of operations that can be used to manipulate these values. Data items have a **value** and a **type** and may be held in what are known as **variables**. Variables have a **name**, various **attributes** and refer to an area of computer store. It is necessary to keep clear the distinction between:

- the name of a variable (its **identifier**),
- where the variable is stored (its **reference** or its **address**),
- the value stored.

The connection between names, references and values is shown diagrammatically in Figure 3.1 using a graphical notation developed by Barron (1977).

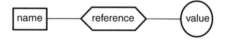

Figure 3.1 Connection between names, references and values.

Typically, an identifier is a combination of letters and digits with the first character being a letter. An exception is Perl where an identifier has a prefix to show whether it is a scalar ($), an array (@) or a hash (%) variable.

Spaces are not normally allowed within identifiers, but as identifiers such as:

```
left link, buffer size, customer account
```

seem quite natural, languages such as Ada, C, C++, Fortran 90 and many Pascal implementations have found a compromise by using the underscore character:

```
left_link, buffer_size, customer_account
```

Although it allows underscores, the convention in Java is to use internal capitals instead as in:

```
leftLink, bufferSize, customerAccount
```

Early languages often restricted the allowed length of an identifier to six or eight characters, but most modern languages have no limit while ANSI C guarantees that at least the first 31 characters in an identifier are significant and Fortran 90 has increased the maximum length of an identifier from 6 to 31.

No consensus seems to have been reached on whether or not upper and lower case letters should be distinct. In C, C++ and Java the case matters, while in Pascal, Fortran 90 and Ada it does not.

3.2 Declarations and binding

One of the most important factors controlling the power, flexibility and efficiency of a language is the time at which different language features are associated with, or **bound** to, one another. This is known as their **binding time**. Binding can take place at compile time, load time or run time. There are two main occasions at which binding takes place at run time: block (i.e. procedure, function or method) entry and statement execution. In general, the ability to bind two features early (for example, at compile time) leads to efficient execution while binding that is delayed until run time leads to more flexibility.

Name-declaration binding

This section looks first at the binding between a variable and its attributes such as its name, its reference (that is, where it is held in store), its current value and its type. In most modern programming languages, variables are introduced into a program by a **declaration**. They can then be used in program statements.

The connection between the use of a name in a statement and its declaration is referred to as **name-declaration binding**. In languages such as Pascal, Java, C, C++ and Ada, we can determine the name-declaration binding by examining the program text alone – there is no need to consider execution of the program. We therefore say that **name-declaration binding occurs at compile time.** The name-declaration binding rules are also called the **scope rules.** Pascal, Java, C, C++ and Ada are said to have **static scope**.

We will look at this through the following example, first in Pascal and then in Java:

```
program Example(input, output);
    var x, y: Real;
    procedure op1;
        var y, z:Integer;
    begin
        . . .
        y := 34;
        x := 27.4;
        . . .
    end{op1};
begin
    . . .
    x := 3.768;
    y := x;
    . . .
end{Example}.
```

Four variables have been declared; x and y of type Real in the main program Example and y and z of type Integer in procedure op1. The main program and procedure op1 are both examples of what are known as **blocks**.

In Pascal, blocks may be nested within other blocks and in this example block op1 is nested within block Example. Essentially, a block is a piece of program text, containing both declarations and statements, which is used to control the visibility of identifiers.

The piece of program text in which an identifier is visible and may therefore be used is known as its **scope**. The use of an identifier is always bound to its most local declaration.

Identifiers declared in a block are not visible from outside that block; hence the Integer variables y and z are not visible outside procedure op1. They are called **local variables**. On the other hand, identifiers declared in enclosing blocks are visible within inner blocks and so the Real variable x can be used within procedure op1 as well as in the main program. In both cases, its use is bound to the declaration of x in the main program. Variables used in one block, but declared in an enclosing block, are called **non-local variables**. A non-local variable which has been declared in the outermost block is often referred to as a **global variable**.

Consider now the declarations of y as a Real variable in block Example and as an Integer variable in block op1. Variables are bound to their most local declaration; hence, the use of the identifier y in the statement:

```
y := x
```

in the main program is bound to the declaration of the Real variable y while the use of y in the statement:

```
y := 34
```

in procedure op1 is bound to the declaration of the Integer variable y. It is not possible within op1 to refer to the Real variable y. This is referred to as a 'hole in the scope'. Ada follows the same rules as Pascal, but it allows the Real variable y to be accessed from within a procedure like op1 by giving it the expanded name of Example.y; that is, the variable y declared in block Example.

The scope rules for methods in a Java or C++ class are exactly the same as those for procedures in a Pascal program. Consider the following Java class declaration:

```
class Example {
    private double  x, y;
    public void op1() {
        int y, z;
        y := 34;
        x := 27.4;
        . . .
    } // op1
    public void op2() {
        x := 3.768;
        y := x;
        . . .
    } // op2
} // Example
```

The methods op1 and op2 are blocks nested within the outer block represented by class Example. As in the Pascal example, the local variables y and z declared in block op1 are not visible outside that block while x and y declared in block Example are visible inside blocks op1 and op2. However, as there is a local declaration of y inside block op1, the use of y inside op1 refers to the local declaration.

When a declaration specifies type information, the binding of names to declarations at compile time (i.e. the static scope rules) means that the binding of names to types (**name-type binding**) is also fixed at compile time. The advantage of this is that it allows type checking to be performed by the compiler; that is, it enables the compiler to check that variables are always used in their proper context. A language with this property is said to be **statically typed**. Furthermore, when there are no loopholes in the type checking, a language is said to be **strongly typed**. Ada and Algol 68 are strongly typed but, as will be seen later, there are loopholes in the type checking of most other widely used languages.

Static typing leads to programs which are:

- **reliable:** because type errors are detected at compile time,

- **efficient:** because type checks do not have to be made at run time,

- **understandable:** because the connection, or binding, between the use of an identifier and its declaration can be determined from the program text.

In **dynamic scope**, the binding between the use of an identifier and its declaration depends on the order of execution, and so is delayed until run time. The difference between static and dynamic scope is best seen through an example. Consider the following outline Pascal program:

```
program Dynamic(input, output);
    var x:Integer;
    procedure a;
    begin
        ... write(x);...
    end {a};
    procedure b;
        var x : Real;
    begin
        ...x := 2.0;...a;...
    end {b};
begin
    ...x := 1; ...b; ...a; ...
end {Dynamic}.
```

As Pascal has static scope rules, the use of the variable x in procedure a is bound to the declaration of the integer variable x in the main program and so the value 1 is output. However, when the name-declaration binding is dynamic, the use of x in procedure a is bound to the most recent declaration of x. Hence, when procedure a is called from procedure b, the use of x in a is bound to the declaration of the Real variable x in procedure b causing 2.0 to be output, while when a is called from the main program, the use of x is bound to the declaration of the Integer variable x in the main program and the value 1 is output.

With dynamic scope, the type of a non-local variable such as x in procedure a therefore depends on where a has been called from. Type checking at compile time is therefore not possible. Many implementations of Lisp use dynamic scope although modern Lisp dialects such as Scheme use static scope. We discuss this further in Chapter 9. Dynamic scope provides few, if any, advantages.

In languages such as Smalltalk, Icon and Scheme, the declaration of a name does not specify type information and a variable can be assigned values of different types. The type of a variable depends on its current value: a value such as 7 has an Integer type and a value such as 94.7 a Real type. Name-type binding is therefore delayed until run time and we have **dynamic typing**. This allows little or no type checking at compile time, but it does allow considerable extra flexibility at run time, even if this flexibility is at the expense of running speed. Dynamically typed languages usually have functions to enable the current type of a variable to be determined at run time so that alternative pieces of code can be executed and type errors avoided. When a program is executed under the control of an interpreter, the interpreter is able to perform any required bindings during program execution. Programs written in dynamically typed languages are therefore usually interpreted rather than being compiled.

Object-oriented languages such as C++ and Java support a controlled form of dynamic binding. An object of a subclass can be used where an object of a superclass is expected. However, the allowed superclass is determined statically, as is the **set** of allowed subclasses, and full type checking can still be done at compile time. This topic is covered in detail in Chapter 8.

Although Lisp and Scheme are dynamically typed languages, recent functional languages such as ML have type definitions and name-type binding occurs at compile time. ML also has a **type inference system**. Although ML is strongly typed, the programmer does not have to declare all the types as the system can work them out for itself from the context of their use. ML also supports what are called polymorphic functions which allow the advantages of early name-type binding to be combined with the flexibility enjoyed by dynamically typed languages. Type inference systems and polymorphic functions are described in Chapter 9.

Declaration-reference binding

A description of the execution of a program in an imperative language is most easily given in terms of the traditional von Neumann computer where a store is composed of individually addressable store locations. During program execution, a program variable is allocated a set of store locations in which its value can be stored. The store locations have a reference (i.e. an address) through which they can be accessed. When a variable is allocated storage, we say that the **declaration** of the variable is bound to a **reference**.

The **lifetime** (sometimes called the **extent**) of a variable is when, during the execution of a program, the variable has storage space allocated to it. There are three times at which a variable can be allocated store locations: load time, block entry and during statement execution.

In most languages, local variables in procedures or methods are allocated space on block entry, i.e. when the procedure or method is called. When we return from the procedure or method call, the space is de-allocated. Hence, in the Pascal program and the Java class Example given earlier, the local variables y and z are only allocated storage when op1 is called and this space is de-allocated when op1 is left.

The Real variables x and y in program Example are allocated storage when program execution starts, that is at load time. The double variables x and y in class Example are allocated storage when an object of class Example is created and that is usually during statement execution. The lifetime of the Pascal Real variables x and y therefore lasts throughout the execution of the program while the lifetime of the Java double variables x and y lasts while the object exists. The local variables y and z declared in op1 on the other hand have a new incarnation each time op1 is called. Consequently, the declarations of y and z may be bound to different store locations (that is, bound to different references) on different calls of op1.

Before proceeding further, it is important to be clear about the distinction between the scope and the lifetime of a variable. The scope property is concerned with name-declaration binding and, in languages like Pascal and Java, is a compile-time feature and so can be discussed purely in terms of the program text. The lifetime of a variable, on the other hand, is concerned with declaration-reference binding which occurs at run time. The distinction between these two properties is shown diagrammatically in Figure 3.2.

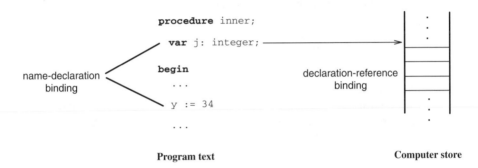

Figure 3.2   Scope and extent.

In object-oriented languages, a class is the definition of the common properties of a set of objects and is part of the program text. We therefore discuss scope in terms of classes. An object is created at run time and is an **instance** of a class. We therefore discuss lifetime in terms of objects.

Binding the declaration of a local variable to a different store location (i.e. reference) each time a procedure or method is entered has the consequence that a local variable does not retain the value it had when the procedure or method was last executed. The initial value of a local variable is, therefore, undefined until it is explicitly given a value.

There are occasions when it is useful for a procedure to 'remember' information from one call to the next. The only way this can be achieved in Pascal is by using global variables, and so to increase the lifetime of a variable its scope must be extended, thereby making it accessible to regions of the program from which we would rather it was hidden.

To handle this problem, Algol 60, C, C++ and Delphi allow the declaration of **static local variables** in addition to ordinary local variables. In Algol 60, these are known as **own variables**. Static local variables obey the same scope rules as ordinary local variables, but declaration-reference binding occurs at the beginning of program execution (that is, at load time) rather than on block entry. This means that a static local variable remains in existence when the procedure in which it is declared is left and its declaration remains bound to the same storage location.

In object-oriented languages or languages with modules there is really no need for static local variables, as information that needs to be held from one method call to the next can be declared at the class or module level. Although that extends the scope of the variable, it is in a controlled way and is usually what is intended.

In Java, objects are created during statement execution using the **new** operator. For example, using the definition of class Example given earlier, execution of:

```
Example anExample = new Example();
```

will cause an object anExample of class Example to be created and space allocated for its attributes x and y. Hence instances of x and y exist for each instance (i.e. object) of class Example. We deal further with declaration-reference binding during statement execution in Section 3.8 when we look at pointers and reference variables.

If an attribute of a Java class is declared to be **static** as in:

```
class Example2 {
    private static int counter = 0;
    . . .
```

then, unlike ordinary attributes, only one instance of counter will exist during execution of the program. It is often referred to as a **class variable** and it can be allocated space at load time. A common use of a class variable is to count how many objects of the class have been created.

Reference-value binding

The binding of a variable to a value occurs as a result of either an input or an assignment statement. Typically, during the execution of a program written in an imperative programming language, a variable will be bound to a succession of different values. Consider, for example, the C++ or Java statement:

```
y = y + 1;
```

whose effect is to increment the value of y by 1. At first sight, this seems trivial until it is realised that the y on the left-hand side refers to a place where a value may be stored (that is, it is a reference) while the y on the right-hand side refers to the current value of y. The binding of a variable to its value involves three bindings:

1. The binding of the variable's name to its declaration (name-declaration binding).

2. The binding of its declaration to a store location (declaration-reference binding).

3. The binding of the store location to a value (**reference-value binding**).

The process of finding the value, given the reference, is known as **dereferencing**. In the assignment statement just given, the y on the right-hand side is dereferenced to find its value so that 1 can be added to it. The resulting value is then assigned to the location whose reference is obtained from the left-hand side. A reference is sometimes called an **L-value** and the value of a variable an **R-value**, where L and R stand for left and right.

It is worth noting at this point that it is the assignment operation, with its notion of updating a store location, that requires locations and references to be introduced into the computational model. When a language has no assignment statement, names can be directly bound to values as will be seen in Chapter 9 which discusses purely functional languages.

Variables must be given a value before they are used in an expression as otherwise the value obtained can vary in each run of the program leading to nondeterministic programs and wrong results. Languages differ in how they deal with this problem. Java gives class attributes a default initial value, but local variables are left undefined. However, the Java compiler does check that they are given a value before they are used. Most modern languages allow variables to be initialised as part of their declaration and this removes many of the problems associated with undefined variables.

Constants

Some data items in a program do not change once they have been given an initial value, and these items should be declared as **constants**. In Pascal, for example, constants are declared in the following way:

```
const pi = 3.14159265;
      lowestprime = 2;
      lastletter = 'z';
```

where the type is determined from the value.

The name-value binding for a constant is shown in Figure 3.3. It has a name and a value, but as a constant identifier cannot appear on the left-hand side of an assignment statement, there is no need for a reference. In Pascal, the name-value binding of a constant occurs at compile time while, with a variable, a value is bound to a reference during statement execution.

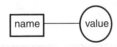

Figure 3.3   Name-value binding for a constant.

Ada, C++ and Java have generalised Pascal's constant declarations and brought them more in line with variable declarations. In these languages, both variables and constants can be given values within a declaration (although in the case of C++, not when we are declaring a data member in a class). Hence, the effect of the declarations:

```
size : Integer := 20;  -- Ada
int size = 20; // C++ or Java
```

is to declare an integer variable whose initial value is 20 whereas the effect of the declarations:

```
size : constant Integer := 20; -- Ada
const int size = 20; // C++
final int size = 20; // Java
```

is to declare an integer constant whose value is always 20. The Java approach is that when an entity is declared as final, it may not be changed. Hence, final variables are constants. The values in Ada, C++ and Java variable and constant declarations may be given by expressions that cannot be evaluated until run time. Consequently, the name-value binding of a constant may have to be delayed until block entry.

If we wish to declare Java constants that can be used throughout a program, we can declare them in a class as follows:

```
public class OurConstants {
    public final static int length = 12;
    public final static int breadth = 6;
    public final static boolean open = true;
}
```

Variables that are declared as **static** are not associated with an object, but with the class. When they are **final**, they are constants. We can use such constants as follows:

```
int area = OurConstants.length * OurConstants.breadth;
```

3.3 Type definitions

The most important attribute of a variable is its type. The characteristics of a type are its allowed values together with the set of operations that can be used to manipulate these values. At the lowest level, data is just a collection of 1s and 0s, but a collection of such bits can be viewed as an integer or floating-point number, an array of numbers, a character or even (although it is of no concern here) an instruction.

The three main kinds of type found in programming languages are: scalar types, structured types and reference types. Scalar types that appear in most programming languages are:

- Numeric data types: integer, floating point and sometimes fixed point and complex.
- A logical type (often called Boolean).
- A character type.

Scalar types can be split into two categories: **discrete** (or **ordinal**) types, where each value (except the maximum and the minimum values) has a predecessor and a successor, and others such as floating-point types for which this is not the case. Integer, Boolean and character types are discrete. Hence, the integer 42 has 41 as its predecessor and 43 as its successor, but it does not make sense to talk about the successor of a floating-point number such as 42.734.

Perl is unusual in that strings are scalar values. Also, although it appears to have integers, all numbers are treated behind the scenes as floating point. There is also no firm distinction between strings and numbers and so the result of an expression such as "3.17" + 1 can be regarded as the string "4.17" or the number 4.17. If a string that does not represent a numerical value is used as a number then it has the value 0.

A distinction can be made between the **built-in** types, which are immediately available to the programmer, and other types, which are defined by the programmer although this distinction is becoming less important. In a language like Ada, new types can be added to the set of built-in types in such a way that a user cannot easily distinguish between the two groups. Similarly, in object-oriented languages such as C++ and Java, new types are defined by means of class definitions.

Although Java is an object-oriented language, simple scalar types (the **primitive types**) such as int, double, char and boolean are not implemented as objects, but are dealt with in the same way as in a procedural language like C.

Specifying type information

In most modern languages, all variables must be declared before they can be used. Variables can be declared to be either one of the built-in types or of a user-defined type. Some languages also have implicit or default declarations. For example, in Fortran, it is assumed that all undeclared variables with names starting with a letter in the range I to N are of type Integer while those starting with any other letters are of type Real. Although this method saves the programmer the somewhat tedious task of making declarations at the start of a program, it does suffer from the serious defect that mis-spelt variable names are taken to be references to new variables. This problem has been officially recognised in Fortran 90 where, if a program unit is prefixed by the statement:

```
IMPLICIT NONE
```

then all identifiers in that unit must be explicitly declared.

Typical variable declarations (using Ada syntax) are:

```
a, b: Integer;
c : array (1 .. 10) of Integer;
```

where c is declared to be an array of 10 integers.

However, instead of giving the array information as part of the variable declaration, it is possible, and preferable, to define a new named type and to declare a variable of that type, as in:

```
type List is array (1 .. 10) of  Integer;
c : List;
```

Details of the new type are thus brought together in one place rather than being distributed throughout the program in separate variable declarations. This is necessary when variables of the same type are to be declared in different parts of a program or are to be passed as parameters to subprograms. Also, by choosing meaningful type identifiers, the reader can be provided with additional information.

The description of name-declaration binding given in Section 3.2 involved the use and declaration of variables. Here, name-declaration binding involves types with the use of the name List in:

```
c : List;
```

being bound to its declaration in:

```
type List is array (1 .. 10) of  Integer;
```

In Ada, a distinction is made between new types (called **derived types**) and **subtypes**. The Ada declaration:

```
subtype Index is  Integer range 1 .. 10;
count : Index;
```

declares a variable count whose possible values are a subrange of the integers. Provided its value does not go out of range, a variable of subtype Index can be used anywhere that a variable of type Integer can be used.

Programs often have variables that are logically distinct although they may be represented in the same way in a computer (for example, as integers). If these variables are declared to be of different types, it is possible to guard against them being combined in ways that are logically inconsistent, and this allows many logical errors to be detected at compile time. The type declaration:

```
type New_index is new  Integer range 1 .. 10;
new_count : New_index;
```

for example, creates a new type called New_index that is distinct from type Integer. Ada uses **name equivalence**; to be of the same type, two variables must be declared with the same type name. The alternative, used in C, is **structural equivalence** where two variables with the same representation are of the same type.

A consequence of name equivalence is that, for each operator available on values of type Integer, there is now a corresponding, but distinct, operator on values of type New_index. Hence, the expression count + 1 has the Integer addition operator while new_count + 1 has the New_index addition operator. Integer literals are available with type Integer and all types derived from type Integer.

Consider now the expression:

```
count + new_count
```

This expression is illegal as the two operands are of different types. Explicit conversion between type Integer and type New_index can be made through the use of what is known as a **type mark**. In the expression:

```
New_index(count) + new_count
```

the type mark New_index is used to convert the value of count from type Integer to type New_index. The type of the expression is, therefore, New_index while the expression:

```
count + Integer(new_count)
```

is of type Integer. By explicitly using the type mark, the programmer is making it clear that there is a reason why the two different types are being combined. For example, distance and time values should not be added, but it is valid to divide distance by time to give velocity.

Types are not just concerned with the set of allowable values, they are also concerned with the set of possible operations. In a language like Pascal, the operations are defined in procedures and functions, but these definitions are spread throughout a program. In languages such as Ada (and in fact in most modern Pascal implementations) the module can be used to group together type information with the definitions of the possible operations. This gives us the notion of **abstract data types** (ADTs).

Object-oriented languages go further. A class is not just the encapsulating mechanism to bring together a type definition with a set of operations. Typically, a module **contains** the declaration of a type while a C++ or Java class **is** the declaration of a type. We will return to this point later.

3.4 Numeric data types

Numeric data types are usually modelled on the machine representation of integer and floating-point numbers. Although this gives the advantage of speed, it does mean that the range and precision of the numbers represented will vary from one machine to the next; thus, a program involving floating-point arithmetic may give different answers on different machines. Java is unusual in this respect as the representation of the numerical values is defined in the language.

The arithmetic operators (+, -, *, /) for addition, subtraction, multiplication and division correspond directly to machine code instructions. However, as computers have different machine code instructions for integer and floating-point arithmetic, the effect of these operators depends on the context in which they are used. Hence, the expression 2 + 3 involves integer addition while 6.5 + 3.7 involves floating-point addition. When the effect of an operator depends on the type of its operands, the operator is said to be **overloaded**.

Languages such as Algol 60, Pascal and Modula-2 have a separate **div** operator for integer division with / being reserved for real division. In Algol 60 and Pascal, the result of evaluating 7 **div** 2 is 3 while the result of 7 / 2 is 3.5. In Modula-2, on the other hand, the operation 7 / 2 is illegal as the / operator is only defined for real operands.

Not all languages have two division operators. Fortran, Ada, C, C++ and Java make do with a single overloaded division operator. In these languages 7 / 2 gives the integer result 3 while real division is obtained by writing 7.0 / 2.0.

The exponentiation operator in Fortran is ** and in Algol 60 it is ↑. As part of the move for simplicity, this operator is not available in Pascal, C, C++ and Java on the grounds that it was used too casually by programmers who did not realise how expensive it was in processing time. When R is a positive number of type REAL, the Fortran expression X ** R is actually evaluated as:

```
EXP(R * ALOG(X))
```

where ALOG is the natural logarithm and EXP is the exponential operator. As both these functions are normally available in other languages, all that is lost is ease of use. In this way, casual use of exponentiation is discouraged. Ada has restored the operator **, but has added the restriction that the exponent must be an integer.

Other operators available with numeric types are the relational and equality operators. The result of a relational expression is of type Boolean. Most languages use <, <=, > and >= for the relational operators, but there is no agreement about 'not equals'; Pascal uses <> while C, C++ and Java use != and Ada and Fortran 90 use /=. The equality operator is represented in C, C++, Fortran 90 and Java as == while = is used for assignment. Earlier versions of Fortran used operators such as .EQ. and .NE. for equality and inequality.

A major difference between integer and floating-point numbers is that integers are always represented exactly while the floating-point representation is only approximate. This is for the same reason that it is not possible to write down a finite decimal expansion for the number one-third. A consequence of this is that the equality operators do not always give the expected result when dealing with floating-point quantities and their use in this context is bad practice.

Integer

The range of possible integers is dependent on the machine hardware and the representation used. Using 32 bits, integers in the range -2^{31} to $2^{31} - 1$ may be represented when the **two's complement representation** is used.

Integers are used by programmers in two contrasting ways: firstly, in the normal mathematical sense, although with a finite range, and, secondly, as counters in a loop or as an array index. The range of allowable integers is usually excessive for the second application while it can at times be insufficient for the first. This has led to several developments.

Languages such as C and C++ have the integer types short and long to provide integers of different lengths, but the actual length of each of these types depends on the implementation. So, on a 16-bit machine, variables of type int typically have the same range as variables of type short on 32-bit machines. It is even possible for a C compiler to implement short, int and long in the same way since it is stated that 'you should only count on short being no longer than long', which seems rather to defeat the object of the exercise. Java, on the other hand, is explicit about the size of integers. It has four integer types: a byte is held in 8 bits, a short is held in 16 bits, an int is held in 32 bits and a long in 64 bits.

Subrange declarations in Pascal and Ada can reduce storage requirements, but their main advantage to the programmer is in the detection of logical errors. For example, given the Pascal declaration:

```
var count : 1 .. 10;
```

then the following:

```
for count := 0 to   10 do
```

will result in the error being picked up at compile time.

Ada has three predefined integer types: Short_Integer, Integer and Long_Integer. The drawback that the allowed range of each is implementation dependent is overcome by not expecting the programmer to use these types directly, but instead to define a derived type. In a declaration such as:

```
type My_Integer is range 1 .. 20000;
```

the compiler will select the most appropriate built-in integer type. Hence, although this type may be derived from type Long_Integer on an implementation on a 16-bit machine and from type Integer on a 32-bit machine, this need not concern the programmer.

Floating-point numbers

Floating-point numbers are the most common type used in mathematical calculations. The name Real has been used to denote this type in most of the older languages while C, C++ and Ada use the term float. Although Java has float, the default is double.

The range and precision of floating-point numbers is determined by the implementation. A floating-point number can be represented by 32 bits, as shown in Figure 3.4: one bit for the sign, seven bits for the exponent and the remaining 24 bits for the mantissa. This gives between six and seven decimal places of accuracy. The representation chosen is, essentially, a compromise, as more bits for the exponent will increase the range and decrease the precision, since there will be fewer bits for the mantissa.

sign   7 bit   24 bit mantissa (m)
bit   exponent (e)   (0.5 <= m < 1)
      (−64 to +63)

Real number = sign x m x 2 ^{e}

Figure 3.4   Representation of a floating-point number.

There are times when more accuracy is required; for example, in certain algorithms used in numerical analysis where errors can accumulate. Languages intended for scientific use, therefore, usually provide a type which gives more precision. In Fortran it is called DOUBLE PRECISION and in C, C++ and Java it is called double. The normal approach taken is to use 64 bits for the floating-point number instead of 32, giving between 14 and 15 decimal places of accuracy. In Java, double is defined as using 64 bits while in C, C++ and Fortran the size depends on the implementation.

Floating-point literals may be written with or without an exponent. Valid examples in Pascal, C, C++, Fortran 90 and Java are:

3.75   5.0   2.5E+7   0.1786E-5   6E+3

The literal 2.5E+7 is read as 'two point five times ten to the power seven'. The number 5.0 is a floating-point literal while 5 is an integer literal. In Java, floating-point literals are of type double; if type float is required then we must write 3.75f. In many languages, there must be at least one digit after the decimal point, hence 5.0, but 5. is allowed in C, C++, Fortran 90 and Java. There are few other differences between languages except that 6E+3 is treated as an integer literal in Ada.

In Ada, although the built-in floating-point type is Float, other floating-point types may be declared. For example, the declaration:

type Real **is digits** 8;

will define a floating-point type which has at least eight significant decimal digits. At first sight, this appears to give great flexibility, but as the computer hardware usually allocates 4 or 8 bytes to a floating-point number, this flexibility is largely illusory. Fortran 90 also allows a programmer to precisely specify the range and accuracy of floating-point numbers.

Complex numbers

Type COMPLEX in Fortran consists of a pair of REAL numbers together with suitable predefined operations. However, it does not occur as a built-in type in most languages and facilities in module and object-oriented languages make it easy to define such a type from its components.

3.5 Logical types

If a program always obeyed the same series of statements in exactly the same order, it would not be a very flexible or powerful tool. Conditional control statements are, therefore, very important. As such statements depend on logical expressions that may be true or false, most languages have a logical type. In Fortran, this is given the name LOGICAL, but in most languages the name given is Boolean in honour of George Boole the Irish mathematician who invented an algebraic approach to logical notation. Theoretically, it is possible to represent Boolean values by a single bit, but this is seldom done as single bits are not usually separately addressable.

In Fortran, the logical values are written as .FALSE. and .TRUE.. In more recent languages, the predefined identifiers false and true are used. C and C++ do not have logical literals as such; a false logical expression returns the integer value 0 while a true logical expression returns the value 1, although any non-zero value is treated as being true. This is a common source of errors by programmers who convert to C or C++ from other languages such as Pascal. As they are used to writing = as the equality operator, rather than ==, it is easy incorrectly to write:

if (a = 3) ...

instead of:

```
if (a == 3) ...
```

Both statements are syntactically correct. The expression a == 3 is only true when a is equal to 3 while the effect of a = 3 is to assign the value 3 to a. Assignments in C and C++ have a value. In this case, it is 3, which is interpreted by the **if** statement as the result true! Having a separate Boolean type is one of the areas where Java has improved on C++.

Examples of the use of the logical operators (**and, or, not**) are given in Chapter 4.

3.6 Character types

Most high-level languages include a built-in character type together with character operations. The main use of characters is as the components of strings. Character values are usually enclosed by single quotes as in:

```
'a'  'A'  ';'  ' '  '3'
```

Apart from input, output and assignment, the main operations on characters involve the relational and equality operators.

Many languages do not define the character set to be used and so this depends on the implementation. In Pascal, all that can be assumed is that the digits and the lower and upper case letters are in their normal order; that is:

```
'0' < '1' < '2' ...< '9'
'a' < 'b' < 'c' ...< 'z'
'A' < 'B' < 'C' ...< 'Z'
```

Ada 83 went one step further than this and stated that type Character gives the 128 characters of the ASCII character set while Ada 95 uses extended ASCII. Java stores char values as 16 bit Unicode characters. In C and C++, a char is held in one byte and can be treated like an integer.

In string manipulation languages such as Perl, strings are treated as scalar types, but the inclusion of strings of characters in languages such as C, C++, Pascal and Ada is accomplished by a data structure such as an array of characters, while in Java there is a String library class. As data structures are the subject of Chapter 7, the discussion of strings is deferred until then.

3.7 Enumeration types

So far, the types discussed have either been built-in types or they have been derived from built-in types, usually by constraining the range of allowed values. Enumeration types are user-defined types and their use leads to more readable programs. For example, consider the construction of a program that deals with the days in a week. One way of doing this would be to define an integer subrange type:

```
type Days = 1 .. 7;
```

and remember that 1 represented Sunday, 2 represented Monday, and so on. However, a much better solution would be to define what is known as an **enumeration type**. This can be accomplished, in Pascal, by the declaration:

```
type Days = (Sunday, Monday, Tuesday, Wednesday,
             Thursday, Friday, Saturday);
```

and in C and C++ by:

```
enum Days {Sunday, Monday, Tuesday, Wednesday,
           Thursday, Friday, Saturday};
```

where the possible literal values of type Days are listed in order. This facility, which was first provided by Pascal, is a good example of the general trend in language design to provide the programmer with facilities to express a solution in terms of the problem to be solved.

The relational and equality operators are available with enumeration types, with the relative values of the enumeration literals depending on their order in the declaration; hence:

```
Sunday < Monday < ... < Saturday
```

In Pascal, successor and predecessor operations (succ and pred) are also available. The value of succ(Monday) is Tuesday while pred(Monday) is Sunday. Sunday has no predecessor and Saturday no successor.

In Section 3.1, the characteristics of a type were defined to be its allowed values together with the set of operations that can be used to manipulate these values. One drawback of using:

```
type Days = 1 .. 7;
```

to represent the days of the week is that all the operations on integers are still available and it does not make sense, for example, to multiply two Days together. Also, it is necessary to ensure that the successor of 7 is 1!

The problem of having too rich a set of operations is removed by using an enumeration type although the reverse problem now exists; that is, all the necessary operations on Days are not available. Thus, additional operations such as dayBefore and nextDay will be needed so that dayBefore(Sunday) is Saturday and nextDay(Saturday) is Sunday. In Pascal, the definition of a new type and its associated operations cannot be grouped together in the program text and so it is not obvious to the reader that they are logically related. This problem is resolved by the use of modules in most Pascal implementations and is discussed in Chapter 5.

In Pascal, C and C++, enumeration values cannot be input or output. This restriction on their use has been lifted in Ada where it is possible to read them in and write them out. It is also possible in Ada to convert an enumeration literal to its representation as a character string and vice versa; thus:

```
Days'image(Friday)  is the string  "FRIDAY"
Days'value("FRIDAY")  is the literal  Friday
```

There is no counterpart of this in Pascal, C or C++.

In Pascal and Ada, type `Boolean` is a predefined enumeration type that is declared behind the scenes as:

```
type Boolean = (false, true);
```

In Pascal, C and C++, the literals in different enumeration types must be distinct. In Ada, however, the following is legal:

```
type Light is (red, amber, green);
type Flag is (red, white, blue);
```

The enumeration literal `red` is said to be **overloaded**. It must always be clear from the context which version of `red` is being used; if it is not, it is necessary to **qualify** the use of `red` and either write `Light'(red)` or `Flag'(red)`.

The `Character` type in Ada is also an enumeration type and this allows other character sets to be defined. In this way, type hexadecimal could be defined as:

```
type Hexadecimal is ('0', '1', '2', '3', '4', '5', '6',
            '7', '8', '9', 'A', 'B', 'C', 'D', 'E', 'F');
```

In Pascal, C and C++, enumeration literals must be identifiers and so the above is not allowed.

Java does not have enumeration types. However, enumeration values are named constants and so the effect can be achieved by defining constants in a Java class definition.

3.8 Reference and pointer variables

Reference variables have an address as their value – that is, a reference or pointer to another data item. Such data types were not available in early languages such as Fortran, Algol 60 and COBOL, although most later languages have included this facility and they have been added to Fortran 90.

In C and C++, we can do arithmetic using pointer values, but that is not allowed in Pascal, Fortran 90 and Ada. Java is even more restrictive. Although objects in Java are always accessed via references (i.e. pointers), we cannot explicitly declare pointer variables.

Typically, pointers can be assigned values, used in equality comparisons and dereferenced. They also have a special value (**nil** in Pascal, **null** in Ada, C, C++ and Java) which indicates that the pointer variable is currently pointing nowhere. This is used to indicate the end of a linked list. Instead of being assigned a null value, pointers in Fortran can have a `NULLIFY` operation applied to them and they can then be checked by the `ASSOCIATED` operation to test whether they are currently pointing at an object.

In most languages, the type being pointed at must be given as part of the pointer declaration and so there is no reduction in compile-time type checking. In C and C++, for example, we can have the declaration:

```
int ci, *cipoint;
```

which declares an integer variable `ci` and a variable `cipoint` whose type is 'pointer to integer'. C and C++ have the operator & to obtain the address of a variable while Delphi has the @ operator. After execution of the assignment statements:

```
ci = 34;
cipoint = &ci;
```

the value of `cipoint` is the address of the variable `ci`. This is shown diagrammatically in Figure 3.5.

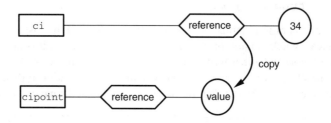

Figure 3.5 Effect of `cipoint` = &ci.

The value of `ci` in an expression can now be referred to in the normal way, as in `ci + 27`, or it can be referred to indirectly by dereferencing `cipoint`, as in `*cipoint + 27`. Both these expressions have the value 61. Note that any change to the value of `ci` is reflected in the value obtained by dereferencing `cipoint`.

C and C++ make extensive use of pointers. The ability to perform pointer arithmetic and thereby manipulate store addresses enables them to perform low-level systems programming and is one of the reasons why they have become the dominant systems programming languages. Although Delphi has the equivalent of the & operator, it does not allow pointer arithmetic.

When there is more than one way of referring to an object – that is, when the object has more than one name as in the case of `ci` – the object is said to have an **alias**. It is generally regarded as a bad idea to have aliases and so Pascal and Ada restrict the use of pointers and have no equivalent of the C & operator. The only operations available with pointer variables in these languages are dereferencing, assignment and comparison for equality.

To declare a pointer type in Pascal, we write:

```
type Integerpt = ↑Integer;
```

Variables may then be declared in the usual way:

```
var pipoint, another : Integerpt;
    pi : Integer;
```

As Pascal has no & operator, neither `pipoint` nor `another` can be assigned the address of an existing integer variable such as `pi`. They can only refer to specially created **dynamic variables**. Hence, to give `pipoint` a value, a new integer object must be created using the predefined procedure new as in:

```
new(pipoint);
```

This call allocates space for a new integer variable and assigns its address to `pipoint`. This is shown in Figure 3.6. The newly created dynamic variable is referred to as `pipoint↑` and can be given a value by writing:

```
pipoint↑ := 17;
```

It should be noted that:

● `pipoint` is of type 'pointer to `Integer`'
● `pipoint↑` is of type `Integer`

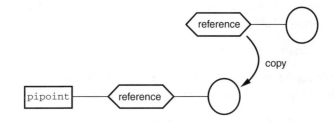

Figure 3.6   Effect of executing `new(pipoint)`.

Normally, declaration-reference binding occurs on block entry. That is when the pointer variable `pipoint` is allocated storage. However, the allocation of storage to `pipoint↑` occurs during execution of the new statement and so we have an example of declaration-reference binding being delayed until statement execution. This is referred to as **dynamic storage allocation**.

Other languages use a similar approach although the syntax is different. In Ada, pointer types are called **access types**. We can have the declaration:

```
type Integerpt is access Integer;
```

and then declare an access variable and give it a value using:

```
pipoint : Integerpt := new Integer;
```

In C, the amount of space required must be stated as in:

```
cipoint = (int *) malloc(sizeof(int));
```

The presence of `(int *)`, which is known as a **cast**, is to ensure that a pointer of the correct type is assigned to `cipoint`. This has been tidied up in C++ which allows:

```
cipoint = new int;
```

The overloading in the meaning of * in C and C++ syntax is confusing. We can declare a pointer variable and assign it a reference in C++ by writing:

```
int *cipoint = new int;
```

To give the integer pointed to by `cipoint` a value such as `17`, we use `*` as the dereferencing operator and have the statement:

```
*cipoint = 17;
```

Hence the text `*cipoint` means different things in the two lines. Features like this show why programs written in C and C++ have a justified reputation for being difficult to understand.

As `cipoint` is a variable of type `int*`, i.e. an `int` pointer, it can be argued that it would have been better to have written:

```
int* cipoint = new int;
```

to emphasise that a variable of type `int*` is being declared. However, that would lead us to believe that:

```
int* cipoint, ci2;
```

would cause two variables of type `int*` to be declared while, in fact, this declares `ci2` to be of type `int`. To declare two pointers, we must write:

```
int* cipoint, *cipoint2;
```

Although we have been discussing pointers to integers, we can declare pointers to any type. Suppose that we have a type `Stype`. We can declare and assign an `Stype` pointer in C++ as follows:

```
Stype *spoint = new Stype;
```

Note that `Stype` could be a C++ class definition, in which case `spoint` is a reference (pointer) to an object of class `Stype`. In Java, if `Stype` is a class definition then after the declaration:

```
Stype spoint = new Stype();
```

`spoint` is a reference (pointer) to an object of class `Stype`. The `*` is not needed as objects in Java are always accessed by reference. This demonstrates that, although Java was derived from C++, they sometimes use the same syntax with different semantics. Hence the declaration:

```
Stype s;
```

in C++ declares a variable `s` of type `Stype` while in Java it declares a variable `s` of type 'reference to `Stype`'.

Garbage

Aliasing is possible in Pascal because after execution of:

```
another := pipoint;
```

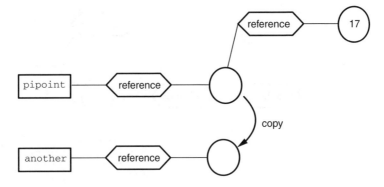

Figure 3.7   Effect of executing `another := pipoint`.

the situation is as shown in Figure 3.7, where `pipoint` and `another` both point to the same integer variable, although we at least have the security of knowing that such aliasing is restricted to dynamic variables. (Aliasing can also be introduced when parameters are called by reference and that is dealt with in Chapter 6.)

If `pipoint` is declared in a procedure, then it is only allocated storage while that procedure is being executed. Consider what happens when a dynamic variable is accessed via `pipoint` and in no other way. On exit from the procedure in which `pipoint` is declared, the dynamic variable will still exist, but it will no longer be possible to access it. In this case, it is said to be **garbage**.

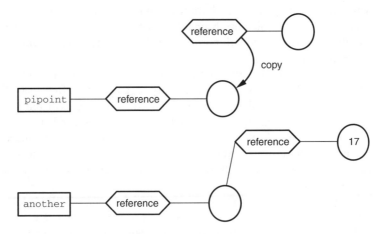

Figure 3.8   Effect of a second call of `new(pipoint)`.

Another way that garbage can be created is by further calls of new. After a second call of `new(pipoint)`, the situation will be as shown in Figure 3.8. As `another` is still pointing to the object created by the original call of `new(pipoint)`, no garbage has been created. However, if this is followed by a call of `new(another)`, the situation shown in Figure 3.9 will arise and garbage will have been created.

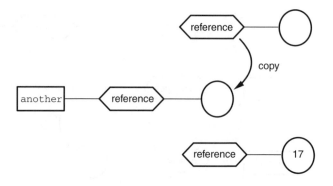

Figure 3.9   Effect of a subsequent call of new(another).

During the execution of a large program, the amount of garbage can build up. To overcome this problem, languages like Pascal have a dispose operation (delete in C++). The effect of:

```
dispose(pipoint);
```

is to deallocate the space allocated to the dynamic variable pointed to by pipoint, so that it can be reused in a later call of new. Thus, it appears that the build up of garbage can be avoided by preceding each call of new by a call of dispose. However, the problem with this is that there may be more than one access path to the dynamic variable, as was shown in Figure 3.7. If the call dispose(pipoint) had been executed in these circumstances, it would have resulted in the pointer variable another pointing to an area of store which had been returned to the system for reuse. This is known as a **dangling reference** and will normally lead to a program either crashing or giving the wrong results.

Errors caused by dangling references are very difficult to track down. The space available for dynamic variables is usually organised as a free space list (also known as the **heap**). A call of new(pipoint), for example, will remove the amount of space required for the dynamic variable from the free space list and assign its address to pipoint. A call of dispose(pipoint) will return the space to the heap so that it can be re-allocated even though the space is still being pointed to by another. However, the space may not be re-allocated immediately and so the value of another↑ may remain unchanged for some time. When the space is eventually re-allocated, there will be no logical reason for the sudden change in the value of another↑. The dispose operation must, therefore, be used with great care.

The solution to the problem of garbage build-up and dangling references is to let the system determine which dynamic variables can no longer be accessed by using an automatic **garbage collector**. A garbage collector has two functions. It first determines those store locations which have been allocated to dynamic variables and which can no longer be accessed, and then it collects these store locations together and returns them to the free space list.

This approach is used in most functional programming languages, but it is unusual in the implementation of imperative languages. A notable exception to this is Java. As it frees the programmer from having to manage the allocation of storage, a garbage collector removes the need for tedious and error-prone coding. When programming in C++ or Delphi, a lot of effort often has to be put into ensuring that there are no **memory leaks**, i.e. ensuring that all parts of an object are deleted when no longer required.

As well as their use with objects, a major use of pointers is with dynamic data structures and they are dealt with in Section 7.4.

Summary

1. Associated with a variable are attributes such as its name, type, reference and current value.

2. Early binding time of an object's attributes leads to efficient programs while run-time binding leads to more flexibility.

3. Static scope is when name-declaration binding occurs at compile time.

4. The characteristics of a type are its allowed values and the set of operations that can be used to manipulate these values.

5. When the type of variables is specified at compile time, a language is said to be statically typed. Static typing enables many logical errors to be detected by a compiler.

6. The lifetime (or extent) of a variable is when, during the execution of a program, that variable has storage space allocated to it.

7. Integer numbers are represented exactly in a computer while the representation of floating-point numbers is only approximate.

8. Enumeration types allow the programmer to express a solution in terms of the problem to be solved.

9. Unlike C++, Pascal and Ada restrict the use of pointers so that they can only refer to dynamic variables. Java does not allow the explicit use of pointers, but all objects are accessed by reference.

10. Dynamic variables are created during statement execution.

11. When a dynamic variable can no longer be accessed, it is said to be garbage. Inaccessible locations may be returned to the free space list either explicitly, by means of an operation such as `dispose`, or automatically by the system invoking a garbage collector.

12. Most imperative languages use the dispose operation (or its equivalent) while Java and functional languages use automatic garbage collection.

3.1 What is the difference between a constant and a variable?

3.2 Although variables may be initialised as part of their declaration in Ada and Java, this is not possible in Pascal. What advantages and disadvantages would result if a Pascal implementation gave all variables a default initial value? Suggest suitable default values for Integer, Char and Real variables. What, if any, are the drawbacks of the choices you have made?

3.3 Distinguish between:

(a) the lifetime and the scope of a variable,

(b) static scope and dynamic scope,

(c) static typing, strong typing and dynamic typing.

3.4 What advantages result from being able to perform type checking at compile time?

3.5 Explain the lifetime of the following in terms of binding and binding times:

(a) a local variable in a Pascal procedure or Java method,

(b) an object in a Java program,

(c) an attribute of an object in a Java program,

(d) a static local variable in a C++ program.

3.6 Why are programs written in dynamically typed languages usually interpreted rather than being compiled?

3.7 When a procedure or method is entered at run time, the local variables do not still have the values they had when the block was last executed. Why is this?

3.8 Distinguish between subtypes and derived types in Ada. What is the advantage of having derived types? Is this advantage worth the added complexity?

3.9 What problems result when the equality operator is used to compare floating-point quantities?

3.10 Define an enumeration type for the months of a year and list a suitable set of operations on values of type Month.

3.11 List the situations in Pascal or Java where values of a discrete type may be used, but not floating-point values.

3.12 What is meant by an alias? Describe the different ways aliasing can be introduced into a program. What problems arise with aliasing?

3.13 Section 3.8 showed how dangling references can be introduced by careless use of dispose. What other source of dangling references exists in languages which contain the equivalent of the C++ & operator?

Bibliography

The description in this chapter has been informal and is based to a large extent on how the features are implemented on present-day computers. This is similar to the approach taken by Ghezzi and Jazayeri (1997). A more theoretical approach is given in the book by Tennent (1981).

Barron, D.W. (1977). *An Introduction to the Study of Programming Languages*. Cambridge University Press.

Ghezzi, C. and Jazayeri, M. (1997). *Programming Language Concepts* (Third Edition). John Wiley & Sons.

Tennent, R.D. (1981). *Principles of Programming Languages*. Prentice-Hall.

Chapter 4

Expressions and statements

The main components of an imperative language are declarations, expressions and statements. Declarations were the subject of the last chapter and this chapter deals with expressions and statements. An expression yields a value, while a statement is a command to carry out some operation that normally alters the state. (Informally, the state can be considered to be the locations in store and their associated values.)

The order of evaluation of an expression depends on the precedence rules. With the exception of the logical operators, there is broad agreement in programming languages as to the order of precedence of the operators. There has also been a trend in language design towards requiring the compatibility of types in assignment statements and to imposing restrictions on mixed-mode expressions.

Structured control statements are an important feature in language design as they have a major impact on how well a language can support structured programming. This chapter discusses such statements in detail with particular attention being given to the development of the **for** statement.

Finally, the advantages of providing exception handling facilities in a language are discussed.

4.1 Expressions

Expressions are composed of one or more operands (that is, variables or constants) whose values may be combined by operators. To evaluate the expression:

```
4.0 + a * b
```

for example, values are substituted for the variables a and b, these values are multiplied together and 4.0 added to the result. At first sight, evaluating an expression appears to be one of the easier operations in computing but there are many subtleties.

For example, the above expression could also be evaluated by adding 4.0 to the value of a and multiplying the result by the value of b. Since these two methods will normally give different values, it is necessary to have precise rules, called the **precedence rules**, to govern the order in which an expression is evaluated. Java, which is typical of many languages, has the following evaluation rules:

1. Evaluate any expressions enclosed within brackets first, starting with the innermost brackets.

2. Apply the operator precedence shown in Table 4.1 within the brackets.

3. If the operators in (2) have the same precedence, apply them in order from left to right.

Rules somewhat similar to these apply in many other languages – for example, Fortran, Ada, C and C++. However, some languages have completely different rules; for example, in APL all operators have the same precedence and expressions are evaluated from right to left. In Pascal, there are fewer levels of precedence and the Boolean operators have higher precedence than the relational operators.

Application of the precedence rules allows a tree structure to be constructed. The tree structure corresponding to the expression:

```
a + b * c / d
```

is shown in Figure 4.1. Here, the values of b and c are first multiplied together, the result is then divided by d and the result of that operation is added to a.

Table 4.1 Java operator precedence (highest at the top).

```
!
*, /, %
+, -
>, <, >=, <=
==, !=
&&
||
=
```

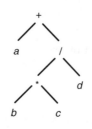

Figure 4.1 Tree structure.

The evaluation of an expression should produce a value and nothing more; that is, it should not change the state of the program. However, if function calls are used in an expression, there is no guarantee that a side effect of the function will not change the state. This practice is bad programming style and should be strongly discouraged. (A further discussion of this topic is given in Chapter 6.)

The action of an operator and a function is very similar, indeed a compiler can treat them both the same except that an operator obeys precedence rules. This is illustrated by operations like abs, which finds the absolute value of its argument. In a language like Ada, abs is an operator while in Pascal abs is a standard function.

Most of the simple operators in expressions are **binary** (or **dyadic**); that is, they operate on two operands and produce a single result. A **unary** (or **monadic**) operator, on the other hand, operates on one operand and produces a single result. Some operators, like + and – , can be both unary and binary under different conditions. For example, consider the two expressions:

```
- a * b + c
+ x / y - z
```

In the first expression, – is used as a unary operator while * and + are binary; however, in the second expression, / and – are binary and + is unary.

Boolean expressions

So far, the expressions used in this chapter have been arithmetic expressions; that is, the operands have been of numeric type and the operators arithmetic. However, expressions can be of different types and one type in nearly every language is Boolean (sometimes known as logical). In a Boolean expression, the value returned must be either true or false. Boolean expressions often involve relational operators, as in:

```
a + b > 0
x <= y
```

However, a Boolean expression can also contain variables of type Boolean and Boolean operators. The common Boolean operators are written as **not**, **and** and **or** in Pascal and Ada and as !, && and || in Java, C and C++. Ada, Java, C and C++ also include exclusive or (**xor** in Ada and ^ in Java, C and C++) while Algol 60 has two extra Boolean operators for implies and equivalence. As these last two operators are not widely used in programs and can be constructed from the other `Boolean` operators, they have not been included in most later languages.

The usual convention is to give **not** the highest precedence (above $*$) with **and** and **or** below the relational operators. This allows Boolean expressions such as:

```
a > b and c + 4 < d -- in Ada
a > b && c + 4 < d // in C, C++ and Java
```

Pascal, on the other hand, to reduce the number of levels of precedence, gives **and** the same precedence as $*$ and **or** the same as $+$. As a result, the above Boolean expression is invalid in Pascal because it would mean attempting to evaluate b **and** c. To achieve the same result as Ada, it is necessary to write:

```
(a > b) and (c + 4 < d)
```

`Boolean` operators are often used in **if** and **while** statements to combine relational expressions; for example:

```
if (i < 0) or (a[i] > a[i+1]) then ...
```

However, in such a case, if $i < 0$ is true, a[i] may not be inside the array bounds, resulting in a run-time error. Logically, of course, there is no need to evaluate the second relation if the first one is true because the overall result is bound to be true by the definition of the operator **or**. This is known as **short-circuit** evaluation and works as follows:

1. Given a **and** b where a is `false`, b is not evaluated.

2. Given a **or** b where a is `true`, b is not evaluated.

Some Pascal compilers take advantage of short-circuit evaluation while others do not, which is not a very satisfactory situation for the programmer. Ada provides distinct `Boolean` operators (**and then**, **or else**) for cases where short-circuit evaluation is desired. The C, C++ and Java operators && and || actually correspond to the Ada **and then** and **or else** operators while & and | correspond to **and** and **or**. However, && and || are virtually always used in C, C++ and Java programs.

Mixed-mode expressions

A previous section showed how operators like $+$ and $-$ may be overloaded; that is, have different meanings depending on their operands. The evaluation of a $+$ b differs if a and b are floating point or if they are integer. The advantage of overloading an operator is that it allows its normal use to continue. The alternative, which is to have a different operator for floating-point and integer addition, would be clumsy.

A further problem of evaluating an expression when the operands a and b are of different types is that languages differ on how they deal with such mixed-mode expressions. Three categories of language can be identified:

1. Languages such as Ada and Modula-2 that forbid mixed-mode expressions.

2. Languages like Pascal and Java that allow 'sensible' combinations such as adding an integer to a floating-point value. The result of such an expression is, as would be expected, a floating-point value.

3. Languages like C and C++ that allow 'unusual' combinations such as the ability to add an integer to a character. A major problem with this approach is that it can lead to unexpected results.

Hence, to add an integer to a floating-point number in a language like Ada or Modula-2, the type conversion must be done explicitly. For example, if a is of type Integer and b is of type Float, their addition must be written in Ada as:

```
Float(a) + b
```

The only disadvantage of this approach is that more has to be written.

4.2 Statements

Statements are the commands in a language which perform actions and change the state. Typical statements are:

- Assignment statements, which change the values of variables.
- Conditional statements, which have alternative courses of action.
- Iterative statements, which loop through a series of statements until some condition is satisfied.
- Procedure and method calls.

This section considers assignment statements and compound statements while conditional statements are considered in Section 4.3, iterative statements in Section 4.4 and procedure and method calls in Chapter 6.

A design aim of Algol 68 was that the number of independent language concepts should be reduced. One idea was that there should be no distinction between statements and expressions and so all statements in Algol 68 have a value. This idea has not been adopted in many later languages because, although it can lead to shorter and more efficient programs, it can also make programs much more difficult to read and understand as it encourages the use of side effects within expressions.

Assignment statements

The general form of the assignment statement is:

```
el := er
```

where el is the expression on the left-hand side of an assignment statement that gives a reference as its result and er is the expression on the right-hand side of an assignment statement that gives a value as its result. The value of the right-hand expression is then assigned to the reference given by the left-hand expression. Assignment is, therefore, an operation on reference-value pairs.

In C, C++ and Java, where the assignment operator is =, statements in general do not have a value, although an assignment such as:

```
el = er
```

is an expression and so can be used within other expressions in the same way as in Algol 68, with the same advantages and disadvantages.

In many languages, there are restrictions on the expression el. For example, many languages only allow a variable name, an indexed variable, a dereferenced pointer variable or the field of a record for el. Languages may also impose restrictions on the compatibility between the type of el and the type of value given by er. As an example, consider the typical Pascal or Ada assignment statement:

```
x := a + b * c;
```

If the type of x is the same as that of the result obtained by evaluating the expression on the right-hand side, then there are no problems. However, some languages state if the two types are not identical, then it is a compile-time error. Such a strict interpretation of assignment compatibility is used in Ada.

Languages such as Pascal and Java have adopted a different approach to assignment compatibility by allowing what is known as **widening**. If x has floating-point type and the right-hand expression has an integer value, then the assignment is valid as, essentially, there is no loss of information in making such an assignment.

However, in the reverse situation, where x is an integer and the right-hand expression has a floating-point value, the assignment would cause a loss of information since the floating-point value must be either truncated or rounded to the integer type. Although such assignments are allowed in older languages (Algol 60 used rounding while Fortran, C and C++ use truncation), languages like Pascal and Java do not allow assignment when information is lost. In Pascal, the programmer is expected to decide what is required and program accordingly, using the standard conversion functions available. To assign the Real x to the Integer i in Pascal, either of the following statements can be written:

```
i := trunc(x);
i := round(x);
```

depending on whether truncation or rounding is required. In Java, a **cast** must be used as in:

```
i = (int) x;
```

where a cast is a type name enclosed in brackets. This conversion causes truncation.

Assignment operators

As assignment statements of the form:

```
a = a + expression
```

occur frequently in computer programs, languages such as C, C++, Java, Algol 68 and Modula-2 provide special short-hand forms. In C, C++ and Java, this can be written as:

```
a += expression
```

Other similar operators are (`-=`, `*=` and `/=`). These assignment operators allow the compiler to generate efficient code without resorting to extensive optimisation techniques.

C, C++ and Java also have increment (`++`) and decrement (`--`) operators. They can be used in two ways. The effect of executing:

```
a = 1; b = ++a;
```

is to set a to 1, increment the value of a by 1 and then assign its value to b. The result is that a and b will both have the value 2. The effect of executing:

```
a = 1; b = a++;
```

is to assign the value of a to b before a has been incremented. Hence, b will have the value 1 and a the value 2. Although such operators allow very compact code to be written, the resulting programs are often difficult to understand when combined with other C and C++ operators as in `*b++`. The meaning of that expression is left as an exercise.

Multiple assignment statements

Many languages allow multiple assignment statements. For example, in Algol 60 the value of the expression in:

```
a := b := c := expression;
```

is evaluated and then assigned to each one of the variables given in the list on the left-hand side.

In languages that treat assignments as expressions, such as Algol 68, C, C++ and Java the assignment operator has very low precedence and is evaluated from right to left. Multiple assignment then comes out naturally. The value of the assignment:

```
c = expression;
```

is the value assigned to c. Hence, in the statement:

```
a = b = c = expression;
```

the expression is evaluated first and its value assigned to c. The value of the assignment:

```
c = expression;
```

is then assigned to b and that value is then assigned to a.

As well as supporting all the C assignment operators given above, Perl allows lists on the left-hand side of an assignment statement. The assignment:

```
($a, $b) = (17, "Hello");
```

will assign 17 to $a and "Hello" to $b. This feature can be used to swap the values of two variables as in:

```
($a, $b) = ($b, $a);
```

Compound statements

The compound statement is vital in languages such as Pascal, C, C++ and Java when constructing structured control statements. In Pascal this is done by the use of **begin** ... **end** brackets, so:

begin S1; S2; ... **end**

can be treated like a single statement. C, C++ and Java use the brackets { } to group statements together as in:

{ S1; S2; ...}

Languages such as Ada and Fortran 90 use explicit terminators for conditional and iterative statements, and so they do not need compound statements. This is a welcome change to students who often forgot the **begin**, **end** or { } brackets. For example, a condition controls a single statement. Hence, in C, C++ or Java, a student may correctly write:

```
if (a < b)
    c = d;
```

and then decide to add a second statement to the condition. A common error is to write:

```
if (a < b)
    c = d;
    e = f;
```

and the student is then bemused when the flow of control does not meet their expectations as this does not do what the indentation suggests. The two statements must be bracketed into a compound statement as in:

```
if (a < b) {
    c = d;
    e = f;
}
```

It is unfortunate that a new language like Java, in order to maintain its close ties with C++, has compound statements rather than explicit terminators. It is interesting that Perl, whose statement syntax is based on C, requires { } brackets even when the condition only controls a single statement.

4.3 Sequencing and control

As the execution of statements is central to imperative languages, sequencing mechanisms are necessary for routing control from one statement to another and for separating individual statements. As was mentioned in Chapter 1, the end of a line terminates a statement in Fortran, Basic and COBOL while a semi-colon is used to either separate statements in Pascal or terminate them in Ada, C, C++ and Java. Conditional and iterative statements are necessary so that the flow of control can vary depending on a program's input data.

Selection

The earliest conditional statements were in Fortran and had the form:

```
IF (C1) L1, L2, L3
```

This is the Fortran arithmetic IF statement. The expression C1 is evaluated and, depending on whether it is negative, zero, or positive, there is a branch to the statement with the integer label L1, L2 or L3. There is also a similar logical IF statement introduced in Fortran 66 which has the syntax:

```
IF (logical expression) statement
```

However, its use was limited as only a single statement can be obeyed if the logical expression is true and that statement cannot be a DO or another IF statement.

Statements containing conditional jumps to statement labels tend not to appear in current languages, even in up-to-date versions of Fortran. Instead, most languages use the **if** statement introduced by Algol 60 as their basic conditional statement; for example:

```
if C1 then S
if C2 then S1 else S2
```

where C1 and C2 are conditions and S, S1 and S2 are statements. The structure of these two forms of the **if** statement is shown diagrammatically in Figure 4.2.

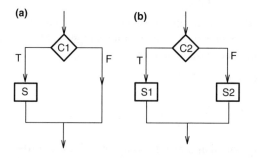

Figure 4.2   Structure of the two forms of an **if** statement.

Often, in a program, a situation arises where several statements are to be obeyed after finding that a condition such as C1 is true. As the statements S, S1 and S2 can be compound statements, this can easily be achieved in Algol 60 without having to resort to explicit jump instructions. Statements such as the Algol **if** statement are called **structured statements** and have the important property that they have only one entry and only one exit point. This property can prove very helpful when trying to reason about a program's effect and in writing well-structured programs.

Although Algol's **if** statements have proved relatively straightforward and easy to use, they can result in a problem known as them **dangling else** because both forms are allowed. For example, in the following statement:

```
if C1 then if C2 then S1 else S2
```

it is not clear whether the single **else** is associated with the first or the second **if** . . . **then**. Therefore, two interpretations are possible:

```
if C1 then begin if C2 then S1 end else S2
```

or:

```
if C1 then begin if C2 then S1 else S2 end
```

Different languages have found different solutions to cope with this ambiguity. Algol 60 forbids conditional statements after a **then** and so extra **begin** . . . **end** brackets must be used. Pascal, C, C++ and Java make the interpretation that the **else** is associated with the innermost **if**; when the other interpretation is required, a compound statement must be used. In Ada, each **if** is paired with a closing **end if**; for example:

```
if C1 then
    if C2 then S1;
    end if;
else S2;
end if;
```

or:

```
if C1 then
    if C2 then S1; else S2;
    end if;
end if;
```

A similar solution is adopted in Algol 68, Modula-2 and Fortran 90.

An **if** statement can be nested inside another **if** statement and this nesting process can be continued as required. In such cases, it is usually better for the nested **if** statement to follow the **else**, as this corresponds much more closely with human processing. When the **if** statement follows the **then** part, the human mind must stack information for later processing and repeated operation will soon exhaust the stacking ability of most humans. Some languages, notably Ada and Modula-2, have an **elsif** construction to assist in the presentation and understanding of cascaded conditional statements.

When a selection from many statements is required, the **case** statement is best used. This was first implemented in Algol W and has been adopted by most subsequent languages. The Pascal version of the **case** statement can be illustrated by calculating the number of days in a month, where January is the integer 1, February 2, etc.

```
case month of
    1, 3, 5, 7, 8, 10, 12 : days := 31;
    4, 6, 9, 11 : days := 30;
    2 : if years mod 4 = 0 then
            days := 29
        else days := 28
end
```

The expression after the word **case** is often called the **selector** and must be of a discrete type. The case labels must be constant values of the same type as the selector expression.

More recent languages, notably Ada, Fortran 90 and Delphi, have made two changes to the basic case statement. The first is the inclusion of a default condition. In standard Pascal, if the expression value is not one of the constant values in the case lists an error will occur; for example, if month had the value zero. Such a default case is covered in Ada by the compulsory inclusion of **others** (DEFAULT in Fortran 90 and **else** in most Pascal extensions), so the programmer must explicitly consider what action is required if an unspecified value is encountered. (Note that **others** is unnecessary if all the discrete type alternatives are covered in the **case** statement.) Secondly, Ada, Fortran 90 and Delphi allow ranges of values to be used for each constant in the case list while in Pascal each value must be given separately.

The following Ada example illustrates these modifications:

```
case ch is
    when '0' .. '9' => put_line("digit");
    when 'A' .. 'Z' => put_line("letter");
    when others => put_line("special character");
end case;
```

The C, C++ and Java version is called the **switch** statement. A major difference from Pascal and Ada is that a **break** statement is required or one case follows through to the next. Omitting the break is used to attach several labels to the same statement as in:

```
switch (month) {
    case 4:
    case 6:
    case 9:
    case 11 :
        days = 30;
        break;
    case 2:
        if (years % 4 == 0)
          days = 29;
        else days = 28;
        break;
    default:
        days = 31;
        break;
}
```

The need for the break statement increases the opportunity for errors. Some experimental languages have increased the range of allowed types in the selector expression to include strings.

4.4 Iterative statements

The essence of making use of the computer's extraordinary speed of operation is to have loops of statements. Such loops are terminated in one of two ways: either by a condition being fulfilled or by completing a fixed number of iterations.

while statement

This is the most common of the statements controlled by a condition. In its simplest form it is:

```
while (C) S // C, C++ or Java
while C do S {Pascal}
while C loop statement_sequence end loop;  -- Ada
```

where C is a conditional expression and S is a statement. Its structure is shown in Figure 4.3. The statement S is normally a compound statement that must eventually make the condition C false if we are not to have an infinite loop. However, it is also possible to exit from a C, C++ or Java loop using a **break** statement and from an Ada loop using **exit**.

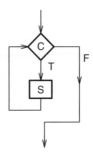

Figure 4.3   Structure of the **while** loop.

Perl has an **unless** loop in addition to a **while** with:

```
unless (C) { statement_sequence }
```

being equivalent to:

```
while (!C) { statement_sequence }
```

A variant of the while loop allows the statement to be executed at least once by placing the test at the end as in the Java, C or C++:

```
do statement_sequence while (C);
```

The Pascal form loops until the condition is true. It is:

```
repeat statement_sequence until C
```

Its structure is shown diagrammatically in Figure 4.4.

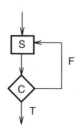

Figure 4.4   Structure of the **repeat** loop.

loop statement

This is a more general form of statement and includes both the **while** and **repeat** statements as special cases. In its Ada form it consists of:

```
loop
    statement_sequence
end loop;
```

The sequence of statements can include an **exit** statement:

```
exit when C;
```

Furthermore, it is possible to have more than one exit from a loop.

The following example shows how an **exit** statement can be used when reading and summing a list of positive numbers where the list is terminated by a negative number:

```
sum := 0;
loop
   get(number);
   exit when number < 0;
   sum := sum + number;
end loop;
```

This **loop** statement illustrates how a programmer can overcome a common problem in computing; that is, performing n and a half loops.

Figure 4.5 shows the structure of a loop with one exit, where S1 and S2 are sequences of zero or more statements. It can be seen from this figure that when S1 is null, it becomes a **while** statement and when S2 is null, a **repeat** statement. Hence, it is not necessary for Ada to include any iterative statement other than the **loop** statement.

for statement

This statement differs from the other **loop** statements in that it is used for an iteration that is to be performed a fixed number of times. Pascal has two forms of the **for** statement:

```
for cv := low to high do S
for cv := high downto low do S
```

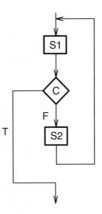

Figure 4.5   Structure of **loop** statement with one exit.

where cv is the control variable, low and high are discrete expressions and S is a statement. These two forms of the Pascal **for** statement are simplified forms of the original and more general Algol 60 **for** statement.

> **for** cv := low **step** increment **until** high **do** S

In the Pascal **for** statement there is an implicit increment. In the first form it is +1 and in the second form it is −1. At first sight, this might appear a major restriction; however, in practice, most **for** statements are used in conjunction with arrays, the control variable being the same as the array subscript. Thus, the majority of cases are covered by step lengths of +1 and −1; the few unusual cases can be written using a **while** loop.

Ada has adopted a similar approach to Pascal. The two forms of the Ada **for** statement are:

> **for** cv **in** low .. high **loop**
> . . .
> **end loop**;

and:

> **for** cv **in reverse** low .. high **loop**
> . . .
> **end loop**;

The structure diagram of the **for** statement shown in Figure 4.6 is constructed on the lines of the Pascal/Ada statement so that the control variable does not go out of range. This is particularly necessary when cv is defined as a subrange variable whose values can only be in the range low to high.

As the **for** statement has evolved from the looping statements of early languages, it is instructive to study its development to understand the advantages and disadvantages of the various forms provided by different languages.

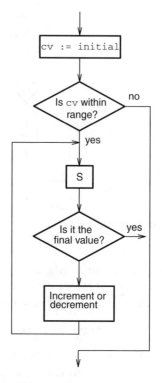

Figure 4.6   Structure of the Pascal/Ada **for** statement.

- Early versions of Fortran used a very restricted DO loop with integer counting and positive increments. In Fortran 66, the loop was always executed at least once. Fortran 90 allows negative increments and a loop to be executed zero times.

- Algol 60 provides a very powerful **for** statement. The initial, final and incremental value can all be expressions and can even be of type Real.

- C has a very complex **for** statement which has been followed in C++ and Java. Its general form is:

> **for** (e1; e2; e3) S

where each of the expressions e1, e2, e3 are optional. This form is equivalent to:

```
e1;
while (e2) {S; e3;}
```

so if the traditional **for** statement to execute a statement n times is required, it is written as:

> **for** (i = 1; i <= n; i++) S

which is equivalent to:

```
for i:= 1 to n do S
```

in Pascal, but is not as obvious to the programmer.

From the use of **for** statements in early languages, several conclusions seem to have been drawn. Firstly, using floating-point values in a counting loop, as Algol 60 did, is likely to lead to error. For example:

```
for i := 0.0 step 0.1 until 6.0 do S
```

does not guarantee that the final value 6.0 will be considered within the loop. Its inclusion or non-inclusion depends on the rounding error and how floating-point numbers are represented in a particular computer. But programs should not be subject to such variations and although programmers could counter such problems (typically by adding a small fraction of the increment to the final value), it is now generally agreed that **for** loops should work with discrete types, since they are counting loops.

It is also better to allow **for** loops to do nothing in certain circumstances rather than to insist, as in Fortran 66, that the statements in the loop must be executed at least once. The increment and final value are best evaluated once, when the **for** loop is first encountered, and not re-evaluated each time around the loop, as was the case in Algol 60. Furthermore, the control variable should only be changed by the increment; that is, no instruction in S should be allowed to alter its value.

The purpose of the changes just outlined is to make the action of a **for** loop very clear to the programmer. By looking at the first line (no matter how complicated S is), the programmer can see the starting point, the increment and the finishing point. This is, in essence, the purpose of the **for** statement. If a more general loop is required then one of the other loop statements should be used.

Ada and Fortran 90 allow an **exit** statement within a **for** loop, but this feature should not be used. In a **for** loop we tell the reader at the beginning of the loop that we are going to go round the loop a certain number of times. If there is an alternative way of leaving the loop, we are going back on that earlier promise and the action of the **for** statement is no longer obvious from the first line.

The scope of the control variable in the **for** statement has also been the subject of some controversy. Ada takes the strong line that the control variable only has scope within the **for** statement and is not available outside it. In Ada, the **for** loop forms a block in which the control variable is implicitly declared. C++ and Java allow the control variable to be declared within the **for** loop as in:

```
for (int i = 0; i < n; i++) S
```

and it is good practice for this always to be done.

Languages that do not have this feature have the problem of deciding what the value of the control variable should be on leaving the loop. The options include the value that failed the loop test (as in Fortran 90) or the last value that was used in the loop statement S. In Pascal, the loop control variable is undefined on exit from the loop. Making the scope of the control variable the **for** loop avoids this problem and seems the best solution.

Languages such as Pascal, Ada, C and C++ which allow enumeration types, permit the use of these types in **for** statements. Given the type declaration:

```
type Month = (Jan, Feb, Mar, Apr, May, Jun, Jul,
              Aug, Sep, Oct, Nov, Dec);
```

the **for** statement:

```
for i:= Jan to Dec do S
```

will iterate through the 12 values Jan, Feb, . . . Dec.

Iterators

A mechanism for iterating over the elements of a data structure is known as an **iterator**. In the Pascal **for** statement:

```
for i := low to high do S
```

the control variable i takes each value in the discrete range low to high in turn and is often used to access the elements of an array. In theory, this can be generalised so that the control variable can range over all the members of a structured data type such as a set, sequence or tree.

For example, given a set of names d, the meaning of the **for** loop:

```
for x in d do S
```

would be to execute the statement S for each name x in the set d. The order in which the names x are selected from the set d is undefined, but that is not a problem. The requirement is to access each element in the set in turn; the precise order in which this is done is unimportant. **for** statements similar to this occur in CLU and Alphard, but both implementations are more complicated than the structure shown here. Perl has a **foreach** statement:

```
foreach $i (@list) { statement_sequence }
```

in which the scalar $i is assigned to each value in the list @list in turn and the body of the **foreach** loop is executed after each assignment.

4.5 goto statement

Controversy has raged over the use of the **goto** statement since Dijkstra's letter to the Communications of the ACM entitled 'Goto Statement Considered Harmful' (1968). Most programmers in the early days of computing made widespread use of the conditional jump. Indeed, it was one of the important features available for constructing the primitive loops of the 1950s and early 1960s. Of the early high-level languages, Fortran and COBOL encouraged the continued use of jumps (**goto** statements) with their associated labels. In Algol 60, with its structured control statements, programs could be written with only a minimal use of **goto** statements, mainly to exit from loops in failure situations.

Since the mid-1970s, the general consensus of opinion has swung strongly against the use of the **goto** statement. Overuse of such conditional jumps in complicated programs can lead to errors that are often obscure and difficult to locate.

Modern high-level languages have usually compromised in their approach to the **goto** statement. With the notable exception of Java, most such languages still include **goto** statements and labels. The use of **break** as a controlled exit from a loop and having **exception handling facilities** (described in the next section) means that there is no need for **goto**.

Recent languages have played down the use of the **goto** statement and have placed restrictions on its use. For example, Algol 60 permits jumps into and out of **if** statements but Pascal and Fortran 90 allow no jumps into any structured statement. Ada goes further than Pascal in not allowing jumps out of procedures.

(4.6) Exception handling

During program execution, 'exceptional' events may occur making normal continuation undesirable or even impossible. Such exceptional occurrences can arise as a result of errors, such as attempted division by zero, erroneous user input, an array subscript going out of bounds, unexpectedly encountering the end of a file or by the need for tracing and monitoring in program testing.

Many programming languages leave the onus of dealing with exceptional events completely with the programmer. It is their responsibility to test for the possibility of such events before they occur and to handle them as they see fit. However, such a policy often leads to complex programs and can obscure the underlying structure of the program.

An alternative strategy is to provide exception handling facilities as part of the language. The first language to do this in a systematic way was PL/I, by including features called ON-conditions. Algol 68 also included exception and default handling facilities but these were restricted to files, and were not available for general program execution. Ada, Java and Delphi provide exception handling facilities of a general nature and they have been added to C++. Exception handling is essential in an embedded language like Ada so that errors that cannot be checked at compile time can be handled at run time.

When an exceptional event occurs, an exception is said to be **raised** (in Ada and Delphi) or **thrown** (in C++ and Java). Normal program execution is interrupted and control is transferred to a specially written part of the program, known as the **exception handler**. A program written to handle the different exceptional events that might occur is called a **fault-tolerant program**.

We will look at exception handling through the facilities provided in Ada and Java. They both have predefined and user-defined exceptions. As an example, we will examine what happens when an array subscript goes out of bounds. In Ada, the predefined exception constraint_error is raised while in Java an ArrayIndexOutofBoundsException is thrown.

In Ada, exception handlers are associated with a statement sequence in what is called a **frame,** which can be a subprogram body, a package body or a block. Consider execution of the statements in the following frame:

```
begin
  ...
  if a(i) < 0 then ...
  ...
exception
  when constraint_error => ...;
end;
```

If the value of the subscript i goes out of bounds, an exception is raised, normal program execution is interrupted and control is transferred to the statements following:

```
when constraint_error =>
```

where remedial action can take place. When the statements in the exception handler have been executed, the frame is left. This is in contrast to PL/I where control is passed back to the point where the exception was raised.

Different exception handlers can exist for each kind of exception. In analogy with the **case** statement, **others** can be included in Ada's exception handling mechanism to catch the exceptions not specifically mentioned at the end of a frame.

In Java, a statement where an exception may occur should be enclosed inside a **try** block.

```
try {
  ...
  if (a[i] < 0)...
  ...
}
catch (ArrayIndexOutofBoundsException e) {
  ...
}
```

If the subscript goes out of range, an exception is thrown and execution of the **try** block is terminated. The exception is then caught by a **catch** block where remedial action can take place. In Java, all exceptions are subclasses of class Exception and so

```
catch (Exception e) { ...}
```

will catch all exceptions.

In both Ada and Java, if an exception occurs in a block that does not have an exception handler for that exception, the exception is propagated to the next level. If the exception occurred in a subprogram or method body, the exception is passed to the block containing the call. Usually when an exception occurs during the execution of a procedure or method it is due to an inappropriate parameter value being passed in the call. Propagating the exception to the calling block means that the error report is passed back to the place where the error was made and where appropriate remedial action can take place. If it cannot be handled there, the exception is thrown again in the calling block. If no exception handler is found, then the system will report a run-time error and stop execution of the program.

Java has two kinds of exception: checked and unchecked. Division by zero or an index out of bounds are unchecked exceptions while most others are checked. If a checked exception may be thrown in a method and will not be caught and handled in that method then the fact that the method can cause an exception to be thrown must be stated in the method declaration. Hence if a call of the method getFile could cause an IOException to be thrown, the declaration of getFile must have the form:

```
public void getFile() throws IOException { ... }
```

In Ada, a user can declare new exception identifiers as follows:

```
overflow, help : exception;
```

A user-defined exception is then activated by a **raise** statement, as in:

```
raise overflow;
```

In Java, an exception is a class and so we can define a new subclass as in:

```
public class StackException extends Exception { ... }
```

We can then throw a StackException object:

```
throw new StackException();
```

As well as being automatically raised when an error occurs, the predefined exceptions may also be activated by a **raise** or **throw** statement. However, it is better not to raise or throw predefined exceptions explicitly, but to declare and use a separate user-defined exception so that there is no confusion as to the cause of an error. The predefined exception could, after all, have been caused by some other reason.

Exception handling in Delphi is similar to that of Java, with exceptions being raised in a **try** block and handled in an **except** clause. Exceptions are classes and user-defined exceptions can be created as subclasses of class Exception.

The syntax of exception handling is very similar in C++ and Java, but the exception handling facilities of C++ are more complex and less general than those of Java. Exceptions in C++ must normally be thrown explicitly, although some operators such as **new** will throw exceptions, in the case of **new** when the system has run out of memory. Exceptions of any type may be thrown rather than just objects of subclasses of class Exception and so we can have statements in a try block such as:

```
if (i < 0)
    throw i;
```

where i is of type int. Due to its complexity, we will not look further at exception handling in C++.

An example

As users of computer systems often make mistakes when typing in data, robust programs must be able to respond to such errors in a sensible way and not immediately crash. If, in Pascal for example, a letter is typed in response to a request for a numerical value, then the program will be terminated with control being passed to the operating system. If a programmer wishes control to remain within the program, then he or she must define special procedures to read the group of characters from which the numerical value is to be constructed character by character. The programmer can then program the appropriate action which is to be taken when an unacceptable character is encountered. This approach is far from satisfactory in a high-level language.

Exceptions are ideal for handling such errors. In Ada, for example, if a letter is typed in response to the input statement `get (x)` when a number is expected, a `data_error` exception is raised. Consider the following loop in which there is an inner block with an exception handler:

```
loop
    begin
        get(x);
        exit;
    exception
        when data_error =>
        skip_line;
        put_line("Error in number, try again");
    end;
end loop;
```

If an error is detected on reading x, control is transferred to the exception handler which, in this case, performs the remedial action of skipping the remaining characters on the current line before giving a new prompt. We then exit from the block in which the exception was raised. As we are still inside the loop, this allows a second attempt to be made to read x.

Overuse

Exceptions should be restricted to the handling of abnormal situations. It is bad programming practice to use them to handle unusual, but normal cases. For example, given the definition of Days in Section 3.7, the function call Days'succ(Saturday) results in a `constraint_error` exception being raised. Such a situation should always be handled by an explicit check as in:

```
if today = Saturday then
    tomorrow := Sunday;
else
    tomorrow := Days'succ(today);
```

rather than with:

```
begin
    tomorrow := Days'succ(today);
exception
    when constraint_error =>
      tomorrow := Sunday;
end;
```

Eiffel

Meyer (1997) takes a very strong line on the action to be taken by an exception handler. He takes the view that only two possible actions are appropriate:

- Tidy up the mess, report an error and terminate.
- Attempt to fix what went wrong and then retry the operation that raised the exception.

A function or procedure should therefore always either carry out the requested action or report failure. This view has been put into practice in the exception handling facilities of Eiffel. As in Ada and Java, when an exception is raised in Eiffel, control is transferred to an exception handler which can attempt to recover from the error. However, in Eiffel, there are only two ways in which an exception handler may be left; by executing a **retry** command (which causes the function or procedure in which the exception occurred to be executed again) or by coming to the end of the handler which causes the exception to be raised in the calling routine.

This approach is reasonable in a sequential language where program termination does not lead to a catastrophe. However, in an embedded or distributed system, it is often not possible for a program to terminate safely when an exception is raised. It must continue, perhaps with reduced capability, while reporting the error so that remedial external action can be taken. As Ada was designed for use with embedded systems and Java with the Internet, this justifies their more flexible approach to exception handling.

Summary

1. An expression yields a value while execution of a statement alters the state.

2. The order of evaluation of an expression depends on the precedence rules used in the language.

3. Side effects in the evaluation of an expression should be avoided.

4. The meaning of an operator can depend on its operands. Such an operator is said to be overloaded.

5. Structured statements should have only one entry and one exit point. This is important when reasoning about a program's effect and in writing well-structured programs.

6. There are two kinds of conditional statement in modern imperative languages: the **if** statement and the **case** (or **switch**) statement.

7. A default condition is not allowed in the Pascal **case** statement, but is permitted in C, C++, Ada, Delphi and Java.

8. There are two kinds of iterative statement in most modern imperative languages: the **while** statement, and the **for** statement.

9. In Pascal and Ada, the **for** statement is restricted to unit steps.

10. The control variable in an Ada **for** statement is implicitly declared while in C++ and Java it may be declared within the loop. In Pascal, the control variable must be declared outside the loop and its value is undefined on exit from the loop.

11. When a run-time error occurs in languages such as Ada, C++, Delphi and Java, an exception is raised. Normal program execution is interrupted and control is passed to the appropriate exception handler.

12. Exception handling is important in embedded systems as they have to be able to recover from errors that occur during program execution.

Exercises

4.1 Compare the precedence of the logical operators **and**, **or** and **not** in Pascal and Ada. List the drawbacks of the precedence rules adopted by each language and outline your preferred solution.

4.2 Under what circumstances will short-circuit evaluation of logical operations lead to results that differ from those obtained from full evaluation?

4.3 Why do languages, such as Ada, not allow mixed-mode expressions and require type conversions to be done explicitly?

4.4 In Algol 68, a statement has a value. What are the advantages and disadvantages of this?

4.5 In Standard Pascal, a positive decision was made not to have a default condition in the **case** statement (although most implementations do provide it). In contrast, in Ada, a default case must be included unless the full range of the **case** expression is already covered by the case labels. Which approach leads to the more reliable programs?

4.6 As it is desirable for structured statements to have only one entry point and one exit point, do you think that Ada and Java should have been restricted so that **exit** or **break** statements are not allowed in **while** and **for** loops?

4.7 Consider the problem of reading and summing a list of positive numbers where the list is terminated by a negative number. An Ada solution, using an **exit** statement, is given in Section 4.4. Compare it with a Pascal solution to the problem.

4.8(a) Describe how the **for** statement differs in Algol 60, Pascal, Ada and C++.

(b) Algol 60 allows the control variable to be changed within a loop. Why was that freedom removed in Pascal?

(c) Is it a major restriction for the increment of the control variable to be restricted to +1 or −1?

(d) What are the advantages of declaring the control variable within the **for** loop, as in Ada, C++ and Java?

4.9 Why is the presence of exception handling facilities important in a language like Ada?

4.10 Once an exception has been handled in PL/I, control is returned to the statement following the exception, while in Ada the frame containing the exception is left. Compare the effect of these two approaches.

4.11 Compare the Eiffel approach to exception handling with that of Ada and Java.

Bibliography

Structured programming and the design of a suitable set of structured control statements was a major issue in language design in the late 1960s and early 1970s following Dijkstra's letter about the **goto** statement (1968). A special issue of *ACM Computing Surveys* (1974) has an interesting series of articles on the topic.

ACM (1974). 'Special Issue: Programming', *ACM Computing Surveys*, **6**(4).

Dijkstra, E.W. (1968). 'Goto statement Considered Harmful'. *Comm. ACM*, **11**, 147–148.

Meyer, B. (1997). *Object-oriented Software Construction* (Second Edition). Prentice-Hall.

Program structure

One of the most important issues that has to be addressed in the design of a language is the support it gives to the control of complexity. This is achieved by hiding unwanted detail and is implemented by dividing programs into self-contained units that can only interact with one another through small strictly defined interfaces.

This chapter looks at the alternative forms of these units and the ways in which they can be combined to form complete programs. In early languages, the principal structuring unit was the procedure. This is a satisfactory unit of decomposition for small programs, but for larger programs, a means of grouping procedures into larger units is needed. This is provided by the module which allowed groups of related procedures and types to be defined together as a single unit. The class, which is central to object-oriented languages, is a special kind of module. Ordinary modules may contain a type definition while a class *is* a type definition. As a further structuring mechanism, languages like Java enable classes to be grouped together in packages.

As well as the logical decomposition of a program into components, we consider its physical decomposition into files whose contents may be compiled separately.

In Chapter 3, we looked at the scope rules governing the visibility of identifiers within a module. In this chapter, we look at inter-module visibility.

5.1 Introduction

An important aim of a modern high-level language is to provide support for the design and creation of reliable systems. This means that the software design process has had a major effect on the constructs and structure of programming languages. Originally, program design concentrated on algorithms, i.e. the sequence of operations or procedures required to carry out a problem. Over the years the focus has changed and there has been a growing acceptance of the importance of understanding a problem and structuring a solution in terms of the information which is to be manipulated. This has culminated in the object-oriented approach.

We will discuss the procedural and object-oriented approaches to design to see why they lead to different ways of structuring a program. However, although their high-level program structure and their approach to problem solving is different, many constructs in a procedural language like Pascal are much the same as those in an object-oriented language like Java. They are both imperative languages which achieve their effect by changing the value of variables. We will therefore be emphasising similarities as well as pointing out differences.

The usual approach to program design in a procedural language is called **programming by stepwise refinement** or **top-down design**. The first step in this process is to produce a top-level algorithm expressed in terms of the problem to be solved. This approach allows the designer to concentrate on the organisation and design of the solution without being distracted by implementation details. Although the statements in the top-level algorithm are not capable of being directly implemented on a computer, they can be regarded as the specifications of subproblems. Thus, the next step is to produce a solution to each of the subproblems by expanding the corresponding specification into a series of more detailed statements, each of which can in turn be considered as the specification of an even simpler problem. This stepwise refinement continues until the subproblems are simple enough for their solution to be written directly in a programming language.

The language features that help support this approach to design are the structured control statement and the procedure. Structured control statements are described in Chapter 4. The advantage of using procedures is that, instead of producing the solution to a subproblem by directly expanding a statement in the top-level algorithm, an appropriate procedure can be defined and then used. In this way, the final main program will not be too different from the original top-level algorithm, since many of the top-level statements will have been implemented by procedure calls. Furthermore, if meaningful identifiers are used for each of the procedures, a reasonable idea of the intent of a program can be gained by reading the relatively short main program. A set of procedure definitions is therefore central to the organisation of a procedural programming language.

Abstraction and encapsulation

The procedure is a major **abstraction** mechanism. By using a procedure, it is possible to concentrate on what the program does without having to bother about how it does it. This ability to **hide unwanted detail** is a major tool in controlling program complexity. Procedures can be considered to be modules that can be joined together to form complete programs. A procedure **encapsulates** a series of program instructions that are hidden from the user. The signature of the procedure (its name and parameters) provides a small well-defined public interface through which the user can make a procedure call and cause the hidden instructions to be executed. However, procedures are rather too small a unit for structuring large programs.

As a result of their size and complexity, large problems must be solved by a team of programmers rather than by a single individual. Each member of the team is set a well-defined task by a team leader, who alone may know the overall design of the system. For this approach to be possible, there must be some mechanism for dividing the problem into separate parts which only interact with one another through small strictly defined interfaces.

A development of the procedural approach is to have modules (known as packages in Ada and as modules in Fortran 90) in which groups of related procedure and type definitions can be encapsulated. Modules have a public interface which gives the information that may be seen and used from outside the module and a private implementation part whose details are hidden. Modules allow a large system to be designed by specifying what each module is to do and what its interface with the rest of the system is to be. Once this has been done, different programmers may implement each of the modules without any need for consultation.

To summarise, we control complexity by raising the level of abstraction in which we can think about the solution to a problem. To achieve this, we hide unwanted detail by encapsulating definitions in modules where implementation detail is hidden behind small well-defined public interfaces. Object-oriented languages are a continuation of this trend. In such languages, a module is a class.

The central belief in the object-oriented approach is that, as the real world consists of entities (i.e. objects) that interact with one another, problems are most easily understood and modelled in terms of a set of communicating objects. There is a further belief in object-oriented development that the objects identified when analysing a problem can be used when we are creating a design and an eventual implementation. A major feature of object-oriented development is that the same concepts of object and class are used in object-oriented analysis, design and programming.

In an object-oriented program, an object is an instance of a **class**. A class defines:

- the attributes of an object,
- the services (operations) offered to other objects,
- the behaviour of an object when one of its services is called.

An object has a hidden state (the values of its attributes) and a public interface (the services it offers to other objects). The implementation of the services is hidden. Each object has a separate identity; the values of its attributes might change, but it remains the same object. Two objects may have the same set of attribute values, but be two distinct objects.

An object-oriented program consists of a set of class definitions. At run time, we have a set of class instances, i.e. objects, that communicate with one another. A **client object** communicates with a **server object** by calling a service that the server object offers at its public interface. An object can act both as a server, by offering services to other objects, and as a client, by calling services offered by other objects.

We look at other object-oriented features such as inheritance and dynamic binding in Chapter 8.

Abstract data types

Most programming languages have a set of built-in or primitive types such as Integer, Real, Character and Boolean, each of which is characterised by an allowed range of values together with a set of operations. Calculations with integers, for example, take place in terms of arithmetic operators (+, −, *, etc.), relational operators (>, <, etc.) and the assignment operator. When solving a problem involving integers, it does not usually help to consider how integers are represented on a computer (for example, in two's complement notation) or how operations such as addition are implemented. In fact, for most purposes, it would be a positive hindrance, as it would introduce unwanted detail.

Problems whose solutions are easily expressed in terms of the built-in types can be tackled in a straightforward manner. Hence, most early imperative languages such as Algol 60 and Fortran were good at carrying out scientific calculations involving integer and floating-point arithmetic and array processing while they were less good at, for example, list processing. Lisp, on the other hand, is excellent at list processing because lists and operations on lists are part of the language. This suggests that the power of a language can be enhanced by extending the number of built-in types. Unfortunately, the number of types required for all possible problems is open-ended, and so a better approach is to have a mechanism through which new types can be created.

Such a mechanism must provide the facilities to:

- declare a new type, give it a name and specify which operations are available to manipulate instances of the type, and
- hide the details of the representation of the type and the implementation of the operations.

By clearly distinguishing between how a type may be used and how it is implemented, users can consider the type from an abstract point of view.

To illustrate this concept, consider a stack of items. The aim is to be able to declare stack variables and to define operations for pushing items on, and popping items off, a stack. Once this has been done, a stack can be regarded as a type and so it is possible to declare stack objects and perform stack operations without considering implementation details.

We can encapsulate the definition of a type and all the procedures needed to manipulate variables of the type inside a module such as an Ada package or a Java class. That way, the implementation of the type can be completely hidden from its users who only see the type name and the allowed operations. This gives us the concept of an **abstract data type** (ADT). While an Ada package can *contain* the definition of a type and its operations, a class in an object-oriented language like Java *is* the definition of a type and its operations. Abstract data types are central to the organisation of programs in both procedural and object-oriented languages.

We compare the Ada, C++ and Java implementations of a stack abstract data type in Chapter 7.

Reuse

Large systems, by their nature, are usually in use for many years and during this time they may undergo substantial modification. Some of the changes will be due to the discovery of errors, but others will be due to changes in the system requirements, which could not be foreseen when the original system was designed. Due to the high cost and the time involved, it is not practicable to redesign large systems from scratch. Hence, systems should be designed and written so that they can be easily modified. The best way of achieving this is for the programs to be written in such a way that the effect of any change is localised. This again points to a solution where the program is designed and implemented in separate parts (modules), each with a clearly defined external interface.

As solutions to different large problems often require solutions to similar subproblems, modules should be capable of being reused. In this way, a library of software components can be made available 'off the shelf' for use in the construction of new programs. Classes are ideally suited to this approach. Hence, Java is a relatively small language, but has an extensive class library. A large part of any Java program consists of calls to the services provided by the library. Often, in the case of other languages, different implementations provide incompatible libraries and the resulting portability problems reduce their usefulness. A major advantage of Java is that it comes with a large standard library which is considered by its users to be part of the language.

5.2 Procedural and object-oriented architecture

To show both the differences and the similarities between a procedural and object-oriented program structure, we will look briefly at a simple outline example in Java, Pascal and Ada before returning to look at alternative architectures in more detail.

A major difference between a procedural and a purely object-oriented language is that in a procedural language, a procedure can exist as a separate entity while in a purely object-oriented language it is always a component of a class. A hybrid language like C++ or Delphi's Object Pascal allows both.

A procedure that returns a value is usually called a **function**. Fortran, Pascal and Ada make a clear distinction between functions and ordinary procedures which in Fortran are called subroutines. The purpose of a procedure is to change the state of the program while the purpose of a function is either to query the current state or to compute a value. A procedure call is a statement in its own right, while a function call is part of an expression and returns a value. A **pure function** is independent of the context in which it is called; for a given set of parameter values, it always returns the same value.

A major idea in language design is that there should be as few distinct concepts as possible. Hence, languages such as Algol 68 and C++ regard a procedure as a special case of a function in which the returned value is void.

In many object-oriented languages (e.g. Java), procedures and functions are called **methods** while in C++ functions defined within a class are called **member functions**. A void member function in C++ or a void method in Java corresponds to a procedure. In this book, we will talk about methods rather than member functions, even when we are talking about C++. We will also refer to procedures, functions and methods as operations.

Java

Let us now consider the implementation of a simple bank account. A program in a purely object-oriented language consists of a set of class definitions. The bank account will therefore be implemented in Java as a class with private attributes and public methods. A simple outline class definition might be:

```
class BankAccount {
    // private attribute declarations
    ...
    public BankAccount() {
      ...
    } // constructor
    public void deposit(int amount) {
      ...
    } // deposit
    public int getBalance() {
      ...
    } // getBalance
} // BankAccount
```

This class has a **constructor**, whose name is the same as the class name and which is used in conjunction with the **new** operator when a BankAccount object is created, and two public methods: a **void** method called deposit whose purpose is to update an account and a method called getBalance whose purpose is to return information about an account.

Let us consider what we have achieved. We have defined a new type. We can now declare BankAccount variables, create BankAccount objects and perform operations on them as if they were a predefined part of the language. BankAccount is therefore an example of an abstract data type. Other classes in our Java program will create BankAccount objects and call their methods. The declarations will have the form:

```
BankAccount bk1 = new BankAccount();
BankAccount bk2 = new BankAccount();
```

This declares two variables bk1 and bk2 whose type is 'reference to a BankAccount object'. Two BankAccount objects are created using the **new** operator and are initialised by executing the BankAccount constructor.

Dot notation is used when calling the methods defined for the objects referred to by bk1 and bk2. We can for example have method calls such as:

```
bk1.deposit(6);
int am1 = bk1.getBalance();
```

which will deposit the value 6 in the bank account referred to by bk1 and then determine its current balance which is assigned to the int variable am1.

Instead of method calls, in some object-oriented systems we talk about objects sending messages to each other. We can therefore say that the messages deposit and getBalance are being sent to bk1. Other terminology is to say that bk1 offers the services deposit and getBalance while the methods are the code used to implement the services.

Pascal

In a procedural language like Pascal, the principal structuring construct is the procedure or function. The bank account and its associated operations can be defined as:

```pascal
program BankAccountEx(input, output);
    type BankAccount = ...
    var bk1, bk2: BankAccount;
        am1: Integer;
    ...

    procedure makeBankAccount (var b: BankAccount);
    begin ... end {makeBankAccount};

    procedure deposit(var b: BankAccount;
        amount: Integer);
    begin ... end {deposit};

    function getBalance(b: BankAccount): Integer;
    begin ... end {getBalance};

begin
    makeBankAccount(bk1);
    makeBankAccount(bk2);
    ... deposit(bk1, 6);
    ... am1 := getBalance(bk1); ...
end.
```

The purpose of procedure makeBankAccount is to initialise a BankAccount variable and therefore corresponds to the constructor in the Java class. Note that the operations makeBankAccount, deposit and getBalance now require a parameter of type BankAccount to determine which BankAccount object is being referred to. Typically, in the call of a procedure or function, we have one more parameter than we would have in the call of the corresponding method in an object-oriented language.

Pascal therefore supports the definition of a new type and the declaration of procedures and functions to perform operations on objects of the type. However, a major difference from the Java solution is that the type and its associated operations are no longer encapsulated in a single entity within which the representation of BankAccount is hidden. Also, as its structure is visible, it is possible to directly access and change the value of a BankAccount object. It is only when the implementation of a type is hidden that it is possible to guarantee that it will only be manipulated through the defined operations, and that users will not take 'efficient' short cuts by manipulating internal details. Also, in a large Pascal program, the definitions of makeBankAccount, deposit and `getBalance` can be far way from the definition of type `BankAccount`, making it difficult for the reader to recognise that they logically belong together.

Ada

An encapsulation mechanism is provided by many Pascal implementations as well as by Ada packages. In Ada, we can have:

```
package BankAccounts is
    type BankAccount is private;
    procedure  makeBankAccount(b: out BankAccount);
    procedure deposit(b: in out BankAccount;
        amount: in Integer);
    function getBalance(b: BankAccount) return Integer;
private
    type BankAccount is ...
end BankAccounts;

package body BankAccounts is
    -- definitions of makeBankAccount,
    -- deposit and getBalance
end BankAccounts;
```

Here we have a package specification and a package body. The signatures of the operations `makeBankAccount`, `deposit` and `getBalance` are declared in the package specification and are visible to users of the package while the operation bodies are declared in the package body and are hidden. Type `BankAccount` is declared to be a **private type** and information about its structure is given in the **private part** of the package specification. This means that, although the identifier `BankAccount` is visible, no information about the structure of `BankAccount` is available to users of the package. The only built-in operations available with a private type are equality and assignment.

By providing a mechanism for structuring and information hiding, a package provides us with a mechanism for defining abstract data types. We can declare variables of type `BankAccount` and make calls of `makeBankAccount`, `deposit` and `getBalance` in the same way as in the Pascal program. However, as nothing is known outside the package about its structure, a `BankAccount` object can only be accessed through the operations `makeBankAccount`, `deposit` and `getBalance`.

5.3 Alternative program architectures

We will now look in more detail at several alternative program architectures. Fortran is an example of a language with subprograms that can be compiled independently, Pascal is a block-structured language, Ada has modules and supports separate compilation, C++ is a hybrid between a procedural and an object-oriented language, and Java is an object-oriented language.

Independent compilation

There have been several different versions of Fortran over the years and the following concentrates on the facilities provided in the early versions as that provides a distinct example of how a program can be structured. It must be emphasised that Fortran 90 provides interfaces which give full type checking across subprogram boundaries. In early Fortran, a program consists of a main program in addition to a series of independent subprograms. A subprogram can be a subroutine (corresponding to a procedure in Pascal) or a function. The structure of a Fortran program is shown in Figure 5.1. Note that the local variable R is only in scope within the main program while S and T are only in scope in the subroutines in which they are declared.

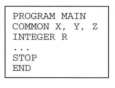

```
PROGRAM MAIN
COMMON X, Y, Z
INTEGER R
. . .
STOP
END
```

```
SUBROUTINE A . . .
COMMON U, V, W
INTEGER S
. . .
RETURN
END
```

```
SUBROUTINE B . . .
COMMON E, F, G
INTEGER T
. . .
RETURN
END
```

Figure 5.1   Structure of a Fortran program.

Subprograms in Fortran can interact with one another via parameters or through a list of COMMON variables. Although the COMMON list must be repeated in each subprogram, the identifiers do not have to be the same in each case, and the lists do not even have to be of the same length. Variables in corresponding positions in each of the COMMON lists share the same locations in store. Hence, any change to the variable U in subroutine A of Figure 5.1 automatically changes the value of the variable X in the main program and the value of the variable E in subroutine B.

As well as allowing subprograms to communicate with one another, COMMON lists are sometimes used to reduce a program's storage requirements. They do this by enabling variables which have no connection with one another to share the same store locations. This is called **overlaying** and was important when Fortran was first designed as the main stores of computers then were small and space was often at a premium. However, such a concept does not aid in the understanding or improve the reliability of programs!

As the subprograms do not depend on one another, they can be compiled independently and held in libraries of pre-compiled routines. Such an approach allows programmers to incorporate tried and tested routines in their programs. Furthermore, if changes need to be made to a subprogram, then only that subprogram has to be recompiled, which is a major advantage when modifications have to be made to large programs containing many subprograms. However, the drawback of this approach is that full type checking across subprogram boundaries is not possible. As each subprogram is compiled independently, it is not possible to check that the type of the actual parameters in a subprogram call matches the type of the formal parameters in the subprogram declaration. This presents a major problem when trying to produce large, reliable systems consisting of many subprograms, which is why Fortran 90 has introduced interfaces so that full type checking can take place. (The difference between independent and separate compilation is discussed in Section 5.4.)

Block-structured languages

In Algol 60 and its many successors (for example, Pascal), an alternative approach has been adopted. Such languages have one monolithic program and procedures can either be declared within the main program or nested within other procedures. This is illustrated by the Pascal program skeleton given in Figure 5.2. We use the term 'procedure' to cover both ordinary procedures and functions.

```
program main ...
   var v, w : Real;

   procedure a ...
      var x, y : Real;

      procedure b ...
         var x, y : Real;
      begin ... end;

   begin ... end;


   procedure d ...
      var w, x : Integer;
   begin ... end;

begin ... end.
```

Figure 5.2 Pascal program skeleton.

Languages that allow the nesting of procedures are said to be **block structured**. As was described in Section 3.2, each procedure in Pascal can be regarded as a block and blocks inherit all the declarations made in enclosing blocks. Algol 60, Pascal and Ada allow the declarations of procedures to be nested while Fortran, C and C++ do not.

The rules governing the visibility of identifiers are called the scope rules and they were described in Chapter 3. The rule that an identifier is always bound to its most local declaration means that a programmer can concentrate on one procedure at a time and choose the most suitable identifiers without worrying if these identifiers are used elsewhere in the program. Hence, within procedure d of Figure 5.2, the integer variable w can be declared and used without worrying that a floating-point variable w has already been declared in an enclosing block.

If identifiers are declared as locally as possible, the number in scope at any particular time is kept to a minimum. To help promote this condition, Algol 60, Algol 68, C++ and Ada allow the nesting of blocks that are not procedures. This is illustrated in the Ada program segment shown in Figure 5.3 where one block is nested within another. As the usual scope rules apply, the integer variable a and the floating-point variables b and d are visible in the inner block while the integer variable b is hidden.

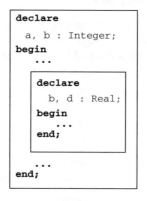

Figure 5.3   Nested blocks in Ada.

In a block-structured language, procedures are declared in an environment created by the enclosing blocks. Although this rules out independent compilation, it does make full type checking possible across procedure boundaries. Reconciling the advantages of being able to pre-compile parts of a program and yet be able to have full type checking has been a major concern of language designers. We describe later how this has been achieved with Ada packages.

As variables used in a procedure can be declared in an enclosing block, there is no indication when a procedure is called that such non-local variables may be accessed or, what is worse, may be changed as a result of the call. To be reliable, programs must be easy to read and understand, and a necessary condition for this is that there are no hidden side-effects. In addition, procedures are used to help support the decomposition of problems into a series of smaller subproblems, each of which can be tackled independently. Procedures should therefore be as self-contained as possible. For these reasons, the use of non-local variables in procedural languages is now generally frowned upon.

To support this, several experimental languages have tightened the scope rules. Alphard has retained block structure, but procedures cannot inherit the names of variables declared in enclosing blocks, although they do inherit the names of types. In Euclid, which was derived from Pascal, procedures have a **closed scope**. (Another name for the usual scope rules is open scope.) In closed scope, declarations are not normally inherited from an enclosing block. Instead, each procedure has an import list indicating which identifiers in the enclosing blocks may be used in the procedure. To prevent the import lists becoming too long, constant, procedure and type identifiers, but not variable identifiers, may be declared to be **pervasive**. Identifiers thus declared are then automatically available in inner blocks without having to be imported.

Modules

Ada is a block-structured language, but in addition to the facilities provided by Pascal, it has packages (modules) in which we can declare types, procedures, functions, variables and constants. The public interface is called the **package specification** and the implementation details are held in a separate **package body**. Package specifications should always be as small as possible, since they form the interfaces between what are otherwise self-contained units. A large interface is often a sign that the decomposition of the problem could be improved.

As an example, consider the following Ada package:

```
package Days is
    type Day is (sun, mon, tues, wed, thurs, fri, sat);
    function next_day(today : Day)   return Day;
    function day_before(today : Day)   return Day;
end Days;

package body Days is
    function next_day(today : Day)   return Day is
    begin
        if today = sat then
            return sun;
        else
            return Day'succ(today);
        end if;
    end next_day;

    function day_before(today : Day)   return Day is
    begin
        if today = sun then
            return sat;
        else
            return Day'pred(today);
        end if;
    end day_before;
end Days;
```

As identifiers declared in a package specification are visible from outside the package, users of the module can declare variables of type Day and call the functions next_day and day_before. The only information about next_day and day_before that is given in the package specification is that needed by the user to call the subprograms properly; namely, the number and type of the parameters and the type of the returned function values. Details of the implementation of the subprograms (the subprogram bodies) are hidden in the package body, since there is no need for a user to have access to this information.

A package specification is an example of an Ada **program unit** while its accompanying body is called a **secondary unit**. An Ada program consists of a series of program and secondary units. One of the program units, the main program, must be a procedure. Variables declared in a package body are allocated space at load time, which allows the separation of the scope and extent of a variable in a way not possible in languages such as Pascal.

To make the items in the visible part of a package available to another program or secondary unit, the unit is prefixed with what is called a **context clause**, as in:

```
with Days; use Days;
procedure main is
    ...
    holiday, working_day : Day;
    ...
begin
    ...
    holiday := sat;
    working_day := day_before(holiday);
    ...
end main;
```

The context clause:

```
with Days; use Days;
```

enables the user to refer to type Day and to the functions next_day and day_before within procedure main. A context clause consists of a **with** clause and an optional **use** clause. When the optional **use** clause is omitted, it is still possible to use the visible information from package Days, but the items have to be referred to by their full names: Days.Day, Days.next_day and Days.day_before. As a procedure or package can import variables and types from several different packages, it can be far from clear where a particular identifier has been declared. It is therefore advisable to give the full name of infrequently used identifiers rather than the abbreviated form made possible by a **use** clause. The structure of this simple Ada program is shown in Figure 5.4.

In Section 5.2, we saw the definition of a type BankAccount whose representation was given in the private part of a package specification. A reasonable question to ask at this point is why Ada package specifications have a private part. Why, for example, can BankAccount not be declared private in the specification and its structure given in the package body? The reason is that an Ada package specification and the units that depend on it may be compiled without the compiler having any knowledge of the

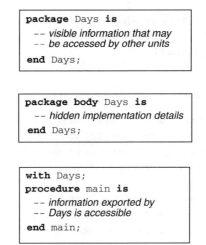

Figure 5.4   Structure of a simple Ada program.

package body, but to achieve this the compiler must know from the specification alone how much space is required for each visible object and type.

The disadvantage of this set-up is that to change the implementation of BankAccount, both the package specification and the body must be modified. This problem can be overcome by the following alternative specification in which BankAccount is an access (pointer) type:

```
package BankAccounts is
   type BankAccount is private;
   procedure makeBankAccount (b: out BankAccount);
   procedure deposit(b: in out BankAccount;
      amount: in Integer);
   function getBalance(b: BankAccount) return Integer;
private
   type ActualBankAccount;
   type BankAccount is access ActualBankAccount;
end BankAccounts;

package body  BankAccounts is
   -- definitions of ActualBankAccount,
   -- makeBankAccount, deposit and getBalance
end BankAccounts;
```

As the size of all access values (pointers) is the same, the compiler knows how much space to reserve for variables of type BankAccount. The representation of type ActualBankAccount can be defined in the package body as knowledge about its size is not required either in the specification or by any program unit that depends on package BankAccounts.

Fortran 90 has modules which achieve the same objective as Ada packages. One difference is that the specification and the implementation parts are declared together in the same program unit.

Hybrid languages

C++ is an incremental development from C and contains procedural as well as object-oriented features. Functions, for example, can exist independently from a class. This has meant that some C++ programmers still really use a procedural style of programming; they may use classes, but only as data structures, not as the principal program structuring mechanism.

A C++ program consists of a main program together with function and class definitions. Identifiers must be declared before they can be used and so functions are declared as a **function prototype** at the beginning of a program by giving their name and parameters while their definitions (i.e. bodies) are given later. A class definition in C++ contains **data members** to define the attributes, and **member functions** through which the attributes may be accessed and changed. In most object-oriented languages, member functions are known as methods and that is the terminology that we will adopt here. In the definition of a class, we normally only give the function prototypes for the methods and define the bodies later. Let us look at this through the following simple example.

```
int checkCents(int c); // function prototype

class Cost {
private:
    int cents, dollars;
public:
    Cost(int d, int c); //constructor
    void add(int d, int c);
    int getDollars() const;
    int getCents() const;
};

// the main program
void main() {
    Cost dress(45, 95);
    Cost *book = new Cost(15, 50);
    . . .
    dress.add(5, 0);
    book→add(3, 15);
    . . .
}

// definition of function body
int checkCents(int c) {
```

```
    if (c < 100)
        return 1;
    else
        return 0;
} // checkCents

// definition of method bodies
void Cost::Cost(int d, int c) {
    dollars = d; cents = c;
} // constructor

void Cost::add(int d, int c) {
    cents += c;
    if (cents > 100) {
        dollars += d + cents / 100;
        cents = cents % 100;
    }
    else
        dollars += d;
} // add

int Cost::getDollars() const {
    return dollars;
} // getDollars

int Cost::getCents() const{
    return cents;
} // getCents
```

A new class, called Cost, with private data members cents and dollars and public methods add, getDollars and getCents has been defined. There is also a method whose name is the same as the class name. This is called a **constructor** and is used to initialise objects when they are created. As information in a class is private by default, the use of the reserved word **private** is not strictly necessary, but makes things more obvious to the reader. The attributes may only be accessed or changed from outside the class by calling one of the public methods. Note that it is possible to define a public attribute, but that defeats the whole purpose.

It is possible for method bodies to be declared within a class definition, but it is more usual only to give the function prototypes and declare the method bodies separately. The **scope resolution operator** :: is used to associate the method names with the appropriate class as shown in the above example.

There are two kinds of method, **selectors** which return information about data members and **modifiers** which modify data members. A method should not be both a selector and a modifier. The **const** after the selectors getDollars and getCents guarantee that they do not modify any of the attributes and so guarantees that they correspond to pure functions.

The constructor is executed when an object is created. For example, the declaration:

```
Cost dress(45, 95);
```

causes a variable (i.e. an object) `dress` of class `Cost` to be created and to have its `dollars` and `cents` attributes initialised to 45 and 95 respectively. The attributes of `dress` may later be changed by the call:

```
dress.add(5, 0);
```

Pointers to classes may also be declared as in:

```
Cost *book = new Cost(15, 50);
```

Here, the type of `book` is 'pointer to a `Cost` object'. The actual `Cost` object is created using the **new** operator and, as before, is initialised using the constructor. We can call the method `add` by deferencing the book pointer and using ordinary dot notation as in:

```
(*book).add(3, 15);
```

but this is rather messy. As this is a commonly required operation, C++ provides us with a special operator and we can write:

```
book→add(3, 15);
```

The different parts of a C++ program are usually held in separate files. We look at that in Section 5.4 where we discuss separate compilation.

A common feature of object-oriented programs is that they contain a large number of very short method definitions. The overhead of making a method call is therefore considerable in comparison to the time taken to execute the method body. In C++, methods can be declared to be **inline**, in which case the compiler may generate in-line code. We therefore get the advantage of a well-structured source program without this causing any inefficiency.

Object-oriented languages

Java was developed from C++, but the core language is considerably simpler. It is also a purely object-oriented language and so, unlike C++, there are no free standing functions. That poses the question of how we represent the equivalent of the main program. There are different answers to this question depending on whether we are writing a Java application (i.e. an ordinary program) or a Java applet.

We will first consider the case of a Java application. An outline Java program corresponding to the C++ program given earlier is:

```
import java.awt.*;

public class Example  extends Frame {
    private Cost dress =  new Cost(45, 95);
    private Cost book =  new Cost(15, 50);
    ...
```

```
public static void main(String [] args) {
    Example ex = new Example();
    ex.setSize(400,200);
    ex.setVisible(true);
} // main

public Example() {
    super("Example");
    ...
    dress.add(5, 0);
    book.add(3, 15);
} // constructor
...
} // Example

class Cost {
    private int cents, dollars;

    public Cost(int d, int c) {
        dollars = d; cents = c;
    } // constructor

    public void add(int d, int c) {
        cents += c;
        if (cents > 100) {
            dollars += d + cents / 100;
            cents = cents % 100;
        }
        else
            dollars += d;
    } // add

    public int getDollars() {
        return dollars;
    } // getDollars

    public int getCents() {
        return cents;
    } // getCents
} // Cost
```

Within class Example there is a rather artificial main method which acts as the main
program. It is declared to be **public**, **static** and **void**. That is where execution
starts. The example assumes that we are using a graphical user interface (GUI) and
which is the reason why Example is a subclass of class Frame. We discuss frames in
Chapter 13 as part of the discussion on graphical user interfaces. All we need to know

just now is that a frame is used to create a window within which a user can interact with the program. The effect of executing main is to create an instance ex of class Example, to give the window associated with ex an appropriate size (using setSize) and to make the window visible (using setVisible). Frames are defined in the awt (abstract windowing toolkit) library package which is imported into the program using the statement:

```
import java.awt.*;
```

In Chapter 13, we discuss how the Swing classes provide an alternative way of defining GUI components. It is not essential to interact with a Java program through a graphical user interface, but that is the normal way in which user interaction takes place.

In the C++ version, the definition of dress and book and the calls of add were given in function main. In the Java example, they have been declared in class Example and the calls to add have been given in the constructor for Example.

The definition of class Cost is very similar to the C++ version. The only real differences are that the visibility of each attribute or method is given separately and that the method bodies are always given within the class declaration. As in C++, when an attribute or method is public, it is visible from outside the class and when it is private, it is only visible from within the class. Java classes can be defined to be within a package. When the visibility of an attribute or method is not given, it is visible from other classes in the same package.

Objects in Java are always accessed by reference. There is therefore no need for the explicit pointer notation used in C++. Hence, the declaration:

```
private Cost dress =  new Cost(45, 95);
```

declares dress to be a reference to a Cost object. It then creates a Cost object which is initialised using the constructor. Ordinary dot notation is used as in:

```
dress.add(5, 0);
```

One of the main selling points of Java is that it can be used to animate web pages. A web page is written in a language called HTML (HyperText Markup Language). If the HTML code for a page contains the following **applet tag** then the applet whose object code is held in file Example.class will be executed when the page is downloaded.

```
<applet archive="AppletClasses.jar"
        code="Example.class" width=400 height=200>
</applet>
```

The Java library classes needed by the applet will be held in the AppletClasses.jar file and both these files will be held in the same folder on disk as the HTML file. The width and height of the area in the web page to be used by the applet is also given.

An applet corresponding to our earlier Java application is given below. We now extend the Applet library class instead of Frame and the constructor for Example is replaced by a void method called init which is invoked when the applet is executed. There is no need for a main method in an applet. The definition of class Cost is unchanged.

```
import java.awt.*;
import java.applet.Applet;

public class Example  extends Applet {
    private Cost dress =  new Cost(45, 95);
    private Cost book =  new Cost(15, 50);
    ...

    public void init() {
        ...
        dress.add(5, 0);
        book.add(3, 15);
    } // init
    ...
} // Example
```

We look further at applets in Chapter 11.

5.4 Separate compilation

Our discussion so far has concentrated on the logical subdivision of a program into its components. Another important feature of programs is their physical decomposition into files whose contents may be compiled separately. We have already seen how early Fortran programs were organised so that each subprogram can be compiled independently. The disadvantage of this approach is that it is not possible to check that the types of the actual parameters in a subprogram call match the type of the formal parameters in the subprogram declaration. Block-structured languages such as Pascal, on the other hand, allow full type checking, but not independent compilation.

When dealing with large systems composed of hundreds of subprograms, it is important to ensure that a change in one subprogram does not necessitate the recompilation of all other subprograms while, if the system is to be secure and reliable, it is important to have full type checking. Ada solves this problem by replacing **independent compilation** by **separate compilation**. As an example, consider the following outline Ada program:

```
package Low is ... end Low;

package Middle is ... end Middle;

with Low;
package body Middle  is ... end Middle;

with Middle;
package High is ... end High;

package body High is ... end High;

with High, Middle;
procedure main is begin ... end main;
```

The packages Low, Middle and High, the package bodies Middle and High, and the procedure main can all be compiled separately and, together with their context clauses, are called **compilation units**. These units are not totally independent, since some depend on information specified in others and their interdependence is given by the context clauses. A package body is always dependent on its specification as identifiers declared in a specification are available in the corresponding body. Similarly, items in package Middle imported into the specification of High are also imported into the body of High. The dependencies are shown diagrammatically in Figure 5.5 where the arrows show the direction in which information is passed.

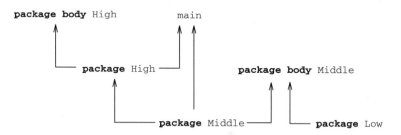

Figure 5.5 Package dependencies.

No unit may be compiled before any of the units on which it depends. As the package specifications of Middle and Low do not depend on the others, they may be compiled first. The body of Middle cannot be compiled until both its specification and the specification of Low have been compiled. Note that the package body of Middle depends on Low while the specification of Middle does not. This is quite a common occurrence as an implementation often requires more facilities than its specification.

The order of compilation is enforced by the **program library** which is associated with each Ada program. It contains information on the compilation units, including the time at which they were compiled. The compilation of the specification of package High, for example, is not done independently, but 'in the context of package Middle'. The compiler uses the information in the program library file to ensure strict type checking across the package boundaries and that, for example, package Middle is compiled before package High.

To illustrate the effect of program modifications on compilation, consider the effect of changing and then recompiling the specification of package Middle. In this case, the body of Middle, the specification and body of High and procedure main all have to be recompiled, since they all depend on Middle either directly or indirectly. This is shown in Figure 5.6. Not much has therefore been gained.

If, on the other hand, it was the body of Middle that was changed and recompiled, then no other unit would need to be recompiled, as units only depend on the specification of a package, not on the body. As most errors and modifications occur in package bodies, with the specifications being fixed at the design stage, the amount of recompilation required in practice is kept to a minimum. This also means that the implementation of a module can be completely changed without requiring the recompilation of the program units that use the module, as long as the interface stays the same. Localising

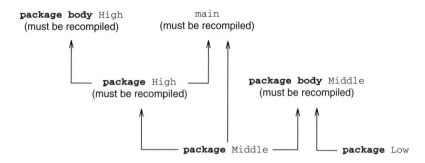

Figure 5.6 Effect of recompiling package Middle.

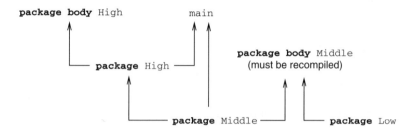

Figure 5.7 Effect of recompiling package Low.

the effects of change is of paramount importance in the maintenance and enhancement of large programs. As an example, the effect of recompiling package Low is shown in Figure 5.7. As it is only used by the body of Middle, the effect is localised.

C++ does not support separate compilation with full type checking, but a convention is used which, when followed, achieves this aim. Consider, for example, class Cost given earlier. The class definition is held in a **header file** with a name such as cost.h while the definition of the function bodies is held in a separate file. Any file containing code which uses the Cost class, must contain the **include directive**:

```
#include "cost.h"
```

In that way, the different files all access exactly the same interface information and full type checking is achieved.

In the same way, C++ libraries consist of header files which contain the public interface, and have names ending in .h, and implementation files. A library item is included in a C++ program using the directive:

```
#include <libraryitem.h>
```

A similar approach is used with C programs.

In Ada , the program library ensures that each program unit was compiled after the units on which it depends. With C++ programs this can be achieved using a **makefile** that holds information on the dependencies between the different files holding the C++ program. After the contents of one or more of these files has been changed, execution of the makefile will ensure that subsequent recompilations occur in the correct order.

It is, however, much better if the type checking across file boundaries and the checks that files are compiled in the correct order are controlled by language rules as in Ada rather than being left to conventions which cannot be enforced. However, **integrated development environments** (IDEs) for C++ can take care of the compilation order automatically, thereby freeing the programmer from an error-prone task.

Java does not physically separate the specification and implementation parts of a class and so, when the implementation of a class is changed, the clients of the class must be recompiled. Cutting down on the required amount of recompilation was therefore less of a priority for the designers of Java than for the designers of Ada and C++. The reason could be that Java is a much simpler language and so recompilation is not as expensive. Also, Java is a much newer language and, as computers become more powerful, there is less need to worry about such optimisations.

5.5 Larger units

Although classes impose a module structure, large programs require a larger scale structuring mechanism. In Java, classes may be grouped into **packages** while in Delphi they are grouped into **units**. A typical outline structure of a Java package definition is:

```
package packageName;
import awt.*;
public class ClassName {
  ...
}
```

Here, we are declaring that `ClassName` is one of the classes in package `packageName` and that it imports all the classes from the library package `awt` (the abstract windowing toolkit). The Java libraries are organised as a set of packages.

Each Java class should be held in a separate file with class `ClassName` being held in a file whose name is `ClassName.java`. The files containing the classes making up a package should be placed in a folder that has the same name as the package. A class in a different package can import class `ClassName` defined in package `packageName` by using the **import** statement:

```
import packageName.ClassName;
```

A class must be declared as **public** if it is to be imported into another package.

We have seen how attributes and methods can be declared to be public or private. When no visibility information is given, attributes and methods are visible to all classes in the current package. This enables the designers of a class to consider two categories of user: trusted users who design other classes in the same package and the rest of the world. Often a set of classes in a package will work together to offer some service. They can be allowed to access each others' attributes while such information can be hidden from all classes declared outside the package.

C++ achieves a similar effect by allowing a class A to declare that a class B or a method c is a **friend**.

```
class A {
    ...
    friend class B;
    friend void c();
};
```

All the methods of class B and the method c can then access the private attributes of A.

Summary

1. In a block-structured language such as Pascal, procedures are declared in an environment created by the enclosing blocks. A procedure call is a statement in its own right, while a function call is part of an expression and returns a value.

2. In a procedural language, a procedure can exist as a separate entity while in a purely object-oriented language it is always a component of a class.

3. To solve a large problem, it must be possible to divide it into separate parts that only interact with one another through small strictly defined interfaces. To ensure that a program can be easily modified, it must be designed so that the effect of any change is localised. These objectives are achieved by the use of modules.

4. A module consists of a collection of related procedure, type and variable declarations.

5. A module in Ada or Fortran 90 can contain the definition of a type while a module (class) in C++ and Java *is* the definition of a type.

6. A module is usually divided into two parts. The public interface describes 'what' the module does while the private implementation part gives details of 'how' the operations are to be carried out. In Ada, these two parts are called the package specification and body.

7. Modules support information hiding. Identifiers declared in the interface part can be used in other modules while identifiers declared in the implementation part are hidden. The ability to hide unwanted detail is our main tool for controlling complexity.

8. A type is characterised by its range of values and the operations that can be performed on objects of that type. Packages in Ada and classes in C++ or Java can be used to define new types. The allowed operations are given in the interface part while the implementation of the operations and the representation of the type are hidden. Types defined in this way are called abstract data types.

9. Ada packages are compiled separately, but in the context of the other packages from which they import information. In this way, type checking can be performed across module boundaries.

10. If the interface part is held in a separate file and is not changed, changing and then recompiling the implementation part of a module does not require any other module to be recompiled.

11. To solve a problem using object-oriented development, the real-world objects concerned are identified and then a high-level solution designed, which is expressed in terms of these objects and their associated operations.

Exercises

5.1 Subprograms in early versions of Fortran can be compiled independently of one another. Pascal procedures and functions may be nested, but cannot be compiled independently. Discuss the advantages and disadvantages of these two approaches and any possible compromises between the two.

5.2 Compare the approach to type checking across subprogram boundaries adopted in Fortran, Pascal, C++ and Ada.

5.3 Compare the program structure of C with that of Pascal and Fortran. Which features do you consider are closer to Fortran and which are closer to Pascal?

5.4 In Exercise 3.10 of Chapter 3, you were asked to list a suitable set of operations on objects of type Month. Give implementations of these operations in Pascal, Ada, C++ or Java.

5.5 Large programs are usually implemented as separate modules. In early languages, subprograms were used as modules. What were the deficiencies of this approach?

5.6 What is meant by information hiding and why is it important in the construction of large programming systems?

5.7 The two principles of information hiding given by Parnas (1972a) are:

- The intended user must be provided with all the information needed to use the module correctly, and nothing more.
- The implementor must be provided with all the information needed to complete the module, but should be given no information about the structure of the calling program.

Describe how packages in Ada, modules in Fortran 90 and classes in C++ and Java support these two principles.

5.8 Distinguish between independent and separate compilation.

5.9 What are the essential features of an abstract data type? What language facilities to support the implementation of abstract data types are available in Ada, but are absent from ISO Pascal.

5.10 Discuss the advantages and disadvantages of the notation used to define an abstract data type in C++ or Java, where a module definition introduces a new type, compared with the notation used in Ada.

5.11 Construct an Ada package and a C++ or Java class that will implement a rational number abstract data type. Compare the solutions. Is being able to overload operators important?

5.12 Construct an Ada package and a C++ or Java class to implement a `Month` abstract data type.

Bibliography

The implementation of modules in modern programming languages is a modification of the SIMULA class concept (Birtwistle *et al.*, 1975). A very influential paper that discusses the way systems should be designed using modules is 'On the Criteria To Be Used in Decomposing Systems into Modules' by Parnas (1972b). Further details on how modules are used in Ada, C++ and Java are available from the standard language texts.

The design of abstract data types in Ada and their use in object-oriented development is described by Booch and Bryan (1992).

Birtwistle, G.M., Dahl, O-J., Myhrhaug, B. and Nygaard, K. (1975). *Simula begin*. Auerbach.

Booch, G. and Bryan, D. (1992). *Software Engineering with Ada* (Third Edition). Benjamin/Cummings.

Parnas, D.L. (1972a). 'A Technique for Software Module Specification with Examples'. *Comm. ACM*, **15**, 330–336.

Parnas, D.L. (1972b). 'On the Criteria to be Used in Decomposing Systems into Modules'. *Comm. ACM*, **15**, 1053–1058.

Chapter 6

Procedures, functions and methods

In a procedural language, a procedure can exist on its own while, in an object-oriented language, a procedure (i.e. method) is always a component of a class. Procedures communicate through their parameters. There are wide variations in parameter passing mechanisms. This chapter looks at and compares the main mechanisms and at the effect they each have in promoting the reliability of programs. We then consider functions and look at the importance of avoiding side-effects.

The chapter also looks at the various methods of storage allocation and relates this to concepts such as the lifetime of a variable, discussed in earlier chapters. Finally we discuss recursion, forward references and how subprograms can be passed as parameters.

6.1 Introduction

The parameters in a procedure declaration are referred to as **formal parameters** while the parameters in the call of a procedure are referred to as **actual parameters**. When a procedure is called, each actual parameter is associated with its corresponding formal parameter. To illustrate this, consider the following C++ example which swaps the values of two integer variables. We have a void function with two formal parameters (first and second) of type int:

```
void swap(int& first, int& second) {
    int intermediate;
    intermediate = first;
    first = second;
    second = intermediate;
} // swap
```

Suppose that we have integer variables higher, lower, his and hers. Each pair can be swapped in the function calls:

```
swap(higher, lower);
swap(his, hers);
```

The types of the corresponding formal and actual parameters must match and this check is performed at compile time. In the first call of swap, the variable higher is associated with the formal parameter first and the variable lower is associated with the formal parameter second. The effect of executing the procedure body is therefore to swap the values of higher and lower.

Procedures allow the user to think at a more abstract level. Thus, once a swap procedure has been declared, it is no longer necessary to think about how to swap two integer variables (or the need for an intermediate). Such a procedure, in effect, adds a new operation to the language. If a collection of such procedures is created, it is not necessary for a programmer to have to start from scratch when writing a new program; instead, the procedures, which have already been written and tested, can simply be incorporated.

Methods

In an object-oriented language like Java, procedures (i.e. methods) always exist as a component of a class. Hence, in our Java BankAccount example in Chapter 5, the variable bk1 is a reference to a BankAccount object and we deposited money by a call such as:

```
bk1.deposit(6);
```

A method call therefore contains a special **target object** which is written to the left of the dot. In the Pascal version of BankAccount, we had the procedure call:

```
deposit(bk1, 6);
```

where an extra parameter is required to determine which BankAccount variable is being updated. The target object in a method call can be regarded as an implicit extra parameter.

The procedural and object-oriented styles lead to different ways in which programs are designed, but from the point of view of parameter passing mechanisms or the scope and lifetime of local variables there is no difference between a procedure and a method. C++, which supports both a procedural and an object-oriented style, uses the same approach for ordinary functions and for member functions, i.e. methods.

We have already discussed the reasons why procedures and functions should be self-contained and should only access local variables and parameters. Method bodies typically access or modify an object's attributes, i.e. non-local variables, and would not therefore seem to be self-contained. However, such methods are self-contained when we consider the target object to be an implicit extra parameter. To correspond to a pure function, a value returning method should not modify object attributes.

Methods are usually declared to be public so that they can be called by an object's clients. When they are declared to be private, they can only be called from one of the other methods in the class. Private methods are then normally called in the same way as procedures in a procedural language. If, for example, `privmethod` was a private method in C++ or Java, we could make the call:

```
privmethod();
```

However, that is a shorthand. We are calling one of the current object's methods and, in Java and C++, the current object can be referred to as **this**. The full call is therefore:

```
this.privmethod();
```

In several languages, including Delphi, the reserved word **self** is used instead of **this**.

A major feature of object-oriented programming is that method calls can be bound dynamically. We delay discussion of that topic until Chapter 8.

Class methods

We normally call methods to update or query the attributes of an object. In Java, when a method is declared to be static, it acts as a class method and it cannot access the attributes of any particular object. A call of the method has the form:

```
ClassName.methodName(parameters);
```

Class methods can be used in much the same way as procedures and functions in a procedural language. Consider, for example, the definition of mathematical operations such as `sin`, `cos`, `exp`, etc. In Java there is a library class called `Math` and such functions are defined there as static methods. To find the square root of a variable x, we write:

```
result = Math.sqrt(x);
```

6.2 Parameters

Parameters can be classified into three groups or **modes**. They can be used to:

- pass information to a procedure,

Table 6.1 Parameter-passing mechanisms.

Language	Mechanism						
	value	constant-value	reference-constant	result	reference	value-result	name
Algol 60	*						*
Fortran 90		*		?	?	?	
Pascal	*				*		
C	*						
C++	*		*		*		
Ada (scalars)		*		*		*	
Ada (others)		?	?	?	?	?	
Java	*						

● receive information from a procedure, or

● pass information to a procedure where it is to be updated before being returned.

Ada and Fortran 90 have three different parameter modes called **in**, **out** and **in out**, corresponding to each of the three cases, but most other languages manage with fewer modes.

To complicate matters further, each mode can be implemented in different ways. In addition, some languages define the mechanism to be used while others leave it up to the compiler writer. This section considers the following mechanisms:

● Passing information in: call by value, constant-value and reference-constant.

● Passing information out: call by result.

● Updating information: call by value-result, reference and name.

Table 6.1 shows the methods used in several different languages. An asterisk in the table indicates that the mechanism is specified by the language and a question mark that it is a possible mechanism.

Passing information in

In **call by value**, the formal parameter acts as a local variable that is initialised with the value of the actual parameter. This mechanism is used in Pascal and C++ and is the only mechanism in C and Java. Consider the C++ function:

```
int total(int val) {
    int sum = 0;
    while (val > 0) {
        sum += val;
        val--;
    }
    return sum;
} // total
```

If max is an integer variable which has been given the value 10, the effect of the call total(max) is to pass a copy of the value of max to the formal parameter val. Within the function, the changes made to val are to this local copy, and so they have no effect on the actual parameter max. Thus, when the program returns from the call, after having summed the numbers from 1 to 10, the variable max will still have the value 10.

In **call by constant-value**, used in Ada and Fortran 90, the formal parameter is a local constant rather than a local variable. The following Ada version of the foregoing procedure requires a local variable as the value of val may not be changed:

```
function total(val : in Integer) return Integer is
    sum : Integer := 0;
    count : Integer := val;
begin
    while count > 0 loop
        sum := sum + count;
        count := count -1;
    end loop ;
    return   sum;
end total;
```

It is now clearer that the actual parameter is not affected by the call. In both call by value and call by constant-value the actual parameter may be a constant or an expression, as only the value of the actual parameter is passed over.

A major drawback of these two methods is that, when the parameter is structured, for example an array, a copy of the complete structure is created, which is expensive in space and time. To overcome this inefficiency, Pascal programmers often pass array or record parameters by reference rather than by value, even when the structure is not being updated. In **call by reference**, it is the address of the actual parameter that is passed. However, this method does not have the advantage of call by value: when only a copy is passed to a subprogram, there is a guarantee that any change to the formal parameter has no effect on the actual parameter.

In Ada, the passing of structured parameters of mode **in** may be implemented by **reference-constant** instead of by constant-value. The difference between call by reference-constant and call by reference is that the formal parameter is a local constant. As a constant cannot be updated, there is no reduction in security. C++ and Delphi have reference-constant as one of their parameter passing mechanisms. Consider the C++ function:

```
float sum(const Matrix& m) { ... }
```

that returns the sum of all the elements in a matrix. We need to access the matrix elements, but we also want to guarantee that none of the elements will be changed as a result of the call. In a call of this function, a reference (pointer) to the matrix is passed over, but the C++ compiler guarantees that the parameter m will not occur in any statements in which it could be modified.

Figure 6.1 illustrates the three methods discussed here for passing information into a procedure.

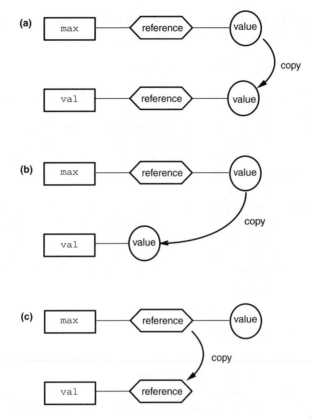

Figure 6.1   Passing information into a procedure: (a) call by value; (b) call by constant-value; (c) call by reference-constant.

Passing information out

Call by result is used in Ada to implement **out** mode parameters for scalar types. The formal parameter acts as an uninitialised local variable which is given a value during execution of the procedure. On leaving the procedure, the value of the formal parameter is assigned to the actual parameter, which must be a variable. This is shown in the following Ada procedure:

```
procedure read_negative(neg_number : out Integer) is
   number : Integer;
begin
   get(number);
   while number >= 0 loop
      put_line("number not negative, try again");
      get(number);
   end loop;
   neg_number := number;
end read_negative;
```

As an **out** parameter may not appear within an expression, it is necessary to have a local variable called number. In the call:

```
read_negative(amount);
```

the value of the integer variable amount is only updated to the value of neg_number when procedure read_negative is left.

Call by result was originally used in Algol W, but with a subtle difference from the mechanism described here. In Ada, the address of the actual parameter is computed on subprogram entry while in Algol W it is not computed until subprogram exit. These two approaches only give different answers in rather contrived situations, as will be seen later in this section.

As call by result means that a local copy must be created within the procedure, it suffers from the efficiency drawbacks that occur with structured parameters, as already discussed. For this reason, Ada allows structured **out** parameters to be passed by reference. As languages such as Pascal and C++ do not have a special parameter mode corresponding to the **out** mode of Ada, they use the same mechanism as that for updating information.

Updating information

Call by value-result is, as might be expected from its name, an amalgamation of call by value and call by result. The formal parameter acts as a local variable which is initialised to the value of the actual parameter. Within the procedure, changes to the formal parameter only affect the local copy. It is only when the subprogram is left that the actual parameter is updated to the final value of the formal parameter. For example, given the following Ada procedure to update a bank account by reading and then adding on the next 10 transactions:

```
procedure update(balance : in out Integer) is
   transaction : Integer;
begin
   for j in 1 .. 10 loop
      get(transaction);
      balance := balance + transaction;
   end loop;
end update;
```

then in the call:

```
update(currentacc);
```

the actual parameter currentacc is only updated when the procedure is left.

In Ada, **in out** scalar parameters must be passed by value-result although structured parameters may be passed by reference. Pascal uses **call by reference**, where the address of the actual parameter (that is, a pointer to the location containing the actual parameter) is passed to the formal parameter. The heading of procedure `update` in Pascal is:

> **procedure** update(**var** balance : Integer);

Within the procedure, any use of the formal parameter is treated as an indirect reference to the actual parameter. Hence, if parameter `balance` in procedure `update` had been called by reference, the actual parameter `currentacc` would have been automatically changed each time there was an assignment to `balance`. C++ also has reference parameters. The heading of `update` in C++ is:

> **void** update(int& balance);

Figure 6.2 illustrates the two methods discussed here for updating information.

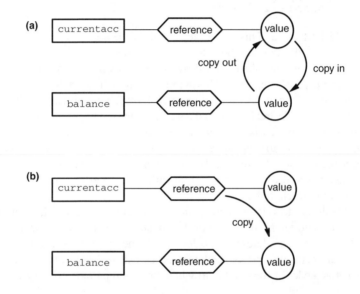

Figure 6.2   Updating information: (a) call by value-result; (b) call by reference.

In Java, parameters are always called by value. This means that values of variables of a primitive type cannot be modified as a result of a method call. However, objects in Java are always accessed by reference and so, when an object is passed as a parameter, it is a reference to the object that is passed by value. This means that it is possible to modify an object's attributes as a result of a method call.

Call by value-result has the same disadvantages with structured types as call by value and so in such circumstances, call by reference would seem to be the better choice. Call by value-result, on the other hand, has the advantage that all references within the subprogram are to local variables, which is faster than the indirect references to non-locals used in call by reference.

Programs should always be written in such a way that they do not depend on whether the mechanism used is call by value-result or call by reference. In most circumstances, the two mechanisms have the same effect, the exception being when an actual parameter is in scope within the body of the called procedure, and is accessed both directly as a non-local variable and indirectly through the formal parameter. This is known as **aliasing** and an example is shown on page 138 in the call of procedure whichmode. Aliasing can lead to errors which are very difficult to find and correct.

Another form of aliasing is when the same actual parameter is passed to two different reference formal parameters. This could happen, for example, with the following call of the swap procedure:

```
swap(this, this);
```

Languages such as Pascal have outlawed such subprogram calls, but it is not clear how calls such as:

```
swap(a[i], a[j]);
```

should be treated. This call is legal unless the values of i and j are equal and so erroneous calls can only be detected at run time.

To avoid the problems raised by aliasing, a variable in Euclid may not be passed as a **var** parameter to a subprogram in whose import list it appears. This has the consequence that call by reference and call by value-result always have the same effect.

In Pascal, Ada and C++, actual parameters passed by reference or by value-result must be variables, but early Fortran and PL/I allow them to be constants or expressions. At first glance, this does not appear to be possible, as the actual parameter must be capable of being updated. In some early implementations of Fortran this led to constants being changed as a result of a subprogram call, with the effect that the resulting errors were difficult to track down.

A solution to this problem with call by reference is for the compiler to allocate a location into which the value of the constant or expression may be put when the call takes place. The address of this location is then passed over to the subprogram. When the parameter passing is implemented as call by value-result, the solution is not to generate code for the result part when the actual parameter is not a variable.

Parameters in C

Scalar parameters in C are always passed by value. (Array parameters are discussed in Section 7.1.) The effect of call by reference can be achieved by having formal parameters of a pointer type and passing the address of a variable as the actual parameter. Hence, the C version of procedure swap is:

```
void swap(int *first, int *second) {
    int intermediate;
    intermediate = *first;
    *first = *second;
    *second = intermediate;
}
```

The parameters `first` and `second` are both value parameters, but the `*` in their declaration indicates that their type is 'pointer to `int`'. The assignment:

```
*first = *second;
```

should be read as 'the value held in the location pointed to by `second` is assigned to the location pointed to by `first`'. A possible procedure call is:

```
swap(&higher, &lower);
```

The `&` operator means that it is not the values of `higher` and `lower` that are passed, but their addresses. The effect is exactly the same as call by reference, the difference being that the C programmer needs to be more aware of what is going on and how parameter passing is being implemented. It can be argued that one of the aims of high-level languages is to hide implementation details so that the programmer can concentrate on the problem to be solved. Thus, this example shows how C is a lower level language than C++.

Call by name

Algol 60 uses call by name as the mechanism for updating information. This involves the equivalent of textual substitution of the actual parameter for each occurrence of the formal parameter. In call by reference, the address of the actual parameter is calculated once at the point of call. In call by name, on the other hand, the actual parameter is passed unevaluated and is recalculated each time the formal parameter is used during the execution of the subprogram. This introduces the possibility of a different address being produced for different uses of the same formal parameter.

In fact, this only leads to different results from call by reference where the programmer is being 'overclever'. Thus, as call by name is much more expensive to implement than call by reference, it has not been used in recent languages.

Comparison of mechanisms

In the following rather contrived example, the effect on `a` and `element` of the call `whichmode(a[element])` depends on how the parameter is passed. It must be emphasised that this example is only given to highlight the differences between the various methods; such tricky programming is not encouraged.

```
...
var element : Integer;
    a : array [1 .. 2] of Integer;

procedure whichmode(x : ? mode Integer);
begin
    a[1] := 6;
    element := 2;
    x := x + 3
end;
```

Table 6.2 Results of different parameter-passing mechanisms.

Mechanism	Result		
	a[1]	a[2]	element
call by value	6	2	2
call by value-result (Algol W)	6	4	2
call by value-result	4	2	2
call by reference	9	2	2
call by name	6	5	2

```
begin
    a[1] := 1; a[2] := 2;
    element := 1;
    whichmode(a[element]);
    ...
```

If the parameter is passed by result, an error will occur as the value of x in the expression x + 3 is undefined. If x was an **out** mode parameter in Ada, this use of x would give a syntax error. The other possibilities are given in Table 6.2.

When the parameter is called by reference, elements of the array a can be accessed in two different ways: either directly as in:

```
    a[1] := 6;
```

or, because the actual parameter is a[element], indirectly as in:

```
    x := x + 3
```

This is an example of aliasing and is the cause of call by value-result and call by reference giving different answers. The reason that call by name gives a different answer from call by reference is that the address of a[element] on procedure entry is different from its address when the statement

```
    x := x + 3
```

is executed. Similarly, as the address of a[element] computed on procedure entry is different from that on procedure exit, the two variants of call by value-result give different answers.

Overloading

Ada, C++ and Java allow more than one procedure or method with the same identifier to be declared in the same scope, but they must have a different parameter profile so that their calls can be differentiated from one another at compile time. Such procedures or methods are said to be **overloaded**. Hence, in Java, the following declarations are allowed:

```
void p(double a, double b) { ...}
void p(int a, int b) { ...}
```

The call **this**.p(2.0, 5.0) is a call of the first method while the call **this**.p(2, 5) is a call of the second. If it is not possible for the compiler to tell from the actual parameters which procedure is being called, then a compile-time error results.

A use of this feature in Ada is in the library of input/output routines where, for example, different put procedures write out values of different types. For example, there is one put routine for type Integer, one for type Float and one for type Character. Thus, in the call put(item), the procedure used will depend on the type of the variable item. Overloading therefore gives a simple straightforward interface for the input/output routines, which is easy for novices to learn and use.

To achieve a similar effect, Pascal 'cheats'. The read and write routines in Pascal appear to be ordinary Pascal procedures but, as they may have parameters of different types (and a variable number of parameters), they do not follow the standard Pascal rules.

In Java and C++, it is common for a class to have several alternative constructors, each with different parameter profiles. In that way, one constructor can initialise an object's attributes with default values while another can use the values passed as parameters.

Default parameters

Value parameters in C++ and **in** mode parameters in Ada may be given a default initial value. Hence, an increment procedure can be written in C++ and Ada respectively as:

```
void increment(int& item, int by = 1, int mul = 1) {
   item = item * mul + by;
} // increment

procedure increment(item : in out integer;
                    by : in integer := 1;
                    mul : in integer := 1) is
begin
   item := item * mul + by;
end increment;
```

In both languages, a call such as:

```
increment(number, 2, 3);
```

will multiply number by 3 and add 2, but if a third actual parameter is not given, as in the call:

```
increment(number, 2);
```

mul is given the default value of 1. When only one parameter is given, both by and mul are given their default values. The parameters with default values must be at the end of the parameter list and so we cannot use the default value for by without also using the default value for mul.

Named parameters

The usual mechanism for pairing actual and formal parameters is by position, with the first actual parameter corresponding to the first formal parameter, and so on. An alternative mechanism, available in PL/I, Fortran 90 and Ada, is to have **named association**. Using named association, the call of the Ada increment procedure can be written in any of the following ways:

```
increment (number, by => 2, mul => 3);
increment (item => number, mul =>3, by => 2);
increment (by => 2, mul =3, item => number);
```

As can be seen, the names of the formal parameters are repeated in the procedure call to indicate the association between actual and formal parameters. Positional and named associations may be mixed, but in such cases all the positional associations must come first. When the formal parameter identifiers are carefully chosen, named association can lead to clearer code, especially when there are a large number of parameters whose relative positions have no intrinsic meaning.

Named association and default parameters are often used together. For example, when real values are written in Ada, parameters are needed to specify the format; that is, the number of digits before the decimal point (fore), the number after the decimal point (aft) and the number in the exponent (exp). A possible statement to write out the value of the real variable size is:

```
put (size, fore => 2, aft => 5, exp => 3);
```

which is more understandable than:

```
put (size, 2, 5, 3);
```

as there is then nothing in the procedure call to indicate which actual parameter corresponds to fore, which to aft and which to exp. It is quite easy, on the other hand, to remember that the first parameter represents the value being written. As fore, aft, and exp have default values, they do not have to be explicitly mentioned in a call of put. This allows calls such as:

```
put (size, aft => 5);
```

where two of the format parameters are given their default value. An advantage of this feature is that a novice user does not have to know about the existence of these extra parameters until he or she becomes more experienced.

6.3 Functions

A function is a special kind of procedure that returns a value. The type of the returned value is usually given in the function heading, as can be seen from the example functions given on page 142 which return twice the value of their integer parameter.

The value to be returned is given in Algol 60, Pascal and Fortran by assigning a value to the name of the function, but this approach has been replaced in most recent languages by the use of an explicit **return** statement. Execution of a **return** statement causes immediate exit from a function, thereby making multiple exit points possible. In contrast, assignment to the name of a function does not cause an exit; such functions are left once their final statement has been executed.

Function calls occur as part of an expression, as in the statement:

```
j := 3 * twice(7);
```

Assuming that the effect of twice is to return twice its argument, this assigns the value 42 to j. If twice was a method declared in a Java or C++ class for which we had an object ob, the call would be:

```
j := 3 * ob.twice(7);
```

The value returned by a function can be regarded as an extra **out** parameter. This approach is most closely followed in Fortran 90 which has a special RESULT parameter.

Languages differ in what can be returned. Algol 60, Java and Pascal do not allow structured values to be returned while Ada, C, C++, Fortran 90 and Algol 68 do. However, as Pascal and Java allow reference (pointer) values to be returned, this is not a problem as we can return a reference to a structured value. Languages which allow functions to be returned as the value of a function are discussed in Chapter 9.

The exact order of evaluation of the operands in an expression is often not specified in the definition of a language so that the compiler writers have a free hand in producing optimal code. Evaluation of the expression:

```
a + b * c
```

will cause the values of b and c to be multiplied together and the result added to a. However, when a, b and c are function calls, the user has no knowledge of the order in which the three calls will take place. It is, therefore, even more important than with procedures that functions have no side effects.

Good programming practice suggests that information should only be passed in to a function via its parameters and that the only effect of the function on the rest of the program should be through the returned value. Ada, in fact, does not allow **out** or **in out** parameters with functions, although both it and most other languages (with the exception of experimental languages such as Euclid) do still allow access to, and modification of, non-local variables. Programmers should not normally indulge in this latter freedom. In C++, when **const** is attached to a function declaration, we have a guarantee that a call of the function will not modify any of its parameters or non-local variables.

In object-oriented languages, value returning methods are normally used to query an object's state and hence access variables that are not local to the function. An example is the getCents and getDollars methods of class Cost given in Chapter 5. However, as we discussed earlier, when we consider the target object to be an extra parameter, we can apply the normal function guidelines.

Example programs – functions

1. Fortran 90

```
FUNCTION TWICE(A)
INTEGER TWICE
INTEGER A
TWICE = A + A
END FUNCTION TWICE
```

2. Algol 60

```
integer procedure twice(a);
  value a; integer a;
  twice := a + a
```

3. Pascal

```
function twice(a : Integer) : Integer;
begin
  twice := a + a
end {add}
```

4. C++

```
int twice(int a) const {
  return a + a;
} // twice
```

5. Java

```
int twice(int a) {
  return a + a;
} // twice
```

6. Ada

```
function twice(a : in Integer) return Integer is
begin
  return a + a;
end add;
```

Operators

Most languages have a set of built-in infix operators such as +, – and * while functions correspond to prefix operators. Thus, a call of add is written as:

```
c := add(2, 3);
```

while the corresponding infix form is:

```
c := 2 + 3;
```

To illustrate the use of these two forms of operators, consider an enumeration type called Day which is declared in Ada as:

```
type Day is (sun, mon, tues, wed, thurs, fri, sat);
```

Consider also a function with two parameters – today of type Day and n of type Integer – that will return the day which is 'n days after today'. In Ada and C++, the names of functions are not restricted to identifiers and we can redefine operators. An example in Ada is:

```
function "+"(today : in Day; n : in Integer)
  return Day is
begin
  return Day'val((Day'pos(today) + n) rem 7);
  --Day'pos converts a Day
  --to the corresponding Integer in the range 0 .. 6
  --while Day'val converts an Integer
  --in the range 0 .. 6 to the corresponding Day
end "+";
```

The corresponding C++ definition has the heading:

```
Day operator+(Day today, int n) const;
```

Assuming that newday has been defined to be of type Day, a possible call of the function in Ada is:

```
newday := "+"(tues, 6);
```

although the more natural approach in both C++ and Ada is:

```
newday := tues + 6;
```

In both cases, newday will be given the value mon. This new definition of + does not replace the existing definitions, but adds to them. It is the overloading property of Ada and C++ that determines, from the type of the parameters (that is, the operands), which of the + operators is intended. If this cannot be decided unambiguously by the compiler, an error is reported. All the + operators have the same precedence. As part of its simplification of C++, Java does not support the redefinition of operators.

Most languages overload operators like +, – and * thereby allowing them to represent either integer or floating-point operations. What Ada and C++ have done is to incorporate this feature into the language and to use it as the basis for extending the available operations in a natural way.

6.4 Storage management

Modern languages are usually implemented in such a way that storage for program code and storage for data items are allocated separately. The area of store set aside to hold the data items used in a call of a procedure is called its **data area** or **activation record**. There are two main storage strategies for allocating data areas; static and block-structured dynamic.

Static storage allocation

This method requires that the maximum size of each data item is known at compile time and that no data item can have multiple simultaneous occurrences. As this second requirement rules out recursive procedures – that is, procedures that can call themselves – Fortran is the only one of the languages discussed in this chapter that can make use of this method. When a Fortran 90 subprogram is recursive, it must be declared as such. Non-recursive subprograms can use static storage allocation.

 With static storage allocation, declaration-reference binding, that is, the allocation of data items to their final store locations – occurs at load time. Although this method is straightforward and allows data items to be accessed efficiently, it does have the drawback that local variables occupy store locations even when the subprogram in which they are declared has not been called. When a procedure is entered for a second or subsequent time, all the local variables have the values they had on the previous exit. Fortran programmers must not make use of this effect, for although Fortran allows such a storage mechanism, the definition of the language does not insist on it and stack storage management may be used.

Stack storage management

In most modern languages, as was outlined in Chapter 3.2, declaration-reference binding for local variables and procedure parameters occurs on block entry. That is the case for both procedural and object-oriented languages. This means that the declaration of a local variable is bound to a different store location each time a block (that is, a procedure) is entered. The storage mechanism that is usually used to implement this type of binding is called **stack storage management**. Using this mechanism, storage is allocated to the main program's data area at load time, while storage for a procedure's data area is only allocated when the procedure is called. On return from the procedure, this storage is de-allocated.

 To illustrate block-structured storage allocation, consider the following skeleton Pascal program:

```pascal
program Main(output);
  var b, d : Integer;

  procedure z;
    var e, f : Integer;
```

```
      begin
         . . .
      end {z};

      procedure y;
        var g, h : Integer;
      begin
         . . .z;  . . .
      end {y};

   begin
      . . .y;
      . . .z;  . . .
   end.
```

The changes that occur in the allocation of storage to the data areas as the execution of this program progresses are shown in Figure 6.3. When execution begins, space is allocated to the data area of Main. It is only when procedure y is called that space is allocated to its data area – that is, to the variables g and h. In procedure y, there is a call of procedure z. On entry to z, space is allocated to its data area. On exit from procedure z and return to y, space for z's data area is de-allocated; at this point, the local variables e and f cease to exist in the sense that they no longer have storage locations allocated. On return from y to the main program, the local variables in y cease to exist in the same way.

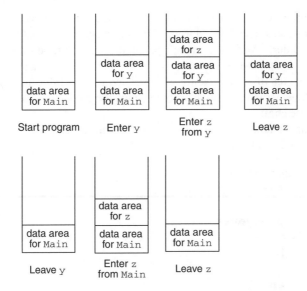

Figure 6.3 Stack storage allocation.

There is now a second call of z, this time from the main program. This call results in space being allocated once again to z's data area. However, as the storage locations allocated are different this time, when z is entered for this second time, its local variables do not inherit their previous values.

This mechanism just outlined results in a stack of data areas called the **run-time stack**. When a procedure is entered, space for its data area is allocated; on exit from the procedure, the data area is popped from the stack. The lifetime of the variables b and d declared in the main program extends throughout the execution of the whole program, while the lifetime of, for example, g and h starts when procedure y is called and ends when it is left.

An advantage of this type of storage allocation is that space is only allocated when it is needed, which is in contrast to static storage allocation, where storage for all data items is allocated at load time. A drawback is that, as the locations allocated to local variables are not fixed, the code generated by the compiler to access them is more complex than in the case of static allocation. However, this approach is so useful that computers have special hardware instructions to ease access to variables allocated storage on the run-time stack.

Provided that the size of all local variables is constant, the relative position of an item within a data area is known at compile time and is called its **offset**. The position of the data area, on the other hand, is unknown until the procedure is entered at run time. When a data area is added to the run-time stack, its base address can be stored in a register as a pointer to the current data area. Local variables may then be accessed using this base address plus the offset determined at compile time.

Data areas

In addition to parameters and local variables, data areas need to hold certain system information, such as the address of the instruction that must be returned to on leaving the procedure. Also, on leaving a procedure, the run-time stack must be restored to its position before the procedure was entered and so each data area must hold a pointer to the data area of the procedure which called it. This information, which links the data areas together in the reverse order in which the procedures were called, is known as the **dynamic chain**.

To understand how the information held in the data area is accessed, consider the following Pascal program:

```pascal
program Main(output);
  var b, d : Integer;

  procedure z;
    var e, f : Integer;
  begin
    . . .
  end {z};

  procedure y;
    var g, h : Integer;
```

```
procedure x;
   var j, k : Integer;
   begin
      . . .
   end {x};
begin
   ...z;  ...x;  ...
end {y};
begin
   ...z;  ...y;  ...
end.
```

In the main program, only variables b and d can be accessed. When executing procedure z, the local variables e and f and the non-local variables b and d can be accessed. When y is being executed, the local variables g and h and the non-local variables b and d can be accessed. As procedure x is nested within procedure y, when x is executed, the non-local variables g, h, b and d can be accessed as well as the local variables j and k.

When procedure z is called from procedure y, three data areas will be on the run-time stack (z, y and Main), but variables in only two of the data areas will be accessible (z and Main). When procedure x is called from y, three data areas will again be on the run-time stack, but this time variables in all three data areas will be accessible. Thus, a mechanism is needed that allows access to certain non-local items, but which restricts access to others.

The rules governing which data areas may be accessed and which cannot are the scope rules, and so this information is known at compile time. A solution is to hold in each data area a pointer to the data area of its textually enclosing block. As that data area will, in turn, contain a pointer to its textually enclosing block, this forms a chain, known as the **static chain**, which links together the accessible data areas. As C, C++ and Java do not allow the nesting of procedure declarations, their implementations do not need a static chain.

The contents of the run-time stack when procedure z has been called from procedure y is shown in Figure 6.4(a). As z and y are both declared in the main program, their static chain pointers both point to the data area of Main. Figure 6.4(b) shows the run-time stack when procedure x has been called from procedure y. As x has been declared locally to y, its static chain pointer points to the data area of y.

Space is allocated for parameters in the data area in the same way as for local variables. For value parameters, the value of the actual parameter is copied into the appropriate location in the data area on procedure entry. With reference parameters, it is the address of the actual parameter that is held in the data area.

6.5 Recursion

Stack storage management is capable of dealing with recursive procedures – that is, procedures that may call themselves. Each time a procedure is called, its data area is added to the run-time stack. With a recursive procedure, this means that there will be

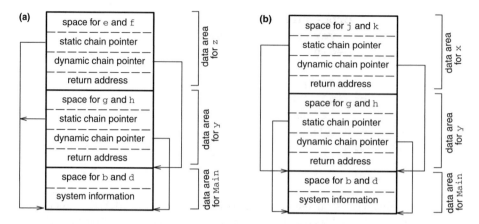

Figure 6.4   Run-time stack: (a) when z has been called from y; (b) when x has been called from y.

several data areas in existence simultaneously, one for each recursive call. This can best be illustrated by considering the following recursive function which calculates factorials. The code is that of C, C++ and Java, although programs written in Pascal and Ada behave in essentially the same way. Most modern languages support recursion, although in Fortran 90 a subprogram must be explicitly declared to be recursive:

```
int factorial(int n) {
   if (n > 1)
      return n * factorial(n - 1);
   else
      return 1;
} // factorial
```

Before looking at the execution of this program, it is important to note that the definition of the factorial function in the program uses the property that factorials can be defined in terms of a simpler version of themselves. In general, n! is n * (n - 1)!. This can be illustrated by considering the value of four factorial (written as 4!), which is 4 * 3 * 2 * 1 or, to put it another way, 4 * 3!.

Consider now, the execution of the call factorial(3). The function factorial is entered and, as n has been given the value 3, the expression:

```
3 * factorial(2)
```

is to be evaluated. This involves a recursive call of function factorial. In this second call of factorial, n has the value 2 and this leads to evaluation of the expression:

```
2 * factorial(1)
```

Function factorial is entered for a third time, but as n has the value 1, the execution of this call is completed, returning the value 1. The program now completes execution of:

```
2 * factorial(1)
```

and so returns from the call factorial(2) with the value 2. Finally, the program completes execution of:

```
3 * factorial(2)
```

and returns to the main program with the answer 6.

The structure of the data areas for the recursive function factorial is shown in Figure 6.5. In each data area, a location is set aside for the value parameter n. When function factorial is entered for the third time, three data areas for factorial are in existence simultaneously. Therefore, three 'incarnations' of n can be considered to be in existence simultaneously with the respective values of 3, 2 and 1. (Note that such a situation does not cause any problems as any reference to n is always to the one in the current data area.) When the program returns from the function calls, the data areas are removed from the stack in the reverse order to that in which they were added.

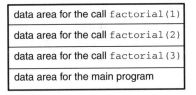

Figure 6.5   Data areas for a recursive function.

Recursive subprograms are most effective when the solution to a problem can be expressed in terms of a simpler version of itself. Such solutions often involve data structures such as linked lists and trees, which can also be defined recursively. This class of problem is discussed in Section 7.4, which deals with dynamic data structures, and in Chapters 9 and 10 which deal with functional and logic programming.

6.6   Forward references

Pascal was designed so that it can be translated by a one-pass compiler. To make this possible, the scope of an identifier extends from its declaration to the end of the block in which it is declared, rather than throughout the whole block. As a consequence, all identifiers, including procedure identifiers, must be declared before they can be used. However, this is not always possible when two procedures are **mutually recursive** – that is, when each calls the other. To get round the problem, **forward declarations** are used in Pascal, as illustrated in the following two procedures exp and operand.

The effect of calling procedure exp is to read and validate an arithmetic expression consisting of a series of zero or more additions where the operands are either a or are bracketed arithmetic expressions with the same form as the overall expression. An example valid expression is:

```
a+(a+(a)+((a+a)+a))
```

Procedure exp calls procedure operand which in turn may call procedure exp:

```
procedure operand(var ca : Char); forward;

procedure exp(var cb : Char);
begin
  operand(cb);
  while cb = '+' do
    operand(cb)
end {exp};

procedure operand;
begin
  read(ca);
  if ca = '(' then
  begin
    exp(ca);
    if ca <> ')' then
      writeln('missing bracket')
  end else
  if ca <> 'a'then
    writeln('missing operand');
  read(ca)
end {operand};
```

The compiler can deal with the call of procedure operand from within procedure exp as it knows the number and type of the parameters of operand from the forward declaration. The actual body of operand is given later in the program, although the parameters are not repeated.

In C, any subprogram called before it has been declared is assumed to be an integer function. When this is not the case then, as in Pascal, a forward declaration (called a **function prototype** in ANSI C and in C++) such as:

```
void operand(char *);
```

must be given before the first call of operand. Function prototypes must always be given in C++ when a function is called before it has been declared and it is good practice to do this in C. Function prototypes are an example of how ANSI C and C++ have increased the amount of type checking done at compile time compared with traditional C.

Ada differentiates between the specification and the body of a subprogram. The declaration:

```
function a(b : Integer) return Real;
```

is of a function specification while:

```
function a(b : Integer) return Real is
begin ... end a;
```

is a function body.

Normally only a subprogram body is declared, although it is always possible for a subprogram specification to be declared as well. This allows subprogram specifications to be used in the same way as forward subprogram declarations in Pascal. The one difference is that the parameters are given in the forward declaration in Pascal, and are not repeated in the actual body, while with Ada they must be given in both situations. Although this requires more writing, it makes programs easier to read.

In Algol 60, Algol 68 and Java the order of declaration of procedures does not matter and so there is no need for forward declarations. This means that more work has to be done by the compiler.

6.7 Subprograms as parameters

So far, this chapter has shown how constants, expressions and variables can be passed as subprogram parameters. In many languages, it is also possible to pass functions and procedures as parameters. These are referred to as **formal functions** or **formal procedures**.

The ability to pass functions as parameters is of central importance in functional languages and is discussed in Chapter 9. It is less widely used in imperative languages, although it is useful in numerical analysis where it allows general mathematical routines to be written. For example, to calculate the value of:

$$\frac{f(x2) - f(x1)}{x2 - x1}$$

for any function f and any value of x1 and x2, the following Pascal function could be used:

```
function slope(f(y : Real) : Real;
   x1, x2 : Real) : Real;
begin
   if x1 = x2 then
      slope := 0
   else
      slope := (f(x2) - f(x1)) / (x2 - x1)
end {slope};
```

A call of this function requires three parameters, the first of which is a Real function with one Real parameter. Given the functions:

```
function straight(x : Real) : Real;
begin
   straight := 2 * x + 1
end {straight};

function tan(x : Real) : Real;
```

```
begin
   tan := sin(x) / cos(x)
end {tan};
```

then possible calls of `slope` might be `slope(straight, 3.8, 3.85)` and `slope(tan, 3.8, 3.85)`. Both of these calls will return `Real` values.

In Fortran, Algol 60, traditional C and in the original definition of Pascal, the type of the parameters in a formal subprogram does not have to be specified and this leads to a loophole in the type checking rules. This omission was rectified for Pascal and C when their standards were produced.

Modula-2 goes further than Pascal and allows procedure types and procedure variables. Thus, it is possible, for example, to have the type declaration:

```
TYPE realfunc = PROCEDURE(REAL) : REAL;
```

and the variable declaration:

```
VAR fx : realfunc;
```

The variable `fx` can take as values functions which have one real value parameter and which return a real value. Given a function similar to `straight`, the assignment can then be:

```
fx := straight;
```

The function `slope` would be written in Modula-2 as:

```
PROCEDURE slope(f : realfunc; x1, x2 : REAL) : REAL;
BEGIN
  IF x1 = x2 THEN
    RETURN 0
  ELSE
    RETURN (f(x2) - f(x1)) / (x2 - x1)
  END
END slope;
```

The call `slope(straight, 3.8, 3.85)` is still possible in this case, but it is also possible to have the call `slope(fx, 3.8, 3.85)` where the function passed depends on the current value of `fx`. In Modula-2, therefore, subprograms are much closer to becoming objects which can be manipulated in the same way as variables. It is permissable, for example, to have arrays of subprograms. Algol 68 and the functional languages go further than Modula-2 and allow functions to be returned as the value of a function.

Procedures and functions may not be passed as parameters in Ada, although a similar effect is achieved by what are called **generics**. Instead of `slope` having three parameters, one of which is a formal function, the Ada equivalent is a **generic function** with two parameters. First, the generic function specification is declared:

```
generic
   with function f(y : Real) return Real;
function slope(x1, x2 : Real) return Real;
```

and then the function body:

```
function slope(x1, x2 : Real) return Real is
begin
  if x1 = x2 then
    return 0;
  else
    return (f(x2 - f(x1)) / (x2 - x1);
end slope;
```

A generic procedure or function is a **template** from which an actual procedure or function may be obtained by what is called **instantiation**. If two Ada functions straight and tan are assumed, two possible instances of the generic function slope are one in which calls of f are replaced by calls of straight and one in which they are replaced by calls of tan. These instances may be produced by the two generic instantiations:

```
function straight_slope is new slope(f => straight);
function tan_slope is new slope(f => tan);
```

Generic instantiation occurs at compile time and results in two completely different slope functions being created; one called straight_slope and the other called tan_slope. In the case of Pascal, on the other hand, there is a single slope function. The equivalent of the Pascal calls of slope(straight, 3.8, 3.85) and slope(tan, 3.8, 3.85) are straight_slope(3.8, 3.85) and tan_slope(3.8, 3.85). The subject of generics is discussed further in Section 7.5.

Summary

1. In Pascal, C and Java, the parameter-passing mechanism of call by value is used to pass information into a subprogram.

2. In call by value, the formal parameter acts as a local variable, while in call by constant-value (used in Ada) it acts as a local constant.

3. Call by value can be expensive in terms of space and time when the parameter is a structured object.

4. Call by reference and call by value-result are used to update the information passed into a procedure. In the absence of aliases, they have the same effect.

5. Ada, C++ and Java allow procedures or methods to be overloaded.

6. The only effect of a function call on the rest of a program should be through its returned value.

7. Ada and C++ allow the redefinition of operators such as +.

8. Stack storage management is required to support recursive subprograms.

9. If the amount of storage required by all local objects can be determined at compile time, it is possible to implement a language so that the relative position of each object within a data area is known at compile time. This was a major goal in the design of Pascal.

10. Pascal was designed so that it can be translated by a one-pass compiler.

11. Procedures and functions can be passed as parameters in Pascal and C, but not in Ada. Ada uses generics to achieve a similar effect.

Exercises

6.1 Compare the parameter-passing mechanisms call by value, call by constant-value and reference-constant for both simple and structured parameters.

6.2 Assuming that j has the value 1, a[1] the value 2 and a[2] the value 3, what would be the effect of the call swap(j, a[j]) when the parameters are passed (a) by value-result, (b) by value-result (Algol W), (c) by reference and (d) by name? Would any of the parameter-passing mechanisms give a different answer if the call was swap(a[j], j)?

6.3 Ada is based on Pascal, but is much larger. Compare the parameter-passing facilities in the two languages with particular regard to the question of whether the introduction of **out** parameters, default parameters and named association is worth the added complexity.

6.4 Parameters in Java are always passed by value, yet a method call can cause the attributes of an object parameter to be updated. Why is this?

6.5 Good programming practice indicates that procedures should be free from side-effects. Why is this even more important with functions? As it is generally agreed that changing non-local variables is undesirable, why is this feature permitted in almost all languages including those which have only recently been defined?

6.6 Describe the advantages of being able to overload procedure and function identifiers. Why is this facility particularly useful with operators?

6.7 Why is static storage allocation not able to support the implementation of recursive procedures?

6.8 Describe how stack storage management can be used in the implementation of procedure entry and exit in a block-structured language. What is the purpose of the static and dynamic chains?

6.9 How has the addition of function prototypes in ANSI C allowed more type checking to be done at compile time compared with traditional C?

6.10 Compare the facility of passing procedures and functions as parameters in Pascal with the use of generics in Ada.

Bibliography

The bibliography at the end of this book gives a list of textbooks on the main programming languages. They all give further information on the structure of subprograms and how parameters are passed in their particular language. Details of the implementation of subprograms, parameter passing and data areas are given in books on compiling such as that by Aho *et al.*(1986). A more general description is given by Pratt and Zelkowitz (1996).

Aho, A.V., Sethi, R. and Ullman, J.D. (1986). *Compilers: Principles, Techniques and Tools*. Addison-Wesley.

Pratt, T.W. and Zelkowitz, M. (1996). *Programming Languages: Design and Implementation* (Third Edition). Prentice-Hall.

Structured data

Chapter 3 looked at simple types. This chapter looks at structured types, which have simpler types as components. The two basic data structures in procedural languages are the array and the record. In object-oriented languages, records are replaced by classes.

All the components (elements) of an array have the same type and the elements are accessed using a computable index. The components (fields) of a record may have different types and are referred to by name. In Chapter 5, we looked at classes as a way of structuring and designing programs and in Chapter 8, we look at how they are used in inheritance hierarchies. In this chapter, we consider them as a way of structuring data and as a way of implementing abstract data types. In C++, for example, a class can be considered as a record in which the components can be operations. An important use of records and classes is in the construction of dynamic structures, such as linked lists and trees, where one or more of the components are of a pointer type.

Strings in many imperative languages are implemented as arrays of characters, which restricts the available set of string operations. In Perl, on the other hand, the character string is a basic type in the language and a full set of string operations are available.

Pascal is unusual in having a `set` data type. Pascal also introduced a `file` data type which has been used as the basis for files in Ada.

7.1 Introduction

A **data structure** is composed from simpler data items. The items from which it is composed are called **components** and they may be simple data items or other data structures.

The early languages, Fortran and Algol 60, had only one kind of data structure, called the **array**, whereas most later procedural languages have both arrays and records. Object-oriented languages have classes instead of records. Figures 7.1 and 7.2 show the major features of arrays and records, respectively. The richness of data structures is obtained by combining the basic data structures in various ways. At the simplest level, such combinations are arrays of records, and records, some of whose fields are arrays, but probably the most interesting and useful extension of the basic data structures is where records and classes are used in conjunction with pointers to form **dynamic data structures**.

Example

```
type   list =   array[1 .. 20] of  Real;
var   a: list;
```

Component type

Homogeneous – all elements are of the same type.

Access to components

This is accomplished by knowing their position in the array; for example, the fourth element in the above array is referred to as a[4]. The array index may be an expression.

Efficiency

Efficient access at run time although not as efficient as simple variables due to the computable index.

Use

If the position of the required components (elements) of a structure has to be computed at run time, then arrays are an appropriate data structure. They are usually used in conjunction with loops and are very important in the solution of scientific or engineering problems.

Figure 7.1   Array features.

The judicious selection of appropriate data structures is central to the production of a well-structured and understandable program.

Example

```
type person =
  record
          name: string;
          age: 0 .. 99;
          sex: (male, female)
   end;
var john: person;
```

Component type

Heterogeneous – mixed types

Access to components

Access is by the name of the component field of the record; for example, `john.age`.

Efficiency

As the field selectors are fixed at compile time, the components of a record may be accessed as efficiently as simple variables.

Use

They are used to group together data items, which are components of a single item in the problem domain.

Figure 7.2   Record features.

7.2 Arrays

Arrays have been widely used as data structures since the earliest programming languages. To specify an array, its attributes must be known, which are:

- The type of its elements: this is a single type since all elements are of the same type.
- The number of components: usually this is given as the number of dimensions with an upper and lower bound for each dimension.
- The type of the subscripts: in some languages this is always integer, although Pascal and Ada allow any discrete type.

In imperative languages, the specification of the attributes of an array are usually given in the declaration. In Pascal, this declaration might be:

```
type Matrix = array [1 .. 10, 0 .. 15] of Real;
var a : Matrix;
```

The name of this array variable is a, its elements are all of type Real, it is two dimensional with bounds 1 and 10 for the first dimension and 0 and 15 for the second dimension, and the subscripts are of type Integer. The elements of an array are accessed using a **computable index** – that is, by evaluating the subscripts that can, in general, be expressions. Hence if i and j are Integer variables with values 3 and 5 respectively, a[i - 1, j + 1] refers to the element at position row 2, column 6. A value can be assigned to an array element in an assignment statement as in:

```
a[i - 1, j + 1] := 25.3;
```

It is a logical error in a program if the value of a subscript goes out of bounds. This leads to a run-time error in Pascal and an exception being thrown in Ada and Java while in C and C++ the program will just access some location outside the array, leading to the program giving wrong results!

A two dimensional array in Pascal and Ada can be considered to be a one-dimensional array, each of whose elements is an array. An alternative way of defining type Matrix in Pascal is therefore:

```
type Row = array [0 .. 15] of Real;
type Matrix = array [1 .. 10] of Row;
```

To emphasise that we have an array of an array, it is possible to refer to elements as a[i - 1][j + 1] instead of a[i - 1, j + 1]. The type of a[i - 1] is Row.

In C and C++, we can declare an array variable arow by writing:

```
double arow[16];
```

In Java, C and C++, the minimum subscript is always zero and so we have created an array with 16 elements whose subscripts are in the range 0 to 15. We refer to individual elements in the same way as in Pascal and so can write arow[j + 1]. In Java an array is an object and is created using the **new** operator. The declaration:

```
double[] arow;
```

declares a variable arow that can refer to an array of elements of type double. An actual array with 16 elements is then created by:

```
arow = new double[16];
```

The creation of an array can be done within the declaration as in:

```
double[] arow = new double[16];
```

To create two-dimensional arrays in C, C++ and Java, we write:

```
double a[10][16]; // C or C++
double[][] a = new double[10][16]; // Java
```

To access the element of array a at position row i, column j in either language, we write a[i][j] in the same way as we saw in the second of the alternative Pascal notations. The value of the first subscript must be in the range 0 to 9 and the second in the range 0 to 15.

It is possible to give a name to an array type in C or C++:

```
typedef double Matrix[10][16];
```

and to then declare a to be of type Matrix as in the Pascal example. Giving names to array types is seldom done in C or C++ and cannot be done in Java.

Array elements can normally be used in a language wherever a variable of that type is allowed. The only major exception to this rule is that languages such as Pascal and Ada do not allow a subscripted variable as the control variable of a **for** statement.

Implementation

As the elements of an array are normally referred to frequently, they need to be accessed quickly and easily, as otherwise a considerable inefficiency will result. There are several ways in which this can be achieved, but the commonest is the **mapping function**. This is a formula that allows a direct calculation of the address of the element required. An array is normally stored with the array elements in contiguous storage locations. For the example of Figure 7.3, the elements of the two-dimensional array are stored in row order, and so the address of element a[i, j] is:

```
Base address + component_size *
   (row_length * (i - first_lower_bound)
              + j - second_lower_bound)
```

In C, C++ and Java, as the lower bounds are always zero, the mapping function is simplified.

Array notation

Languages have varied in their notation for array elements. In Fortran and Ada, the subscripts are contained in round brackets as in a(i), while other languages such as Pascal, C, C++ and Java have followed Algol 60's lead and have used square brackets as in a[i]. The argument in favour of square brackets is that arrays and their subscripts can clearly be distinguished from those parts of a program that use round brackets – that is, expressions and function calls. The counter argument for round brackets is that they make arrays look like functions, and this is not unreasonable as they are both mapping functions: an array selects a particular element from a table whereas a function performs the same process using an algorithm.

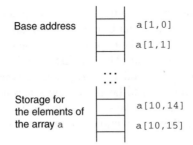

Figure 7.3   Possible storage for elements of the array a.

Accessing arrays in C and C++

Consider again the C or C++ declaration:

```
double arow[16];
```

Elements of an array can be accessed very efficiently in C and C++ using pointers. If the identifier b is declared as:

```
double *b;
```

then the assignment:

```
b = &arow[0];
```

will assign the address of arow[0] to b. This assignment can also be written as:

```
b = arow;
```

since the identifier arow can be considered to be a constant double pointer whose value is the address of arow[0]. The array element arow[i] can now be referred to, using pointer arithmetic, as * (arow + i) or as * (b + i). As arow is a constant, its value cannot be changed, but b is a variable and so it is possible to step through the elements of the array arow by incrementing the value of the double pointer b.

Hence, instead of:

```
double total = 0.0;
for (int i = 0; i < 16; i++)
    total += arow[i];
```

it is possible to write:

```
double total = 0.0; b = arow;
for (int i = 0; i < 16; i++)
    total += *b++;
```

This gives very fast access to the array elements and is one of the reasons why it is possible to write very efficient C and C++ programs. Execution of *b++ gives us the value pointed to by b and then updates the value of the pointer b so that it points to the next element in the array. The compiler knows how many bytes are allocated to a double value and so can add the correct number when evaluating the expression b++. A major change from C++ to Java is that Java does not allow pointer arithmetic.

Using pointers to access arrays can lead to some common, but subtle pitfalls. Suppose that we have the following function that returns a double pointer:

```
double* fun() {
    double arow[16];
    ...
    return arow; //wrong!!
} // fun
```

This is syntactically correct, but arow is a local variable and so the space for the array is de-allocated when we leave the function. We are therefore returning a pointer to space that is no longer allocated, i.e. we have a dangling reference. The solution is to declare arow as:

```
double *arow = new double[16];
```

As space for the array is now allocated on the heap, it remains in existence after we leave fun.

In C, parameters are always passed using call by value, but as an array identifier is a pointer, this is equivalent to arrays being passed by reference.

Name-size binding

Another important matter is the time at which the required amount of storage for an array is determined. The binding of the name of an array variable to its required amount of storage is referred to here as **name-size binding**, and there are three possibilities.

Static arrays (compile-time binding)

In this case, the size is fixed when the array variable is declared and it cannot change at run time. It is simple to compile and is fast at run time. This method is used in Pascal because, for reasons of efficiency, a design decision was made in the original language definition that the size of all objects should be known at compile time. Chapter 6 showed how, on block entry, storage can be allocated to data areas on the run-time stack and how it is important that the relative position of all items within the data area is known at compile time. With static arrays, this is indeed the situation.

There are disadvantages of this method however: it is inflexible and arrays must be declared the maximum size they can ever attain, which can lead to considerable wastage in storage space.

Semi-dynamic arrays (binding on block entry)

In this case, the size of an array is not determined until block entry. In Ada, for example, we can have the declarations:

```
type Matrix is array(Integer range <>,
                     Integer range <>) of Real;
a, b : Matrix(1 .. m, 1 .. n);
```

where m and n are declared and given values in an enclosing block. The relative position of all of the items in the data area is no longer known at compile time as the size of a and b can differ each time the block is entered.

However, the size of the arrays is fixed and is known on block entry. Hence, when the block is entered at run time, storage for the arrays can be allocated on the run-time stack beyond the end of the block's data area. Within the data area we can have fixed size pointers which will point to where the arrays a and b are held. As the relative position of the pointers within the data area is known at compile time, they can be used to provide indirect access to the array elements. When the block containing the array declarations is left, the space for the data area and for the arrays is de-allocated as normal.

Most languages allow semi-dynamic arrays. The advantage is that arrays can be created to exactly the size required by the particular problem.

Dynamic arrays (binding during statement execution)

There are two kinds of dynamic array. In Java, for example, space is allocated to an array during statement execution. After the declaration:

```
double[] arow = new double[16];
```

space is allocated on the heap in a sequence of contiguous store locations. That means that array elements can still be accessed using a mapping function as discussed earlier. Suppose that we subsequently wish arow to point to an array with 20 elements, the effect of:

```
arow = new double[20];
```

is to allocate space on the heap for a completely new array and for the previous array to become garbage. In Java, space for an array is always allocated on the heap while in C, C++ and Fortran 90 allocation on the heap can be used as an alternative to semi-dynamic arrays.

The alternative is to have **extensible arrays**. This is a very flexible arrangement for the programmer and ideally suited to interactive languages where it may be required to add new array elements at any time. It is not surprising, therefore, that an interactive language like APL should feature such arrays. Other languages that make use of extensible arrays are SNOBOL 4, Icon and Perl. As will be seen in Section 7.5, there is a close connection between extensible arrays and strings of variable length and we delay implementation issues until then.

Array parameters

In Pascal, the number of elements is part of the definition of the type of an array. Consider the problem of finding the sum of the elements of an array of 20 floating-point numbers. In Pascal, this could be declared as:

```
type List = array[1 .. 20] of Real;
```

and a suitable function would be:

```
function sum(a : List) : Real;
var i : Integer;
   total : Real;
begin
  total := 0.0;
  for i := 1 to 20 do
    total := total + a[i];
  sum := total
end {sum};
```

However, if the problem is extended to find the sum of the elements in an array of 40 floating-point numbers, a completely new function must be defined. This was a major problem in early versions of Pascal although it did not occur in earlier languages such as Fortran, Algol 60 and C where the size of the array could be passed as a parameter.

The ISO Pascal standard has solved this problem by introducing what are known as **conformant array parameters**. Function sum now becomes:

```
function sum(a : array[low .. high : Integer]
                 of Real) : Real;
var i : Integer;
   total : Real;
begin
  total := 0.0;
  for i := low to high do
    total := total + a[i];
  sum := total
end {sum};
```

If b is of type List, the function call sum(b) will cause low and high to be given the values 1 and 20, respectively. The function sum is, therefore, now able to accept one-dimensional arrays of Real elements of any size.

If the parameter a is a variable parameter then, when the function sum is called, only a pointer to the actual array parameter is passed together with values for low and high. The size of all objects is therefore still known at compile time. When the parameter a is a value parameter, on the other hand, a copy of the actual parameter is passed. As there can be several calls of sum, each with an actual array parameter of a different size, the amount of space to be reserved within the data area of sum can no longer be fixed at compile time. Value conformant array parameters must therefore be implemented in a similar way to semi-dynamic arrays.

Ada has **constrained** and **unconstrained** array types. The declaration:

```
type List is array(Integer range <>) of Real;
```

declares an unconstrained array type List. An array variable b can then be declared as:

```
b : List(1 .. 20);
```

The size of a particular array can be found by using what are called its attributes. Hence, b'first is 1, b'last is 20 and b'range is the range 1 .. 20. These attributes can be used in the body of a function so that arrays of differing sizes can be dealt with. The Ada function for sum is:

```
function sum(a : List) return Real is
  total : Real := 0.0;
begin
  for i in a'range loop
    total := total + a(i);
  end loop;
  return total;
end sum;
```

Array attributes are also available in Java and the equivalent method definition is:

```
double sum(double[] a) {
  double total = 0.0;
  for (int i = 0; i < a.length; i++)
    total += a[i];
  return total;
} // sum
```

Note that we give the structure of the array parameter in the heading, rather than defining a new type. As arrays are objects, we always pass a reference to an array object in Java. Array parameters in C++ are also passed by reference, but as array attributes are not available, we have to pass the size of the array as a second parameter. To ensure that the array is not modified as a part of the call, we can pass the array by reference-constant. The C++ function heading is:

```
double sum(const double a[], int length);
```

Alternatively, as array parameters in C++ are treated as pointers, we can write:

```
double sum(const double* a, int length);
```

Name and structural equivalence

Chapter 6 explained that, when a function or procedure is called, the types of the actual and formal parameters must match. This leads to the question of when two arrays are of the same type. Consider the following Pascal declarations:

```
type First = array[1 .. 10] of Integer;
     Second = array[1 .. 10] of Integer;
var a : First;
    b : Second;
    c : array[1 .. 10] of Integer;
    d, e : array [1 .. 10] of Integer;
    f : First;
```

As can be seen, there are six array variables, all of which have 10 elements of type Integer. Structurally, these six array variables are all the same, but are they all the same type? In the original definition of Pascal, this problem was not addressed and so the answer was left up to the compiler writers.

Two approaches can be taken to this problem. If **structural equivalence** is assumed, then all six variables are of the same type. An alternative approach, known as **name equivalence**, assumes that two variables only have the same type if they have the same type name. The ISO Pascal standard adopts name equivalence as the criterion and so a, b, c and d all have different types while a and f are of the same type as are d and e.

Name equivalence is also used in Ada, but as the Ada declaration:

```
d, e : array(1 .. 10) of Integer;
```

is equivalent to:

```
d : array(1 .. 10) of Integer;
e : array(1 .. 10) of Integer;
```

the variables d and e are of different types, which seems rather counter-intuitive.

The question of name and structural equivalence in Pascal was first discussed in a paper by Welsh *et al.*(1977) and interested readers might like to consult this document. As the size of an array is not part of the type information in C++ and Java, these languages use structural equivalence for arrays, although they do use name equivalence for classes.

Operations on complete arrays or slices of arrays

Array aggregates are especially useful in initialising an array. Given the Ada declaration:

```
type Vector is array (1 .. 6) of Integer;
a : Vector;
```

the following assignments are allowed, each having the same effect:

```
a := (7, 0, 7, 0, 0, 0);
a := (1 => 7, 2 => 0, 3 => 7, 4 .. 6 => 0);
a := (1 | 3 => 7, others => 0);
```

We can achieve a similar effect in C++ using either of the declarations:

```
int a[] = {7, 0, 7, 0, 0, 0};
int a[6] = {7, 0, 7};
```

When the size of the array is given and the aggregate has insufficient values, the remaining values are initialised to zero. In C++, aggregates can only be used to initialise an array within a declaration.

In the Java declaration:

```
int[] a = {7, 0, 7, 0, 0, 0};
```

space is allocated for a new initialised array of 6 elements.

Many languages allow operations on **slices** of an array. The commonest situation is in a two-dimensional array where a row or a column is to be used as the slice. In Pascal and Ada, a two-dimensional array is an array of arrays and so the concept of a row slice is a natural one. A row of a two-dimensional array can be passed as a one-dimensional array parameter to a procedure or function, but it is not possible to treat a column as a slice. In Ada, a slice can be part of a one-dimensional array. For example, given the declaration:

```
a, b : Vector;
```

an assignment such as:

```
a(1 .. 3) := b(4 .. 6);
```

sets the first three elements of a to the values of the fourth, fifth and sixth elements of b, respectively.

In Ada and C++, arrays or records may be returned as the values of functions and this gives us the ability to define operations on complete arrays. As an example, consider the problem of adding two vectors together. In Ada, this can be accomplished by the function:

```
function add(left, right : Vector) return Vector is
   total : Vector;
begin
   for i in left'range loop
     total(i) := left(i) + right(i);
   end loop;
   return total;
end add;
```

If a, b and c are all of type Vector, a possible function call is:

```
c := add(a, b);
```

However, when the function is called '+' instead of add, the following statement can be written:

```
c := a + b;
```

This gives a natural way of dealing with vector arithmetic. A similar redefinition of the + operator can be made in C++.

Languages such as PL/I and APL have built-in operations on complete arrays. However, the approach in modern languages is not to have lots of predefined operations, but to provide facilities through which abstract data types can be defined.

Associative arrays

A drawback of an ordinary array is that the computable index must be a scalar type whose values are consecutive. Associative arrays allow us to generalise from this to give us a data structure in which the index (called the key) can be a value of any type. An associative array can be thought of as a set of *key*, *value* pairs.

Associative arrays are very important within string processing languages, but the advantage of the object-oriented approach is that we can always extend a language by providing a class that implements associative arrays. Such a class, Hashtable, exists in the util package of the Java standard library.

Suppose that we want to hold information about a group of people whom we identify by name and that we have a class called PeopleInfo to contain the information that we want to hold about each person. The key of the associative array will be a String representing a name while the associated value will be an object of class PeopleInfo. We can add people to the associative array using the following code:

```
Hashtable persons = new Hashtable();
PeopleInfo p1, p2, p3;
...code to give a value to p1, p2 and p3 ...
persons.put("J Smith", p1);
persons.put("F Bloggs", p2);
persons.put("A Brown", p3);
```

Now to retrieve the information held on F Bloggs, we can write:

```
PeopleInfo inf = (PeopleInfo) persons.get("F Bloggs");
```

All Java classes are subclasses of class Object. Class Hashtable allows both the key and the value to be objects of any kind by defining them to be of class Object and so we need to use a cast to convert the retrieved information to be an object of class PeopleInfo.

Associative arrays are implemented by what are known as hash tables. (Hence the name of the Java class.) There is a special function called a **hash function** that takes a key and converts it into a position in the hash table. That is how we decide where to put an item in the hash table. When we want to retrieve an item, we again apply the hash function to the key and that tells us where the item is stored.

In Perl, the key of an associative array must be a scalar value, but as strings are scalars in Perl that is not too much of a restriction. Perl code with much the same effect as the above would be:

```
$persons{"J Smith"} = $p1;
$persons{"F Bloggs"} = $p2;
$persons{"A Brown"} = $p3;
```

and we can then retrieve information by writing:

```
$inf = $persons{"F Bloggs"};
```

The notation is therefore very close to conventional array notation.

7.3 Records and classes

A **record** is a structured type that is composed of heterogeneous elements of data. The definition of a record specifies the name and the type of the various components or **fields** of the record.

In data processing problems, a file consists logically of a set of records. The original use of records was in languages like COBOL, where they were used to define the structure of records held on file. They had a similar use in PL/I where they were called **structures**. However, in languages such as Pascal, Ada and C, the prime use of records is not in the solution of file processing problems, but to allow logically related data items to be grouped together as one structured variable. Being able to structure data in this way is central to the construction of understandable programs. The individual items in a record are accessed by name (using dot notation) and not by computable index as in an array. Hence, after the Pascal definitions:

```
type Date =
  record
     day : Integer;
     month : Integer;
     year : Integer
  end;
var adate : Date;
```

we can access the components of the variable `adate` as `adate.day`, `adate.month` and `adate.year`.

In C and C++, a record is called a **struct** and the components are called **members**. Type `Date` can be defined as:

```
struct Date {
    int day;
    int month;
    int year;
};
```

To declare a variable of type `Date` in C we have to write:

```
struct Date adate;
```

while in C++ we can just write:

```
Date adate;
```

In the traditional use of records, the fields are variables. However, an extension is to allow the fields also to be operations. That is how classes are implemented in languages such as C++ and Java. In C, a struct can only have **data members**, while in C++ a struct may also have **function members**. In fact, the term struct only exists in C++ for backward compatibility with C and the term class is virtually always used. The only difference between a struct and a class in C++ is that in a struct, the data members are visible (public) by default while in a class they are hidden (private).

As C++ is a hybrid between a procedural and an object-oriented language, it is possible for a C++ programmer to use classes purely as a way of defining data structures. Such programmers then often believe that they are writing object-oriented programs. However, object-oriented programming is much more than that. It is a way of designing solutions and structuring programs in which classes and objects are the central concept, not just another data structuring device.

The traditional way of describing classes is as extensions to records. However, for those brought up on the object-oriented approach, records can be considered to be classes whose attributes are public and which have no operations.

Stack example

Fields of a record (or the attributes of a class) can be of any type, including arrays or records. Consider, for example, the problem of defining a stack of characters. We look at how this can be done in Pascal, Ada, C++ and Java as an example of how data abstraction, encapsulation and information hiding are used in the definition of structured data types in each of these languages. The Pascal representation is:

```
type CharStack =
  record
    val : array [1 .. 20] of Char;
    head : 0 .. 20
  end;
var a, b : CharStack;
    ch : Char;
```

The two fields of the record CharStack represent the elements of the stack in the array val and the pointer to the top of the stack in the integer head. Thus, the representation of the stack is contained wholly within the record.

Typical operations on a stack are push and pop which, respectively, add an element to the top of the stack and remove the top element from a stack, an initialise operation and operations to test if the stack is empty or full. Possible definitions in Pascal for initialise, isEmpty and pop are:

```
procedure initialise(var stack : CharStack);
begin
  stack.head := 0
end; {newstack}

function isEmpty(var stack : CharStack) : Boolean;
begin
  isEmpty := stack.head = 0
end; {isEmpty}
```

```
procedure pop(var stack : CharStack; var x : Char);
begin
  if isEmpty(stack) then
    writeln('Error: stack empty')
  else
  begin
    x := stack.val[stack.head];
    stack.head := stack.head - 1
  end
end; {pop}
```

The head and val fields of parameter stack are accessed using dot notation. Typical calls of the operations are:

```
initialise(a); initialise(b);
push(a, 'f'); push(b, 'g');
pop(a, ch);
```

This shows a typical way of using records. We define a new type and then have a set of procedures and functions to manipulate variables of that type. In our example, an abstraction of a stack has been created. Users of type CharStack no longer have to concern themselves with the details of the components out of which type CharStack has been composed or the implementation of the operations that manipulate CharStack variables. Such user-defined types are referred to as abstract data types.

A problem in standard Pascal is that the definition of the type and the associated operations are not grouped together as a logical whole. That problem is solved in Ada by the use of packages. The type name and the specification of the associated operations are given in a package specification and the stack representation is hidden in the private part. The Ada version of type CharStack is:

```
package Stacks is
  type CharStack is private;
  procedure push(st : in out CharStack;
                 x : in Character);
  procedure pop(st : in out CharStack;
                x : out Character);
  function isEmpty(st : CharStack) return Boolean;
private
  type Values is array(1 .. 20) of Character;
  type CharStack is
    record
      val : Values;
      head: Integer range 0 .. 20 := 0;
    end record;
end Stacks;
```

The implementations of push, pop and isEmpty are given in the package body. As the name of the type is visible to users of the package, objects of type CharStack may be declared. However, as the type is private, the only way such objects may be examined or changed is through the defined operations, as in:

```
with Stacks; use Stacks;
procedure main is
    a, b : CharStack;
    ch : Character;
begin
    . . .
    push(a, 'f'); push(b, 'g');
    pop(a, ch);
    . . .
end main;
```

As the value of head is set to zero by default, both a and b initially represent empty stacks and so we do not require a special operation to initialise a stack.

As CharStack is a private type, the only built-in operations available on objects of type CharStack are equality and assignment. However, the predefined equality operator cannot be used to compare two stacks for equality as it would compare elements beyond the current top of stack pointer, as well as the elements that are currently on the stack. To deal with such situations, Ada has **limited private** types. When a variable such as CharStack is declared to be limited private, neither predefined equality nor assignment is available. If required, a new function =, which only compares the relevant elements in the array of characters, can be defined, but the assignment operator : = cannot be redefined, and so if assignment is still required an assign procedure must be declared.

In this example, the stack has been represented as an array. An alternative representation would be a linked list. This can be achieved by changing the hidden representation of the stack and the implementation of the operations. Users of the package will see the stack abstract data type in exactly the same way as before and do not need to be aware that the representation has been changed.

In C++, the operations on the stack can be defined as **member functions**. The definition of CharStack becomes:

```
class CharStack {
    char val[20];
    int head;
public:
    CharStack(); // constructor
    void push(char x);
    char pop();
    int isEmpty() const;
};
```

Class CharStack has member functions push, pop and isEmpty. Only the function prototypes are given in the class definition with the bodies being defined separately as we saw in Chapter 5. As information in a class is private by default, the representation of the stack by the data members is hidden from users and may only be accessed through calls of the member functions. Variables of class CharStack may be declared and manipulated as follows:

```
main() {
  CharStack a, b;
  char ch;
  . . .
  a.push('f'); b.push('g');
  ch = a.pop();
  . . .
}
```

Two objects a and b of class CharStack representing empty stacks are created. We can then push characters onto and pop characters from the stacks.

In the definition of CharStack, the stack is of a fixed size. It is possible to modify the definition so that stacks of different sizes may be declared. The class definition now becomes:

```
class CharStack {
  char *val;
  int head;
  int maxSize;
public:
  CharStack(int size);
  ~CharStack() {delete val;}
  void push(char x);
  char pop();
  int isEmpty() const;
};
```

Space for the stack is now allocated during execution of the constructor which is defined as:

```
CharStack:: CharStack(int size) {
  val = new char[size];
  head = -1;
  maxSize = size;
} // constructor
```

Two stacks, one with 50 elements and the other with 100 elements, can now be declared as:

```
CharStack a(50), b(100);
```

and used in exactly the same way as before. The implementations of push, pop and isEmpty are unchanged. The member function:

```
~CharStack() {delete val;}
```

in the class definition is known as a **destructor**. It ensures that, whenever space for a `CharStack` object is de-allocated, the storage referenced on the heap by its `val` attribute is reclaimed.

The Java version of CharStack is similar to the second C++ example, but as garbage collection is automatic in Java, there is no need for a destructor operation. The outline Java code is:

```java
public class CharStack {
   private char[] val;
   private int head;
   private int maxSize;

   public CharStack(int size) {
     val = new char[size];
     head = - 1;
     maxSize = size;
   } // constructor

   public void push(char x) { ...}
   public char pop() { ...}
   public boolean isEmpty() { ...}
} // CharStack
```

We can then create a `CharStack` object with:

```java
CharStack a = new CharStack(50);
```

The method calls to manipulate the stack are as shown above for C++.

Note that the definition of pop in C++ and Java not only returns a value, it also modifies the stack attributes. It is not possible to declare pop as a function in Ada because function parameters must be of **in** mode and, as it is changed, the `CharStack` parameter must be of mode **in out**. In Java, on the other hand, parameters of a primitive type are always passed by value and so a value returning method must be used. Our usual rule is that a method should **either** return a value **or** modify the attributes, not both. A purer approach is therefore to split pop into two operations: `top` which returns a value and to redefine pop so that it removes an element from the stack, but does not return a value.

Variant records

Static typing supports reliability at the expense of flexibility. Consider a problem in which there is a need for a list containing both postgraduate and undergraduate students. In a dynamically typed language, there is no difficulty; some of the components of the list will be of type `undergraduate` and others of type `postgraduate` and type checks are made at run time to ensure that the components are always used correctly. This is not possible in a statically typed procedural language as all the components of a list must have the same type.

Languages, such as Pascal and Ada, solve this problem by means of **variant records**. In Pascal, a variant record has a fixed part, with fields as in a normal record, followed by a variant part, in which there are alternative fields. For example:

```
type Status = (undergraduate, postgraduate);
   Student =
     record
       {fixed part}
       name : String;
       {variant part}
       case kind : Status of
         undergraduate : (advisor : String);
         postgraduate : (course : String;
                         supervisor : String)
   end;
```

The field kind is called the **tag field** and in this example there are two alternatives. The tag field determines whether there is a single field, advisor, in the variant part or two fields, course and supervisor.

Given the declaration:

```
studentlist : array[1 .. 3000] of Student;
```

and assuming that the array has been suitably initialised, the following code will print out the name and advisor of the i'th student when the student is an undergraduate and the name, course and supervisor when the student is a postgraduate.

```
write(studentlist[i].name);
if studentlist[i].kind = undergraduate then
   writeln(studentlist[i].advisor)
else
   writeln(studentlist[i].course,
           studentlist[i].supervisor)
```

Pascal's method of using variant records can unfortunately lead to insecurities and inconsistencies. These arise if the tag field is changed without changing the variant fields that depend on the tag.

Ada allows similar variant records, although with some syntactic differences, and the insecurities of the Pascal construction are removed by not allowing the tag field to be changed independently of the dependent fields in the variant part. Variant records are still, however, a rather untidy feature. In Chapter 8, we look at how dynamic binding handles this problem in object-oriented languages.

7.4 Dynamic data structures

A very different kind of data structure is obtained by using records and classes in conjunction with pointer variables. Components of a record or class can be specified to be of a pointer type and that allows data structures in which individual records are linked to others. Thus, in Pascal, a simple linear linked list can be written as follows:

```
type Ptr = ↑Node;
   Node =
       record
           data : Char;
           next : Ptr
       end;
   var p, listhead : Ptr;
       ch : Char;
```

Note that the above type declaration is one of the few places in Pascal where an identifier (Node) can be used before it has been declared.

The Pascal procedure new was introduced in Chapter 3. The effect of a call of new(p) is to create a record of type Node which is pointed at by the pointer variable p. This is shown in Figure 7.4. The value 'A' can be assigned to the data field and **nil** to the next field by writing:

```
p↑.data := 'A'; p↑.next := nil
```

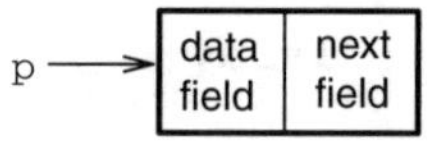

Figure 7.4   Creating a node.

The nodes can be linked together to form a linked list. The normal approach to dealing with linked lists and other dynamic data structures is to define a set of procedures and functions to perform the standard operations of adding a node, deleting a node, searching for a node etc. The following procedure will add a node to the beginning of a linked list:

```
procedure add(c : Char; var head : Ptr);
   var p : Ptr;
begin
   new(p); p↑.data := c;
   p↑.next := head;
   head := p
end {add};
```

Procedure add can be used to create a linked list as follows:

```
listhead := nil;
read(ch);
while ch <> ' ' do
begin
   add(ch, listhead);
   read(ch)
end;
```

The variable `listhead` points to the beginning of the linked list. When `listhead` is **nil**, we have an empty list. The end of a non-empty list is denoted by a node whose next pointer is **nil**. Figure 7.5 shows the state of the linked list after each cycle round the loop as the characters A, B and C followed by a space are read in.

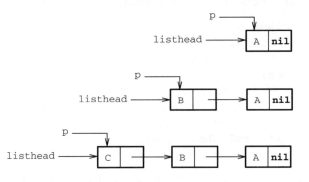

Figure 7.5 Stages in building a linked list.

Ada follows much the same pattern as Pascal although the syntax is different. As a name cannot be used before it has been declared in Ada, it is necessary to write:

```
type Node;
type Ptr is access Node;
type Node is
   record
      data : Character;
      next : Ptr;
   end record;
```

Dynamic variables in Ada can be given initial values when they are created. Thus, instead of the Pascal:

```
new(p); p↑.data := c; p↑.next := head
```

the following can be written:

```
p := new node'(data => c, next => head);
```

C, C++ and Java

In C and C++, it is possible to define a node using a **struct** as in the C code:

```
struct Node {
   char data;
   struct Node * next;
};
```

It should be noted that the declaration is **self-referential**, i.e. within the definition of Node, we have a reference to Node. We do not therefore need two types (a node and a pointer to a node) as we do in Pascal and Ada where self-referential types are not allowed.

As we need to define operations to manipulate our lists, it is better in C++ to use classes. Also, the user interface is improved if we define a List class which makes use of class Node. Class Node becomes:

```
class Node {
  char data;
  Node * next;
public:
  Node (char c, Node * p) {
    data = c; next = p;
  } // constructor
  friend class List;
}; // Node
```

Classes are not always completely independent of one another. In this case, the List class needs to access hidden information in class Node. To achieve this, class Node declares class List to be a **friend**. Class List is now:

```
class List {
  Node * head;
public:
  List() {
    head = NULL;
  } // constructor
  void add(char c);
  void remove(char c);
  int inList(char c) const;
}; // List
```

We have operations to add an item, remove an item and to check if an item is in the list. Typically, a larger set of operations will be available. The implementations of add and inList are:

```
void List::add(char c) {
  head = new Node(c, head);
} // add

int List::inList(char c) const {
  Node * temp = head;
  while (temp != NULL) {
  if (temp→data == c)
    return 1;
  temp = temp→next;
  }
  return 0;
} // inList
```

The implementation of function `inList` directly accesses `Node` attributes. To declare an empty list and to then add a node, we write:

```
List aList;
aList.add('a');
```

Java's lack of pointers might be thought to lead to problems with linked lists. However, as objects in Java are always accessed by reference, there is no need for explicit pointers. Classes `Node` and `List` become:

```
class Node {
   char data;
   Node next;
   public Node (char c, Node p) {
      data = c; next = p;
   } // constructor
} // Node

class List {
   private Node head;
   public List() {
      head = null;
   } // constructor

   public void add(char c) {
      head = new Node(c, head);
   } // add

   public void remove(char c) { ...}
   public boolean inList(char c) { ...}
} // List
```

The attributes in class `Node` have not been declared as private and so are visible to other classes defined in the same package. That is why they can be used in the definition of method `inList`. This replaces the **friend** feature of C++.

Trees

Dynamic data structures can be considerably more complicated than simple linked lists. One structure that they model in a particularly appropriate way is the tree. In a tree structure there is more than one pointer field in each record. A type declaration in Pascal for a binary tree could be:

```
type Ptr = ↑Node;
   Node =
      record
         data : Char;
         left, right : Ptr
      end;
```

The effect of new(root), where root is of type Ptr, is shown in Figure 7.6.

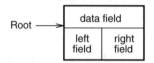

Figure 7.6   Creating a tree node.

Both lists and trees can be conveniently defined recursively. For example, a binary tree can be defined as follows:

> A binary tree is either null or it consists of a special node, called the root, which has a value and two descendants, called the left subtree and the right subtree. The left subtree and the right subtree are themselves binary trees.

As trees can be defined recursively, they are most easily manipulated using recursive procedures. To illustrate how this may be done, consider the problem of printing out a binary tree representing an algebraic expression in what is known as **reverse Polish notation** where an operator follows its two operands. This can be achieved by using the following recursive Pascal procedure:

```
procedure revPolish(p : Ptr);
begin
   if p <> nil then
   begin
      revPolish(p↑.left);
      revPolish(p↑.right);
      write(p↑.data)
   end
end;
```

Assuming that root points to the tree shown in Figure 7.7, the procedure call revPolish(root) will cause the contents of the tree to be printed out in the order:

    a b c + / d *

Tracing through the execution of revPolish(root) is left as an exercise for the reader.

The use of records and pointers does entail a good deal of detailed programming on the part of the programmer, but that can largely be hidden by the judicious use of modules and classes to encapsulate the required operations. An alternative method of approaching dynamic data structures is with functional languages and this issue is taken up again in Chapter 9.

7.5   Parametrised types

In our examples of a stack, a linked list and a tree, the data held in each element or node was a character. However, the algorithms for manipulating stacks, lists or trees do not

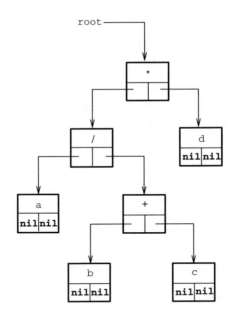

Figure 7.7   A binary tree.

depend on the type of the elements. For example, a package or class that implements
a stack of characters is essentially the same as one that implements a stack of integers
or some other type. That leads us to the notion of a type that has another type as a
parameter.

In Ada a **generic package** for a stack can be defined which has the type of the stack
element as a parameter. Such a generic package gives an abstraction of a stack that is
independent of the element type. As the stack operations are independent of the type of
the element, once the package has been shown to be correct for an element of one type,
it can be guaranteed to work for elements of any other type. This has the advantage
of making the program text shorter and hence easier to read. A similar effect can be
achieved in C++ with **class templates**, but there is no such facility in Java.

Generic procedures and functions were discussed in Chapter 6. Generic procedures,
functions and packages in Ada are templates that have to be instantiated to produce actual
procedures, functions or packages. As an example, consider the following generic stack
package. It has two generic parameters: Item for the element type and size for the
size of the array:

```
generic
   type Item is private;
   size : Integer;
package Stacks is
   type Stack is limited private;
   procedure push(st : in out Stack; x : in Item);
   procedure pop(st : in out Stack; x : out Item);
   function isEmpty(st : Stack) return Boolean;
```

```
private
  type Values is array(1 .. size) of Item;
  type Stack is
    record
      val : Values;
      head : Integer range 0 .. size := 0;
    end record;
end Stacks;
```

The implementations of push, pop and isEmpty are given in the package body in the normal way. A package with the properties of our earlier stack of characters can be produced by the instantiation:

```
package StkChar is new Stacks(Item => Character,
                              size => 20);
```

while a stack of integers can be produced by:

```
package StkInt is new Stacks(Item => Integer,
                             size => 20);
```

As instantiation takes place at compile time, static type checking is not compromised in any way.

Packages StkChar and StkInt may now be used as follows:

```
with StkChar, StkInt;
use StkChar, StkInt;
procedure main is
   a, b : StkChar.Stack;
   d : StkInt.Stack;
   ch : Character;
begin
   ...
   push(a, 'f'); push(b, 'g');
   pop(a, ch);
   push(d, 42);
   ...
end main;
```

The identifiers push and pop are overloaded, but their parameters make it clear which version is being employed.

7.6 Strings

Character strings and their manipulation played a very minor role in the early scientific languages and it was SNOBOL 4 that actually showed how character strings could be manipulated in a programming language. However, it was soon realised that the unrestricted manipulation of strings brings with it considerable penalties in the slowness of the run-time program.

String operations are best divided into two categories. The first category consists of string comparisons, the selection of a substring, searching for a substring and the moving of strings. The second category of operations includes the replacement of substrings within a string and appending one string to the end of another. The operations in the first category cause few problems, as strings remain the same length throughout. Operations in the second category, on the other hand, have the potential of dynamically altering the length of the strings.

In Pascal and Ada, strings are simply arrays of characters and since arrays are not extensible in these languages, the length of a string cannot be changed once it has been created. In Pascal, a string is typically declared as:

```
type Name = packed array [1..8] of char;
```

The reserved word **packed** used in this declaration indicates that the compiler should allocate the minimum amount of space possible for objects of type Name, even though this may increase the time required to access individual array elements. The need to declare this requirement explicitly has not been carried over into other languages.

In standard Pascal, the length of an array is part of the type and so any attempt to assign or compare strings of different lengths gives an error at compile time. This means that trailing blanks must always be inserted in string constants. Hence, if person is of type Name, four trailing blanks are required in the assignment:

```
person := 'Alan    '
```

A similar assignment is necessary in Ada, although strings of different length may be compared. Hence, the expression:

```
person < "James"
```

is legal in Ada while in standard Pascal three trailing blanks are needed, as in:

```
person < 'James   '
```

Most recent Pascal implementations have relaxed this requirement.

In languages with fixed length strings, only the first category of string operations is allowed, although Ada does permit some second category operations provided that the length of the string is not changed. Examples are:

```
person := "James ";
person(2 .. 5) := "immy";
```

C and C++ also represent strings as arrays of characters, but they are variable up to a maximum defined length. The null character, represented as \0, is used as an explicit string terminator and space must be set aside for it in all strings. The null character is used to recognise the end of the string and so, assuming stra and strb have been defined as arrays of characters, a string can be copied by the following loop:

```
for (int i = 0; strb[i] != '\0'; i++)
   stra[i] = strb[i];
stra[i] = '\0';
```

There is a standard library of functions to manipulate C and C++ strings. For example, string assignment is not built into the language, but can be achieved by a library call such as:

```
strcpy(stra, strb);
```

Care must be taken to ensure that the length of `stra` is sufficient to receive all the characters being copied to it as no check is done at run time.

Delphi has a `String` type that supports strings of varying length. However, to support compatibility with C, it also includes strings that are variable up to a maximum defined length and which are terminated by the null character. They are declared as:

```
type Cstring = array [0.. maxSize] of Char;
```

Routines are available to convert between the two kinds of string.

In languages like Ada and C++, it is of course possible to define a string abstract data type so that string processing is easier and is more secure. That is how strings are defined in Java, where a string is an object. Many string operations in Java make it appear that `String` is a primitive type like `int`, `double` or `char`. We can for example write code such as:

```
String st = "Hello";
```

but that is actually shorthand for:

```
String st = new String("Hello");
```

As `String` variables are references to `String` objects, after the statement:

```
String another = st;
```

both `another` and `st` will refer to the same `String` object; a copy has not been made. This does not cause any problems because `String` objects are constants in Java and cannot be modified once they have been created.

Examples of Java `String` methods are: comparison for equality (`equals`), extraction of a substring (`substring`) and deciding whether one string is less than another (`compareTo`). To decide whether one string is greater than another, we start with the leftmost pair of characters. If a decision can be made, no more comparisons are made. If the first pair of characters is the same, then the second pair of characters is compared and so on.

Both Java and Ada also have a **catenation** operator (`&` in Ada and `+` in Java) which is useful in constructing a string with a constant and a variable part. However, as Java strings are constants, a Java statement such as:

```
stra += "Hello";
```

is shorthand for:

```
stra = new String(stra + "Hello");
```

and a completely new string is created rather than the existing string being extended. If the length of `stra` is large, this can be a very expensive operation. The Java `String` class is not therefore suitable for extensive text processing. For that, Java has another class called `StringBuffer` which allows strings to grow in length. If `str` is a `StringBuffer` object, then the operation:

```
str.append("Hello");
```

will add `"Hello"` to the end of `str`. Other methods include `insert` which can be expensive as characters are moved up to make space. There are conversion methods between `String` and `StringBuffer` objects and so, if extensive string processing is required, a `String` should first be converted to a `StringBuffer` where the processing can take place, and then the result can be converted back to a `String`.

Java is unusual in that all input and output involves strings. If we wish to write a number, we must first convert it to a string. That is easily achieved using the catenation operator as, for example, when x is an integer with the value 43, the expression:

```
"Value = " + x
```

yields the string `"Value = 43"`. Operations are also available to convert a string to a number. For example, if s is a `String` variable, the effect of:

```
int val = Integer.parseInt(s);
```

is to convert the string of characters contained in s to an integer value. If the string does not contain a character representation for an integer, an exception is thrown. All objects in Java also have a `toString` method which provides a string representation of the object.

Pattern matching

The built-in string types in procedural and object-oriented languages are not suitable for creating applications such as a text editor where strings can vary arbitrarily in length. SNOBOL 4, on the other hand, has the character string as a basic type. No bounds are placed on the string's length and so, if strings get longer, extra storage is allocated. All the string operations in the first and second category are then potentially available. In SNOBOL4, substrings are selected by pattern matching. The statement:

```
TEXT 'programme' = 'program'
```

will find the first occurrence of `'programme'` in the string TEXT and replace it by `'program'`. To replace all occurrences, the statement could be written:

```
LAB1 TEXT 'programme' = 'program'  :S(LAB1)
```

The S here stands for success and so, if a successful replacement is made in TEXT, a jump is made to the statement labelled LAB1. The statement:

```
TEXT 'programme' = 'program'
```

is therefore repeated until no more replacements can be made.

The Perl statement:

```
$text =~ s/programme/program/g;
```

will replace all occurrences of 'programme' by 'program' in the string variable $text. If the g at the end is omitted, only the first occurrence is replaced. Perl allows complex patterns to be specified using **regular expressions**.

String implementation

The easiest method of implementing a string is as a contiguous series of characters. The size can be fixed at compile time or on block entry with the string being allocated space on the run-time stack (as in Ada) or the size can be fixed during statement execution with the string being allocated space on the heap (as in Java). A mapping function can give rapid access to individual array elements. That leaves the question of how variable length strings are to be implemented. It is straightforward to implement strings which are variable up to some maximum length as is done in C, but there is still the problem of what happens when a string is to be extended beyond that length.

A possible implementation is to use a linked list of characters. However, that is expensive in terms of space and, although substrings can easily be inserted or deleted, accessing elements is slow. An alternative approach, used in the Java StringBuffer class, is to allocate space in contiguous locations for some initial maximum size. Then, when more space is required, a further sequence of contiguous locations equal to the current length of the string is allocated and linked on to the end. A mapping function can then still be used to access individual elements. Inserting and deleting substrings is expensive in time as string elements are moved to make space, but appending and searching for substrings is efficient.

7.7 Sets

A **set** is an unordered collection of distinct elements of the same type. This is in contrast to both lists and arrays, which are ordered collections of possibly non-distinct elements.

Very few of the major languages have included the set as a standard data structure. The notable exception is Pascal. If a set consists of days of the week, the following declarations can be written in Pascal:

```
type Day = (sun, mon, tues, wed, thur, fri, sat);
   Weekset = set of Day;
var w1 : Weekset;
     d : Day;
```

We can represent a set value by listing the elements as in [mon, thur, sat] or by giving a range as in [mon .. fri]. The empty set is represented by []. After the assignment:

```
w := [mon, thur, sat];
```

we can test if the value of d is a member of set w1 by writing:

```
if d in w1 then ...
```

In addition, the normal mathematical set operations are available.

A Pascal set is implemented as a string of bits. This is satisfactory if the number of possible elements in the set is small, as in the Pascal example given at the beginning of this section when it was 7, but implies a restriction on the overall set size in Pascal implementations.

When the set size is unbounded, more elaborate storage methods, such as hashing, have to be resorted to. This is particularly necessary when a set can contain a large number of different integers or character strings. Java's HashTable class is well suited to that approach.

Ada, Java, C and C++ allow operations on bit strings which can be manipulated like sets. Systems programming languages are prime examples of languages that need to be able to manipulate bit patterns. The approach taken in Ada is to represent a bit pattern as a Boolean array. The Boolean operators **and, or** and **xor** can be applied to such arrays. For example, given the declarations:

```
type bytestring is array (1 .. 8) of Boolean;
    a, b, c : bytestring;
    t : constant Boolean := true;
    f : constant Boolean := false;
```

the execution of the statements:

```
a := (f, f, f, t, t, t, t, t);
b := (t, f, t, f, t, f, t, f);
c := a and b;
```

will result in c being assigned the value (f, f, f, f, t, f, t, f), which can be used to represent the bitstring 0001010.

In C, C++ and Java, we can directly manipulate the bit pattern used to represent an integer value. Operators include: left and right shifts (<< and >>), bitwise complement (~), bitwise and (&), bitwise or (|) and bitwise exclusive or (^).

7.8 Files

Files are large collections of data that are kept on secondary storage devices. They are liable to have an extensive lifetime, which will normally be longer than the run of the computer program that created them. In data processing applications, the logical structure of a file is usually considered to be a collection of records. Hence, in languages such as COBOL and PL/I the primary purpose of records (structures) is to describe information held in files.

Files were not explicitly represented in early scientific languages. Pascal was, therefore, unusual in having a file type defined in the language, although this approach has been followed by most of its successors. A file in Pascal can be thought of as an ordered collection of homogeneous data. A typical Pascal file definition is:

```
type Stream = file of Entities;
```

where Entities can be of any type except another file.

There are two main differences between a Pascal array and a Pascal file. Firstly, the size of an array is given as part of its declaration while a file is unbounded. Secondly, the time to access an element in an array is independent of its position, whereas with Pascal files the access is sequential, mirroring the way that sequential files are accessed on a backing store.

In Pascal, file variables usually correspond to external disk files. In such cases, the variable must be listed as a parameter in the program heading as well as being declared as a variable, as in:

```
program ex(old, new);
  type Stream = file of ...;
  var old, new : Stream;
```

Local files may also be declared both within the main program and within a procedure. The normal rules governing the lifetime of an object apply to files and so a file declared within a procedure will come into existence when the procedure is entered and will cease to exist when the procedure is left. The main use of local files is in the temporary storage of information of unknown size. When the maximum size is known an array is used.

Operations on files are usually given by a set of predefined functions and procedures. Operations are required to open files for reading and writing, to determine the current position within a file, and to read and write information. As files are, therefore, primarily associated with the input and output of data, a detailed discussion of files is delayed until Chapter 13, which discusses input and output.

Summary

1. The judicious selection of appropriate data structures is as important as top-down design in the production of a well-structured program.

2. All components of an array have the same type and are accessed using a computable index.

3. In Pascal and C, the size of an array is determined at compile time. In Ada, determining the size of an array can be delayed until block entry while in Java it can be delayed until statement execution.

4. In C and C++, pointers can be used to access elements of an array.

5. In Pascal and its successors, a two-dimensional array is an array of arrays.

6. The components of a record can have different types and are accessed by name.

7. Records enable logically related data items to be grouped together as one structured variable.

8. Pascal is strongly typed except in the case of variant records. This problem is overcome in Ada.

9. Classes in C++ are **structs** that have function members as well as data members. Classes allow the operations on a data structure to be incorporated with the definition of the data structure.

10. Dynamic data structures are built from records (or classes) that have one or more fields (or attributes) of a pointer type.

11. The representation and manipulation of strings is determined by whether the language design allows operations that potentially increase the string length.

Exercises

7.1 Arrays and records are both aggregates of data. How do they differ? What information would you expect in the declaration of (a) an array and (b) a record?

7.2 Describe how a mapping function can be used to find the storage location of an array element. What is meant by the base address in such a situation and how is it used by the compiler? Given the following Pascal array declarations, what would be suitable mapping functions?

```
var x : array[2 .. 10] of Real;
    a : array[1 .. 7, 0 .. 5] of Integer;
```

In what locations, relative to the base address, would you expect to find x[7] and a[3, 2]?

7.3 Why was a decision made in the design of Pascal that the size of all objects should be known at compile time?

7.4 Discuss the concept of dynamic bounds in an array, explaining the meaning of the terms static array, semi-dynamic array, dynamic array and extensible array. Give examples of languages that implement arrays in each of these ways. What are the advantages and disadvantages of each method to the programmer and to the implementor?

7.5 In Pascal, a two-dimensional array can be regarded as a one-dimensional array, each of whose elements is itself a one-dimensional array. What advantages does this give? How is the concept extended to three- and higher-dimensional arrays?

7.6 Give an example of a Pascal procedure with a one-dimensional array as a formal parameter together with a call of the procedure in which the corresponding actual parameter is a slice of a two-dimensional array. Definitions of appropriate one- and two-dimensional array types should also be given.

7.7 How could the definition of Pascal variant records be improved so that type insecurity does not arise?

7.8 Show how a queue can be represented by a record (or class) with three fields, one of which is an array whose elements are the items in the queue and the other two are used to indicate the front and rear of the queue. Use this structure to define two operations, one to add a new element to the rear of the queue and the other to delete an element from the front of the queue.

7.9 Lists may be implemented as arrays or as linked lists. Which is to be preferred when solving:

(a) a problem that requires the elements of the list to be accessed in a random order,

(b) a problem that requires the elements of the list to be accessed sequentially,

(c) a problem that requires the ordering of a list of ordered elements to be retained during the insertion and deletion of elements.

7.10 Modify procedure revPolish, given in Section 7.4, so that it will print the algebraic expression in forward Polish notation, where the operator precedes its two operands.

7.11 Why are recursive algorithms particularly appropriate for the manipulation of structures such as lists and trees?

7.12 Given the Ada declaration:

        a : **array**(1 .. 7) **of** Character;

the effect of the assignment:

        a(4 .. 6) := a(3 .. 5);

is to make a copy of the value of a (3 .. 5) before the assignment takes place. If a initially has the value CORECAT, what will its value be after the assignment?

7.13 Consider the following C++ program fragment:

```
int * fun(int x) {
    int y[10];
    for (int i = 0; i <= 9; i++) {
        y[i] = x;
    return y;
} // fun

void main() {
    int* a;
    a = fun(4);
    ...
```

Explain why the call:

```
a = fun(4);
```

causes a dangling reference to be created. Why would a dangling reference not have been created if the declaration of the array y had been:

```
int* y = new int[10];
```

Why are dangling references very dangerous and difficult to track down when they occur?

7.14(a) Discuss the facilities that programming languages have provided for string handling. Contrast a language like Pascal, which has primitive string operations, with a language like Perl.

(b) Why are string handling operations divided into two categories and what are the operations in each category?

7.15 Describe how a linked list could be used in the implementation of a set. Outline procedure declarations for the insert and delete operations.

Bibliography

There are a large number of textbooks on the representation and manipulation of data structures, several of which are given below. The first volume of Knuth's *The Art of Computer Programming* in 1968 was the earliest book to make a systematic approach to data structures and a new edition has recently been published (Knuth 1997). It is a pity that only three volumes of this monumental series were published.

Another influential book was *Algorithms + Data Structures = Programs* by Wirth (1976) which emphasised that data structures are at least as important as algorithms in the construction of programs.

Most recent texts emphasise the importance of data abstraction and take all their examples from one particular language, usually Pascal, C++ or Java. Often the same author has produced a series of texts, each one dealing with a different language, as in the case of Weiss.

Hoare, C.A.R. (1972). 'Notes on Data Structuring' in *Structured Programming*, Academic Press, pp. 83–174.

Knuth, D.E. (1997). *The Art of Computer Programming, Volume 1: Fundamental Algorithms* (Third Edition). Addison-Wesley.

Weiss, M.A. (1996). *Algorithms, Data Structures and Problem Solving with C++*. Addison-Wesley.

Weiss, M.A. (1998). *Data Structures and Problem Solving using Java*. Addison-Wesley.

Welsh, J., Sneeringer, M.J. and Hoare, C.A.R. (1977). 'Ambiguities and Insecurities in Pascal', *Software Practice and Experience*, **7**, 685–696.

Wirth, N. (1976). *Algorithms + Data Structures = Programs*, Prentice-Hall.

Chapter 8

Inheritance and dynamic binding

Modularity, data abstraction, encapsulation and information hiding have already been discussed. This chapter deals with the additional object-oriented concepts of inheritance, inclusion polymorphism and dynamic binding. Inheritance is a major tool for software re-use.

The chapter starts by introducing the concept of inheritance and describes how a subclass may add attributes and operations to those it inherits from its superclass and how it may redefine operations. Inheritance can be used for two purposes: the inheritance of implementation or the inheritance of behaviour. We strongly advocate that it should only be used for the inheritance of behaviour. Inclusion polymorphism and dynamic binding, where the decision about which version of an operation is to be used is delayed until run time, is then examined. We look at abstract classes, at multiple inheritance and at how interfaces in Java achieve a similar effect.

We discuss how inheritance can provide a loophole to information hiding and at the problem of fragile superclasses. It is important that dynamic binding does not introduce errors at run-time and we examine how contravariant parameters can ensure type safety, although that does not guarantee behavioural inheritance.

8.1 Introduction

A language like Ada 83, which supports data abstraction, encapsulation and information hiding, is often described as being **object based**. In an object-based language, an object has a hidden local state and public operations acting on that state. A **class-based** language such as CLU has the following additional properties:

- a module is a class,
- a class corresponds to a type,
- a class defines the properties of an object,
- an object is an instance of a class.

An **object-oriented** language is a class-based language in which new classes do not have to be created from scratch, but can inherit attributes and operations from existing classes. The new class is said to be a **subclass** and the class from which it is derived, a **superclass**. As a superclass can itself be a subclass, a class hierarchy can be created. A subclass can add new attributes and operations to the ones it inherits and can redefine (override) inherited operations. When an operation originally defined in a superclass is redefined in a subclass, the decision about which version is to be called is made at run time, that is, we have **dynamic binding**.

Inheritance provides an excellent tool for software re-use, as existing software is re-used in the creation of the new class. It also leads to faster software development as new components are created by modifying and extending existing components rather than starting from nothing. However, it is important that there is a conceptual link between a subclass and a superclass. This is best expressed by the is_a relationship which means that an object of a subclass should also conceptually be an object of the superclass. We can then regard the subclass as a **specialisation** of the superclass and the superclass as a **generalisation** of the subclass. The conceptual relationship is important because an object of a subclass can be used in a program where an object of its superclass is expected.

The origin of the object-oriented approach lies with Simula and the ideas were carried forward into Smalltalk. Although there are a large number of experimental object-oriented languages, the most widely used are extensions or developments of traditional procedural languages. For example, C++ was developed from C, Delphi from Pascal, Ada 95 from Ada 83 and OOCOBOL from COBOL. These languages are hybrids and have a procedural subset.

Eiffel and Java, on the other hand, are purely object-oriented languages although Java is a development from C++ and the syntax of Eiffel is greatly influenced by Pascal. In Smalltalk, everything is an object. This purity has not been carried over into Java and Eiffel where, for reasons of efficiency, simple scalar types such as integer and floating point are implemented as they would be in a procedural language.

8.2 Inheritance

Consider the following definition of class `Person` in Java:

```
public class Person {
    protected String theName;

    public Person(String name) {
        theName = name;
    } // constructor

    public String getInfo() {
        return theName;
    } // getInfo

    public String detailInfo() {
        return "Details are:" + this.getInfo();
    } // detailInfo
} // Person
```

The method `detailInfo` returns the concatenation of two strings and contains the call **this**.`getInfo()`. The presence of **this**, which denotes the current object, is not strictly necessary as we could just have written `getInfo()`. However, its presence emphasises that even when we are calling a local method, we are still calling a method offered by an object.

We can declare a reference to a `Person` and create a `Person` object:

```
Person girl = new Person("Sue");
```

After the declarations:

```
String stra = girl.getInfo();
String strb = girl.detailInfo();
```

`stra` will refer to the string `"Sue"` while `strb` will refer to the string `"Details are:Sue"`.

We now want to define the classes `Student` and `Professor`, in which `Student` is a `Person` with a registration number while a `Professor` is a `Person` with a department. To define these new classes, we do not have to start from scratch, but can extend class `Person`. `Student` and `Professor` will then be subclasses of the `Person` superclass. In C++ and Ada 95, a superclass is known as a **base class** and a subclass is known as a **derived class**.

We can show the relationship between `Person`, `Student` and `Professor` in the UML class diagram of Figure 8.1. A UML class diagram shows the static relationships between classes. Each class is represented as a rectangular box divided into three parts: class name, attributes and operations. Private, public and protected attributes and operations are prefixed with –, + and # respectively. Relationships are represented as lines between classes. The relationships in Figure 8.1 show that classes `Student` and

Professor inherit from, i.e. are subclasses of, class Person. The diagram also shows that class Student inherits the attribute theName and the operation detailInfo, adds a new attribute theRegNum and method getRegNum and redefines method getInfo.

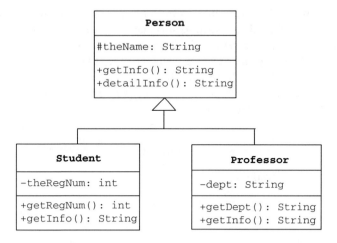

Figure 8.1   UML class diagram.

UML is used in the analysis and design phases of object-oriented development and is independent of any particular object-oriented programming language. Once we have created a UML class diagram, it is straightforward to represent the classes in an object-oriented language. Indeed many UML tools will automatically generate outline classes in languages such as Smalltalk, Java or C++ from class diagrams.

Remember that there should be a logical relationship between a subclass and its superclass. That is the case in our example as we have the relationships:

- Student is_a Person
- Professor is_a Person

A possible Java definition of class Student is:

```java
public class Student extends Person {
    private int theRegNum;

    public Student(String name, int reg) {
        super(name);
        theRegNum = reg;
    } // constructor

    public int getRegNum() {
        return theRegNum;
    } // getRegNum
```

```
        public String getInfo() {
            return theName + "," + theRegNum;
        } // getInfo
    } // Student
```

We show that `Student` inherits from `Person` by using the reserved word **extends**. Only the new attribute `theRegNum`, the new method `getRegNum` and the redefined method `getInfo` together with a new constructor are given in the `Student` subclass. The attribute `theName` and the method `detailInfo` are inherited from the `Person` superclass. When a `Student` object is created and its constructor is executed, the constructor of the superclass is called using **super** to initialise the inherited attributes.

We can now declare woman to be a reference to a `Student` and create a `Student` object using **new**:

```
    Student woman = new Student("Mary", 2000153);
```

After the declarations:

```
    String stra = woman.getInfo();
    String strb = woman.detailInfo();
```

`stra` will refer to the string `"Mary,2000153"` while `strb` will refer to the string `"Details are:Mary,2000153"`.

It is often the case that a subclass will need access to members of a superclass that should be hidden from clients of the superclass. That is the reason for the reserved word **protected** in the definition of `Person`. It indicates that the attribute `theName` is visible to methods of a class such as `Student` that is derived from class `Person`.

Inheritance in other object-oriented languages follows the approach described above. In C++, for example, we show that class `Student` inherits from class `Person` by writing:

```
    class Student: public Person { ... };
```

Apart from minor syntactic differences, the definitions of `Person` and `Student` in C++ closely resemble the Java version. One difference is that in Java all classes are a subclass of class `Object`. Class `Object` has methods such as `toString` and `equals` that are available for all classes although they will often be redefined in subclasses. Delphi has `TObject` as a common superclass, but there is no common superclass in C++.

In Chapter 7, we looked at `CharStack` as an example of how an Ada package can support the implementation of an abstract data type. `CharStack` was implemented as a record, but the representation was hidden. The radical approach to turning Ada 95 into an object-oriented language would have been to make a package a type. This has not been done. However, Ada 95 does support inheritance. When we are to inherit from a type in Ada 95, it must be represented as a **tagged record**. The definition of `Person` becomes:

```
    package Persons is
        type Person is tagged private;
```

```
procedure personInit(p : in out Person;
                     name : in String);
function getInfo(p : in Person) return  String;
function detailInfo(p : in Person) return  String;
private
   type Person is tagged record
      theName : String;
   end record;
end Persons;
```

The procedure bodies are defined in the package body as usual. Now, to derive a `Student` from `Person` we have:

```
with Persons; use  Persons;
package Students is
   type Student is new  Person with private;
   procedure studentInit(p : in out Student;
                         name : in String;
                         reg : in Integer);
   function getRegNum(p : in Student) return Integer;
   function getInfo(p : in Student) return String;
private
   type Student is new  Person with record
      theRegNum : Integer;
    end record;
end Students;
```

Although inheritance is supported in this way, Ada 95 is not class based and an extra parameter is required in the procedures to determine the object being referred to. It is possible to write Ada 95 programs in an object-oriented style, but it is an option rather than being central to the language.

8.3 Polymorphism and dynamic binding

In object-oriented systems we have **inclusion polymorphism**, that is, a reference to an object of a subclass can be used anywhere that a reference to an object of its superclass is expected. That means that the following Java assignment is legal:

```
Person p = new Student("George", 204503);
```

Although the type of `p` is 'reference to `Person`', it now refers to an object of one of the subclasses of `Person`. This enables us to create flexible systems, but raises the issue of what happens when we call a method such as `getInfo` that is defined in the `Person` superclass and then redefined in the `Student` subclass.

In this context, it is important to distinguish between **overloading** and **overriding**. In Java, when a method is redefined in a subclass with exactly the same parameter profile as the original method in the superclass then we have overriding and the binding of method calls occurs at run time, i.e. it is dynamic. If the new method has the same name, but a different parameter profile, then we have overloading as described in Chapter 6 and the binding occurs at compile time, i.e. it is static.

Let us look at this through an example. Suppose that we have the following declarations in Java:

```
Person p1 = new Person("Fred");
Student sp = new Student("George", 204503);
String s1 = p1.getInfo();
String s2 = sp.getInfo();
Person p2 = sp;
String s3 = p2.getInfo();
```

The first two calls of getInfo are no different from those in the last section and so s1 refers to the string "Fred" while s2 refers to the string "George,204503". However, what about s3? The type of the variable p2 is 'reference to Person'. Inclusion polymorphism means that it is possible for p2 to refer to an object that belongs to a subclass of Person. That is the case here because, after the assignment to sp, p2 refers to a Student object.

The question is now which version of getInfo is used in the call of p2.getInfo(): the one defined in class Person or the one defined in class Student. If we have static binding then, as p2 is a reference to a Person, the version is the one defined in class Person and so s3 would now refer to the string "George". However, we have dynamic binding and so the version depends on the class of the object to which p2 is currently referring. As p2 is currently referring to a Student object, s3 refers to the string "George,204503".

Let us now consider execution of the Java statement:

```
s3 = p2.detailInfo();
```

The method detailInfo defined in class Person and inherited by class Student is executed. Execution of detailInfo involves a call of getInfo. As p2 currently refers to a Student object, it is the version of getInfo defined in class Student that is called and so the registration number is printed as well as the name.

C++

C++ supports both static and dynamic binding of function members. In C++, when a member function is defined in the superclass to be virtual as in:

```
virtual char* getInfo() { ... }
```

then it may be overridden in a subclass giving us dynamic binding. If the reserved word **virtual** is omitted then the binding is always static. The reason for this is that dynamic binding does incur run-time overheads and, as C++ is used as a low-level systems programming language, the programmer is given the choice of using the more efficient static form when dynamic binding is not required.

Delphi not only requires methods that are to be overridden to be declared as **virtual**, but also requires the overriding method to be declared as **override**. When this is not done, we have static binding.

Objects in Java are always accessed by reference. Hence the C++ equivalent of the Java declarations of sp and p2 is:

```
Student *sp = new Student("George", 204503);
Person *p2 = sp;
```

Assuming that getInfo was defined to be virtual in the C++ version of class Person, the call p2→getInfo() will cause the member function defined in class Student to be called in the same way as was described for Java. However, objects in C++ do not have to be accessed through pointers and so the question now arises of what happens when we write:

```
Student sp("George", 204503);
Person p2 = sp;
```

As a Student object has an extra attribute, it requires more space than a Person object and so there is a problem in assigning the value of sp to p2. What happens is that we get **slicing**: only the attributes of the sp object defined in the superclass are copied. Binding is now static and the call p2.getInfo() calls the method defined in class Person and so returns the string "George". Hence, to achieve dynamic binding in C++ we must use pointers to objects or have them as reference parameters. The space problem does not then arise as all pointers are of the same size.

Type checking

It should be noted that full type checking in Java, C++ and Delphi is still performed at compile time. An expression such as:

```
int r = p2.getRegNum();
```

is picked up as an error by the compiler as getRegNum() is not one of the methods defined in class Person and the type of p2 is 'reference to Person'. This guards against possible run-time errors since, although the statement has a valid interpretation when p2 is referring to a Student object, it does not have a valid interpretation when p2 is referring to either a Person or Professor object.

Ada 95 supports dynamic binding. To get round Ada's strict type checking, when the type of a procedure or function parameter is written as Person'Class then the actual parameter can be of type Person or any of the types derived from Person such as Student and Professor.

Heterogeneous data structures

Dynamic binding allows us to set up heterogeneous arrays without compromising type safety. Suppose that we have the Java declaration:

```
Person[] pList = new Person [100];
```

Each array element can refer to a `Person`, `Student` or `Professor` object. If we assume that all the array elements have been given values, we can process the elements of the array in the loop as follows:

```
for (int i = 0; i < 100; i++) {
    String st = pList[i].getInfo();
    // process string st ...
}
```

The version of the method `getInfo` called each time round the loop depends on whether the object referred to by `pList[i]` is currently a `Person`, a `Student` or a `Professor`. As long as we restrict ourselves to calling the operations defined in class `Person`, everything is fine and we have full static type checking.

However, suppose that we know that `pList[3]` refers to a `Student` object and we want to perform one of the extra operations defined in class `Student`. We can use a **cast** to convert a reference to a `Person` to a reference to a `Student`:

```
Student s = (Student) pList[3];
```

However, if `pList[3]` does not currently refer to a `Student`, a `ClassCastException` will be thrown. Great care must therefore be exercised when using a cast. It is possible to check the class of an object using the `instanceof` operator. We can write:

```
if (pList[3] instanceof Student) ...
```

The `instanceof` operator and casting should be used very sparingly; polymorphism and dynamic binding leads to much clearer and more robust code. In Ada 95, it is possible to determine the type of an object by examining its `Tag` attribute but, like `instanceof` in Java, this should seldom be used.

We looked in Section 7.5 at parametrised data types. A similar effect can be achieved using dynamic binding. In Java, all classes are subclasses of class `Object` and so we can, for example, declare a `Stack` class, the type of whose elements are references to class `Object`:

```
public class Stack {

    private Object[] val;
    private int head;
    private int maxSize;

    public Stack(int size) {
        val = new Object[size];
        head = -1;
        maxSize = size;
    } // constructor

    public void push(Object x) { ... }
    public Object pop() { ... }
```

```
    public boolean isEmpty() { ... }
} // Stack
```

Once we have created an instance of class `Stack`, we can push elements of any class on to it. Suppose, however, that we restrict ourselves to pushing elements of class `String` on to a particular `Stack` object. In that case, we know that when we `pop` an element it will be a string and we can use a cast to convert a reference to an `Object` to a reference to a `String`. We therefore have simulated the effect of a parametrised `Stack` class. However, we do not get the static type checking that we get with generics in Ada or class templates in C++. It is up to the programmer to code carefully so that run-time errors do not occur due to the inappropriate use of a cast and this will often require the addition of explicit checks at run time.

Inheritance is a powerful feature and there is a temptation to use it to solve all programming problems, including those for which better solutions exist. Hence, although their effect can be simulated by inheritance, parametrised data types are an important addition to a robust programming language. We feel that it is only a matter of time before they will be introduced into Java.

Message passing

Programming in an object-oriented style requires a different approach to problem solving. To emphasise the central position of the object and the dynamic nature of object interaction, the object-oriented community has developed a new vocabulary. The object-oriented view is that objects send **messages** to one another and, on receiving a message, an object decides (at run time) which of the available **methods** (that is, operation bodies) should be used in response. An object may send a message to itself. The call of `getInfo` in the body of `detailInfo` is written as **this**`.getInfo()` to emphasise that point.

Implementation of dynamic binding

In a procedural language, procedure calls are implemented by inserting the procedure's start address and parameter information into the code at compile time. How then do we deal with dynamic method calls where the decision about the method to be called is delayed until run time? At compile time, we can create a **method access table** for each class. This table will contain the required calling information for each method in the class. If the class is a subclass, the table will contain information for the inherited methods as well as the new methods. When a method has been redefined in the subclass, information about the redefined method is held.

The method access table for class `Person` will contain calling information for methods `getInfo` and `detailInfo` while the method access table for class `Student` will contain calling information for the inherited method `detailInfo`, the new method `getRegNum` and the redefined version of `getInfo`. All this information is known at compile time. When a `Person` object is created at run time, it contains the object's attributes plus a link to the `Person` method access table. Similarly, a `Student` object will contain a link to the `Student` method access table. This is shown in Figure 8.2

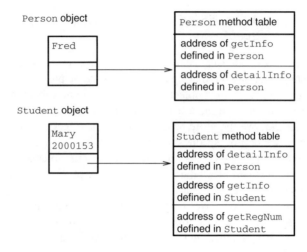

Figure 8.2   Implementation of dynamic binding.

where we have a `Person` object whose name is `Fred` and a `Student` object whose name is `Mary` and whose registration number is `2000153`.

When we have the Java call `p2.getInfo()`, we access the object currently pointed to by `p2`. Hence, even though `p2` may be of type `Person`, when `p2` is referring to a `Student` object, it is the `Student` method access table that is accessed. This gives us dynamic binding.

8.4   Comparing the procedural and object-oriented approach

Suppose that we have different kinds of shape and we want to do various things with these shapes, such as draw them, calculate their area, move them and so on. In the procedural approach, the solution would be organised in terms of procedures (`draw`, `area`, `move`, etc.) with one procedure for each kind of operation that we wished to carry out. A particular shape would be specified as a parameter of the procedures. Hence, in C for example, the `draw` procedure might have the structure:

```
void draw (Shape s) {
    switch (s.kind) {
        case LINE: /* code to draw a line */ ...
        case RECTANGLE:
            /* code to draw a rectangle */ ...
        case CIRCLE: /* code to draw a circle */ ...
        default: /* error message */ ...
    }
} /* draw */
```

where `Shape` is a `struct` that has a data member `kind` to determine which shape is being dealt with. To add a new shape we add a new case to the switch statement. As we will have many such procedures (to calculate area, etc.) adding a new shape requires changing many procedures.

In the object-oriented approach, the focus changes entirely. Instead of the organisation being in terms of shape operations, the solution is organised in terms of the shapes themselves. Each shape has a class definition where we define its required attributes and operations. We ensure that all the shapes offer a common set of operations by having a Shape superclass from which all the different subclasses inherit. We add a new shape by defining a new subclass in which the Shape operations can be redefined and new operations added. No existing operation code needs to be modified.

This leads to an inheritance hierarchy such as that shown in the UML diagram in Figure 8.3. In the definition of class Shape we put all the common properties about shapes, their height, width, position, how to move them, etc. A subclass such as Polygon inherits information from Shape and redefines or adds methods that are specific to polygons. The subclass Rectangle inherits from its Polygon superclass and give definitions for operations such as how to draw itself or calculate its area.

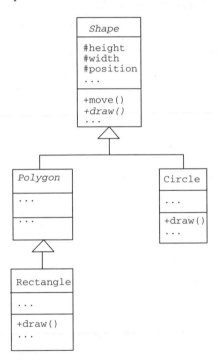

Figure 8.3 UML inheritance hierarchy.

8.5 Abstract methods and classes

Let us now consider in more detail the definition of class Shape in Java. Its outline structure is:

```
public abstract class Shape {
    // declaration of protected attributes
    // and public operations
    // common to all shapes
    ...
    public abstract void draw();
    // definition of other abstract methods
    ...
}
```

One of the things that we want to do with our shapes is draw them. However, we cannot draw an arbitrary shape and so it is not possible to define a body for draw in class Shape. Hence draw is defined in class Shape as an **abstract method**, i.e. as a method that has no body. Each kind of shape is drawn differently and so the subclasses will all define their own implementation of the draw method. Virtual methods in Delphi can be declared to be abstract while the equivalent in C++ is to give a virtual method an empty body in which case it becomes a **pure virtual function**. In Eiffel a method is made abstract by being declared to be **deferred**.

When a class such as Shape contains one or more abstract methods, we cannot create objects of the class as there is no code for some of the methods. Class Shape is an example of an **abstract class**. Its purpose is to define a common interface for all its subclasses. In a UML diagram such as that shown in Figure 8.3, abstract classes and methods are written in italics.

We can define a class such as Line which inherits from Shape and which defines a body for the draw method:

```
class Line extends  Shape {
    ...
    public void draw() {
        // code to draw a line ...
    } // draw
} // Line
```

Although Shape is an abstract class, we can still have a declaration such as:

```
Shape ashape;
```

because ashape is only a reference to Shape, not an actual Shape object. As we cannot have Shape objects, ashape must refer to an object of a subclass of Shape. We can, for example, write:

```
ashape = new Line(...);
```

In the call:

```
ashape.draw();
```

we ask ashape to draw itself. If ashape is currently pointing at a Line object, a line is drawn.

An abstract class will typically contain several abstract methods. When we inherit from an abstract class, we must give definitions for all its abstract methods if we wish to create object instances. If we do not, then the subclass is also an abstract class (as is likely to be the case with `Polygon` in our example).

If the subclass `Line` adds a new operation such as `length` then the call:

```
ashape.length();
```

is a syntax error because the type of `ashape` is 'pointer to `Shape`' and only those methods given in class `Shape` may be called. To be able to make the above call, we would need to define `length` in class `Shape` as an abstract method.

To summarise:

- A superclass reference variable may point to a subclass object.
- The only methods available are those listed in the superclass.
- However, methods defined in a superclass may be redefined (overridden) in the subclass and it is the redefined version that is used.

8.6 Multiple inheritance

Multiple inheritance is a controversial issue in object-oriented programming languages. In multiple inheritance a subclass can inherit from more than one superclass. C++ and Eiffel allow multiple inheritance while Java and Ada do not. An example of multiple inheritance is shown in the UML class diagram in Figure 8.4 where a `Circle` class inherits from both a `Shape` and a `Moveable` superclass. Although multiple inheritance appears to be a natural way to describe many problems, it does lead to code that can be difficult to understand, as it is often far from clear in which class a method has been defined. Updating code that uses multiple inheritance is far from simple.

Another problem with multiple inheritance is where a method with the same name and parameter profile is inherited from two different superclasses. If only one of the methods has a body and the other is abstract then there is no problem; the problem arises when they provide alternative implementations. The solution in Eiffel is that, when a method is inherited from two superclasses, one of the methods must be renamed in the subclass. Otherwise, we have a syntax error. In C++, the scope resolution operator `::` is used to resolve any possible ambiguity. Neither language makes use of the fact that nothing need be done if one or both of the methods is abstract.

Java achieves the advantages of multiple inheritance without its disadvantages by using **interfaces**. An interface is like an abstract class which has no attributes and in which **all** the methods are abstract. A class that **implements** an interface guarantees that it will provide implementations for these methods. An interface for a moveable shape could be:

```
interface Moveable {
    public void horiz(int val);
    public void vert(int val);
} // Moveable
```

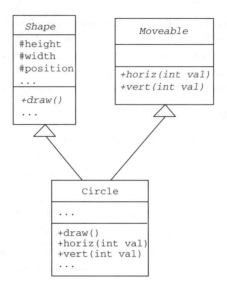

Figure 8.4   Multiple inheritance.

A Java class can only inherit from one superclass, but can implement several interfaces as in the example:

```
public class Circle extends Shape
    implements Moveable, Resizing {
    . . .
} // Circle
```

Class `Circle` must provide implementations for the `horiz` and `vert` methods of `Moveable` and for the abstract methods listed in the `Resizing` interface or we have a syntax error. There is no problem when the same method name appears in more than one interface. As none can have a body, there can be no conflicting implementations.

8.7   Problems with inheritance

Information hiding and inheritance

The purpose of a class is to hide implementation detail and provide clients with a strictly defined interface. A class can be considered to have two kinds of client; those who use its services and those who create subclasses. Information hiding is about restricting access while inheritance involves giving subclasses access to the inner workings of a superclass. There is therefore a conflict between information hiding and inheritance.

There are two main ways in which a subclass can compromise the security provided by a superclass:

● A protected attribute in a superclass may be used purely for internal purposes and the designer of the superclass may have decided that there should be no public methods to access or change its value. A subclass can overturn that design decision by providing such methods.

- A set of protected attributes may have rules relating their values and so they should only be changed as a group. A subclass can add a method to allow one of the attributes to be changed independently.

As an example of the second problem, consider a class Date that has full checks to ensure that only valid dates can occur:

```
class Date {
    protected int day, month year;
    public Date(int d, int m, int y) {
        // check that d, m and y make a sensible
        // date before creating the object
        ...
    } // constructor
    public void tomorrow() { ... }
    ...
}
```

Unfortunately, a subclass can add a method or redefine an existing method to modify a date without checking that the new date is valid, thereby corrupting an important design feature of the superclass.

The solution is to treat subclass designers as users of the subclass who are only given a strictly defined interface. Attributes, such as day, month and year would then be **private**, not **protected**. The superclass can have **protected** methods through which subclasses can access and modify the private attributes. In the Date example, the protected methods would only allow a complete date to be updated, not individual attributes. A superclass designer can also decide that certain methods may not be redefined in a subclass. That can be achieved in C++ by omitting the word **virtual** while in Java a method can be declared to be **final**. Indeed a whole class can be defined to be **final** in which case no subclasses can be defined. Methods in the Java standard library classes are often declared as **final** so that users cannot change their behaviour.

If private attributes can be accessed through protected methods, a subclass can still make their values available to ordinary clients, even though the designer of the superclass wanted them kept private. Inheritance therefore provides a loophole to information hiding. Superclass designers must therefore pay particular attention to how much information is to be made available to subclasses. Packages in Java offer a solution to this problem. As we saw in Section 5.5, when no visibility information is given, an attribute or method is visible to classes defined in the same package, but is hidden from classes defined in other packages. Classes defined in the same package are likely to have the same designer. We can therefore consider subclasses defined in the same package as the superclass to be trustworthy and they can be allowed access to information denied to the untrustworthy subclasses defined outside the package.

An alternative view is that subclass designers should be free to create subclasses in ways not thought of by the superclass designer. That is the approach taken by

Eiffel which separates the notion of inheritance and information hiding. Attributes and methods are not declared as being private, protected or public. A subclass inherits **all** the attributes and methods of its superclasses while information hiding is implemented by each class having an **export list** which lists the attributes and methods visible to ordinary clients. (When an attribute is exported, it may be used, but not modified by the client.) It is possible for a subclass to export less information than its superclass.

A related problem is that of a **fragile superclass**. If we change the definition of a superclass then we need to examine all the subclasses to ensure that they still work properly. If, on the other hand, the subclasses have a strictly defined interface to the superclass, and that interface is unchanged, then we have a guarantee that the subclasses are not affected.

Breaking strong typing

There are problems with the Java inheritance rules concerning arrays. When a Student is a subclass of Person, the Java language definition states that an array of Student objects is a subclass of an array of Person objects. Suppose that we have the method:

```
public void  update(Person [] pList) {
    pList[2] = new Person(...);
} // update
```

If we have the declaration:

```
Student[] sList = new Student[100];
```

and make the call update(sList), then sList[2] now refers to a Person rather than a Student. The call sList[2].getRegNum() is syntactically correct, but will give an error at run time.

8.8 Behavioural inheritance

Behavioural inheritance is concerned with the subtype–supertype relationship and with inclusion polymorphism, i.e. the possibility of using an object of a subtype anywhere an object of the supertype is expected. In all widely used object-oriented languages, subtypes are derived from supertypes by means of inheritance. Subtypes therefore correspond to subclasses and supertypes to superclasses. This is not the only approach and some experimental languages have separate type and class hierarchies, but as they are not widely used, we do not consider them here.

If it is to ensure that using an object of a subclass where an object of a superclass is expected does not introduce run-time errors, a language must impose restrictions on inheritance. The subtype–supertype relationship can be defined by the **weak form of the principle of substitutability**:

> S is a subtype of T if substituting an object of type S wherever an object of type T is expected does not introduce the possibility of type errors occurring at run time.

The following **syntactic conditions** guarantee the weak form of the principle of substitutability:

1. All services in the superclass are present in the subclass.

2. Additional services and attributes may be present in the subclass.

3. If a service is redefined in the subclass then the new service must be compatible with the original service in the superclass.

We must now define what is meant by compatible. Two services are compatible if:

(a) they have the same number of parameters,

(b) the type of each input parameter in the redefined service is a supertype of (or the same type as) the corresponding parameter in the original service,

(c) the type of each output parameter in a redefined service, including the returned value if any, is a subtype of (or the same type as) the corresponding parameter in the original service.

Condition (b) is known as the **contravariance rule** and is counter-intuitive in its handling of input parameters. Covariance, where the type of a parameter in a redefined service may be a subtype of the corresponding parameter in the original service, seems more natural.

The need for contravariance can be demonstrated using the following example which is expressed in Java syntax:

```
public class Vehicle {
    protected int licNum;

    public Vehicle(int ln) {
        licNum = ln;
    } // constructor

    public int getNumV() {
        return licNum;
    } // getNumV

    public boolean eq(Vehicle v) {
        return v.getNumV() == licNum;
    } // eq
} // Vehicle

public class Car extends Vehicle {
    private int numSeats;

    public Car(int ln, int numS) {
        super(ln);
```

```
        numSeats = numS;
    } // constructor

    public int getNumS() {
        return numSeats;
    } // getNumS

    public boolean eq(Car v) {
        return (v.getNumS() == numSeats)
            && (v.getNumV() == licNum);
    } // eq
} // Car
```

Let us now consider execution of the following program segment:

```
Car c1 = new Car(27, 4);
Car c2 = new Car(27, 5);
Vehicle v1 = c1;
Vehicle v2 = new Vehicle(27);
if (v1.eq(c2)) ...

...

if (v1.eq(v2)) ...
```

Class Vehicle has a method eq which compares two vehicles for equality. It seems natural to want to override this method in subclass Car so that we can compare two cars for equality and assume that dynamic binding will ensure that the correct method is called.

This is not, however, possible in Java. The method eq in class Car overloads rather than overrides the method eq defined in class Vehicle because Car is not a supertype of Vehicle as would be required to satisfy the contravariance rule, but is a subtype. Hence, although v1 is referring to a Car object, the binding is static and so the call v1.eq(c2) causes the function eq defined in Vehicle to be called, giving the result true. The call v1.eq(v2) has the same effect. Most object-oriented languages, including Java and C++, actually handle the contravariance rule by requiring that, for a method to be overridden, the types of corresponding formal parameters must be the same, but that makes no difference to this example.

Let us now consider the effect if covariance had been used. The method eq in class Car would now override its counterpart in class Vehicle. With v1.eq(c2) there is no problem. As v1 refers to a Car object, the call of eq is dynamically bound to the method defined in Car and the value false is returned. If v2 was currently referring to a Car object there would also be no problem with v1.eq(v2). But v2 is currently pointing to a Vehicle object and so when the eq method in Car is executed with parameter v2, an attempt is made to execute v2.getNumS(). As no such operation is defined for in Vehicle, we have a run-time error.

As covariance does lead to more flexible systems, it is used in Eiffel. The Eiffel approach is to have a second level of checking where a complete program is analysed to detect all possible situations where the use of covariance **could** lead to a run-time error.

Need for further conditions

Inheritance should be restricted to situations where the is_a relationship holds. The alternative is **implementation inheritance** where the prime aim is the re-use of code and there may be no logical connection between a subclass and its superclass. Consider, for example, a Stack and a Queue. As the only difference between a Stack and a Queue is the semantics of the remove operation, it is possible, though far from desirable, to define a Stack class as being derived from a Queue superclass:

```java
public class Queue {
    protected int[] vals;
    protected int first, last, numElements;

    public Queue() { ... }
    public void add(int item)
        {... // add element to back of Queue ...}
    public int remove()
        {... // return front element of Queue ...}
} // Queue

public class Stack extends Queue {
    public Stack(){ ... }
    public int remove()
        { ... // return top element of Stack ...}
} // Stack
```

The redefined service remove in Stack has the same parameter profile as the original service in Queue and a reference to a Stack object can be used anywhere a reference to a Queue object is expected without causing a run-time error.

The behaviour of the redefined service is, however, different and we do not have the relation Stack is_a Queue or wish to regard Stack as a subtype of Queue. Inheritance is therefore being used inappropriately; we only have implementation inheritance.

We therefore see that, although satisfying the syntactic conditions means that the use of **inclusion polymorphism** does not introduce run-time errors, it does not guarantee behavioural inheritance. In behavioural inheritance, we want an object of a subtype to have all the properties of an object of the supertype and for it to be usable as an alternative for the supertype object. A definition of the subtype–supertype relationship which satisfies behavioural inheritance is the **strong form of the principle of substitutability**.

> S is a subtype of T if, for each object s of type S, there is an object t of type T such that, for all programs P defined in terms of T, the behaviour of P is unchanged when s is substituted for t.

Unfortunately this is almost impossible to enforce in a programming language although support is given in Eiffel where we can make assertions about the behaviour of a class and can have pre- and post-conditions and invariants about each method. The assertions associated with a superclass also apply to its subclasses; invariants and post-conditions may be strengthened in a subclass while pre-conditions may be weakened. (This is another example of the contravariance rule.) As the post-conditions for the `remove` operation in `Stack` and `Queue` are not compatible, we see that the subtype–supertype relationship does not exist.

Private inheritance

In C++, we normally have **public inheritance** and write:

```
class Subclass: public  Superclass { ... };
```

All the public methods of the superclass are then available to clients of the subclass. However, the C++ default is **private inheritance** where the public and protected information in the superclass can be used in the implementation of the subclass, but the public methods of the superclass are not available to clients of the subclass. Inheritance is therefore being used purely for code re-use, i.e. we have implementation inheritance. When private inheritance is used, an object of the subclass cannot be used where an object of the superclass is expected.

An example of this is where a `Stack` is to be implemented as a linked list. A linked list has operations, such as being able to insert an element anywhere in the list, that are not applicable to a stack. Assuming the presence of a `LinkedList` class, we can write:

```
class Stack: private  LinkedList { ... };
```

The operations manipulating the linked list can be used in the implementation of the `Stack` class, but are not available to clients of `Stack` objects. We do not have the relationship `Stack is_a LinkedList`. Instead, we have the **aggregation** or has_a relationship and so a much better solution is to define the linked list as an attribute of class `Stack`:

```
class Stack {
    LinkedList theList;
    ...
}; // Stack
```

Private inheritance is not available in other widely used object-oriented languages.

Restriction

Traditionally, we think of subtyping in terms of restriction, i.e. an integer subrange is a subtype of integer and a `Square` is a subtype of `Rectangle`. We have the relation `Square is_a Rectangle`. A value of type `Square` can appear anywhere a value of type `Rectangle` is expected and so defining subtypes by restriction presents no problem in, for example, a purely functional language.

There is, however, a major difference between a value and an object. We do not change a value, we get a new value. An object, on the other hand, has an identity and, although its attributes may be given new values, it remains the same object. There are, therefore, things that we can do with Rectangle objects, such as changing their length while keeping their breadth constant, which we cannot do with Square objects. A Square object cannot, therefore, appear anywhere a Rectangle object is expected.

Restriction should not therefore be used in the definition of subtypes in object-oriented languages. The object-oriented notion of a subtype is where we give **more** information. An example is class Car which has subclasses RacingCar and SaloonCar, each of which has extra attributes and services. All objects of class RacingCar and all objects of class SaloonCar are also objects of class Car. However, because we give more information in the definition of RacingCar, not all Car objects belong to the RacingCar class.

Because subclasses usually have more attributes and operations than their superclass, some authors argue that the subclass/superclass terminology is confusing and should be avoided. Hence C++ and Ada use the terms *base class* and *derived class* while Eiffel uses *heir* or *descendant* instead of subclass and *parent* or *ancestor* instead of superclass.

8.9 Conclusion

We have seen how inheritance supports software re-use and enables new classes to be derived from existing base classes. Dynamic binding gives great flexibility. However, when the definitions of the attributes and operations of a class are distributed over an inheritance hierarchy, it can make a program more difficult to understand and hence to maintain.

Inheritance can therefore be overused. It is now generally accepted that using inheritance purely to inherit implementation details is not a good idea and that aggregation with its has_a relationship gives a much better way of re-using implementation details. Also, although parametrised types can be modelled using inheritance, that solution is error-prone and does not give us the type checking support provided when a language supports parametrised types.

Summary

1. A subclass inherits the attributes and operations of its superclass. It can add new attributes and operations and override existing operations.

2. Inheritance provides an excellent tool for software re-use as new components can be created by extending and modifying existing components.

3. Inclusion polymorphism means that a reference to an object of a subclass can be used anywhere a reference to an object of its superclass is expected.

4. When a method is overridden in a subclass, the decision about which version is to be called is made at run time, i.e. we have dynamic binding.

5. In Java, all operations can be overridden unless they are explicitly declared to be final. In C++ and Delphi, methods which may be overridden must be declared to be virtual.

6. Although they support dynamic binding, full type checking is still performed in Java, C++, Ada and Delphi at compile time.

7. Dynamic binding allows heterogeneous data structures to be created.

8. As an abstract class contains one or more abstract methods, we cannot declare objects of an abstract class. Its purpose is to define a common interface for all its subclasses.

9. In multiple inheritance, a subclass can inherit from more than one subclass. Java provides interfaces as an alternative to multiple inheritance. An interface is like an abstract class, but it has no attributes and all its methods are abstract.

10. Inheritance should only be used where there is a conceptual relationship between a subclass and its superclass.

Exercises

8.1 Distinguish between an object-based, a class-based and an object-oriented language. How would you categorise Ada 83 and Ada 95?

8.2 Discuss the importance of inheritance in object-oriented programming.

8.3 As one is concerned with exporting information and the other with hiding information, is there a conflict between the ideas of inheritance and those of information hiding?

8.4 Why do C++ and Java classes have both private and protected members?

8.5 The skeleton of a class for an integer queue has been given. Write the code for the method bodies.

8.6 What is the difference between overloading and overriding? Compare the overloading facilities of Ada, C++ and Java.

8.7 In Section 8.3, we defined pList to be an array of Person. Explain why an element pList[i] can refer to a Student object. In the call pList[i].getInfo(), what determines which version of the method getInfo is called? What would happen in C++ or Java if we made the call pList[i].getRegNum()?

8.8 Describe how C++ and Java manage to combine dynamic binding with compile-time type checking.

8.9 Describe the advantages that dynamic binding gives compared with the use of variant records.

8.10 In this chapter we saw how we could define a Java Stack class whose elements are references to class Object. This enabled us to have a stack whose elements were objects of any class. In Chapter 7, we saw the definition of a generic Stack. Compare these two approaches from the point of view of flexibility, understandability, run-time efficiency and, most important of all, the creation of robust code.

8.11 What problems can arise with multiple inheritance? How does Java provide the advantages of multiple inheritance without the disadvantages that you have identified?

8.12 Give arguments for and against automatic garbage collection in the languages C++ and Java.

8.13 The contravariance rule is counter-intuitive in its handling of input parameters with the covariance rule being the more obvious. Through an example, explain how covariance can lead to a run-time error.

8.14 Distinguish between behavioural and implementation inheritance. Can implementation inheritance always be replaced by aggregation?

Bibliography

A more general introduction to object-oriented programming has been given by Cox and Novobilski (1991) while object-oriented software construction using Eiffel is described by Meyer (1997). The definitive description on using UML is given by Booch *et al.* (1998).

Object-oriented programming is an active research area and a large number of languages have been developed. Many, such as Flavors, are based on LISP. An article by Wolf (1989) compares Flavors with C++.

Cardelli (1984) investigated the conditions that guarantee the weak form of the principle of substitutability while Clark (1995) discusses the conflict between type safety and inheritance.

Booch, G., Rumbaugh, J. and Jacobson, I. (1998). *The Unified Modeling Language User Guide*. Addison-Wesley.

Cardelli, L. (1984). 'A semantics of multiple inheritance'. *Semantics of Data Types*, LNCS 173, Springer-Verlag, pp. 51–67.

Clark, R.G. (1995). 'Type Safety and Behavioural Inheritance'. *Information and Software Technology*, **37**(10), 539–545.

Cox, B.J. and Novobilski, A. (1991). *Object Oriented Programming* (Second Edition). Addison-Wesley.

Meyer, B. (1997). *Object-oriented Software Construction* (Second Edition). Prentice-Hall.

Wolf, W. (1989). 'A Practical Comparison of Two Object-Oriented Languages'. *IEEE Software*, **6**(5) 61–68.

Chapter 9

Functional languages

···

Up till now, the discussion has concentrated on imperative languages with only passing references to languages such as Lisp. This chapter looks at languages that achieve their effect by the evaluation of expressions, rather than by changing the value of variables through assignment.

It starts by introducing the concepts of functional programming using a functional subset of Ada. This approach has been taken so that we can pinpoint and discuss features, such as the absence of side-effects, the presence of higher-order functions and operations on structured values, that are absent from many imperative languages without the issues being confused by the introduction of the syntax of a new language.

Lisp is described in some detail and it is shown that, although Lisp contains all the necessary features of a functional language, it also contains imperative features such as assignment. The principal differences between Lisp and its dialect Scheme are then discussed.

The chapter then goes on to consider FP whose main impact has been in exploring new ideas in functional programming rather than as a practical system. The chapter concludes with an examination of ML as a representative of a modern functional language and compares constructs in ML with their counterparts in Scheme.

9.1 Introduction

Von Neumann influence

The languages discussed so far in this book are often referred to as imperative languages. A program written in an imperative language achieves its effect by changing the values of variables by means of assignment statements. The design of imperative languages has been closely tied to the design of conventional computers, which follow what is known as the von Neumann design, where a store has individually addressable locations.

Since machine code programs achieve their effect by changing the contents of store locations, a variable in an imperative programming language can be regarded as an abstraction of the von Neumann computer store location.

Machine code programs are executed by carrying out machine code instructions in sequence with conditional and unconditional jump instructions being used to alter the flow of control. Similarly, the execution of a program in an imperative language is carried out by executing statements in sequence with conditional and loop statements being used to alter the sequence of control. The influence of the von Neumann computer on the design of imperative languages is therefore clear. As imperative languages are closely tied to the design of conventional computers, they can be implemented efficiently.

With the decreasing cost of computer hardware, radically different designs have become possible. One likely outcome of this is that multiprocessor systems will eventually become the norm. It is even possible that conventional machines of the future will have as many processors as store locations or that the whole concept of the store location will disappear.

It is therefore clear that using currently available hardware as a model is not the only way to design a computer language. Other computational models can be used and, if they are found to provide a successful way of describing computations, it may be possible to design computer hardware to fit the computational model rather than the other way round.

Functional languages

The computational model used in functional languages is the **lambda calculus**. This provides functional languages with a well-defined semantics, making it much easier to formally reason about the correctness of functional programs than programs written in an imperative language.

The mathematical function is central to functional programming languages. A function definition such as:

```
f(x)  =  10  *  x
```

gives a rule showing how each element in the **domain** of the function f can be mapped to an element in the **range** of the function by multiplying it by 10. If the domain of this function is the set of all integers, then the range will also be the set of all integers. For example, f(1) = 10, f(2) = 20 and f(30) = 300; so the **application** of the function f to the integer 2 results in the integer 20. This corresponds closely to function calls in imperative languages. Languages based on mathematical functions are said to be **functional** or **applicative** as they achieve their effect by the application of functions.

What then are the significant differences between a functional and an imperative programming language? Functional languages are only concerned with values and expressions and so the concept of a store location is not required. The assignment statement, fundamental to imperative languages, does not exist in a purely functional language. Assignment causes a change in the value of an existing object. Application of a function, on the other hand, causes a new value to be returned.

A major problem with assignment is that when it is used in conjunction with reference parameters or non-local variables in subprograms it can lead to side-effects and aliasing. As a simple example of this, consider the following Ada function that modifies a non-local variable:

```
function strange return Integer is
begin
   a_global := a_global + 1;
   return a_global;
end strange;
```

Different calls of `strange` return different results and so the relational expression

```
strange = strange
```

gives the value `false`! Side-effects of this nature make it difficult to reason about the correctness of programs and therefore to ensure that they are reliable.

By doing away with assignment, it is possible to ensure that functions do not have side-effects and behave like mathematical functions. The precise order in which functions are called then no longer matters; calling a function with a certain parameter will always give the same answer. This is called **referential transparency** and makes it much easier to reason about the correctness of programs. It also makes it possible for different expressions to be evaluated concurrently on a multiprocessor system. Determining which parts of an imperative program may be executed concurrently is, on the other hand, very difficult due to the interaction of their various parts via shared store locations.

Program structure

The main components of a functional language are a series of primitive functions together with a mechanism for defining new functions from existing ones. A functional program usually consists of a series of function definitions followed by an expression which involves application of the functions. To illustrate the structure of a functional program, consider the problem of finding the difference between the largest and the smallest of three integer numbers. A solution to this problem can be written in a functional subset of Ada:

```
function max(a, b : Integer) return Integer is
begin
   if a > b then
      return a;
   else
      return b;
   end if;
end max;

function min(a, b : Integer) return Integer is
```

```
begin
  if a < b then
    return a;
  else
    return b;
  end if;
end min;

function difference(a, b, c : Integer)
  return Integer is
begin
  return max(a, max(b, c)) - min(a, min(b, c));
end difference;
```

with a possible call being:

```
put(difference(10, 4, 7));
```

A function definition that only contains function calls does not specify an order in which the calculation must be carried out. The calls of min and max can therefore occur in any order or they may be carried out concurrently. Synchronisation, which is often a problem in concurrent systems, is automatically dealt with. Consider that in the execution of:

```
max(a, max(b, c))
```

both calls of max were taking place concurrently. When the value returned by the inner call is required by the outer call, execution of the outer call is suspended until the inner call is completed. Execution of the outer call is then reactivated.

As programs in functional languages state 'what' is to be done rather than 'how' it is to be done, they are at a higher level than imperative languages, and this makes it possible to produce simpler solutions for many problems, especially problems involving symbolic manipulation. Another major reason for this is the central position of the list data structure, which is ideal for the representation and manipulation of symbolic data. Languages like Lisp and Scheme are list-processing languages while most imperative languages can be considered to be scalar-processing languages, since their built-in operations act on scalar rather than on structured values. The main application area of Lisp is artificial intelligence where problems typically involve symbolic manipulation rather than numeric computation.

Operations on lists

Lisp is concerned with atoms, lists and functions. There are two kinds of atom: symbolic atoms that correspond to identifiers and numeric atoms that correspond to numbers. The elements of a list are either atoms or they are other lists. Lists, in Lisp, are written in brackets with the elements separated by a space or a new line.

Hence:

```
(ALPHA BETA GAMMA)
(12 14 16)
((A B) (HELLO THERE) 94)
```

are all lists with three elements. A diagrammatic representation of these lists is shown in Figure 9.1. Lists allow the straightforward representation of hierarchical symbolic information and, as they can be defined recursively, they are ideally suited to being taken apart and constructed by recursive functions.

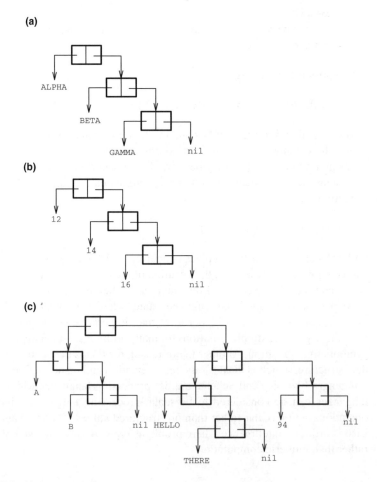

Figure 9.1   List representation.

Modern imperative languages such as Pascal, Java, C++ and Ada allow linked-list structures to be created, but as list processing in such languages involves the direct manipulation of references, it is largely concerned with details of 'how' linked lists can be represented and manipulated rather than the higher level of 'what' they represent.

In imperative programs, structured objects are usually declared and then given initial values. Then, during program execution, the values of individual elements of a structured object are changed. In functional programs, in contrast, where the concept of modifying store locations does not exist, new copies of an object (that is, new values) are created, rather than an existing object modified. This results in run-time overheads and the need for garbage collection, but leads to conceptually simpler solutions.

As lists are of such importance in functional languages, it is important to have functions to extract elements from a list and to construct a list from its components. Two important functions are head, which gives the first element in a list and tail, which returns the list containing all elements except the first. Hence, the **head** of the list:

```
(ALPHA BETA GAMMA)
```

is the atom ALPHA while the **tail** of the list is:

```
(BETA GAMMA)
```

Note that the head of the list:

```
((A B) ( HELLO THERE) 94)
```

is the list (A B).

Another important function is cons which will put back together a list which has been taken apart by head and tail. Hence, if x is the name of a list, the function call:

```
cons(head(x), tail(x))
```

produces the original list. The functions head and tail can be defined in terms of cons. Assuming an item a and a list x, the definitions can be written as:

```
head(cons(a, x)) = a
tail(cons(a, x)) = x
```

If the empty list is represented by **nil**, the following function will test if an integer is a member of a list of integers. (It is assumed here that the type IntegerList has already been suitably declared.)

```
function isMember(x : Integer; a : IntegerList)
  return Boolean is
begin
  if a = nil then
    return false;
  elsif x = head(a) then
    return true;
  else
    return isMember(x, tail(a));
  end if;
end isMember;
```

Function isMember is an example of a recursive function. If the list a is empty, the value false is returned as x cannot be a member. If the first element in the list is x, then true is returned. If neither of these conditions holds, isMember is applied to the tail of the list. In this way, either x is found or the number of elements is exhausted and isMember is eventually applied to the empty list. Where imperative languages usually use loops to achieve repetition, functional languages always use recursion.

Dynamically typed languages

Most modern imperative languages are statically typed. Although this reduces the flexibility of a language, it allows many logical errors to be picked up at compile time. Early functional languages opted for flexibility rather than reliability and are dynamically typed. This approach is illustrated in the following example.

Using type-free notation, function isMember could be re-written as:

```
function isMember(x, a) is
begin
   ...
end isMember;
```

The body of the function is unchanged. In a call of the function the actual parameter corresponding to a must be a list as the functions head and tail are applied to it. If an atom was passed over instead, this would lead to an error when the function was called. The cost of the increased flexibility is, therefore, that some errors, which would be picked up in a statically typed language at compile time, are not picked up in a dynamically typed language until the program is executed.

Dynamically typed languages usually include Boolean functions which enable run-time checks to be made on the current type of an expression. This can prevent type errors although at the expense of run-time efficiency.

Higher-order functions

An important feature of functional languages that is missing from many imperative languages (with the notable exception of Algol 68) is that functions can accept functions as parameters and return functions as results. Functions with this property are called **higher-order functions** and the languages **higher-order languages**.

As an example of a higher-order function, consider the problem of applying a function f to each element in the list (x1 x2 ...xn) so that the new list (f(x1) f(x2) ...f(xn)) is produced. Using the type-free notation, this could be achieved by the function:

```
function map(f, x) is
begin
   if x = nil then
      return nil;
   else
      return cons(f(head(x)), map(f, tail(x)));
```

```
        end if;
      end map;
```

The higher-order function map has two parameters, a function f and a list x. If there is a function:

```
function timesTen(x) is
begin
   return 10 * x;
end timesTen;
```

then if aList is the list:

```
(17 24 59)
```

the effect of the call:

```
map(timesTen, aList)
```

would be to produce the list:

```
(170 240 590)
```

Execution of a purely functional program

Due to the absence of side-effects, the execution of a functional program can be viewed as replacing a function call by the corresponding body in which formal parameters have been replaced by actual parameters. This process is called **reduction** and can be shown by tracing the execution of the function call given in the previous example:

```
map(timesTen, (17 24 59))
=> cons(timesTen(17), map(timesTen, (24 59)))
=> cons(170, cons(timesTen(24), map(timesTen, (59))))
=> cons(170, cons(240, cons(timesTen(59),
   map(timesTen, nil))))
=> cons(170, cons(240, cons(590, nil)))
=> cons(170, cons(240, (590)))
=> cons(170, (240 590))
=> (170 240 590)
```

Replacing a function call by the corresponding body is referred to as the **application of a rewrite rule**.

9.2 Lisp

To most people outside the functional programming community, the language regarded as the archetypal functional programming language is Lisp, and so it comes as a surprise to find that Lisp is not a purely functional language. It does have a functional core and this is considered before some of its imperative features are examined.

One striking difference between Lisp and imperative languages is the simplicity of its syntax. In place of a large number of language constructs, Lisp has function application. Values to be manipulated by a Lisp program are known as **symbolic expressions** or **S-expressions**. An S-expression is an atom or a list where a list is written as a sequence of atoms or lists, separated by spaces and enclosed in brackets. The S-expression:

```
(TIMES 10 2)
```

is interpreted as applying the built-in function TIMES to the two numerical atoms 10 and 2.

Certain atoms in a Lisp system represent predefined functions while others represent what are called **special forms**. Special forms do not follow the usual rules of function application and, indeed, their effect often differs from one system to the next.

New functions can be defined using the special form LAMBDA. The function to multiply a value by 10 can, for example, be written as:

```
(LAMBDA (X) (TIMES 10 X))
```

An S-expression whose first element is LAMBDA is called a **LAMBDA expression**. The LAMBDA special form takes two parameters, in this case the lists (X) and (TIMES 10 X). The first parameter gives the parameters of the function being created while the second parameter gives the function body.

To give a function a name, the special form DEF is used, as in:

```
(DEF TIMESTEN (LAMBDA (X) (TIMES 10 X)))
```

DEF has two parameters. The first is an atom representing the new name and the second is a LAMBDA expression indicating the function to which the name is to be bound. The value of TIMESTEN is, therefore, a function. In some Lisp implementations, DEF takes as its parameter a list of functions to be defined. However, for the purposes here, it is assumed that DEF can only deal with one function at a time.

Lisp systems are normally interactive with functions being defined and then applied. For example, once TIMESTEN has been defined, either of the following two S-expressions could be used to multiply the number 2 by 10:

```
(TIMESTEN 2)
```

```
((LAMBDA (X) (TIMES 10 X)) 2)
```

A typical Lisp session will continue with the definition and application of other functions. As the definition of a function can use any existing function, complex new functions can be built up in a hierarchical manner.

In most imperative languages, expressions are written using infix notation. In Lisp, prefix notation is used. Hence, instead of A + B, the built-in function PLUS is used to add two numbers and it is written as (PLUS A B). The S-expression:

```
(PLUS A (TIMES B C))
```

corresponds to the infix expression A + B * C. There is no need in Lisp to define an order of evaluation of operators as all expressions are fully parenthesised. In the purely functional subset of Lisp, there is no assignment. Hence, once parameters such as X have been bound to a value in the call of a function, that value may not be changed.

The S-expression is central to Lisp. It is the only data structure in the language and a Lisp program is itself an S-expression. This allows Lisp functions to be manipulated or even created by other Lisp functions. Although it is a powerful feature of Lisp, this facility is not available in all functional languages, and so is not a central feature of functional programming.

Due to the importance of lists, quite a few of the predefined functions manipulate lists; for example CAR and CDR are the head and tail functions, and CONS is the list constructor function. The names CAR and CDR are not meaningful and are a hangover from the machine code instructions used to implement these functions in the first implementation of Lisp! The names head and tail are much more expressive.

When an S-expression such as (A B C) is written, it is interpreted as a request to apply the function A to the arguments B and C. To treat (A B C) as a list that can be passed as an argument to a function, the special form QUOTE must be used, as in:

```
(CAR (QUOTE (A B C)))
```

No attempt is now made to apply the function A and the function CAR is applied to the list (A B C). The result of the application is the atom A.

The use of QUOTE in this way allows a parameter to be passed over unevaluated and so is similar to call by name. The default mechanism in Lisp is call by value. Strictly speaking, numbers should also be quoted, as in:

```
(TIMESTEN (QUOTE 2))
```

but most Lisp systems do not insist on this. They also usually allow (QUOTE X) to be abbreviated to 'X.

The empty list is referred to by the special form NIL. Other predefined functions are the predicates or Boolean functions. ATOM tests if its argument is an atom, NULL tests if its argument is NIL, EQ compares two atoms for equality and NUMBERP tests if its argument is a numeric atom. The special form T represents true while NIL can be used to represent false.

Instead of the notation **if ... then ... else**, Lisp has the special form COND. This takes a list of pairs where the first element of each pair is a Boolean expression. COND is evaluated by evaluating the first element of each pair in turn until one is true. The result is the value of the corresponding second element of the pair. The following function to test for membership of a list of atoms makes use of COND:

```
(DEF ISMEMBER (LAMBDA (X A)
  (COND ((NULL A) NIL)
    ((EQ X (CAR A)) T)
    (T (ISMEMBER X (CDR A)))
  )
))
```

If the list A is empty, NIL (false) is returned, while if the head of the list is X, T is returned. If neither of these conditions is true the third condition T, which is always true, is evaluated and this leads to a recursive call of ISMEMBER where X is tested to see if it is a member of the tail of the list. The effect of evaluating:

```
(ISMEMBER 24 '(17 24 59))
```

will therefore be T.

The predefined function MAPCAR corresponds to the function map defined earlier. The effect of evaluating:

```
(MAPCAR 'TIMESTEN '(17 24 59))
```

is the list (170 240 590). An advantage of using higher-order functions such as MAPCAR is that they reduce the need to program recursion explicitly. Another useful function is LIST which takes a list of expressions and returns a new list, each of whose elements is the result of evaluating the corresponding element in the original list. The effect of evaluating:

```
(LIST (TIMESTEN 17) (TIMESTEN 24) (TIMESTEN 59))
```

is the same list as we obtained from our MAPCAR example.

Having looked at the functional core of Lisp, consider now the Lisp solution to a simple problem. Given an S-expression such as:

```
(TIMES 4 (POWER X 3))
```

the aim is to produce the S-expression that represents its derivative with respect to X, that is, in this case, to produce the list:

```
(TIMES 12 (POWER X 2))
```

The program should also be able to handle expressions in the form (POWER X 3), but to keep the program simple it is assumed that it only has to deal with correctly formed expressions and that special cases are dealt with normally. Hence the result of differentiating:

```
(TIMES 3 (POWER X 1))
```

will be:

```
(TIMES 3 (POWER X 0))
```

which when differentiated gives:

```
(TIMES 0 (POWER X -1))
```

The proposed solution in Lisp uses two functions, the first of which selects the third element from a list:

```
(DEF THIRD (LAMBDA (Y)
          (CAR (CDR (CDR Y)))
     ))
```

The main function DERIVE consists primarily of an example of the COND special form and carries out different actions depending on whether the first atom in the list Y is POWER or TIMES. The DERIVE function is given below followed by an explanation of its action through an example call:

```
(DEF DERIVE (LAMBDA (Y)
  (COND
    ((EQ (CAR Y) 'POWER)
    (LIST 'TIMES (THIRD Y)
      (LIST 'POWER 'X (DIFFERENCE (THIRD Y) 1))
    ))
    ((EQ (CAR Y) 'TIMES)
    (LIST 'TIMES (TIMES (CAR (CDR Y))
      (THIRD (THIRD Y))) (THIRD (DERIVE (THIRD Y)))
    ))
    (T 'ERROR)
  )))
```

Consider the call:

```
(DERIVE '(POWER X 4))
```

As the first element in the list is the atom POWER, this results in the evaluation of:

```
(LIST 'TIMES (THIRD Y)
  (LIST 'POWER 'X (DIFFERENCE (THIRD Y) 1)))
```

This gives a list whose first element is the evaluation of 'TIMES (that is, the atom TIMES), whose second element is the result of evaluating (THIRD Y), which is 4, and whose third element is the list obtained by evaluating:

```
(LIST 'POWER 'X (DIFFERENCE (THIRD Y) 1))
```

As (THIRD Y) is 4, the value of:

```
(DIFFERENCE (THIRD Y) 1)
```

is 3 and so the final result is the list:

```
(TIMES 4 (POWER X 3))
```

The reader should now trace the effect of the function application:

```
(DERIVE '(TIMES 4 (POWER X 3)))
```

Scope rules

Most imperative languages have static scope where the association of the use of an identifier with its declaration can be seen from the program text. Many versions of Lisp, on the other hand, have dynamic scope, where the use of an identifier is bound to its most recent definition during program execution.

In most circumstances in Lisp, static and dynamic scope have the same effect, but they can give different results with higher-order functions. For example, consider the following two definitions:

```
(DEF BASE (LAMBDA (F A)
   (PLUS (F 10) A)
))
(DEF TWODIGIT (LAMBDA (A B)
   (BASE '(LAMBDA (C) (TIMES A C)) B)
))
```

In the function definition:

```
(LAMBDA (C) (TIMES A C))
```

the atom A is what is called a **free variable**. As it is declared within function TWODIGIT, it might be expected to be bound to the value of the first parameter in a call of TWODIGIT. The effect of the function call:

```
(TWODIGIT 2 3)
```

would then be 23. However, this is not the result obtained. Application of the function TWODIGIT in fact gives:

```
(TWODIGIT 2 3)
=> (BASE '(LAMBDA (C) (TIMES A C)) 3)
=> (PLUS ((LAMBDA (C) (TIMES A C)) 10) 3)
```

It is only now that the LAMBDA expression is evaluated and the free variable A is associated with the most recent occurrence of A, that is, its appearance as a parameter of function BASE. As this A has been bound to the value 3, the effect of the function application is 33, not 23, giving:

```
=> (PLUS (TIMES 3 10) 3)
=> (PLUS 30 3)
=> 33
```

This problem would not have arisen if the atom *A* had not been used in two different contexts; for example, if BASE had been defined as:

```
(DEF BASE (LAMBDA (F X)
   (PLUS (F 10) X)
))
```

This shows that care must be exercised in writing higher-order functions in a language with dynamic scope if unexpected results are to be avoided.

Scheme

Scheme is a popular dialect of Lisp which has been very influential in the development of Lisp systems in general. Scheme programs are more readable than their Lisp counterparts, as Scheme makes use of more meaningful identifiers and special forms are replaced by reserved words. The reserved word DEFINE, for example, replaces the special form DEF, operators such as + and * replace PLUS and TIMES, the empty list is written as (), true and false are written as #T and #F respectively, and the convention with predicates is that the identifiers always end with ? as in ATOM?, NULL?, EQ? and NUMBER?.

Hence, the function TIMESTEN is defined in Scheme as:

```
(DEFINE TIMESTEN (LAMBDA (X) (* 10 X)))
```

The reserved word ELSE can be used in conditional expressions which leads to a more readable construct. The ISMEMBER function in Scheme becomes:

```
(DEFINE ISMEMBER (LAMBDA (X A)
  (COND ((NULL? A) #F)
     ((EQ? X (CAR A)) #T)
        (ELSE (ISMEMBER X (CDR A)))
   )
))
```

Two important features of Scheme are that it has a block structure, allowing the declaration of local identifiers, and that the scope rules are static.

Although LAMBDA expressions can be treated as ordinary values in Lisp and higher-order functions are possible, the full use of such features requires static scope rules since, as has been shown, dynamic scope can lead to unexpected results. A full discussion of higher-order functions is delayed until the section on ML as Scheme and ML deal with higher-order functions in essentially the same way.

Imperative features of Lisp

As has already been indicated, Lisp is not a purely functional language. It has, for example, two assignment operators SET and SETQ. The function call:

```
(SETQ A 'B)
```

will assign the symbolic atom B to A while:

```
(SET A 'C)
```

will assign the symbolic atom C to the value of A. When the value of A is the symbolic atom B, the effect of the function call (SET A 'C) is to assign the symbolic atom C to B. Note that the immediate effect of assignment is that the order of function application becomes important.

The connection between SET and SETQ is that the effect of:

```
(SET 'A 'B)
```

is the same as the earlier use of SETQ.

SET and SETQ are often used in conjunction with the PROG special form which has an arbitrary number of parameters. The first parameter is a list that defines local variables while the other parameters correspond to the statements of an imperative language. There is even a GO function which causes transfer of control to a label!

The following function uses the PROG feature to calculate the sum of the elements in a list X. It can be seen to have more in common with an imperative Pascal solution (with a rather unhelpful syntax) than with a functional solution. Writing the equivalent (and simpler) recursive function is left as an exercise.

```
(DEF SUMLIST (LAMBDA (X)
  (PROG (TOTAL)
    (SETQ TOTAL 0)
    LOOP
    (COND ((NULL X) (RETURN TOTAL))
      (T (SETQ TOTAL (PLUS TOTAL (CAR X)))
    ))
    (SETQ X (CDR X))
    (GO LOOP)
))))
```

Concluding remarks

For programmers brought up in the imperative style, Lisp programs are not easy to read. This has led to the suggestion that Lisp really stands for Lots of Infuriating Superfluous Parentheses. However, this situation has been ameliorated by modern Lisp systems which provide an editor to help ensure that the proper matching of brackets is achieved, and a pretty printer to lay out programs in a readable form. Modern dialects such as Scheme are also more readable due to their use of reserved words.

Lisp systems are interactive and support a development environment where new functions can easily be constructed, tested and modified. This gives many advantages, but one of the central themes in the construction of large reliable programs is that they should be easy to read, even if this means that they are more difficult to write. This is evident in both the design of imperative languages such as Ada and in how the languages are used. Lisp programs have the advantage of being much shorter than their equivalent imperative programs, but ease of understanding is not helped by many Lisp programmers who give mathematical conciseness a higher priority than software engineering concerns of ease of understanding.

Having an acknowledged language standard is another area where Lisp falls short. There are almost as many dialects of Lisp as there are of Basic, although there has been an attempt to make Common Lisp the standard. However, Common Lisp is very large and seems to combine the features of all other Lisp dialects rather than be selective.

Many Lisp systems treat function calls at the outermost level differently from inner calls. Hence, instead of writing (TIMES 10 2), it is possible to write TIMES (10 2) or use the predefined function EVAL and write:

```
EVAL(TIMES 10 2)
```

Before using a Lisp system, a programmer must discover how that particular system deals with such features. Although the differences may be minor they are off-putting to the novice or casual user.

9.3 FP systems

The FP language or, more correctly, group of languages have been proposed by Backus (1978) as an alternative to the Lisp style of functional programming. The intention behind FP is that it is a vehicle for new ideas rather than a language which is to be implemented and used.

Data values in FP are either atoms or sequences and the elements of a sequence can themselves be a sequence. Sequences are written in angular brackets with the elements separated by commas. A sequence in FP is therefore the counterpart of a list in Lisp.

FP systems are purely functional languages and so the only operations are the definition and application of functions. Application of a function G to a value X is written as G:X. Higher-order functions are replaced by what are known as **functional forms** which provide the main mechanism of creating new functions from existing ones. Functions themselves may not be higher order.

As an example of the use of a functional form, consider the following FP alternative to the Lisp MAPCAR higher-order function. (It is assumed that function TIMESTEN has already been defined.) Instead of:

```
(MAPCAR 'TIMESTEN '(17 24 59))
```

the functional form APPLYTOALL is used in FP to create a new function from the existing TIMESTEN. This new function can be given a name such as TIMESTENALL in a function definition:

```
DEF TIMESTENALL = APPLYTOALL TIMESTEN
```

The effect of the function application:

```
TIMESTENALL : <17, 24, 59>
```

is to apply the function TIMESTEN to each element in the sequence. Hence:

```
APPLYTOALL TIMESTEN : <17, 24 59>
=> <TIMESTEN : 17, TIMESTEN : 24, TIMESTEN : 59>
=> <170, 240, 590>
```

An interesting point to note in the definition of a function in FP is that there is no mention of parameters or variables. There is only the combination of functions. In fact, FP programs do not contain any variables.

Once all the elements have been multiplied by 10, the sequence containing all but the first element can be produced by using the above function combined with the tail function TAIL. The combination is performed by the **composition functional form** o.

```
DEF TAILTENS = TAIL o (APPLYTOALL TIMESTEN)
```

The effect of applying the function H o G to X is the same as first applying G to X and then applying H to the result. Hence, the effect of:

```
TAILTENS : <17, 24, 59>
```

is the same as:

```
TAIL : (APPLYTOALL TIMESTEN : <17, 24, 59>)
```

An FP system contains a set of primitive functions together with a set of functional forms. Existing functions can be combined using functional forms to create new functions, but it is not possible to define new functional forms. A function may only have one parameter, but as that parameter may be a sequence, this is not a restriction. The function +, for example, takes as its parameter a sequence of two numbers and returns their sum as a numeric atom.

To create interesting functions, the ability to make choices must exist. This is achieved in FP systems by the **condition functional form** which is written as →. Assuming that the function P is a predicate, the effect of:

```
(P→H; G) : X
```

is that if P : X is true, H is applied to X, otherwise G is applied to X. Another important functional form is **construction**. The result of the function application:

```
[F1, F2, ..., FN] : X
```

is the sequence:

```
<F1 : X, F2 : X, ..., FN : X>
```

These functional forms can be used to define, for example, a function ISMEMBER, which accepts a sequence consisting of a number and a sequence and determines if the number is a member of the sequence. Hence:

```
ISMEMBER : <3, <7, 3, 9>>
```

will give the value true as 3 is a member of the sequence <7, 3, 9>. The definition of ISMEMBER is:

```
DEF ISMEMBER = (NULL o SEC → F;
               (EQ o [HEAD, HEAD o SEC] → T;
               ISMEMBER o [HEAD, TAIL o SEC]))
```

The function SEC selects the second element of a sequence while HEAD selects the first element. T is a function which always returns the value true and F is a function which always returns the value false. The primitive function NULL tests if its argument is the empty sequence while EQ takes a sequence of two elements as its argument and tests if they are equal. Note again that the function definition consists solely of functions and functional forms.

The effect of the function application:

```
ISMEMBER : <3, <7, 3, 9>>
```

is to first evaluate:

```
NULL o SEC : <3, <7, 3, 9>>
```

to determine if the sequence being examined is empty. This evaluates to:

```
NULL : (SEC : <3, <7, 3, 9>>)
=> NULL : <7, 3, 9> => false
```

As the value is `false`, the following is now evaluated:

```
EQ o [HEAD, HEAD o SEC] : <3, <7, 3, 9>>
=> EQ : ([HEAD, HEAD o SEC] : <3, <7, 3, 9>>)
=> EQ : <HEAD : <3, <7, 3, 9>>,
     HEAD o SEC : <3, <7, 3, 9>>>
=> EQ : <3, HEAD : (SEC : <3, <7, 3, 9>>)>
=> EQ : <3, HEAD : <7, 3, 9>>
=> EQ : <3, 7> => false
```

As this also has the value `false`, the value of the function is obtained by evaluating:

```
ISMEMBER o [HEAD, TAIL o SEC] : <3, <7, 3, 9>>
=> ISMEMBER : ([HEAD, TAIL o SEC] : <3, <7, 3, 9>>)
=> ISMEMBER : <HEAD : <3, <7, 3, 9>>,
     TAIL o SEC : <3, <7, 3, 9>>>
=> ISMEMBER : <3, TAIL : (SEC : <3, <7, 3, 9>>) >
=> ISMEMBER : <3, TAIL : <7, 3, 9>>
=> ISMEMBER : <3, <3, 9>>
```

`ISMEMBER` is now applied to this new sequence and as the second Boolean expression gives the value `true` this time, the value returned by `ISMEMBER` is `true`.

The advantage of FP systems is that they are amenable to formal mathematical reasoning due to their regular and simple structure. On the other hand, they are too simple to be effective programming languages and their primary interest is as a vehicle for the radical re-examination of what languages need to contain. Their major impact is therefore on the design of more conventional functional languages.

9.4   Modern functional languages

ML is presented here as an example of a modern functional language. A continuing debate in computing science is over the importance of static typing. Lisp, Scheme and FP are dynamically typed, but functional languages, such as ML, can be fully type checked at compile time.

In ML, the definition of a function such as `Timesten` can be written as:

```
fun Timesten(n : int) : int = 10 * n;
```

When a function is defined, the ML system responds with its functionality which in this case is:

```
val Timesten = fn : int → int
```

that is, `Timesten` is a function that takes one integer parameter and returns an integer result.

Brackets are not necessary in function application and so the application of `Timesten` to the number 2 can either be written as `Timesten(2);` or as `Timesten 2;` which results in:

```
20 : int
```

being typed out – that is, both the the result and its type are given. As function application has higher precedence than addition, the result of `Timesten 2 + 3;` is 23. Brackets can, as usual, be used to alter precedence and so the result of `Timesten(2 + 3);` is 50.

An important feature of ML is that it has a **type inference system**. It is strongly typed, but the programmer does not always have to give the types as the system can work them out for itself. In the case of `Timesten`, the function can be written as:

```
fun Timesten(n) = 10 * n;
```

As 10 is an integer, the type of `n` and the type of the returned value must be `int` and so the ML system will respond, as before, with the functionality:

```
val Timesten = fn : int → int
```

However, it is often better to explicitly add type information as that can make a program easier to understand.

Names are bound to values in **value declarations** as in:

```
val ten = 10;
```

which causes the system to respond with:

```
val ten = 10 : int
```

A function is a value just as an integer constant is a value. An alternative way of defining `Timesten` is therefore:

```
val Timesten = fn n => 10 * n;
```

where:

```
fn n => 10 * n
```

is an example of a **function expression** which corresponds to a LAMBDA expression in Lisp or Scheme. In this case, the function expression defines an anonymous function which takes an integer parameter `n` and returns an integer result whose value is `10 * n`. In the value declaration, the function expression is bound to the name `Timesten`. The reason why the system described the functionality of `Timesten` as:

```
val Timesten = fn : int → int
```

should now be clear.

A function or LAMBDA expression can be used anywhere a function name can be used. Hence the calls in ML and Scheme:

```
(fn n => 10 * n) 2;
((LAMBDA (N) (* 10 N)) 2)
```

both give the result 20.

Lists

As one might expect, ML has lists as a built-in data structure together with functions such as hd, tl and cons (written as the right associative infix operator : :). Lists are written in square brackets and the elements are separated by commas as in [7, 3, 9] which is syntactic sugar for 7 : : 3 : : 9 : : **nil**. All the elements in a list must have the same type.

An IsMember function to check whether or not an integer is in a list of integers can be defined as:

```
fun IsMember(x : int, y : int list) : bool =
        if y = nil then false
        else if x = hd(y) then true
        else IsMember(x, tl(y));
```

The functionality of IsMember is:

```
val IsMember = fn : (int * (int list)) → bool
```

showing that the function takes two parameters, an integer and a list of integers (an int list) and returns a value of type bool. (Strictly speaking, functions in ML have only one parameter which, in the case of IsMember, is a pair consisting of an integer and a list of integers. It can, however, be convenient to refer informally to a function having more than one parameter.)

The above definition is not the usual way of defining a function in ML. Instead **pattern matching** is used. Lists can be classified as being empty or non-empty and IsMember can be defined using separate definitions for each of the two cases:

```
fun IsMember(x : int, nil : int list) : bool = false
  | IsMember(x : int,
                first :: rest : int list) : bool =
        if x = first then true
        else IsMember(x, rest);
```

The appropriate definition is selected by pattern matching of the parameters. The symbol nil is the pattern representing the empty list and so if the list being examined is empty, the result of the function is false. The pattern first : : rest represents a non-empty list as it has at least one element, namely first. Due to the properties of the : : operator, the parameter first must represent the head and rest must represent the tail of the list.

Consider now the function call:

```
IsMember(3, [7, 3, 9]);
```

The second definition is selected with the head of the list, 7, being matched with first and the tail, [3, 9], with rest. As the value of x = first is then false, IsMember is applied to the tail of the list. In this second call of IsMember, the head of the list is 3 and so true is returned. If the call had been

```
IsMember(3, [7, 6, 9]);
```

then the first definition would eventually be selected giving the result `false`.

In our earlier definitions of `IsMember` in dynamically typed languages, the function was defined for lists of any type. For full static type checking, the only concern with `IsMember` is that the type of the item being searched for is the same as the type of the elements in the list. The type inference system of ML can infer this requirement from the definitions, allowing a general `IsMember` function to be written as:

```
fun IsMember(x, nil) = false
  | IsMember(x, first :: rest) =
      if x = first then true
      else IsMember(x, rest);
```

The functionality is now:

```
val IsMember = fn : (''a * (''a list)) → bool
```

indicating that if the first parameter is of type `''a`, then the second parameter must be of type `list of ''a`, where `''a` is what is known as a **type parameter**. There are two kinds of type parameter in ML, written with a single or with two quotes. The difference is that a type parameter of the form `''a` can only be substituted by a type for which equality of values can be tested.

Functions which can take parameters of more than one type are said to be **polymorphic**. Although generic functions in Ada are similar, they have to be instantiated with an actual type before they can be applied, as we saw in Section 6.6. This is not necessary in ML as `IsMember` can be applied directly. Therefore, the test whether a character is present in a list of characters would be written:

```
IsMember("a", ["a", "e", "i", "o", "u"]);
```

Higher-order functions

Higher-order functions are central to ML which, like Scheme, has static scope rules. As an example of a higher-order function, consider:

```
fun map(f, nil) = nil
  | map(f, first :: rest) =
      f(first) :: map(f, rest);
```

The functionality of `map` is:

```
val map = fn : (('a -> 'b) * ('a list)) → ('b list)
```

that is, the first parameter of `map` is a function which has a `'a` parameter and returns a `'b` result while the second parameter is a `'a list` and the returned value has type `'b list`.

The effect of the application:

```
map(Timesten, [17, 24, 59]);
```

is to print out:

```
[170, 240, 590] : int list
```

As has already been stated, functions in ML take only one parameter. Consider now the function:

```
fun Times m n : int = m * n;
```

Its functionality is:

```
val Times = fn : int → (int → int)
```

that is, Times takes one integer parameter and its result is a function which takes an integer and returns an integer. The structure of this function may be more clearly seen using a functional expression:

```
fun Times m = fn n : int => m * n;
```

The result of the function call Times 10; is the function:

```
fn n : int => 10 * n
```

This function can, in turn, be applied to an integer as in:

```
(Times 10) 2;
```

which gives the result 20. Function Timesten may now be defined as:

```
val Timesten = Times 10;
```

The equivalent definitions of TIMES and TIMESTEN in Scheme are:

```
(DEFINE TIMES (LAMBDA (M) (LAMBDA (N) (* M N))))
(DEFINE TIMESTEN (TIMES 10))
```

Function map can be re-written in this notation:

```
fun map f nil = nil
  | map f (first :: rest) =
      f(first) :: map f rest;
```

Its functionality is now:

```
val map = fn : ('a -> 'b) -> (('a list) → ('b list))
```

that is, its parameter is a function which takes a 'a and returns a 'b and its returned value is a function which takes a 'a list and returns a 'b list.

A function to multiply all the elements in a list by 10 can now be defined as:

```
val Timesten_all = map Timesten;
```

The result of Timesten_all([17, 24, 59]); is the list [170, 240, 590].

In the section on FP, functions were composed using the functional form o. This is also allowed in ML, where we have the compose operator o. Function Tailtens can be defined as:

```
val Tailtens = tl o Timesten_all;
```

The result of Tailtens([17, 24, 59]); is the list [240, 590]; that is, the result of first applying Timesten_all to the list and then applying tl to the result.

Data types

The ability to construct data types is a powerful feature of ML. Data types are not defined by how they can be represented, but by the constructor operations used to construct them, together with the definitions of selector operations used to manipulate and examine them.

This is best illustrated by looking at the standard example of a stack. A new type is defined by having a **datatype** declaration where a type is defined in terms of its constructors. For a stack with items of an unspecified type, this might be written:

```
datatype 'a stack = new_stack
        | push of ('a * 'a stack);
```

Here, a stack has been defined in terms of the constructors new_stack, which represents a new empty stack, and push, which has two parameters and is the means of constructing a new stack from an item and an existing stack. The functionality is given as:

```
datatype 'a stack = new_stack | push of 'a * ('a stack)
con push = fn : ('a * ('a stack)) → ('a stack)
con new_stack = new_stack : 'a stack
```

The definition of the stack is completed by defining top, which returns the top element of a stack, pop, which returns the stack obtained by removing the top element, and is_empty, which tests to see if the stack is empty. The definitions are:

```
exception top_err;

fun pop(new_stack) = new_stack
  | pop(push(a, b)) = b;

fun top(new_stack) = raise top_err
  |top(push(a, b)) = a;

fun is_empty(new_stack) = true
  | is_empty(push(a, b)) = false;
```

The two patterns to be matched are: new_stack, which represents an empty stack and push(a, b), which represents a stack with at least one item. Consider the definition:

```
top (push(a, b)) = a
```

This states that if we have a stack constructed by pushing a onto an existing stack, then the top element of the resulting stack is a.

A stack value can be bound to a name as in:

```
val s1 = push(29, push(4, new_stack));
```

The result of top(s1); is then 29. It is an error to try to find the top element of an empty stack. ML allows exceptions to be declared and then raised as was shown in the definitions of the exception top_err and the function top. The effect of calling top(new_stack) is that the system reports an error with the message:

```
Failure: top_err
```

The definitions of pop, top and is_empty, together with the constructors push and new_stack, fully define a stack without giving any representation information. Such an approach can be difficult for imperative programmers to get used to as the definition of a stack and its associated operations in a language like Ada or Java can only be given in terms of some concrete representation. The above set of definitions can be considered as the specification of a stack. The power of ML is that, once the full specification has been given, then that is the solution.

Lazy evaluation

In ML and Lisp, parameters are called by value, that is, the parameters are evaluated before being passed to a function. It can, at times, be useful for parameters to remain unevaluated until they are required. This is called **lazy evaluation** and is similar to call by name in Algol 60.

With lazy evaluation, infinite data structures become possible. Consider the following function definitions:

```
fun generate100(m) =
    if m <= 100 then m :: generate100(m + 1)
    else nil;

fun lowsquares(nil) = nil
  | lowsquares(first :: rest) =
    if first <= 5 then
        first * first :: lowsquares(rest)
    else nil;
```

Function generate100 generates a list of the integers from m to 100 inclusive. Function lowsquares takes a list of integers and generates a list of squares, stopping when either the end of the list is reached or when an integer greater than 5 is encountered. Using call by value, the function application:

```
lowsquares(generate100 1);
```

is very inefficient as it first generates the list of integers from 1 to 100 and then only uses the first few in producing the list of squares.

Using lazy evaluation, function generate100 only generates those integers required by lowsquares, the rest of the list remains unevaluated. Consider now the function:

```
fun generate(m) = m :: generate(m + 1);
```

which generates an *infinite* list of integers. With lazy evaluation this is no problem and the call

```
lowsquares(generate 1);
```

produces the list of the first five squares while, of course, using call by value, it would lead to infinite recursion.

Lazy evaluation allows interactive I/O to be implemented in a purely functional language. Data to be input can be considered as a list. The current input is the head of the list while the rest of the list (which has not yet been input) is left, as yet, unevaluated.

The language described in this chapter is referred to as Standard ML and it does not support lazy evaluation. A lazy version of ML, called LML has been produced (Johnsson, 1984). The language Haskell also uses lazy evaluation.

Summary

The main differences between ML and Scheme are:

- Static strong typing: this gives the advantage that many errors are found at compile time instead of run time. As such errors are often logical errors, debugging is made much easier. Furthermore, the existence of polymorphic functions removes many of the restrictions that arise with static typing in conventional imperative languages.

- Pattern matching: using pattern matching as an alternative to conditional expressions allows the different parts of a function definition to be given separately. This both makes it easier to construct the definitions and leads to a layout which is much easier to read and understand than Lisp's nested parentheses.

- Data types: there are similarities in the definition of data types in ML and Ada but their definition in ML is at a much higher and abstract level.

9.5 Concluding remarks

Functional languages are a major vehicle for Computing Science research into new language features and concepts. Their simple mathematical form is both attractive to theoreticians and provides a good foundation on which to build and experiment with new ideas. A downside of this is the large number of functional languages, many of which are only used within the organisation in which they were created.

Another strand of research is the demonstration that everything can be done in a purely functional way. Haskell, for example, even achieves interactive input and output without the use of side-effects. Also, early implementations of functional languages were criticised for being much slower than their imperative counterparts. This has led to a great deal of research into the efficient implementation of functional languages so that it is no longer really an issue.

Lisp has been widely used in artificial intelligence for several decades, but is not regarded as a functional language by functional programmers because its users make heavy use of side-effects. However, with the exception of Lisp, functional languages are little used outside universities or research groups. The reasons for this have been discussed by Wadler (1998) who suggests that a major reason is that researchers have concentrated their efforts on the development of new systems and on program analysis. He suggests that more emphasis should be placed on providing support for the application of existing systems and on software development methods. Object-oriented analysis and design methods are an important complement to object-oriented programming, but there seems to be little corresponding work in the functional programming field.

This situation could change. The simple structure of functional languages and their lack of side-effects make them amenable to mathematical reasoning. This could make them increasingly important in the development of secure safety-critical systems. They can also be used in the specification and design phases of the software life cycle where the aim is to provide a precise definition of what is to be achieved. As the resulting specifications and designs are executable, they can be used in rapid prototyping, where the aim is to provide an initial solution that has the correct effect and can be used to test a design. The experience gained in producing the prototype can then be used to help in the design of an efficient full implementation.

Another consequence of their lack of side-effects is that functional languages are much more amenable to having their different parts securely executed in parallel. The language Erlang (Armstrong *et al.*, 1996) was specifically designed for building robust distributed and concurrent systems and perhaps points the way to the future for functional languages.

Summary

1. A program written in an imperative language achieves its effect by changing the values of variables by means of assignment statements. A functional program, on the other hand, achieves its effect by creating new values by the evaluation of expressions.

2. As side-effects cannot occur in a purely functional language, calling a function with a certain parameter will always give the same answer. This is called referential transparency.

3. A functional program consists of function definitions and expressions that involve application of the functions.

4. Functional languages are much better at dealing with structured values, such as lists, than are imperative languages.

5. Most functional languages allow functions to accept functions as parameters and to return functions as results. Such functions are said to be higher-order functions.

6. Values manipulated by a Lisp program are known as S-expressions. An S-expression is an atom or a list of S-expressions.

7. Expressions in Lisp are fully parenthesised and prefix notation is used rather than conventional infix notation.

8. Lisp is not a purely functional language, as assignment is possible.

9. FP is a purely functional language and was designed as a vehicle for trying out new ideas in functional programming. Functional forms are used to create new functions.

10. FP function definitions contain neither parameters nor variables. It is only possible to have a combination of functions.

11. An advantage of FP systems is that they are amenable to formal mathematical reasoning. This is due to their regular and simple structure.

12. ML and Scheme have static scope rules which means that they can make full use of higher-order functions.

13. ML differs from Lisp and FP in that it can be fully type checked at compile time. The programmer does not, however, have to specify all the types, as ML has a type inference system which determines what the types must be.

14. Functions are defined in ML by a set of alternative definitions which cover all possible cases. The appropriate definition is chosen by means of pattern matching.

15. Instead of the generics of Ada, ML supports polymorphic functions.

16. Lazy evaluation allows interactive I/O to be implemented in a purely functional language such as Haskell.

Exercises

9.1 It is possible to write programs in a functional subset of Ada. What features would have to be added to Ada to make it a useful functional language? What features should be removed?

9.2 What properties of functional languages make them better able to exploit the parallelism which results from multiprocessor systems than is possible with imperative languages?

9.3 What is the difference between predefined functions and special forms in Lisp?

9.4 Evaluate by reduction, the function applications:

```
(ISMEMBER 24 '(17 24 59))  (Lisp)
IsMember(24, [17, 24, 59])  (ML)
```

9.5 Describe the difference between static and dynamic scope rules. Under what circumstances will they lead to different results?

9.6 Why are languages like Lisp and ML better able to solve problems which require the manipulation of lists than languages such as Pascal and Java?

9.7 Compare functional forms in FP with higher-order functions in Lisp.

9.8 What are the differences between polymorphic functions in ML and generic functions in Ada?

9.9 Write ML and Scheme functions to:

(a) sum the elements in a list of integers,

(b) determine the length of a list,

(c) take a list of integers and return the list from which the negative numbers have been removed.

What is the functionality of each of these functions?

9.10 Construct a higher-order function `filter` which takes a list and returns the list containing only those elements for which a certain condition holds. Hence, if ge0 was a Boolean function to determine if an integer was greater than or equal to 0, the function `filter ge0` would be an answer to question 9.9(c). What is the functionality of `filter`?

9.11 Using the ML definition of a stack as a guide, define a queue data type where elements join the queue at one end and leave the queue at the other end.

9.12 A Lisp program to differentiate a simple expression has been given. Give an implementation in ML.

9.13 Define an ML function `generate10` which generates a list of integers from m to 10 inclusive. Using the definition of `lowsquares` given in the text, evaluate by reduction, the function application :

```
lowsquares(generate10 1);
```

(a) without lazy evaluation,

(b) using lazy evaluation.

Bibliography

Detailed descriptions of functional programming are given by Reade (1989) and Thompson (1999) who use ML and Haskell respectively as their main language.

There are many textbooks on Lisp. The book by Winston and Horn (1988) uses the Common Lisp dialect which is the nearest there is to a standard version of the language. A very influential book on the teaching of programming using Scheme is by Abelson and Sussman (1985). The Revised Report on Scheme is given in Kelsey et al.(1998).

The paper by Backus (1978) has been very influential. As well as introducing FP, it gives a critique of the advantages of the functional style over imperative von Neumann based languages. A description of modern functional languages, including purely functional languages such as Haskell and Miranda, is given by Hudak (1989). The version of ML described in this chapter is known as Standard ML (Milner et al., 1997). Functional programming in Erlang is described in Armstrong et al.(1996).

Abelson, H. and Sussman, G.J. (1985). *Structure and Interpretation of Computer Programs*. MIT Press.

Armstrong, A., Virding, R., Wikstrom, C. and Williams, M. (1996). *Concurrent Programming in Erlang* (Second Edition). Prentice Hall.

Backus, J. (1978). 'Can Programming be Liberated from the Von Neumann Style?'. *Comm. ACM*, **21**, 613–641.

Hudak, P. (1989). 'Conception, Evolution, and Application of Functional Programming Languages'. *ACM Computing Surveys*, **21**, 359–411.

Johnsson, T. (1984). 'Efficient Compilation of Lazy Evaluation'. *ACM SIGPLAN Notices*, **19**(6), 58–69.

Kelsey, R., Clinger, W. and Rees, J. (1998). 'Revised Report on the Algorithmic Language Scheme'. *ACM Sigplan*, **33**(9), 26–76.

Milner, R., Tofte, M., Harper, R. and MacQueen, D. (1997). *The Definition of Standard ML - Revised*. MIT Press.

Reade, C. (1989). *Elements of Functional Programming*. Addison-Wesley.

Thompson, S. (1999). *Haskell: The Craft of Functional Programming*, (Second Edition). Addison-Wesley.

Wadler, P. (1998). 'Why No One Uses Functional Languages'. *ACM Sigplan*, **33**(8), 23–27.

Winston, P.H. and Horn, B.K.P. (1988). *Lisp* (Third Edition). Addison-Wesley.

Logic programming

....

Logic programming is almost synonymous with Prolog. Indeed, the name Prolog stands for PROgramming in LOGic. This chapter is, therefore, mainly concerned with the Prolog language. The approach that Prolog takes to logic programming means that it is primarily concerned with goal-oriented programming. This is very different from problem solving in a procedural or object-oriented language and can cause difficulties when programmers experienced in these languages first encounter Prolog.

The chapter opens with a discussion of the goal-oriented approach of Prolog. The basics of Prolog are then illustrated by means of an example program that defines family relations. This example is then extended to show how unification, backtracking, recursion, negation, data abstraction and information hiding are handled.

Backtracking is an important feature of Prolog and the use of the cut operation to control this process is examined.

Finally, a Prolog program that performs simple symbolic differentiation is presented.

10.1 The Prolog approach

The majority of programming languages concentrate on **how** operations are carried out. Prolog, on the other hand, is concerned with **what** is to be done. It is **goal oriented**; that is, the programmer defines the problem to be solved – the goal. The programmer is not expected to give a detailed solution of how such a goal can be achieved; this is left to the Prolog system itself. Such a design feature has evolved in part because Prolog was developed in an artificial intelligence environment where practitioners are encouraged to think in terms of the goals rather than the means of satisfying such goals.

A Prolog program describes how a goal can be satisfied by giving a list of subgoals whose achievement will result in the fulfilment of the goal. As alternative subgoals can be provided, there may be more than one way in which a goal may be achieved. A subgoal may be an assertion, which evaluates to either true or false, or, alternatively, achieving a subgoal may require the Prolog system to generate and then try to achieve further subgoals.

Execution of a Prolog program, therefore, amounts to trying to satisfy a goal. It starts by trying to satisfy the list of subgoals and, if failure occurs, it **backtracks** and tries an alternative set of subgoals. If the system runs out of alternatives, then it has failed to achieve the goal. The power of Prolog lies in the fact that the selection of goals and backtracking are built in, while in most other languages such operations would have to be explicitly programmed.

Prolog programs have both a **declarative** and a **procedural** meaning. The declarative (or descriptive) meaning is concerned with the objects and their relationships, as defined by the program. The procedural meaning is concerned with how and in what order such relationships are evaluated to obtain a solution. Ideally, programmers should restrict their attention to the declarative meaning and leave the matter of the efficiency of the search processes to the implementation. That leads to much shorter and more easily understood programs. Unfortunately, there are many situations where the order of evaluation is important for reasons of efficiency and so, in practice, the purely declarative approach is not sufficient.

Prolog programs are significantly slower than programs written in traditional imperative languages, but it is possible that, in the future, efficient Prolog implementations will be provided by re-examining basic computer architecture. Just how successfully new computer architecture can be designed to support logic languages like Prolog is, however, still a matter of speculation.

10.2 The basics of Prolog

This section gives an overview of Prolog, looking at its basic mechanisms and illustrating them by an example. Problem solving in Prolog is achieved by identifying the basic objects to be manipulated and describing the relationships between these objects. This is accomplished using **facts** and **rules**.

- The facts about objects are declared to be always true.
- The rules about objects and their relationships state that a statement is true if certain stipulated goals and subgoals are satisfied.

Finally, a Prolog program can be asked **questions**. These questions are about objects and their relationships and are concerned with the satisfying of goals. A question may be concerned with a single goal or a series of goals. In some circumstances, more than one answer will satisfy the goals and Prolog can be programmed to find as many solutions as the programmer desires, and are available.

To illustrate how Prolog programs are written, here is an example that defines family relations. The details of the family can be described by the following facts:

```
male(philip).
female(elizabeth).
male(charles).
female(anne).
male(andrew).
male(edward).
female(diana).
male(william).
male(harry).
parents(charles, elizabeth, philip).
parents(anne, elizabeth, philip).
parents(andrew, elizabeth, philip).
parents(edward, elizabeth, philip).
parents(william, diana, charles).
parents(harry, diana, charles).
```

where `parents(A, B, C)` means the parents of **A** are mother **B** and father **C**. Such facts can be represented in many different ways. For example, instead of:

```
parents(charles, elizabeth, philip).
```

the following two binary relationships could be used:

```
mother(charles, elizabeth).
father(charles, philip).
```

Similarly `male(philip)` could be expressed as the binary relationship:

```
sex(philip, masculine).
```

The information on this family can be extended by adding new facts and also by adding rules. For example, the concept of a person being someone's brother can be introduced. This could be defined by the following rule:

```
brother(X, Y):- male(X),
                parents(X, M, F),
                parents(Y, M, F).
```

This rule should be interpreted as stating that if it is the case that the result of evaluating all three subgoals:

```
male(X),
parents(X, M, F),
parents(Y, M, F).
```

which make up the **body** of the rule is true, then it is the case that the result of evaluating the **head** of the rule:

```
brother(X, Y)
```

is also true. Note that the commas between the conditions are the same as the logical **and**. Note also that Prolog has the convention of starting variables with capital letters and values with lower case letters. As there is no assignment, variables in Prolog are different from variables in an imperative programming language like Pascal. They correspond more closely to Pascal parameters than to Pascal variables.

Questions, unification and backtracking

A Prolog program can be asked questions at any stage. Writing:

```
?- parents(william, diana, charles).
```

asks the question 'Is it the case that the parents of **william** are **diana** and **charles**?'. In this case, the answer to the question is 'yes' as the question can be matched to one of the sets of facts.

Facts, rules and questions are examples of **clauses** in Prolog. A Prolog program consists of a set of clauses with each clause being terminated by a full stop. A clause is considered to have a **head** and a body. Facts are clauses with a head but no body; questions have no head only a body; and rules have both a head and a body. The body part of a clause gives a list of the subgoals. If it is a question, then it asks if such goals are true; if it is a rule, then it is defining the goals that can be satisfied to make the clause head true.

Here is a slightly more complicated question:

```
?- brother(edward, anne).
```

The Prolog proof process involves generating subgoals and instantiating (that is, re-placing) Prolog variables by values. Using the rule:

```
brother(X, Y) :- male(X),
                 parents(X, M, F),
                 parents(Y, M, F).
```

the substitutions **X** ← **edward** and **Y** ← **anne** are made and the following subgoals attempted:

```
male(edward),
parents(edward, M, F),
parents(anne, M, F).
```

The first subgoal is true, as it matches one of the facts. The program must now find values for **M** and **F** so that it can match:

```
parents(edward, M, F)
```

Matching this subgoal to the fact:

```
parents(edward, elizabeth, philip)
```

causes the substitutions **M** ← **elizabeth** and **F** ← **philip**. The same substitutions for **M** and **F** must be made in the third subgoal giving:

```
parents(anne, elizabeth, philip)
```

which can be seen to match one of the facts. As the three subgoals have been satisfied, so has the original goal. The process of finding a suitable set of values which can be substituted for variables, so that a goal can be matched to a fact or to the head of a rule, is called **unification**. The matching used by Prolog systems does not exactly correspond to unification in logic. However, the differences are minor and subtle.

Straightforward questions such as the one just examined would be of little interest in a general problem-solving situation and the questions asked would almost certainly contain variables. Thus, a question like:

```
?- brother(X, anne).
```

would require a slightly more complex matching process, since it requires a value for **X** that satisfies the goal. After making the substitution **Y** ← **anne**, the subgoals are:

```
male(X),
parents(X, M, F),
parents(anne, M, F).
```

The first fact with which **male(X)** can be matched is **male(philip)**. Therefore, the substitution **X** ← **philip** is made and the following goal attempted:

```
parents(philip, M, F)
```

As there is no fact that matches this goal, it fails. The program must now backtrack and attempt an alternative way of achieving the goal **male(X)**. This time, the substitution **X** ← **charles** is tried, which satisfies both the subgoals **male(charles)** and **parents(charles, M, F)** as one of the facts is:

```
parents(charles, elizabeth, philip)
```

As the third subgoal matches the fact:

```
parents(anne, elizabeth, philip)
```

the Prolog system will respond with something like:

```
X = charles
```

If a semicolon is typed in response to this answer, the system will attempt to find further matches for the original question by backtracking to find other ways of matching the subgoals. In this case, the other answers are **andrew** and **edward**. The semicolon is the logical **or** and can be used elsewhere in Prolog with this meaning.

An alternative to asking 'Who is the brother of **anne**?' is 'Who is **edward** the brother of?'.

```
?- brother(edward, X).
```

The matching process will again give the answer:

```
X = charles
```

If the system is asked for further matches, it will eventually give the match **edward**. Such a result means that the original rule for brother(X, Y) was insufficiently specified, and it must be redefined to exclude people being considered brothers of themselves.

As backtracking is such an intrinsic part of Prolog, here is a more complicated example to show how the backtracking process operates. Suppose that the facts are:

```
mother(jane, george).
father(john, george).
brother(bill, john).
```

and the rules are:

```
parent(X, Y) :- mother(X, Y).
parent(X, Y) :- father(X, Y).
uncle(Z, Y) :- parent(P, Y), brother(Z, P).
```

If the goal is:

```
?- uncle(X, george).
```

the steps in the solution process are as follows.

1. The substitutions **Y ← george** and **Z ← X** result in the subgoals:

```
parent(P, george), brother(X, P).
```

2. Using the rule:

```
parent(X, Y) :- mother(X, Y).
```

the goal **mother(P, george)** is attempted and, as this is matched by the fact mother(jane, george), the substitution **P ← jane** takes place.

3. The subgoal **brother(X, jane)** is now attempted, but it fails as there is no fact with which it can be matched.

4. The system must now backtrack to **parent(X, Y)** and try the alternative rule:

```
parent(X, Y) :- father(X, Y).
```

The goal is now **father(P, george)** and this is matched by the fact **father(john, george)** and so **P ← john**.

5. The goal **brother(X, john)** is now attempted, which is matched with the fact **brother(bill, john)** giving **X** ← **bill**.

6. The goal in the original question is now satisfied since both its subgoals are satisfied. The Prolog system will respond with something like:

```
X = bill
```

An important factor in all backtracking techniques is the ordering; in Prolog's case, the ordering of the subgoals and the facts. Order is necessary so that the search can be carried out systematically and to prevent the occurrence of infinite loops. Ordering also influences the speed of the searching process and good choices can have a considerable effect on the efficiency. For example, a good heuristic is to place those subgoals that are liable to be most difficult to satisfy as early as possible since this will normally reduce the amount of backtracking.

Recursion in Prolog

Recursion plays a central role in Prolog, as it does in functional languages. As with all recursive situations, there must be a rule to halt the recursion in addition to a recursive rule. For example, the rule:

```
child(X, Y) :- mother(Y, X).
child(X, Y) :- father(Y, X).
```

says that **X** is a child of a parent **Y**. Such a relation can be generalised to **X** is a descendant of **Y**, and this can operate over as many generations as necessary. In Prolog, descendant could be defined as follows:

```
descendant(X, Y) :- child(X, Y).
descendant(X, Y) :- child(X, Z),
                    descendant(Z, Y).
```

This defines both the recursive definition and the definition which halts the recursion. Both of these definitions are needed, since without the first one, the recursion will be infinite, while the first one alone is an incomplete and restricted definition of descendant. The two definitions are often considered together to form a *procedure*.

Negation

Some Prolog implementations provide **not** as a built-in procedure. If such a facility is available, it is used as a prefix operator, as in:

```
?- not typhoid(bill).
```

However, care must be taken in interpreting the answer to this question, as negation is not the same as in mathematics.

Prolog uses the **closed-world assumption** and thus assumes that all the facts about the world are included in the model. Anything not derivable is therefore false. When Prolog has to process **not typhoid(bill)**, it tries to prove that bill has typhoid and it then negates the result. The **not** goal therefore succeeds in two situations:

1. When **bill** has definitely not got typhoid.

2. When it cannot prove **bill** has typhoid.

The problem of using the closed-world assumption with negation is that the negation of anything not derivable is considered true.

10.3 Data objects

As in most languages, both simple and structured data objects are allowed in Prolog. Simple data objects are numbers and character strings (also known as **atoms**).

Chapter 7 showed how records in Pascal can be represented by a tree. Structured data objects in Prolog are also of this nature. The Pascal record:

```
type Name = packed array [1 .. 12] of Char;
     Fullname =
       record
          forename : Name;
          surname : Name
       end;

     Student =
       record
          person : Fullname;
          age : Integer
       end;
```

could be represented in Prolog as an object with the structure:

```
student(fullname(Forename, Surname), Age)
```

The name part of a structure in Prolog is called a **functor**. Hence, **student** and **fullname** are functors. The components of a structure are given in brackets.

A structure can be used in facts and rules, as in:

```
attends(student(fullname(mary, smith), 20), stirling).
attends(student(fullname(joe, brown), 25), stirling).
maturestudent(Surname) :-
    attends(student(fullname(Forename, Surname), Age),
       University), Age > 23.
```

Prolog can then be asked questions like:

```
?- maturestudent(X).
```

to which the answer is:

```
X = brown
```

A database can be built up from a collection of Prolog facts and the questioning facility used to query the database and the matching mechanisms used to retrieve structured information.

An important structure in Prolog is the list. It is defined using the special functor **.** as is shown in the following list representation, which is built from the four atoms **p**, **q**, **r** and **s**:

    .(p, .(q, .(r, .(s, [])))))

where **[]** represents the empty list. As lists are used so frequently in Prolog, a special notation is available. The above list can be written as:

    [p, q, r, s]

As is the case in functional languages, a Prolog list consists of a head, which may be any Prolog object, in this case **p**, and a tail which must be a list, in this case **[q, r, s]**. A list with the head **X** and the tail **Y** can be written as **[X | Y]**, which allows pattern matching operations on lists in the same way as is done with the **::** operator of ML. Prolog considers lists to be binary trees and the list **[p, q, r, s]** is represented as the tree shown in Figure 10.1.

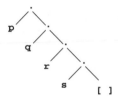

Figure 10.1   The structure of a list.

Prolog can be used to support the ideas of data abstraction and information hiding by means of what are called **selector relations**. Such relations are used to access components of a structure as illustrated in the following example which selects the **forename** of a **student**. The selector **forename** can be defined by means of the clause:

    forename(student(fullname(Forename, Surname),
        Age), Forename).

although, as the definition of **forename** does not depend on the values **Surname** and **Age**, this would normally be written as:

    forename(student(fullname(Forename,_),_), Forename).

where each occurrence of the underscore character represents a different (anonymous) variable.

In Prolog, the scope of a variable is restricted to the clause in which it is used. Hence, both occurrences of **Forename** refer to the same variable, but the identifier **Forename** has no significance outside this clause, and of course it has no connection with the functor **forename**. Conventional software engineering wisdom would suggest that it is inadvisable to use two identifiers that only differ in the case of their first letter. Such usage does, however, seem to be common practice in Prolog.

The result of asking the question:

```
?- S1 = student(fullname(john, smith), 18),
             forename(S1, X).
```

will be:

```
X = john
```

while the answer to:

```
?- attends(Person, stirling), forename(Person, mary).
```

is:

```
Person = student(fullname(mary, smith), 20)
```

This illustrates that once selectors such as **forename** have been defined, the user no longer needs to know about the structure of **student**. If, during the development of a program, the structure is changed, then all that is needed is a change to the definitions of selectors such as **forename**. Their use could continue unchanged. Hiding the representation of a structure in this way does, however, remove some of the advantages of pattern matching.

10.4 Efficiency in Prolog

From a theoretical standpoint, all the user needs to know about the execution of a Prolog question clause is that it terminates. It is not too difficult for logic languages to attain this goal in theory, but if they wish to be considered seriously as practical programming languages, they must do more than guarantee termination – they must search reasonably efficiently.

When Prolog is asked a question, a simple backtracking strategy is instituted which is normally **depth-first tree search** with subgoal evaluation from left to right. It is, therefore, of some importance to think about the order in which the goals are listed, as the ordering of the subgoals in a rule is likely to have a considerable bearing on its speed of execution. Such considerations are far from trivial and in complex search problems of the type likely to be encountered in an Expert System, the ordering and methods of searching are often the crux of the solution process.

Allowing automatic backtracking relieves the programmer of the problems of designing a detailed search algorithm. This is satisfactory in small problems or when the searching is not too deep. However, it soon becomes clear to a programmer that complete reliance on the Prolog search mechanisms produces some very inefficient programs. Prolog gives the programmer some control of the backtracking process by the **cut** facility. The cut operation, indicated in a Prolog program by **!**, is used to stop backtracking.

For example, consider the rules:

```
R :- G1, G2, !, G3.
R :- G4.
```

where **G1**, **G2**, **G3** and **G4** are goals and **!** is a cut (or pseudo-goal). When the cut is encountered, **G1** and **G2** will have already been satisfied. The cut ensures that they are frozen in that state, since no further backtracking is allowed. If goal **G3** fails, we will not therefore try to achieve either **G1** or **G2** in some other way. Furthermore, it will not consider the other rule for **R**; that is, it will not try to achieve goal **G4**.

One example where cuts are useful is in rules that have mutually exclusive clauses. A function which is $-1, 0, +1$ when its argument is negative, zero or positive, respectively, can be expressed in Pascal as:

```
if x < 0 then
    F := -1
else if x = 0 then
    F := 0
else
    F := +1;
```

The Prolog rules without cuts could be:

```
f(X, -1) :- X < 0.
f(X, 0) :- X = 0.
f(X, 1) :- X > 0.
```

but this could lead to unnecessary inefficiencies and backtracking due to the exclusive nature of the three clauses. A more efficient Prolog implementation would be:

```
f(X, -1) :- X < 0, !.
f(X, 0) :- X = 0, !.
f(X, 1).
```

Here, the use of cuts prevents the program from trying alternatives that cannot succeed. Hence, if the condition **X < 0** is satisfied, neither of the alternatives will ever be tried.

The objection to cuts is that they can change the nature of a Prolog program. Provided that it terminates, a Prolog program without cuts has the same declarative and procedural meaning. As has been seen, the procedures may be slow, but they will arrive at the correct answer. When cuts are included, there is no longer a guarantee that the declarative and procedural meanings are the same. When the use of cuts does not affect the declarative meaning, they are called **green cuts**. In other words, if the cuts are removed the answers will be unchanged, and so the cuts are achieving improved efficiency without any disadvantages. Cuts that affect the declarative meaning are called **red cuts**. The use of this type of cut is more dangerous and they can easily lead to errors since the program's meaning cannot be deduced from the program without cuts.

10.5 A Prolog example

Chapter 9 looked at a Lisp program that performed simple symbolic differentiation. This section looks at a Prolog solution to this problem.

Suppose that an expression such as:

```
4 * power(x, 3)
```

is to be converted into **12 * power(x, 2)** and:

```
power(x, 3)
```

to be converted into **3 * power(x, 2)**. To differentiate an expression **Y** with respect to **X**, giving the result **E**, the heads of the rules will have the form **derive(Y, X, E)**. A first attempt at the rules might be:

```
derive(A * F, X, A * C) :- integer(A), derive(F, X, C).
derive(power(X, N), X, N * power(X, N-1)) :- integer(N).
```

where the goal **integer(N)** succeeds when **N** is instantiated to an integer number. The first rule defines the derivative of **A * F** with respect to **X** (where **A** is an integer) to be **A** times the derivative of **F** with respect to **X**. The second rule defines the derivative of **power(X, N)** with respect to **X** to be **N * power(X, N - 1)**. These rules deal with the differentiation, but do not carry out the necessary arithmetic. Using these rules, the result of:

```
?- derive(4 * power(x, 3), x, E).
```

is:

```
E = 4 * (3 * power(x, 3 - 1))
```

Arithmetic is performed by means of the **is** operator. The effect of:

```
P is N - 1
```

is to evaluate the expression **N - 1** and associate its value with **P**.

The **is** operator is used in the following two modifications to the rules for **derive**:

```
derive(A * F, X, G * B) :-
    integer(A), derive(F, X, D * B), G is A * D.
derive(power(X, N), X, N * power(X, P)) :-
    integer(N), P is N - 1.
```

The required Prolog program is therefore short, although its effect is not immediately obvious. Consider the matching process for the question:

```
?- derive(4 * power(x, 3), x, E).
```

The aim here is to match this with:

```
derive(A * F, X, G * B)
```

which means that after the substitutions:

> **A ← 4, F ← power(x, 3)** and **X ← x**

the three subgoals to be achieved are:

> **integer(4), derive(power(x, 3), x, D * B)**
> and **G is 4 * D**

The first subgoal is achieved, but the second subgoal:

> **derive(power(x, 3), x, D * B)**

does not match with the first rule for **derive** and so Prolog tries to match it with the second:

> **derive(power(X, N), X, N * power(X, P))**

On making the substitutions:

> **X ← x, N ← 3, D ← 3** and **B ← power(x, P)**

the new subgoals are:

> **integer(3)** and **P is 3 - 1**

The goals **integer(3)** and **P is 3 - 1** (yielding **P ← 2**) are achieved. Prolog has, therefore, succeeded in matching **D * B** to:

> **3 * power(x, 2)**

The third of the original three subgoals is:

> **G is A * D**

and so **G** is 12. **E** has, therefore, been matched with:

> **12 * power(x, 2)**

The Prolog program to solve this problem is much shorter than the Lisp solution, which in turn is much shorter than a solution in an imperative language like Java. This is because much more of the processing is carried out behind the scenes by the Prolog system.

10.6 Concluding remarks

The newcomer can face problems in trying to acquire a Prolog programming style and technique. The book by Bratko (1999) includes a chapter on the subject and suggests that clauses should be short, with only a few goals in their body. The more general guidance in Bratko's book is not dissimilar from the advice on structuring a program that would be given to a new programmer using any language. Prolog does support the implementation of top-down design principles with the subgoals acting as subdivisions of the tasks. Each subgoal can then be subdivided again if further refinements are required.

Case analysis can be implemented conveniently by alternative rules or clauses for the same predicate. Since there is no such thing as a global variable in Prolog, the ideas of information hiding are easier to implement than in many procedural languages.

For many programmers, Prolog often poses readability problems, which is partly due to the fact that it can be highly recursive. Although recursion is a powerful and useful programming tool, it does not always aid the transparency of the code. Prolog also lacks a module structure to impose form and structure on programs. This seems an area where improvements are required.

Objections to Prolog have mainly come from three types of programmer. Firstly, the users of imperative languages have attacked its inefficiencies and claimed that it is unrealistic to consider Prolog as a serious language for the practical programmer. However, the speed of modern hardware means that Prolog, although still slower than other languages, is fast enough for many applications. Also, some of the inefficiency caused by the von Neumann architecture of traditional computers may be removed by new hardware configurations.

The second group of objectors are the orthodox mathematicians and logicians who find that the use of cuts and negation (based on the closed-world assumption) take Prolog away from the realm of a pure logic language. Their objection is valid, but misplaced, since programming languages are not pure mathematical objects, but practical tools for solving problems, and a pure logic language can never be that.

Finally, there initially were a lot of objections to Prolog from the artificial intelligence community. This is ironic because it is in AI that many of the most suitable applications for the language exist. The reason for such objections is probably due to the strong hold that languages like Lisp have for AI practitioners. It does seem that in the last few years there have been serious attempts to look at both functional and logic languages objectively and examine their strengths and weaknesses. Such moves are welcome and will help to remove the attitude of mind that sees Prolog and Lisp as competitors.

These two languages take different approaches to problem solving and should be viewed as alternatives rather than rivals.

Summary

1. Logic programming is almost exclusively carried out in Prolog.

2. Prolog is a declarative language and is goal oriented.

3. A program in Prolog consists of clauses, which can be of three types: facts, rules and questions.

4. Facts about objects are declared to be always true.

5. A rule about objects and their relationships gives the goals and subgoals that must be satisfied to make the head of the rule true.

6. Questions require a goal or series of goals to be satisfied and invoke a process of matching. If a goal fails, an alternative is tried by backtracking.

7. The operations of selecting goals and backtracking are carried out by the Prolog system itself. However, the efficiency of these operations can be influenced by the ordering of the subgoals in a rule.

8. Recursion is an important feature of many Prolog rules.

9. Prolog is well suited to problems in artificial intelligence.

10. Efficiency in Prolog can be improved by cuts, which are used to limit backtracking.

11. Prolog uses the closed-world assumption and assumes that anything not derivable is false.

Exercises

10.1 Using the facts and rules given at the beginning of Section 10.2 for family relations:

(a) Explain in detail how the goals in the following Prolog questions are achieved:

```
?- brother(william, harry).
?- brother(X, william).
```

(b) Define a rule for **sister** and show the steps in answering the questions:

```
?- sister(X, edward).
?- sister(X, william).
```

(c) How can the **brother** and **sister** rules be altered so that a person is not considered to be their own brother or sister?

10.2 Given the facts:

```
loves(john, jane).
loves(bill, jane).
loves(james, jane).
loves(mary, bill).
loves(jane, james).
```

and the rule:

```
goodmatch(X, Y) :- loves(X, Y), loves(Y, X).
```

show the backtracking involved in answering the question:

```
?- goodmatch(A, B).
```

10.3 Given the facts:

```
district(stirling, dunblane).
region(central, stirling).
country(scotland, central).
continent(europe, scotland).
```

define a rule whose head is **within(X, Y)** and which expresses the fact that **Y** is within the geographical region **X**. Show how this can be done using **district**, **region**, **country** and **continent**. How can the facts be redefined and recursion used to simplify the definition of **within**?

10.4 An object **X** is a member of a list **L** if **X** is the head of **L** or if **X** is a member of the tail of **L**. Use this definition of membership to define **member(X, L)** and then trace the actions required by the Prolog question:

```
?- member(X, [john, bill, fred, peter]), X = fred.
```

10.5 Compare and contrast functional languages, logic languages and object-oriented languages as exemplified by ML, Prolog and Java, respectively. Discuss areas in which they each have particular strengths and weaknesses.

10.6 Give an example to show how the ordering of the subgoals in a Prolog rule can make a significant difference in the efficiency of processing of a question.

10.7 Define the minimum function as two rules whose head is **minimum(X, Y, Minval)**. Give an initial definition without a cut and then show how its efficiency can be improved by using a cut.

10.8 Discuss the difference between green and red cuts and give an example of each.

10.9 Compare the use of pattern matching in ML and Prolog.

(**Bibliography**)————————————————————————————

An introduction to the use of logic in problem solving has been given by Kowalski (1979), whose ideas were a major influence in the development of Prolog.

   One of the most interesting books on Prolog is by Bratko (1999). The amalgamation of functional and logic programming languages has been actively researched. A review of that field with an extensive bibliography is given by Hanus (1994).

Bratko, I. (1999). *Prolog Programming for Artificial Intelligence* (Third Edition). Addison-Wesley.

Hanus, M. (1994). 'The integration of functions into logic programming'. *J. Logic Programming*, **19/20**, 583–628.

Kowalski, R. (1979). *Logic for Problem Solving*. North-Holland.

Chapter 11

Concurrency and networking

This chapter looks at the language features that are used to support concurrent and distributed processing. It starts with a description of the concepts involved and how processes can pass information to one another and synchronise their actions.

We do not only write concurrent programs so that they can run faster on parallel hardware. They are also used to deal with problems that require several separate tasks to be done at the same time. That does not require more than one processor as the operating system can allocate time slices to each of the tasks so that they only *appear* to be occurring in parallel.

Tasks often need to communicate with one another. The two main methods of communication are shared variables and message passing. This chapter looks at how the problems associated with shared variables can be overcome using critical regions and how this is implemented in Java and Ada 95. As an example of message passing, Ada 95 is discussed and it is shown how the rendezvous mechanism achieves both communication and synchronisation.

In a distributed system, computers communicate over a communications network. Networks are now central to the way computers are used and much of the appeal of Java is that it provides high-level support for network programming. We first consider Java applets and then look at distributed programming and how an object-oriented approach can ease the problems involved.

Finally, the chapter considers the problems encountered in real-time systems and the facilities that Ada 95 provides in this area.

(11.1) Introduction

During the execution of a sequential program, statements are executed one at a time in some predefined order. In a concurrent system, several program fragments are viewed as being executed in parallel. When several processors are available, this is called **multiprocessing**; when there is only one CPU, and so there is only pseudo-concurrency, this is called **multiprogramming**.

Each program fragment is called a **process** or a **task** and has its own **thread of control**. Even when there is only a single processor, it is conceptually easier to consider each thread as if it had its own separate processor.

Multiprocessing is important in certain application areas such as weather forecasting, but these areas form only a small part of the computer market. For many years, there has been a belief amongst some computer scientists that, in order to increase processing power, multiprocessors would become the dominant computer architecture. Programming languages with features to support parallel programming would therefore become of central importance. This has not happened. One reason is that CPUs have continued to increase significantly in power while dropping in cost. A second reason is that modern computers are in fact multiprocessor machines, but usually have a single CPU together with special purpose hardware to control disks, graphics, sound, etc. Multiprocessing of this nature is transparent to an applications programmer.

The use of networks has become of central importance and that does of course involve multiple CPUs. However the driving force of networking has been communication together with the desire to access and share resources rather than a need to increase processing speed. Making a program run faster is not therefore the only reason why we might want to construct concurrent programs. Indeed, if we have only one processor, a concurrent program will run more slowly than an ordinary sequential program due to the synchronisation and communication overheads.

Possible reasons for concurrent programming are:

- to make a program run faster when several processors are available;
- to handle several different tasks at the same time;
- to describe distributed programs, e.g. programs that communicate over a network;
- to ease the design process when a problem is most easily described in terms of a set of communicating concurrent objects.

We look briefly at each of these points before considering how the problems that arise can be handled. The purpose of this chapter is not to give a general introduction to the topic of concurrency, but to focus on the high-level language constructs that have been designed to support the concurrent and distributed execution of programs.

Parallel hardware

When several processors are available, an obvious use of concurrency is to make a program run faster. Often, the precise order in which certain program statements are to be executed is unimportant. For example, if a, b, c and d refer to different variables, and it is assumed that there is no aliasing, the order in which the assignments:

```
a := a + 5; b := d * 6; c := d - 94
```

take place does not matter; so, when we have three processors, the three statements could be performed in parallel. An optimising compiler can be used to determine which statements do not interfere with one another or, alternatively, this decision could be left to the programmer using a notation like the Algol 68 **collateral** statement. When statements in Algol 68 are separated by commas instead of semicolons, the order of execution is not specified. Hence, the statement:

```
begin
    a := a + 5, b := d * 6, c := d - 94
end
```

can be used as an indication to the compiler that code can be generated for parallel execution. However, care must be taken when using such constructs. As the statements in:

```
begin
    a := a + 5, b := d * 6, c := b - 94
end
```

are not independent of one another, the result depends on the precise order in which the assignments are carried out.

In general, identifying the components of a sequential program that can be correctly executed in parallel is far from easy due to the possibility of side-effects. That problem does not, of course, arise with purely functional languages as, due to referential transparency, the order in which expressions are evaluated does not matter.

A common situation in programming is a loop in which the same calculations are performed in turn on the different elements of an array as in:

```
for i := 1 to   100 do
    a[i] := 3 * b[i]
```

Although languages like Pascal impose an order on the processing of the elements in arrays a and b, the order does not in fact matter: given 100 processors, each of the 100 assignment statements could be performed in parallel.

High-performance computers sometimes include what are known as **array processors,** which allow the same operation to be applied simultaneously to different pieces of data – for example, array elements. In applications where a large amount of time is spent processing arrays, the use of an array processor can significantly speed up the processing.

Several extensions to Fortran have been designed to aid the identification of loops in which an array processor can be used, but the simplest language solution is to allow complete arrays as operands. The above loop would then reduce to the single statement:

```
a := 3 * b
```

which can be evaluated using a loop on a single processor machine, while it is clear that it is safe to perform the operations on each of the elements in parallel when an array processor is available. APL, which has many operations that act on complete arrays, is well suited for use with an array processor.

Other parallel architectures include **multiprocessor systems**, where a set of processors all share the same memory, but where each processor can act independently, and **distributed systems** where the processors do not share memory, but communicate over a **communications network**. The processors can be in the same room or be many miles apart. Examples of distributed systems are:

- a network of diskless workstations with a central file server;
- computers connected to the Internet through which they access a database.

Distributed systems introduce extra problems; as the processors become more distant, there is an increase in communication delays and in the possibility of communications failure. However, they support the creation of fault-tolerant systems because, when one processor in the network fails, work can be carried out on another.

Doing more than one thing at a time

Modern operating systems enable several different tasks to appear to be performed simultaneously. For example, many users may interact with a single computer or a single user at a personal computer may have programs running in different windows.

In a system with only one processor, only one process may be active at any given moment while all others are suspended. The speed of the computer allows each program to be given sufficient slices of time for it to appear to have sole control of the system. Operating systems usually use **pre-emptive scheduling** in which a process is **interrupted** after a fixed time so that another process can be scheduled.

When there are more processes ready to run than there are available processors, a scheduling algorithm is needed to decide which processes are to be chosen. In the multiprogramming case, only one processor is available and so the scheduling algorithm has to choose one process. Simple approaches to this problem include:

- allowing the process that has been waiting longest to go next, or
- attaching a priority to each process and allowing the process with the highest priority to be the one to proceed.

Whichever method is used, it is important that it allows what is called **fair scheduling** to operate, where all waiting processes are eventually given a chance.

Concurrency and process interaction introduce many new problems into programs, such as the management of shared resources and the possibility of deadlocks. Another major problem is that, when several processes are executing concurrently, it is not always possible to predict their relative speeds or, on a single processor system, the order in which they may be scheduled, and this may change with the system load. Running the same program with the same data may not, therefore, always give the same results. Such programs are said to be **non-deterministic** and are clearly very difficult to debug.

As the processes in a concurrent system need not be independent, there must be some means through which they can pass information to one another and through which their actions can be **synchronised**. For example, one process may have to wait for results to be produced by another process before it is able to continue. The usual assumption is that processes normally proceed independently and only interact with one another infrequently. We look at different approaches to process synchronisation and communication in Section 11.2.

Operating systems must be able to respond to external events. This will often require that the currently running process is interrupted and another process scheduled to handle the external event. This is especially important with real-time control systems where a system may, for example, have to react extremely quickly to sensor readings.

Other examples of external events include user interactions such as pressing a key on a keyboard or clicking a mouse. Most modern application programs are written to interact with their users through a **graphical user interface** (GUI). The user clicks on a button, selects an item in a menu or types data into a text box and so the application program must be able to receive and deal with events. Such programs are said to be **event driven**.

Traditionally, event handling was only the concern of low-level systems programmers, but graphical user interfaces have meant that event driven programming has moved from being an advanced topic to one that is taught in elementary courses. Thankfully, the operating system or a language's run-time system performs the low-level processing of the external events before passing them on to the appropriate application program. In that way, event handling can be dealt with at a level of abstraction that is understandable to the applications programmer. Typically, the program has an **event loop** in which it waits for an **event** such as a mouse click to occur so that it can be handled. In languages such as Java and Delphi, the programmer does not have to explicitly program the event loop as the languages provide direct support for event handling. We will look at this in detail in Chapter 13 where we deal with graphical user interfaces.

Networks

In offices, it is normal for computers to be connected through a **local area network** (LAN) which will then be connected to other networks. The Internet is the combination of all these networks. As it is now common for home computers to be connected to the Internet, we can consider computers to be no more than nodes on a network with inter-computer communication central to their use. For most users, use of a network is either transparent (files for example may be on a central file-server, but the operating system makes it appear as if they were on a local disk) or is through browsers such as Netscape or Internet Explorer. Users are therefore able to access information over a network without the need to know about new language features or concepts.

The implementation of these high-level services does require knowledge of special language features. A common approach in distributed systems programming is to have the concept of **clients** and **servers**, both of which may be considered to be objects. The client and server objects may exist on separate computers connected by a network. The client makes calls on methods offered by the remote server as if they were local calls. These local calls are then mapped onto calls of the methods in the remote server objects. We look at such an approach in Section 11.3.

Communicating concurrent objects

A set of communicating processes has many similarities with a set of communicating concurrent objects, where each object has a local state, local processing ability and communicates with other objects by message passing. In a sequential program, there is a single thread of control and we have **passive objects** which are only executed when one of their methods is called by another object. In a concurrent object-oriented program, we also have the concept of an **active object**, i.e. an object with its own execution thread. A concurrent system can be implemented as a set of active objects.

In Java, we talk about **multi-threading** as several threads of execution can occur in parallel. Java has a library class Thread that includes a method run, a method start to begin execution and a method stop to terminate execution. We can define an active object in Java either by instantiating a subclass of class Thread or by declaring an object that implements the Runnable interface. To implement this interface, an object must define a run method. We can therefore have a class ActiveC, defined as:

```
public class ActiveC  implements Runnable {
   ...
   // definition of a run method
   ...
} // ActiveC
```

An active object activeO can then be instantiated by passing an instance of class ActiveC to the Thread constructor:

```
Thread activeO = new  Thread(new ActiveC());
```

The activeO thread is started by the call activeO.start() which causes its run method to be executed. Execution of the activeO thread terminates either when we exit from its run method or when its stop method is called.

Delphi is very similar; an active object is an instance of a subclass of the abstract class TThread. A method execute, corresponding to run in Java, must be defined in the subclass. Several C++ libraries support threads, but as they are part of a C++ implementation rather than the C++ language, there is a lack of standardisation.

Concurrency in design

In many situations, the design of a program is most easily expressed in terms of a set of communicating concurrent objects, even when the resulting implementation is known to be sequential. A good example of this is simulation, which attempts to model a real-life situation in which several activities occur in parallel and interact with one another. When used in simulation, concurrency is not being used to promote efficiency; rather, it is being used because it leads to a more natural representation of the solution to a problem. The first language designed to support this approach to simulation was Simula, the original object-oriented language. The approach of object-oriented development is, therefore, well suited to concurrent as well as sequential systems.

11.2 Process synchronisation and communication

A simple way of achieving synchronisation is for a process to execute an instruction (often called a **wait instruction**) so that the process is suspended until another process sends a signal to wake it up. However, care must be taken to avoid a situation where two processes are each waiting for a signal from the other and so neither is able to continue. Such a situation is called a **deadlock**.

There are two main ways in which processes can communicate with one another: they can either access the same variable, called a **shared variable,** or they can send messages. A major problem with shared variables is when one process starts reading the value of a structured shared variable and, halfway through, the operating system schedules another process which updates the structured variable. When the first process is eventually resumed and reads the rest of the variable, the process will have inconsistent information.

This problem can be overcome by the notion of **critical regions** of programs within which access to shared variables takes place. At any one time only one thread of control may be executing a particular critical region. If a second thread wishes to enter the region, it is suspended until the first thread has left the critical region. This is called **mutual exclusion** and is often implemented by means of a **monitor** module, which provides procedures for the safe updating of shared variables. Communication using shared variables is obviously best suited to systems in which the threads physically share store.

Message passing is suited to distributed as well as to shared-memory systems. There are two approaches to message passing; synchronous and asynchronous. In **synchronous message passing**, synchronisation is achieved as well as communication because a sending process has to wait for its message to be accepted and a receiving process may have to wait for a message to be sent. Synchronous message passing was proposed by Hoare (1985) in the experimental language CSP (Communicating Sequential Processes) and is the basis for the Ada **rendezvous** mechanism.

In **asynchronous message passing**, the sending process continues execution after sending a message. Asynchronous message passing is more flexible, but gives the programmer less control over the order of events. It can be constructed from synchronous message passing primitives by the introduction of a buffer process to de-couple the two communicating processes.

We use the standard producer/consumer problem to illustrate how the passing of information and process synchronisation can be implemented in C, Java and Ada 95. A consumer process must wait for a piece of information to be produced while a producer process cannot pass a new piece of information until the previous piece has been consumed.

Unix pipes

C is a sequential language. Separate sequential C programs can, however, run concurrently and their effect combined by the use of the Unix **pipe** mechanism, where the output from one program becomes the input to another. Consider the Unix command:

```
A1 | A2 | A3
```

where A1, A2 and A3 are three programs and | represents a pipe. The output from program A1 becomes the input to program A2, and the output from A2 becomes the input to program A3. The pipe is a very powerful feature of Unix which allows complex actions to be performed by linking together a series of simple programs.

The solution to the producer/consumer problem is to have two sequential programs, representing the producer and the consumer respectively, linked by a pipe which acts as the buffer, as in:

```
producer | consumer
```

The C code for the producer program is:

```c
#include <stdio.h>
main () {
  char c;
  int more = 1;
  while (more) {
    ... code to generate next item ...
    putchar(c);
  }
}
```

while the C code for the consumer is:

```c
#include <stdio.h>
main () {
  char c;
  int more = 1;
  while (more) {
    c = getchar();
    ... code to consume next item ...
  }
}
```

Communication is achieved through the normal I/O commands. Program consumer cannot read information until it has been output by program producer, although there is no explicit synchronisation between the two programs.

In writing programs producer and consumer, the programmer does not have to take into account the fact that they are to be run in parallel. Concurrency has therefore been left completely in the hands of the operating system, rather than being explicitly catered for in the program code.

Monitors

To see how a monitor can ensure safe communication of information via shared variables, we look at Java and Ada 95. A monitor can be implemented as an object. To provide a critical region, we must guarantee that only one thread may be actively executing a method in the monitor object at any one time. This is achieved in Java by defining a class which has all its public methods **synchronised** and all its attributes private while in Ada 95 we use an instance of a **protected type**.

A possible Java program to implement the producer/consumer problem is given below. We have a `Producer` and a `Consumer` class which both extend class `Thread`. These classes have, as an attribute, a reference to a monitor object of class `Buffer` which provides the critical region and holds the shared variable. A **lock** is associated with each monitor object. At any one time, only one thread can hold the lock for a particular monitor and therefore have access to the shared variable. If a second thread wishes access, it is suspended until the first thread has left the monitor and so has released its lock.

The Java definitions of `Producer` and `Consumer` are:

```java
public class Producer extends Thread {
    private Buffer buffPRef;
    private int x;

    public Producer(Buffer b) {
        buffPRef = b;
    } // constructor

    public void run() {
        while (true) {
            ...code to produce an item x ...
            buffPRef.give(x);
        }
    } // run
} // Producer

public class Consumer extends Thread {
    private Buffer buffCRef;
    private int x;

    public Consumer(Buffer b) {
        buffCRef = b;
    } // constructor

    public void run() {
        while (true) {
            x = buffCRef.take();
            ...code to consume item x ...
        }
    } // run
} // Consumer
```

In Ada 95, an active object is declared to be an instance of a **task type**. The Ada version of the Java `Producer` class is:

```
task type Producer(buffPRef: PtBuffer);

task body Producer is
  x : Integer;
begin
  loop
    ... code to produce an item x ...
    buffPRef.give(x);
  end loop;
end Producer;
```

As with packages, an Ada task is declared in two parts: a specification and a body. An instance of task `Producer` is automatically started when the block in which it is declared is entered. There is therefore no need for the equivalent of a `run` method. Type `PtBuffer` is a pointer to the protected type `Buffer`.

The following Java class `Buffer` defines a monitor object. The shared variable `contents` is declared to be private and so can only be accessed through calls of the methods offered by class `Buffer`. Mutually exclusive access to `contents` is guaranteed as only one of the synchronised methods, `give` and `take`, may be being executed by a thread at any one time:

```
public class Buffer {
  private int contents; // the shared variable
  private boolean bufferEmpty = true;

  public synchronized void give(int item) {
    try {
      while (!bufferEmpty)
        wait();
    }
    catch (Exception e) {...}
    contents = item;
    bufferEmpty = false;
    notify();
  } // give

  public synchronized int take() {
    try {
      while (bufferEmpty)
        wait();
    }
    catch (Exception e) {...}
    bufferEmpty = true;
    notify();
    return contents;
```

```
    } // take
  } // Buffer
```

Suppose that a `Producer` thread is executing and makes the call:

```
    buffPRef.give(x);
```

Once a `Producer` thread has entered `give`, it may be unable to proceed because the buffer is not empty. The thread can then suspend itself by calling the `wait` method which, in Java, must always occur within a **try/catch** block. The thread is put on the monitor's wait list and releases its lock. The `Consumer` thread may then obtain the lock and execute `take`, thereby changing the condition. Before leaving the monitor, a thread should call either `notify` or `notifyAll`. A call of `notify` wakes up the thread that has been longest in the monitor's wait list so that it may try to re-acquire the lock. A call of `notifyAll` wakes up all the threads in the monitor's wait list so that they may all try to re-acquire the lock. If there is no waiting thread, a call of `notify` or `notifyAll` has no effect.

The following Java applet can act as the main program:

```
public class ProduceConsume extends Applet {
  private Buffer buff;

  public void init() {
    buff = new Buffer();
      // instantiate the monitor object
    Producer produce = new Producer(buff);
    produce.start();
    Consumer consume = new Consumer(buff);
    consume.start();
  } // init
} // ProduceConsume
```

Execution of the applet's `init` method causes the monitor object `buff` of class `Buffer` to be instantiated and its attribute `bufferEmpty` set to `true`. The thread objects `produce` and `consume` (of the `Thread` subclasses `Producer` and `Consumer`) are then instantiated and passed a reference to the `Buffer` object. They are then explicitly started by calls of their `start` methods. This causes their `run` methods to be executed. Note that `produce` and `consume` are active objects while `buff` is passive.

Although the execution of this Java program is not carried out using true concurrency, when designing programs of this nature it is better to consider that the `produce` and `consume` threads actually run in parallel. In this way, the problem can be considered at an abstract level and implementation details can be ignored.

Suppose that the `consume` thread is first to access the `buff` monitor. It calls method `take` and, as `bufferEmpty` is true, it executes a call of `wait`. It is therefore suspended and loses its lock on `buff`. After executing the code to produce an item, the `produce` thread calls `give` and acquires the lock. As `bufferEmpty` is `true`, the call of `wait` is not made and hence `contents` is given a value.

Before the produce thread leaves give, it sets bufferEmpty to false and calls notify. This wakes up the consume thread. Hence, once the produce thread has left the monitor, the consume thread may re-acquire the lock and resume execution of take. Execution of take resumes inside the **while** loop but, as bufferEmpty is now false, the loop is left and so wait is not called. The shared variable is therefore read and bufferEmpty is reset to true.

The two threads can now proceed in parallel with produce producing the next item while consume is consuming the last one. The use of wait, together with the Boolean bufferEmpty, provides synchronisation and means that produce cannot give a new item until consume has removed the previous one, and that consume cannot attempt to take an item which has not yet been produced.

As Java only supports single inheritance, a subclass of Thread may not inherit from any other class. Hence, instead of defining Producer and Consumer as subclasses of class Thread, they can be defined as implementing the Runnable interface. We can have:

```
public class Producer  implements Runnable { ... }
```

The body of class Producer is unchanged. The thread object is then instantiated by passing an instance of class Producer to the Thread constructor:

```
Thread produce = new Thread(new Producer(buff));
```

The thread is started, as before, by a call of its start method.

In Ada 95, the Buffer monitor is declared to be a protected type. A protected type has private attributes and three kinds of public operations: procedures, functions and **entries**. A thread can only execute a procedure or an entry if it has exclusive access to the monitor. As a function is only used to read the attributes in the monitor, more than one thread can be simultaneously executing a function, but a function can only be executed while no procedure or entry is being executed. The difference between a procedure and an entry is that an entry can have a **barrier condition**. The entry can only be executed when the barrier condition is true.

In Java, a thread starts executing a method in a monitor and then typically tests a condition to determine whether it should proceed or call wait. In Ada 95, on the other hand, the condition is tested **before** the thread enters the monitor. If the barrier condition is false, the thread is forced to wait in a queue. Once execution of an entry has been completed, the barrier conditions of the waiting threads are re-evaluated in turn until one evaluates to true. In Java, on the other hand, a thread typically has to call notify before it exits from a method in a monitor. Synchronisation in Ada 95 is therefore more abstract as it has replaced explicit calls of wait and notify by a new language feature: the barrier condition.

The Ada 95 code for the buffer monitor is:

```
protected type Buffer is
  entry give(item : in  Integer);
  entry take(item : out  Integer);
end Buffer;
```

```
protected body Buffer is
   contents: Integer;

   bufferEmpty: Boolean := true;

   entry give(item : in  Integer)
      when bufferEmpty is
   begin
      contents := item;
      bufferEmpty := false;
   end give;

   entry take(item : out  Integer)
      when not bufferEmpty is
   begin
      item := contents;
      bufferEmpty := true;
      end take;
   end Buffer;
```

Initially, bufferEmpty is true and so only the give entry can be executed. If the Consumer thread calls take, it is suspended. Once the Producer thread has completed execution of give, the barrier condition for take is re-evaluated. As it is now true, the Consumer thread can now enter the monitor and take an item.

When we have several producers and consumers, more than one thread can be suspended. The suspended threads will be waiting, in the case of Java, for a call of notify and, in the case of Ada 95, for another thread to leave the monitor. Suppose that:

- we have a thread produce and two Consumer threads, consumeA and consumeB;
- the produce and consumeA threads are waiting, with consumeA having waited the longest;
- the consumeB thread is executing take, calls notify (in the Java case) and exits from take.

There is no problem in the Ada 95 case. Only the barrier condition for the give entry will be true and so only the produce thread will be able to enter the monitor.

In Java on the other hand, consumeA will be woken up, can re-acquire the lock and hence resume its execution of take. The value of bufferEmpty is true and so wait is called. We now have deadlock as no more calls of notify will be made and so the produce thread is never woken up. The solution is to call the method notifyAll rather than notify. That causes both waiting threads to be woken up. If the consumeA thread acquires the lock first, it executes wait and so the produce thread is able to acquire the lock and give a new item to buff. The drawback of notifyAll is the time wasted scheduling non-productive threads such as consumeA.

An alternative solution, used in Modula-2, is to maintain two wait lists and for wait and notify to have the conditions notFull and notEmpty as parameters. A Consumer thread will wait on the condition notEmpty and be woken up by a Producer thread calling notify(notEmpty). A Producer thread will wait on the condition notFull and be woken up by a Consumer thread calling notify(notFull). In that way, a Consumer thread can only wake up a Producer thread and vice versa.

A further problem is when **priorities** are attached to threads as this introduces the possibility of **starvation**: a thread with a low priority may never be executed if there is always a higher priority thread waiting to be scheduled.

Larger buffers

The produce and consume threads may vary in the time they take to produce or consume items. If a larger buffer is used, the producer can produce items ahead of schedule as long as items are not put in a full buffer. The consumer can catch up when the producer slows down. The shared variable is now a queue of items, with the first item inserted in the buffer being the first to be removed. The revised definition of class Buffer is given below. It assumes the presence of a Queue class with methods add, remove, isFull and isEmpty. Classes Producer and Consumer remain unchanged:

```
public class Buffer {
  private Queue contents = new Queue();

  public synchronized void  give(int item) {
    try {
      while (contents.isFull())
        wait();
    }
    catch (Exception e) {...}
    contents.add(item);
    notify();
  } // give

  public synchronized int take() {
    try {
      while (contents.isEmpty())
        wait();
    }
    catch (Exception e) {...}
    notify();
    return contents.remove();
  } // take
} // Buffer
```

A similar extension can be made in the Ada 95 case.

Monitors have been found to be an effective way of implementing mutual exclusion. A major advantage, when they are implemented as a class, is that their internal details are hidden and protected from the processes that use them. However, it is essential to program them with great care so that deadlock does not occur. A program may appear to work correctly, but then deadlocks unexpectedly when a certain combination of circumstances occurs. Also, as they are concerned with protecting access to shared variables, they are not suited to situations where the processors do not physically share memory.

Brinch Hansen, the originator of the monitor concept, has complained that Java does not implement a monitor construct, but only provides a style in which a monitor may be written (Brinch Hansen 1999). A programmer can add ordinary methods or public attributes to a class that was intended to implement a monitor thereby compromising its security. An important feature of language design is to create constructs that reduce the opportunity for programmers to make mistakes. It would therefore be better if the definition of Java was changed so that, if a class contained a synchronised method, then all its public methods must be synchronised and all its attributes must be private. Such a rule could easily be checked at compile time.

The rendezvous

In Ada, it is possible for tasks to communicate directly with one another without the use of shared variables. A task is entered by means of an entry call in the same way as an instance of a protected type. Indeed, the calling task need not know whether it is calling an entry defined in a protected type or in a task. Task entries may have a **guard**, corresponding to the barrier condition in a protected type. However, there is a major difference. A task has its own thread of control and so may not be in a position to accept the call because it is busy doing something else. An entry call cannot proceed until the called task is able to execute an **accept** statement to accept the call – that is, when there is a **rendezvous**. An entry call is therefore used both for inter-task communication and for synchronisation.

The rendezvous mechanism can be illustrated by looking at an Ada program where a producer communicates directly with the consumer. Instead of defining a task type and then declaring a task instance, we can just declare a task. We look later at the Ada implementation of a buffer task type where the buffer can contain several items:

```
procedure produce_consume is

task Producer;

task Consumer is
    entry give(item : in  Integer);
end Consumer;

task body Producer is
    x : Integer;
```

```
begin
  loop
    ... code to produce an item x ...
    Consumer.give(x);
  end loop;
end Producer;

task body Consumer is
  x : Integer;
begin
  loop
    accept give(item : in Integer) do
      x := item;
    end give;
    ... code to consume item x ...
  end loop;
end Consumer;

begin
  ...
end produce_consume;
```

Tasks Producer and Consumer are started by calling procedure produce_consume. If two processors are not available, then a decision must be made about which task is to be scheduled first. As the tasks have equal priority, the scheduling order is not defined by the Ada language, although in circumstances where it is important, it is possible to allocate different priorities to different tasks. The order in which the tasks are executed in this case does not matter.

First, consider task Consumer. The entry give is declared in the specification of Consumer and so, as it is visible from outside the task, it can be called by other tasks. An entry is called in the same way as a procedure with information being passed by parameters. The statements to be executed when an entry is called are given by an **accept** statement in the task body.

In the execution of the body of task Consumer, the first statement in the loop is:

```
accept give(item: in  Integer) do
  x := item;
end give;
```

This indicates that Consumer is ready to accept a call of the give entry. If no such entry call has been made, the execution of task Consumer is suspended.

Meanwhile the Producer task will have been executing the code to produce an item before eventually executing the statement:

```
Consumer.give(x);
```

If `Consumer` is sitting waiting to accept this call, a rendezvous exists between the tasks `Consumer` and `Producer`. Task `Producer` is suspended while the body of the **accept** statement is executed. This ensures that the body of the **accept** statement acts as a critical region. If this critical region did not exist, the value of x might be changed by subsequent execution of instructions in `Producer`, before the parameter passing had been successfully completed.To ensure that the execution of `Producer` is not delayed for too long, the critical region should be kept as short as possible. Once the body of the **accept** statement has been executed, the rendezvous is over and both tasks are free to continue in parallel.

Task `Producer` starts producing the next item while task `Consumer` executes code to consume the item. If a new item is produced and the call:

```
Consumer.give(x);
```

takes place before `Consumer` is ready to accept the call, then `Producer` is suspended until `Consumer` is ready. Similarly, `Consumer` is suspended at its **accept** statement if it is ready before `Producer`. Thus, Ada uses the rendezvous mechanism to achieve both communication and synchronisation with messages being passed as the parameters of an entry call. Message passing can be implemented on distributed systems as well as on systems involving shared memory.

To allow `Producer` to produce items ahead of schedule, we can implement an Ada `Buffer` task. This task will contain two entries, `give` and `take`. The buffer can be filled by a sequence of `give` entries or emptied by a series of `take` entries, as long as there are safeguards against adding an item to a full buffer or taking an item from an empty buffer.

Instances of `Buffer` must be able to accept either a `give` or a `take` entry. This is achieved by what is known as a **select** statement, which in this case contains two **select alternatives**. The tasks `Producer` and `Consumer` have the same structure as in the monitor example. We use a queue to hold the information in the buffer. The following assumes that a type `Queue` has been defined and has operations `add`, `remove`, `isFull` and `isEmpty`:

```
task type Buffer is
  entry give(item : in   Integer);
  entry take(item : out   Integer);
end Buffer;

task body Buffer is
  contents : Queue;
begin
  loop
    select
      when not isFull(contents) =>
        accept give(item : in   Integer) do
          add(item, contents);
        end give;
    or when not isEmpty(contents) =>
```

```
            accept take(item : out Integer) do
                remove(item, contents);
            end take;
        end select;
    end loop;
end Buffer;
```

The buffer acts like a queue with the first item inserted in the buffer being the first item to be removed. Each of the **select** alternatives is guarded by a **when** condition to ensure that items cannot be added to a full buffer or removed from an empty one. Statements guarded in this way are called **guarded commands**.

To execute the **select** statement, the guards are first evaluated. If the value of a guard is false, the select alternative is said to be **closed** and the corresponding **accept** statement is not considered further. If the value of a guard is true, the select alternative is said to be **open**. When only a give entry call has been made and the buffer is not full, then the give entry is accepted. Similarly, when only a take entry call has been made and the buffer is not empty, the take entry is accepted. In the situation when both entry calls have been made and both guard conditions are satisfied, one of the calls is selected arbitrarily (that is, in a non-deterministic manner) and the other has to wait. If no give or take entry call corresponding to an open **select** alternative has been made, the buffer task is suspended until one is.

Comparison between monitors and the rendezvous

The rendezvous approach is at a higher level of abstraction than the use of a monitor and hence is easier to understand and use. Its main disadvantage is that it often requires a larger number of processes than when monitors are used. In the producer/consumer example with multiple items in the buffer, we showed how an active Ada buffer process could replace a passive buffer monitor. Therefore, although the rendezvous solution is conceptually simpler, it would seem to lead to higher run-time overheads when insufficient processors are available. That is why protected types were introduced into Ada 95.

In Ada, the tasking overhead is high. However, just because a source program describes a solution in terms of three processes, this does not mean that it must be implemented in that way. It is possible for an optimising Ada compiler to remove processes, such as an active buffer, and to move the code to the calling tasks. This gives the advantage of being able to view a solution as if it involved separate processes without this necessarily leading to slower execution.

(11.3) Internet programming

Many object-oriented languages such as Java and Delphi have library classes that provide facilities so that programs can access web pages and remote databases and can communicate with one another across a network. The use of library classes to extend the capabilities of a language and to hide low-level details is, of course, one of the main advantages of the object-oriented approach. However, in some cases, C++ for example, the available library facilities are part of a particular implementation rather than a feature of the language.

Animating web pages

A page on the Internet can be visited by giving its URL (Uniform Resource Locator) to a web browser. An example URL is:

```
http://www.cs.stir.ac.uk/~rgc/cpl/index.html
```

which is where you can find information about this book. Web pages are written in HTML (hypertext mark-up language) and can contain hypertext links to other web pages. An example HTML document is given below.

```
<HEAD>
<TITLE>Page with Java applet</TITLE>
</HEAD>
<BODY>
You can get information on this book
<A href="http://www.cs.stir.ac.uk/~rgc/cpl/index.html">
  here</A>.
<P>
A simple Java applet is being executed below:
<P>
<APPLET archive="appletclasses.jar"
  code="Trivial.class" width=200 height=50>
</APPLET>
</BODY>
```

This HTML code will cause a web page with one hypertext link and one Java applet to be created. The code:

```
<A href="http://www.cs.stir.ac.uk/~rgc/cpl/index.html">
    here</A>
```

contains the hypertext link. Clicking on the word "here" in the generated web page will cause the web page with the quoted URL to be opened.

One of the selling points of Java is that it can be used to animate web pages. The HTML code:

```
<APPLET archive="appletclasses.jar"
    code="Trivial.class" width=200 height=50>
</APPLET>
```

causes a Java applet called `Trivial` to be executed. The Java applet's object code is held in file `Trivial.class` while the Java library classes needed by the applet are held in the `appletclasses.jar` file. Both these files are held in the same folder as the HTML file.

Although this applet was translated and its object code form is held on a computer (a web server) in Stirling, a person anywhere in the world can access and run the applet using a web browser. The browser will first download the applet into the person's local computer and then run it on that computer. This is possible because Java programs are translated into machine independent object code called bytecode. To run the bytecode, you require a browser that contains a `bytecode` interpreter, but that is standard for modern browsers. Note that this would not have been possible if the Java applet had been translated into machine code because the machine code for one kind of computer will not run on a different kind of computer.

There are dangers in executing programs that have been downloaded over a network. They might contain a virus or could perform actions that could corrupt your files. Java applets come with a guarantee that this will not happen. Applets are only able to access the files of the site from which they were downloaded. Also, as applets are interpreted, the interpreter can ensure that they do not carry out improper actions.

Another way of animating web pages is to use JavaScript, a scripting language developed by Netscape. JavaScript code is unusual in that it does not exist independently, but must always be embedded within an HTML document. As with Java and Perl, the syntax of JavaScript is based on C and, like Perl, its variables do not have a type. Its big advantage is that as the JavaScript code is part of a web page, it can directly access, and make use of, the properties of the web page in which it is embedded.

Using URLs

As well as supporting the creation of applets, the Java class library contains a `net` package that has features that enable Java programs to access other machines in a network. Package `net` contains, for example, a URL class that enables us to access the information held at a particular URL. Delphi also has classes that allow programmers to interact with HTML files. In Java, we can create a URL object:

```
URL cpl =
    new URL("http://www.cs.stir.ac.uk/~rgc/cpl/");
```

We can then create another URL object relative to this:

```
URL trivialRef = new URL(cpl, "Trivial.html");
```

That is equivalent to:

```
URL = new URL(
    "http://www.cs.stir.ac.uk/~rgc/cpl/Trivial.html");
```

If the string given to a URL constructor does not correspond to a valid URL, then a `MalformedURLException` is thrown. The constructor of a URL object should therefore always be executed within a **try/catch** block.

Once we have a URL object, we can call its methods. For example, a call of `trivialRef.getHost()` will return the String value `"www.cs.stir.ac.uk"` while `trivialRef.getFile()` will return the String value `"/~rgc/cpl/Trivial.html"`.

We can also open a network connection between our program and the URL referred to by `trivialRef` by creating an object of class `URLConnection`:

```
URLConnection trivConnection =
    trivialRef.openConnection();
```

Many web pages contain HTML forms through which a user enters data, i.e. writes to the web page. The `URLConnection` class has `getInputStream` and `getOutputStream` methods which enable us to read or write to the URL in the same way as we can read and write to files.

Common Gateway Interface

With Java applets, we download a program from a remote computer and run it on our local computer. The more common approach to network programming is where a program on one computer (the client) will call the services provided on a remote computer (the server). Execution of these services will occur on the remote computer with the results being returned to the calling computer. In this way, we can have a truly distributed system. Distributed databases are perhaps the most common use of this approach, and both Java and Delphi provide substantial support for that area.

A user can enter data into an HTML **form** in a web page and the data is sent to the web server where an interface program will process the data before responding in some way. An example is a search engine. When a user submits a query, an interface program is executed on the search engine's web server. This interface program will extract the query information and execute the search engine program with the query as input data. The results of the search are then passed back to the interface program which typically creates a new web page to display the results to the user.

The interface program must conform to a standard known as the **Common Gateway Interface** and is referred to as a **CGI program**. Perl is the most widely used language for writing CGI programs although such programs can be written in any language and other common examples are C and C++. The advantage of Perl is that it provides the necessary text processing capabilities and, in addition, has a library of built-in operations to make CGI programming easier. Let us look at this through a very simple example. The following form can appear as part of any HTML document:

```
<FORM ACTION =
   "http://www.cs.stir.ac.uk/cgi-bin/rgc/simple">
   Hello, what is your name?
   <INPUT Name = "myname">
   <P>
   <INPUT Type = submit Value = "Submit name">
</FORM>
```

The resulting web page will contain a string asking for your name, a textbox where you can type in a response and a button labelled `Submit name`. A CGI program, whose address is given in the form's `ACTION` field, must be associated with each form. If you type the name `Jenna` into the textbox and click on the submit button, then the following URL is sent:

```
http://www.cs.stir.ac.uk/cgi-bin/rgc/simple?myname=Jenna
```

This causes the CGI program held in file `simple` to be executed. The input parameters are given after ? and they are represented as name, value pairs. Hence, in this example, the `myname` parameter is given the value "Jenna". The program in `simple` can be written in any suitable language; the following is a Perl version:

```
#!/usr/bin/perl
use CGI ":standard";
$name = param("myname");

print <<FirstPart;
Content-type: text/html

<HTML>
  <HEAD>
  <TITLE>Hello</TITLE>
  </HEAD>
  <BODY>
  <H1>Hello
FirstPart
print $name;
print <<Remaining;
  </H1>
  </BODY>
</HTML>
Remaining
```

The first line is to tell the system that the file is in Perl while the second brings in the contents of the Perl CGI library. The `param` operation extracts the value of the `myname` parameter (i.e. `Jenna`) which we save in $name. We could now do an arbitrary amount of processing before constructing the web page that is to be returned to the user, but in this simple example we do not do anything here. We use print statements to output the HTML code that will generate the web page. The following rather strange syntax is used to bracket the text being output:

```
print <<SomeLabel;
...
SomeLabel
```

The `Content-type` line indicates the kind of output being generated. The body of the generated web page depends on the input parameter and so in our example we get:

Hello Jenna

All the difficult work has therefore been done behind the scenes, but that is typical of Internet programming in Java and Delphi where the support libraries provide a level of abstraction that allows the programmer to get on with the task in hand without having to worry about the details of network protocols.

CGI programs must be held in special folders and so, if you are creating a CGI program, you need to contact your system administrator to find out where it can be located.

Clients and servers

The Java classes `URL` and `URLConnection` are both oriented towards accessing web pages using the HTTP protocol. The Java `net` package also has `Socket` and `ServerSocket` classes to provide a wider range of facilities. (Delphi has classes `TClientSocket` and `TServerSocket`.) The `Socket` class supports the client end of a connection while the `ServerSocket` class supports the server end. This book is not about how a range of library classes can provide low-level facilities. It is more concerned with language facilities that can raise the level of abstraction and so we will not look into programming with sockets.

The obvious level of abstraction is to allow a program to call the procedures offered on a remote computer as if they were ordinary local procedures and for all the networking complexity to be hidden behind the scenes. This led to the concept of the **Remote Procedure Call** (RPC). In an object-oriented context, that is equivalent to a client object making calls of methods offered by a remote server object as if the server was local. This is known as **Remote Method Invocation** (RMI). There must, of course, be some underlying mechanism through which the local calls are mapped to calls of the actual methods in the remote server.

One approach is **CORBA** (Common Object Request Broker Architecture), an internationally defined standard that is not dependent on any particular programming language or computer architecture. Central to the implementation of CORBA is the **Object Request Broker** (ORB) which handles all the networking.

A server object in CORBA must have an associated interface which is defined in a language called **IDL** (Interface Definition Language) whose syntax is based on C++. An IDL interface defines the services that may be offered to clients, but does not provide any implementation. The interface is then implemented by one or more server objects. Mappings have been defined between IDL and language such as C++, Java, COBOL, Ada 95 and Delphi. The idea is that, through the IDL interface, a client object written in one language can call a service provided by a server object written in another language. The client does not need to know which language has been used to implement the service.

Compiling an IDL interface causes language specific **stub** and **skeleton** code to be generated. Suppose that the client object is written in Java and the server object in C++. At the server end, the generated C++ skeleton code is used to handle client requests that are received from the ORB and to pass them on to the server object. At the client end, the client object uses the generated Java stub code to communicate with the server object via the ORB. The stub code will include a reference to a **proxy object**. The client makes local method calls to the proxy object and these calls are then, behind the scenes, passed on to the remote server object. A very simplified version of the CORBA architecture is shown in Figure 11.1.

Other similar approaches are Microsoft's DCOM and a Java specific mechanism known as Java RMI. In Java RMI, a separate IDL is not required as ordinary Java interfaces can be used.

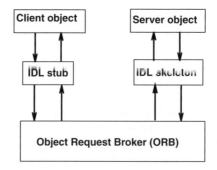

Figure 11.1   Simplified CORBA architecture.

11.4 Real-time programming

The central feature of a real-time system is that it must respond to external inputs or events, such as **interrupts**, sufficiently quickly so that an appropriate response can be made and no information is lost. What is meant by the phrase 'sufficiently quickly' depends on the application and the response time could be required to be within microseconds, seconds or even days.

An example of a real-time system is a computer system controlling a chemical process. If the input from its sensors showed that pressure was building up to an unacceptable level, then the computer system would have to initiate action such as opening valves or lowering the temperature within a very short time period. It is therefore essential that the input of information and the resulting calculations are completed sufficiently quickly so that a suitable response can be made before the chemical plant blows up.

Real-time programming is one of the last bastions of the assembly language programmer as it usually requires access to low-level machine facilities. This includes the ability to access absolute memory locations, such as those used in handling external devices and in processing interrupts. Few mainstream high-level languages, with the notable exceptions of Ada and occam, have these facilities although several others, such as C, C++ and Coral 66, achieve the effect through calls to special system routines. A further problem occurs in multiprocessor systems when trying to define what exactly is meant by time – each processor is likely to have its own internal clock and they may all 'tick' at different rates.

When a computer is embedded in, and used to control, non-computer equipment the system is known as an **embedded system**. An example of such a system is process control in a chemical plant where the computer system is part of a much larger control system. Most embedded systems are also real-time systems and, indeed, some writers treat the two words synonymously. Ada was specially designed for use in real-time embedded systems.

In general, real-time programming has all the problems of concurrent programming with the added problem of time. To help solve such problems, it is usual for different processes to be given different priorities, for clearly the process handling an emergency situation such as the one described for the chemical plant must be given top priority and must not be suspended to make way for routine processing.

To give a specific example of real-time programming, suppose that, when a sensor in the chemical plant detects abnormal pressure levels, it sends an interrupt to the computer system. This interrupt appears to a running Ada program as an entry call. Each possible hardware interrupt is associated with a memory address and this association is shown in the specification of the task which is to handle the interrupt by a **for** ... **use at** ... definition. This allows hardware interrupts to be dealt with in exactly the same way as an entry call. Such a task specification has the form:

```
task Pr_interrupt_handler is
   entry pressure_warning;
   for pressure_warning use at allocated_location;
end Pr_interrupt_handler;
```

So that the interrupt can be handled in Ada, there must be a task body waiting to make a rendezvous with the pressure_warning entry call. The Ada task body will have the form:

```
task body Pr_interrupt_handler is
begin
   accept pressure_warning;
   ... perform appropriate action ...
end Pr_interrupt_handler;
```

There must be a waiting **accept** statement for each interrupt which may be received by the system. By using a **select** statement, one task can be used to handle several interrupts.

Time can be introduced into an Ada program through the **delay** statement. Execution of the statement:

```
delay 4.0;
```

will delay a task by at least four seconds. Note that there is no guarantee that the task will be started immediately after four seconds have elapsed for, in a multiprogramming environment, some other task may be chosen by the scheduler. A similar delay in a C program is achieved by the library routine call sleep(4) or, in Java, Thread.sleep(4000).

To guarantee that some operation is carried out every four seconds, a simple solution in Ada would seem to be:

```
loop
   ... code to carry out some operations ...
   delay 4.0;
end loop;
```

The problem with this solution is that the time to go round the loop is:

four seconds + time for operations + delay due to scheduler

which together could be considerably more than four seconds.

The answer to this problem is to use **absolute** rather than **relative** time. Absolute time is provided in Ada by the predefined package Calendar, which defines the abstract data type Time. The representation of type Time is implementation dependent and is hidden, but functions in package Calendar allow the extraction from values of type Time the components year, month, day and the time within a day in seconds. Absolute time is provided by the function clock, which returns the current value of Time. The package also provides overloaded definitions of +, – and the relational operators, so that Time arithmetic may be carried out.

With start_time having been declared as a variable of type Time, the problem of carrying out an operation every four seconds may now be programmed as:

```
start_time := clock;
loop
   ... code to carry out some operations ...
   start_time := start_time + 4.0;
   delay until start_time;
end loop;
```

The delay will be less than four seconds as it takes into account the time spent in carrying out the operations. It has, of course, been assumed that the operations in the loop are executed in less than four seconds.

delay statements may be incorporated into **select** statements. Hence, in the process control example, the action to be taken by the interrupt handler when the pressure is too high might be to reduce the temperature knowing that, when the process returns to normal, a second interrupt will be received. If this interrupt is not received within twenty seconds, the task will initiate emergency action. This could be programmed as the task body:

```
task body Pr_interrupt_handler is
begin
   loop
      accept pressure_warning;
      reduce_temperature;
      select
         accept pressure_ok_signal;
      or
         delay 20.0;
         emergency_shut_down;
      end select;
   end loop;
end Pr_interrupt_handler;
```

The loop ensures that, once this body has finished handling a pressure_warning interrupt, it is ready to handle a similar subsequent interrupt.

Summary

1. In a concurrent program, several sequential program fragments (processes) are viewed as being executed in parallel. When the processes are not independent of one another, a mechanism is needed through which they can communicate and through which their actions can be synchronised.

2. Many concurrent programs run on single processor machines and so only pseudo-concurrency exists. In such circumstances, concurrency is not being used to promote efficiency, but because it leads to a more natural solution.

3. Processes can communicate through shared variables or by message passing.

4. To get round the problem of one process updating a shared variable while another process is examining it, critical regions are used. Only one process may be executing a procedure in a critical region at any one time. In object-oriented languages, critical regions are implemented by means of a monitor class.

5. In Ada, processes are implemented by tasks. A task is entered by means of an entry call which must then be accepted by means of an **accept** statement.

6. Two Ada tasks communicate when one task executes an entry call that the other is ready to receive. If one task is not ready to take part in this rendezvous, the other task must wait. Synchronisation is thereby achieved. Communication between tasks is achieved using the parameters of the entry call.

7. The Ada **select** statement enables a task to be in a position to accept alternative entry calls. The select alternatives may have Boolean guards.

8. Java applets can be used to animate web pages. Using a web browser, applets can be downloaded from a remote computer and executed on the local computer.

9. When data is sent from a web page to a web server, it is processed by a CGI program running on the server. Results can be returned to the user by the CGI program generating a web page.

10. Resources on the web are accessed through their URL. Languages like Java and Delphi contain classes that allow network connections to be made through URLs.

11. Distributed programs make use of the client–server paradigm.

12. CORBA supports distributed programs whose parts are written in different languages and implemented on different hardware.

13. The central feature of a real-time system is that it must respond to external inputs sufficiently quickly so that an appropriate response can be made.

14. Delay statements delay a process by at least the stated time. There is, however, no control over how quickly a process will be re-activated after the delay has expired.

11.1 Should a language include constructs to indicate that certain program segments may be executed in parallel or should such decisions be left up to the compiler?

11.2 Identify the features of languages such as Pascal, Ada and C++ that make it difficult to determine which parts of a program are independent of one another and so may be executed in parallel.

11.3 Outline the problems associated with shared variables and indicate how they may be overcome.

11.4 Section 11.2 gives the definition of a Java monitor class for a single element buffer. An item may not be put in a full buffer or removed from an empty buffer. What changes would have to be made to the definition of class `Buffer` if:

(a) The same item can be read several times, but a new item cannot be put in `Buffer` until the previous one has been read at least once.

(b) New items can be inserted before the previous one has been read.

11.5 Repeat question 4, but this time modify the Ada 95 protected type `Buffer`.

11.6 In our rendezvous example, we saw a `Consumer` task accept an entry call from a `Producer` task during which the consumer was given an item. Rewrite the example so that the `Producer` task accepts an entry call from a `Consumer` task during which the consumer takes an item.

11.7 You are accessing a web page that contains or refers to a Java applet, JavaScript code and a CGI program. Which of these items is executed by the web browser and which by the web server?

11.8 The web page at:

```
http://www.cs.stir.ac.uk/~rgc/cpl/Trivial.html
```

causes the `simple` CGI script given in Section 11.3 to be executed. Try it for yourself. Now construct your own version of this page using a copy of the Perl CGI program in your own CGI special folder.

11.9 Design two outline Ada tasks, one for an alarm and one for a person. The sleeping person task should be ready to receive a call from the alarm task and will either return the value `off` and get up or return the value `snooze` and go back to sleep. The alarm task will terminate when the value `off` is returned. If `snooze` is returned, it will delay for two minutes before calling the person task again. This is repeated until the alarm task is switched off.

Bibliography

An important early synchronisation primitive was the semaphore which was introduced by Dijkstra (1968). Monitors were introduced and developed by Brinch Hansen (1973) and Hoare (1974) and are based on the SIMULA class concept. A full description of CSP is given by Hoare (1985).

The book by Burns and Davies (1993) is recommended for those readers who want a more detailed introduction to the concepts of concurrency. Concurrent programming in Java is described by Lea (1997) while the rendezvous concept and buffering between producers and consumers is described in most Ada texts.

Briot *et al.*(1998) provide a survey of object-oriented languages in concurrent and distributed systems while Schwartz and Christiansen (1997) give an introduction to the use of Perl in CGI programming. A review of the client/server approach and a comparison between CORBA and the DCOM alternative is given by Lewandowski (1998). The use of CORBA is described by Baker (1997).

Baker, S. (1997). *CORBA Distributed Objects*. Addison-Wesley.

Brinch Hansen, P. (1973). *Operating System Principles*. Prentice-Hall.

Brinch Hansen, P. (1999). 'Java's Insecure Parallelism'. *ACM Sigplan*, **34**(4), 38–45.

Briot, J.-P., Guerraoui, R and Lohr, K.-P. (1998). 'Concurrency and Distribution in Object-Oriented Programming'. *ACM Computing Surveys*, **30**(3), 291–329.

Burns, A. and Davies, G. (1993). *Concurrent Programming*. Addison-Wesley.

Dijkstra, E.W. (1968). 'Cooperating Sequential Processes' in *Programming Languages* (F. Genuys, Ed.), Academic Press.

Hoare, C.A.R. (1974). 'Monitors: An Operating System Structuring Concept'. *Comm. ACM*, **17**, 549–557.

Hoare, C.A.R. (1985). *Communicating Sequential Processes*. Prentice-Hall.

Lea, D. (1997). *Concurrent Programming in Java*. Addison-Wesley.

Lewandowski, S.M. (1998). 'Frameworks for Component-Based Client/Server Computing'. *ACM Computing Surveys*, **30**(1), 3–27.

Schwartz, R.L. and Christiansen, T. (1997). *Learning Perl* (Second Edition). O'Reilly.

Chapter 12

Syntax and semantics

This chapter describes the use of Backus–Naur form and syntax diagrams in the definition of the syntax of programming languages. Examples are given of how sentences in a language can be derived from its grammar and how a BNF grammar imposes a phrase structure on the derived sentences.

Although the syntax of a programming language is always defined formally using a notation such as BNF, the semantics are still usually defined in English. Methods do, however, exist for formally describing the semantics of programming language constructs and brief outlines of two approaches, denotational and axiomatic semantics, are given. As these methods require a higher level of mathematical sophistication than is assumed, they have not been used in this book.

12.1 Syntax

The **syntax** (or **grammar**) of a programming language describes the correct form in which programs may be written while the **semantics** denotes the meaning that may be attached to the various syntactic constructs. Finding methods and notations to express the formal syntax of a language is a much simpler problem than formalising the semantics. Therefore, in the definition of a programming language, the syntax is usually expressed formally in a variant of BNF, which stands for Backus–Naur Form or Backus–Normal Form, while the semantic description is given in English.

BNF is an example of a **metalanguage**; that is, a language used to define other languages. The first language whose description used the combination of a syntax description in BNF and a semantic description in English was Algol 60 (Naur *et al.*, 1960), and the same approach is still used today. When the syntax of a language is expressed in a simple and unambiguous notation such as BNF, it is clear to the language user and implementor alike which constructs are legal and which are not.

A BNF definition consists of a set of **nonterminals**, a set of **terminals** and a series of **production rules** (also known as **productions** or **rewrite rules**). A nonterminal is defined in a production rule, while a terminal is a symbol in the language being defined. In a production rule, the nonterminal on the left-hand side, known as the **left part**, is defined in terms of a sequence of nonterminals and terminals on the right-hand side, known as the **right part**.

Some example production rules are:

```
<digit> ::= 0|1|2|3|4|5|6|7|8|9
<letter> ::= a|b|c|d| ... x|y|z
<identifier> ::= <letter>
            |<identifier><digit>
            |<identifier><letter>
```

In BNF, a nonterminal is written within angle brackets < and >, the symbol ::= means 'is defined as' and the symbol | means 'or'.

These definitions define <digit> to be one of the symbols 0, 1, ... 9, <letter> to be a lower case letter and <identifier> to be either a single letter, an identifier followed by a letter or an identifier followed by a digit. Hence, ch1 is an identifier as it can be **derived** from <identifier> as follows:

```
<identifier>
<identifier><digit>
<identifier><letter><digit>
<letter><letter><digit>
c<letter><digit>
ch<digit>
ch1
```

At each stage, the leftmost nonterminal has been replaced by the right part of one of its defining production rules. The sequence of terminals and nonterminals produced at each stage in a **derivation** is known as a **sentential form**. The final sentential form, which does not contain any nonterminals, is known as a **sentence**. The structure of a derivation is best shown by what is known as a **derivation tree**. The tree showing how ch1 is derived from <identifier> is given in Figure 12.1.

A complete programming language is defined by starting with a nonterminal such as <program>, known as the **start symbol**, and from which all possible programs can be derived by replacing the left parts of production rules by one of their corresponding right parts. In practice, derivation trees are created in one of two ways. In the **top-down** approach, the required sentence is derived from the start symbol as was done in the derivation of ch1. In the **bottom-up** approach, the starting point is the required sentence which is reduced to the start symbol by replacing right parts by their corresponding left parts. Both approaches are used in the **syntax analysis** phase of compilers.

A grammar defining a programming language always has a finite number of production rules, but the use of recursion in, for example:

```
<identifier> ::= <identifier><digit>
```

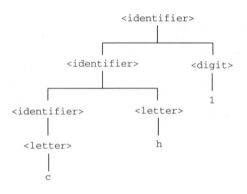

Figure 12.1   Derivation tree for an identifier.

allows an infinite number of possible programs. When recursion is included in a production rule, the same care must be exercised as would be necessary in a recursive procedure. There must, for example, be a nonrecursive alternative so that the recursion can terminate. A production rule such as:

```
<identifier> ::= <identifier><letter>
```

is said to be **left-recursive** because the nonterminal being defined, that is, `<identifier>`, is the leftmost symbol in the right part. Similar definitions exist for **right-recursive** and **self-embedding** production rules.

A BNF grammar is said to be **context-free** as the left part always consists of a single nonterminal. This means that the left part can always be replaced by one of its alternative right parts, irrespective of the context in which the left part appears.

As a further example of the use of BNF, consider:

```
<exp> ::= <exp> + <term>
        | <exp> - <term>
        | <term>
<term> ::= <term> * <factor>
         | <term> / <factor>
         | <factor>
<factor> ::= ( <exp> )
           | <identifier>
```

which defines algebraic expressions. The derivation for the expression:

```
a * (b + c)
```

is:

```
<exp>
<term>
<term> * <factor>
<factor> * <factor>
```

```
<identifier> * <factor>
a * <factor>
a * (<exp>)
a * (<exp> + <term>)
a * (<term> + <term>)
a * (<factor> + <term>)
a * (<identifier> + <term>)
a * (b + <term>)
a * (b + <factor>)
a * (b + <identifier>)
a * (b + c)
```

and the corresponding derivation tree is shown in Figure 12.2.

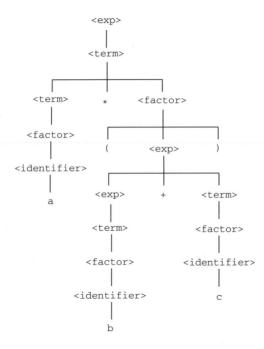

Figure 12.2 Derivation tree for an expression.

From the derivation tree in Figure 12.2, it can be seen that a structure, known as a **phrase structure**, has been imposed on the sentence a * (b + c). A subtree of the main tree defines a **phrase**. Hence, for example, b + c and (b + c) are phrases. It should be noted that the phrase structure imposed by the grammar mirrors the grouping of symbols normally expected in an algebraic expression as evaluation of a * (b + c) takes place by first adding together the values of b and c and then multiplying the result by a.

As the definition of <exp> and <term> are left-recursive, the grammar defines evaluation of a + b + c to take place by first evaluating a + b and then adding c to the result. The grammar also defines multiplication and division to have a higher precedence than addition and subtraction. To convince themselves that this is the case, readers are encouraged to produce the derivation trees for a + b + c and for a + b * c and to examine the phrase structure which has been imposed on these two sentences.

Ambiguity

A problem arises when a BNF definition defines an **ambiguous** grammar, that is, a grammar that allows different interpretations for the same sentence. The classic example of ambiguity in programming languages is the so-called 'dangling else' problem. This occurred in the original definition of Algol 60 as conditional statements were defined so that the **else** part was optional. Consider the definition:

```
<statement> ::= <conditional statement>
          | begin <statement> end
<conditional statement> ::= if <condition>
        then <statement>
        | if <condition> then <statement>
        else <statement>
```

Two different derivation trees exist for the conditional statement:

```
if <condition> then if <condition> then <statement>
   else <statement>
```

and they are given in Figure 12.3. The problem is knowing to which **then** the **else** belongs. As there are two interpretations, the grammar is ambiguous. The approach taken with the revised version of Algol 60 was to insist that only unconditional statements could follow the reserved word **then** and so the above statement would have to be written as either:

```
if <condition> then
begin
  if <condition> then <statement> else <statement>
end
```

or as:

```
if <condition> then
begin
  if <condition> then <statement>
end
else <statement>
```

depending on which interpretation was required. A general discussion of this problem was given in Section 4.3.

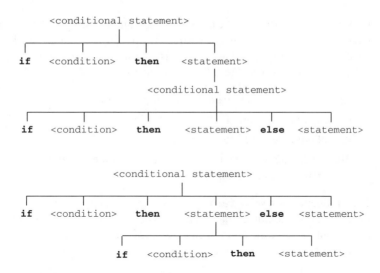

Figure 12.3 Derivation trees for conditional statement.

General proofs that a given grammar is unambiguous are not possible, but a simple and useful rule is that a grammar is always ambiguous if it is both left- and right-recursive with respect to the same nonterminal.

EBNF

Several variants of the BNF notation have been used in language definitions, for example replacing : : = with →, not using angle brackets and enclosing terminals within quotes. Hence, instead of writing:

```
<exp> ::= <exp> + <term>
```

the rule might be written as:

```
exp → exp '+' term
```

The following extensions to BNF (called EBNF) are of a more substantive nature and were used in the definitions of Pascal and Ada:

- Optional constructs are enclosed in square brackets [ ].
- Zero or more repetitions of a construct are indicated by braces, { }.
- Round brackets, ( ), can be used for grouping items together.

Their main effect is to replace left-recursion by iteration.

The BNF definition for an algebraic expression has already been given. The equivalent EBNF production rules are:

```
exp ::= term { ('+' | ' - ') term }
term ::= factor { ('*' | '/' ) factor }
factor ::= '(' exp ')' | identifier
```

EBNF production rules can be presented diagrammatically by what are known as **syntax diagrams**. These diagrams are particularly useful for students at the early stages of understanding the syntax of a language as they are easier to follow than production rules.

Syntax diagrams have the following properties:

- Arrows are used to indicate the direction of flow.
- Rectangular boxes are used for nonterminals.
- Round boxes are used for terminals.
- There is a diagram for each nonterminal. A nonterminal is defined by the possible paths through its defining diagram.

The production rules for `factor`, `term` and `exp` are shown as syntax diagrams in Figure 12.4. It should be noted that the syntax diagrams are recursive; `exp` is defined in terms of `term`, which is defined in terms of `factor`, which may, in turn, be defined in terms of `exp`.

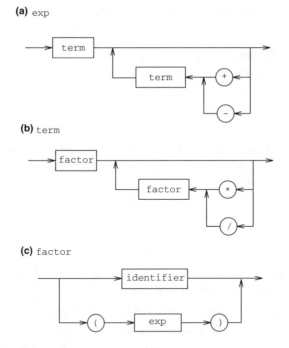

Figure 12.4   Syntax diagrams for `exp`, `term` and `factor`.

Syntax-directed compiling

The production rules used in the definition of a language are embedded in modern compilers and control the syntax analysis phase of the compiler. Such compilers are said to be **syntax directed**.

During the derivation of a sentence, there is often a choice as to which right part should be used to replace a left part and it is often far from obvious which alternative should be chosen. Programming languages are therefore usually defined using a restricted form of context-free grammar so that the choice is always obvious.

If, using the top-down approach, it is always clear which of the possible right parts should be chosen by looking one symbol ahead, then the grammar is said to be LL(1). When syntax is defined using EBNF, it is much easier to put a grammar into LL(1) form than when BNF is used. If, using the bottom-up approach, it is always clear, by looking one symbol ahead, which part of a sentential form should be reduced, then the grammar is said to be LR(1). LL(1) and LR(1) grammars are always unambiguous and lead to languages which can be efficiently compiled. Such issues are taken into account by language designers. The language Pascal, for example, was designed in such a way that its syntax could be defined by means of an LL(1) grammar.

12.2 Semantics

In contrast to the early progress made in the formal definition of syntax, the task of formulating a suitable definition for the semantics of programming languages has presented many problems. Attempts have been made by researchers to arrive at a readable, concise and unambiguous notation for the definition of semantics, and, although considerable progress has been made, an easily understandable solution to the semantics of programming languages is still not available.

BNF was first used in the definition of Algol 60, but as the Algol 60 committee was unable to come up with a solution to the semantic problem to match the BNF syntactical description, they resorted to the English language for the semantic explanations. Unfortunately, the use of English prose is ambiguous, so that two readers can often arrive at different interpretations of a typical sentence. However, the semantics in the ISO and ANSI definitions of recent programming languages are still defined in English.

One approach, called operational semantics, defines a simple abstract machine that has a set of data structures and operations whose semantics is assumed to be known. The semantics of a programming language can then be defined by the rules governing how programs written in that language can be executed on the abstract machine. Although the abstract machine is unlikely to be similar to any existing computer, the operational semantics of a language can be of direct benefit to the language implementor. This approach does, however, often involve too much implementation detail to be of much use to the language user.

Two other formal methods used to describe the semantics of a language are the **denotational** approach and the **axiomatic** approach. The notations used with these approaches are not easy to follow and require a higher level of mathematical sophistication than is assumed in this book. However, for completeness, a brief overview of each approach is given.

Denotational semantics

In denotational semantics, information is given about the effect of program execution and not about how the execution is to be carried out. Therefore, unlike the operational approach, it is of more use to language designers than to language implementors. The following description does not attempt to be rigorous, but only to give an idea of what is involved. Difficult points, such as the handling of errors, are ignored.

Language constructs are modelled by appropriate mathematical objects, usually numbers or functions, whose meaning is already known. Consider, for example, a language which only consists of constant declarations and expressions. A series of declarations is modelled as a function that maps identifiers to their associated values; this kind of function is known as an **environment**. A new pair is added to the environment by the function **bind**, which takes an identifier, a value and an environment and returns a new environment to which the new identifier/value binding has been added. A declaration can then be defined by the semantic function D:

$$D(\textbf{const i = e}, \text{ env}) = \text{bind}(\textbf{i}, \text{ E}(\textbf{e}, \text{ env}), \text{ env})$$

which takes the declaration **const i = e** and an environment env, and returns a new environment which differs from env in that a binding between the identifier **i** and the value obtained by evaluating the expression **e** has been added. The semantic function E takes an expression and an environment and returns the value obtained by evaluating the expression in that environment. During the evaluation of the expression, the value of any identifiers encountered are determined by looking them up in the environment using a lookup function which takes an identifier and an environment and returns the value to which that identifier is currently bound. As purely functional languages consist of only declarations and expressions, their semantics can be fully defined without the need to introduce the concept of a computer store.

When commands, such as the assignment statement, exist in a language, the notion of a store is necessary and functions such as E must include the current store as a parameter. In the declaration of a variable, an identifier is bound to the address of a store location (a reference) and this binding is added to the environment. The store, itself, is modelled in a similar way to the environment, but this time as a function which maps references to their associated values. A function set can be defined which takes a reference, a value and a store and returns a new store to which the reference/value binding has been added.

Consider now the assignment statement. Its effect is to modify the store. The semantic function C takes a command, an environment and a store and returns a new store. The definition:

$$C(\textbf{i := e}, \text{ env}, \text{ st}) = \text{set}(\text{lookup}(\textbf{i}, \text{ env}), \text{ E}(\textbf{e}, \text{ env}, \text{ st}), \text{ st})$$

is interpreted as stating that the effect of executing the command **i := e** in the environment env and store st is to create a new store which differs from st in that the reference bound to the identifier **i** (found by looking up **i** in the environment env) is bound to the value obtained by evaluating the expression **e** in the environment env and store st. As the definition of assignment is in terms of a new store, rather than in terms of a modification to the old store, this is obviously not intended as a model for a possible implementation. The difference between the old and the new store does, however, define the *effect* of the assignment operation.

Denotational semantics is hierarchical in nature with high-level features being defined in terms of lower level features whose meaning has already been defined. The effect of an **if** statement can be defined as:

```
C(if e then s1 else s2, env, st)
    = E(e, env, st) → C(s1, env, st);
              C(s2, env, st)
```

This is interpreted as stating that the effect of executing the **if** statement in the environment env and store st is first to evaluate the expression **e** in env and st and, if the value is true, to return the store obtained by executing the command **s1** in env and st and, if the value is false, to return the store obtained by executing the command **s2** in env and st. It has been assumed that evaluation of the expression **e** does not produce any side-effect, that is, modify the store.

A **while** statement can be defined in a similar way, with iteration being defined using recursion. The definition:

```
C(while e do s, env, st)
    = E(e, env, st)
    → C(while e do s, env, C(s, env, st)); st
```

is interpreted as stating that the effect of executing the **while** statement in environment env and store st is first to evaluate the expression **e** in env and st and, if the value is false, then the **while** statement has no effect and the result is the original store st. If the value is true, the **while** statement is again executed, this time using the store obtained by executing the command **s**.

Axiomatic semantics

The axiomatic method, which is based on symbolic logic, uses **rules of inference** to deduce the effect of executing a construct. The meaning of a statement, or group of statements, S is described in terms of:

1. the condition P (the **pre-condition**) that is assumed or asserted to be true before S is executed, and

2. the condition Q (the **post-condition**) which can be deduced to be true after execution of S.

This is usually written as:

```
{P} S {Q}
```

The post-condition that holds after the execution of one group of statements   1, of course, act as the pre-condition for the next.

Consider the assignment statement **x := x + 1**. If the condition **x ⩾ 0** is true before execution of this statement, then **x > 0** will be true after execution of the statement. This is written as:

```
{x >= 0} x := x + 1 {x > 0}
```

Assertions about a structured statement can be deduced from assertions about its components. The rule of inference for the **if** statement is:

$$\{P \text{ and } \mathbf{e}\} \ \mathbf{s1} \ \{Q\}, \ \ \{P \text{ and not } \mathbf{e}\} \ \mathbf{s2} \ \{Q\}$$

$$\{P\} \ \mathbf{if \ e \ then \ s1 \ else \ s2} \ \{Q\}$$

which states that, when P is true before the **if** statement is executed, Q will be true after the statement is executed if either:

- Q is true after **s1** is executed, provided that P and **e** were both true before **s1** was executed, or

- Q is true after **s2** is executed, provided that P was true and **e** was false before **s2** was executed.

Unlike the other two approaches, the meaning of a statement S is, therefore, not described directly. Instead, the effect of executing S is described indirectly by the relationship between P and Q. This means that the axiomatic method is of most use in verifying and reasoning about the effect of programs. Using axiomatic semantics, program verification of:

$$\{P\} \ S \ \{Q\}$$

consists of proving, using rules of inference like the one shown above, that if the pre-condition P is true before S is executed, the post-condition Q is true after S has been executed.

Instead of being used to verify the correctness of an existing program, axiomatic semantics can be used in program construction by constructing the program and its proof at the same time. The starting point is the pre- and post-conditions, from which the statements which satisfy these assertions are to be constructed. In order to support this approach to program construction, assertions are included in some programming languages, an example being Eiffel.

As operational, denotational and axiomatic semantics are useful under differing circumstances, they can be seen to be complementary to one another, rather than being competitors.

Summary

1. The syntax of a programming language is usually defined using BNF.

2. BNF is an example of a metalanguage, that is, a language used to define other languages.

3. A BNF definition consists of nonterminals, terminals and a series of production rules. Sentences in the language are derived from a special nonterminal known as the start symbol.

4. A BNF grammar imposes a phrase structure on sentences.

5. An ambiguous grammar allows different interpretations for the same sentence.

6. The production rules used in the definition of a language are often used to control the syntax analysis phase of its compiler.

7. In most language reference manuals, the semantics of language constructs are not described formally; rather, they are given in a natural language such as English.

8. There are three approaches to formal semantics: operational, denotational and axiomatic.

9. In denotational semantics, language constructs are modelled by appropriate mathematical objects whose meaning is already known.

10. In axiomatic semantics, rules of inference are used to deduce the effect of executing a language construct.

Exercises

12.1 Give BNF definitions for:

(a) an unsigned integer number,

(b) an unsigned real number, where there must be at least one digit before and after the decimal point.

12.2 Using the definition for `<exp>`, `<term>` and `<factor>` in Section 12.1, give a derivation tree for the expression a * b + c.

12.3 Section 12.1 gives a BNF definition for an algebraic expression. Extend this definition so that the expressions can include the relational operators >, >=, <, <=, = and ! = which all have a lower precedence than the arithmetic operators.

12.4 For each of the following grammars, in which `<start>` is the start symbol, determine the language (the set of sentences) which is generated:

(a) `<start> ::= a | a <start>`

(b) `<start> ::= a | a <next>`
    `<next> ::= a <start>`

(c) `<start> ::= a <start> | a <next>`
    `<next> ::= b | b <next>`

(d) `<start> ::= a <start> b | ab`

12.5 List all the valid sentences with one, two or three characters which can be derived from the EBNF grammar:

```
sequence -> 'A' { 'B' | 'C' } [ 'D' ]
```

Represent the EBNF grammar as a syntax diagram and give an equivalent grammar in BNF.

12.6 How is the 'dangling else' problem dealt with in Pascal?

12.7 When there are alternative right parts, it can be far from obvious, even with very simple grammars, which one is to be chosen at each stage. As an example, derive the sentences abag and aabg using the following grammar in which <sentence> is the start symbol.

```
<sentence> ::= a <first> | <second> g
<first> ::= <third> g | b <first> | a <first>
<second> ::= <third> b | <third> <second>
<third> ::= a
```

12.8 Using the grammar:

```
<sentence> ::= p <char> <continue>
           | r <char> <continue>
<char> ::= a | b
<continue> ::= , <char> <continue> | ;
```

in which <sentence> is the start symbol, derive the sentence:

```
p a, b, a;
```

Why was this straightforward? At each stage, how many symbols ahead must be scanned to determine which of the alternative right parts was to be used?

Bibliography

Most programming language texts include a definition of the language's syntax using either BNF or syntax diagrams, while an introduction to language grammars is given in most books on compiling such as that by Aho *et al.*(1986). Books on semantics are far from simple. One that is more accessible than most is by Nielson and Nielson (1992).

Aho, A.V., Sethi, R. and Ullman, J.D. (1986). *Compilers: Principles, Techniques and Tools*. Addison-Wesley.

Naur, P. *et al.* (eds) (1960). 'Report on the Algorithmic Language ALGOL 60'. *Comm. ACM*, **3**, 299–314.

Nielson, H.R. and Nielson, F. (1992). *Semantics with Applications*. John Wiley & Sons.

Chapter 13

Input, output and GUIs

In the second edition of this book, we described input and output (I/O) as the Cinderella of language design. Well, Cinderella has been to the ball and met her Prince Charming. His name is GUI. Graphical user interfaces (GUIs) are now the usual way in which users interact with application programs and they can dominate the structure of the resulting programs. We look at how languages provide GUI components such as buttons, menus and windows, how they handle events such as mouse clicks and at the support that they provide for event loop programming.

I/O routines must be able to deal with a wide range of different peripheral devices and so, for reasons of simplicity, languages abstract away from the physical details. Most languages provide support for input and output through a set of predefined or library routines rather than by special statements in the language.

When dealing with files, both input and output are dealt with in terms of sequences of records. When the information is in human readable form, each record usually corresponds to a line of text. Until the advent of graphical user interfaces, interactive I/O was dealt with in the same way as accessing sequential files on disk. The problems caused by this are discussed. Binary files and direct access files, where records may be written or read in any order, are then considered.

13.1 Introduction

Until recently, menu-driven systems, mouse input, multiple windows and icons were regarded as being part of an operating system or an application package, rather than being features of a high-level language. That situation has now completely changed and an important part of the appeal of Java, Delphi and Visual Basic is the support that they give for the creation of graphical user interfaces. The simplest way of regarding files, menus, windows, buttons etc. is as objects. Object-oriented programming is therefore central to modern input/output systems and languages such as C++, Java and Delphi have an extensive hierarchy of library classes to deal with both interactive and file I/O. Such library classes are regarded by users as a central and intrinsic part of these languages.

Until the advent of GUIs, the commands for the interactive reading and writing of human readable information dealt in terms of lines of text and the language facilities had not changed much from the days when batch processing was the norm and the standard devices were a card reader and a line printer. That is how languages such as Pascal, Ada 95, C++ and Fortran deal with interactive I/O and the facilities are very similar to those used with text files. Languages such as Java support this approach as an alternative to using a GUI.

The operations required to implement graphical user interfaces are very complex and difficult to program. However, the complexity can be hidden by encapsulating the operations into library classes and by extending language implementations to provide the necessary run-time support. That allows GUIs to be added to existing languages. In this way, Delphi has built GUI facilities on top of Object Pascal while many C++ implementations provide the necessary extensions.

Graphical user interfaces have a major impact on the structure of a program. The resulting programs are **event driven**. They typically wait for some user interaction, handle the interaction, carry out some processing in response and then wait for further user interaction. That is, the program reacts to events sent to it by the user. This is implemented by means of an **event loop**. In a language such as Java, the event loop does not have to be explicitly programmed as it is provided, behind the scenes, by the Java virtual machine.

No matter how the user interacts with a computer, an important part of the input process is to convert information from an external human readable form, such as text, to a suitable internal representation. With integer data, for example, the external representation is a series of digit characters with a possible leading $+$ or $-$ sign. Reading an integer involves reading such a character string and converting it into the computer's internal representation for integer numbers (for example, two's complement). Similarly, when results are output the internal representation has to be converted back into the appropriate character string. Java is unusual in that it makes these two stages explicit. All input and output of textual information in Java involves character strings and separate conversion routines are then used to convert between a string and an integer, floating-point number, etc.

Input and output devices (I/O devices) are much slower than the central processor. To prevent I/O instructions slowing down the operation of the whole computer, they are executed concurrently with processing by the CPU, and buffers are used to hold intermediate information. This process is normally handled by the operating system and is transparent to the programmer, the exception being when the language is to be used for systems programming. Even then, programmers do not need to get involved with low-level detail, unless they wish to, because systems programming languages usually have different levels of I/O instructions.

13.2 Input and output of text

Traditional text based input/output is based on an abstraction of the peripherals used in the early days of computing. In the original definition of Fortran, for example, it was assumed that input came from punched cards and output went to a line printer. These devices can be considered as delivering or receiving a series of fixed-length records, with each record being regarded as a line of characters divided into fields. Similarly, information held in a file on backing store can be considered as a series of such records and so can be dealt with in the same way.

The abstraction used in ISO Pascal is that all I/O, even when it involves a terminal, is considered to be to or from a sequential file; that is, a file in which the records may only be accessed in the order in which they were originally written. A Pascal program automatically declares two variables, called input and output, which are of the predefined type Text and which are associated with what are called the **standard input and output devices**; usually the keyboard and terminal screen. Type Text is a file of lines where each line consists of a sequence of characters terminated by an end-of-line indicator. A Text file is not the same as a file of characters since the implementation of the end-of-line indicator depends on the particular operating system used, and systems differ in the way that they represent the end of a line. This abstraction of text I/O is used in many languages, examples being Ada, C, C++ and Java.

To write a character string followed by the values of the integer variables item and number to the standard output device in Pascal, we have:

```
write('ANSWERS =', item, number)
```

which is shorthand for:

```
write(output, 'ANSWERS =', item, number)
```

The default layout is implementation dependent, although the number of columns to be used in writing a value can be specified, as in:

```
write('ANSWERS =', item : 9, number : 7)
```

In C, high-level I/O is provided by a standard library called stdio. To control layout a format specification is incorporated within the print statement. Hence:

```
printf("ANSWERS =%9d%7d", item, number);
```

causes ANSWERS = to be output followed by the value of item in the next 9 columns and the value of number in the following 7. The format %d indicates that an integer number is to be printed. Other formats are possible, such as %s for string, %c for character and %f for floating-point number. Fortran has separate FORMAT statements as in:

```
      PRINT 51, ITEM, NUMBER
   51 FORMAT ('ANSWERS =', I9, I7)
```

but Fortran 90 also allows the format to be incorporated into the PRINT statement. The main advantage of format specifications is that it makes it straightforward to output tables of information.

Input and output in C++ uses a different library from C, namely `iostream`. This library declares two variables `cin` and `cout` which are associated with the standard input and output devices. The variables are respectively of type `istream` and `ostream` which represent input and output streams of characters in which the end-of-line indicator is treated specially. They therefore are similar to type `Text` in Pascal. We output values to the standard output device using the insertion operator << as in:

```
cout << "ANSWERS =" << item << ' ' << number;
```

Note that we need to explicitly output a space to separate the two numerical values as the minimum possible number of columns is used. To set the number of columns for a number we write:

```
cout << "ANSWERS ="
        << setw(9) << item << setw(7) << number;
```

Languages differ in how they output the end of line indicator. In Fortran, each `PRINT` statement causes information to be written on a new line while, in most languages, values are written on the current line. To output an end-of-line indicator in Pascal, `writeln` is used instead of `write`. Ada has a special procedure called `new_line` while in C, C++ and Java we output the character \n. The end-of-line indicator is treated internally as a single character even in operating systems such as Microsoft Windows where it is physically represented as two separate characters.

Input is usually **free format** with the strings representing numbers being separated by spaces or new lines. In Pascal, for example, the statement to read two values is:

```
read(item, number)
```

which is shorthand for:

```
read(input, item, number)
```

The statement:

```
readln(item, number)
```

will read two values and then skip all the remaining characters in the line up to and including the end-of-line indicator. In C, we must indicate the type of each item input in a format statement as in:

```
scanf("%d%d", &item, &number);
```

In C++, the extraction operator >> is used to 'extract' values from the stream `cin` and we write:

```
cin >> item >> number;
```

In early versions of Fortran, we always had to specify the format of input data although recent versions allow free format.

When reading data, it is often important to determine if the current position is at the end of a line. As the end-of-line indicator is read as the space character in Pascal and is skipped in Ada, these languages have predefined Boolean functions (eoln in Pascal and end_of_line in Ada) to indicate when we are at the end of a line. In C, C++ and Java the end-of-line indicator has the value \n and so we can just test for that character.

I/O in Pascal was not designed with interactive input in mind. A statement such as readln(item) reads the value of item, skips the rest of the characters on the line, including the end-of-line indicator, and then inputs the first character on the next line into what is known as the file buffer variable. In interactive input, this character may not yet have been typed in and so cannot be read. In early implementations of Pascal, this caused programs to hang up at unexpected times, waiting for input. Most recent implementations of Pascal solve this problem by using what is called **lazy I/O**, where the reading of the next character into the file buffer variable is delayed until it is required.

Languages differ in what may be read and written. In Pascal, for example, items of type Char, Integer, Real and Boolean, together with packed arrays of Char, may be written, but Boolean variables may not be read and strings have to be read in as a series of individual characters.

High-level text I/O in Ada is provided by the package Text_Io, which provides facilities at a similar level to Pascal I/O. This package defines procedures called get and put to read and write characters or strings. The get and put routines to read and write integers, fixed point numbers, floating-point numbers and the values of enumerated types are declared in local generic packages Integer_Io, Fixed_Io, Float_Io and Enumeration_Io, which are declared within package Text_Io. However, these packages must be instantiated before such I/O can take place. (The instantiation of generic packages was looked at in Section 7.5.) For example, to be able to read and write integers, the following must be written:

```
with Text_Io; use  Text_Io;
procedure example is
  . . .
    package Int_Io is new  Integer_Io(Integer);
    use Int_Io;
  . . .
```

Calls of get and put to read and write character, string and integer values may now be made in procedure example. As Ada allows procedures and functions to be overloaded, the type of the parameter determines which version of get or put is required. The drawback of this approach is that students need to learn about generic instantiation early in an Ada course.

Reading and writing text files

Files are not only used for communication between different programs on the same computer, but for the transfer of information between computers with different operating systems. As systems can, for example, differ in how they represent the end-of-line indicator, this transfer can cause problems. However, it is usually possible to achieve the transfer of a file of records, where each record consists of a line of printable (non-control) characters. If the end-of-line indicator used in the transmitting system is known to the network, a series of records can be sent. On receipt of each record, the receiving system can insert its own end-of-line indicator.

To read or write information to a file, we need to do two things. We must associate the name of the physical file on disk with some logical file name which we will use within our program and we must open the file for reading or writing. Usually, when an existing file is opened for writing, it is replaced, while if no such file exists, it is created.

We look at opening files in several languages. In each case, we use the identifiers `oldFile` and `newFile` for the logical file names and the character strings `input.txt` and `output.txt` for the names of the actual files on disk. Although, in each case, we use a string constant for the names of disk files, we can use a string variable instead and so the association between logical and physical files can be set up and changed during program execution.

In systems that support graphical user interfaces, we typically want to be able to open a window in which we can browse and navigate through the available folders on disk to determine which file is to be opened. Setting up such a facility is complicated, but is provided in languages like Java and Delphi as part of the standard library.

In Ada, logical file names are declared to be of type `File_Type`, as in:

```
oldFile, newFile: File_Type;
```

Ada files may have the mode `in_file` or `out_file` and the procedure call:

```
open(oldFile, in_file, "input.txt");
```

will cause the logical file called `oldFile` to be associated with the backing store file whose name is `input.txt` and for that file to be opened for reading. The call:

```
create(newFile, out_file, "output.txt");
```

will create a new file with the name `output.txt` and will associate that file with the logical file `newFile` so that it can be written to. The same approach is used in C where logical file names are declared to be pointers to type `FILE`, as in:

```
FILE *oldFile, *newFile;
```

We then have the calls:

```
oldFile = fopen("input.txt", "r");
newFile = fopen("output.txt", "w");
```

If a file cannot be opened, the null pointer is returned. In C++, we declare input and output file streams as in:

```
ifstream oldFile;
ofstream newFile;
```

As `ifstream` and `ofstream` are classes, we use dot notation to associate `oldFile` and `newFile` with `input.txt` and `output.txt` and to open the files:

```
oldFile.open("input.txt");
newFile.open("output.txt");
```

In Java, we declare the variables:

```
BufferedReader oldFile;
PrintWriter newFile;
```

and then associate them with the physical files and open the files using the statements:

```
oldFile = new BufferedReader(
    new FileReader("input.txt"));
newFile = new PrintWriter(
    new FileWriter("output.txt"), true);
```

which is rather over-complicated.

In ISO Pascal, the way in which logical file names are associated with physical files on disk is up to the operating system. This association is fixed and cannot be changed during program execution, for there is no equivalent in standard Pascal of the open and close procedures found in most other languages. This defect has been rectified in most Pascal implementations, an example being Delphi. In Pascal, to open the file associated with oldFile for reading, the command is:

```
reset(oldFile)
```

and to open the file associated with newFile for writing, the command is:

```
rewrite(newFile)
```

The statements to read and write data to files are normally the same as those used with interactive I/O, the difference being that the logical file name is given as an extra parameter. In Ada, for example, overloaded versions of get and put are used for file I/O as in:

```
get(oldFile, item); put(newFile, item);
```

Numerical data in a text file is represented as a character string, but if item is, for example, of type Integer, the system will convert the character string representing the integer to the internal representation of an integer. In Java, we separate these two operations and read and write operations always involve strings. Hence, assuming that info is a String variable, the statements:

```
info = oldFile.readLine();
newFile.println(info);
```

input and output lines of characters. On input, we can then extract numerical items from string info while, on output, we first convert a series of numbers into a string and then write out the string.

In Ada, to close the file associated with newFile, the command is close(newFile). The commands for closing files in other languages are very similar although, of course, in an object-oriented language like C++ and Java we write newFile.close(). Files should be explicitly closed before a program is terminated to ensure that the contents of the intermediate input and output buffers have been emptied.

Input and output is an area where users can easily make errors at run time. Possible errors include:

- trying to open a file that does not exist or is already open,
- trying to read past the end of a file,
- encountering a string that does not correspond to a number when performing numeric input.

Languages like C++ set flags when things go wrong and it is then the responsibility of the programmer to test the status of the appropriate flag before attempting an operation. A much better approach is used in Ada and Java, where the file and exception handling facilities are integrated so that a program is always informed when an error has occurred and can therefore take remedial action. In Ada, package `Io_Exceptions` contains the definition of several predefined exceptions. In Java, we perform I/O in a `try` block and errors cause an `IOException` to be thrown. We can then handle the exception to recover from the error.

13.3 Graphical user interfaces

Users usually interact with an applications program by using the mouse to perform operations such as pressing buttons, choosing items in a menu or selecting a text box into which information may be typed. A program providing GUI facilities needs to be able to define these graphical components, to specify where they are to be displayed in a window and to handle user events such as mouse clicks and keyboard input.

Graphical components

There is general agreement in languages and systems as to the graphical components that should be provided and standard frameworks have been developed for the handling of user events. However, programming these facilities is very difficult and either a high level of abstraction or support from a development system is required if they are to be incorporated into ordinary programs.

Questions arise as to how much control a program should have over the appearance or position of the graphical components, especially when the implementation details are dependent on the operating system being used. As it was designed to be independent of any particular operating system, Java allows a programmer to take a very abstract view. Using the classes declared in the abstract windowing toolkit (AWT), a programmer can declare, for example, objects of class `Button`, but does not have to say what a button looks like or define its size and its actual appearance depends on the system on which it is being displayed.

When the Java `Swing` classes are used to define graphical components instead of the AWT, a programmer can specify the **look and feel** of the graphical components by making a call such as:

```
UIManager.setLookAndFeel(
    UIManager.getCrossPlatformLookAndFeelClassName());
```

Several standard look and feels are available. This causes the components to have the same appearance on all platforms.

Using either the AWT or the Swing classes, the precise positioning of graphical components can be left to what are known as **layout managers**. The simplest layout manager is FlowLayout in which components are placed in a row one after the other in a window. When there is no more room in a row, a component is placed at the beginning of the next row. Other layout managers support more complex layouts. although the precise details are still left to the system. Although this means that the programmer does not have fine control over layout, it can be argued that this is the correct level of abstraction as it is all too easy for the programmer to get bogged down in inconsequential detail.

We discussed in Chapter 1 whether Visual Basic and Delphi are languages or development environments. We will not repeat the discussion here, but briefly consider the facilities they provide for graphical user interfaces. A major difference from Java is that both Visual Basic and Delphi are closely tied to Microsoft Windows and have language features that make direct use of Windows facilities.

To create a Visual Basic or Delphi program, we start by creating a user interface. We specify what the interface is to look like by using graphical tools to draw it using standard components in a window known as a **form**. A program may contain several forms. We therefore do not do any programming in the conventional sense, but interact with a visual development environment which provides the necessary tools to select and place graphical components in a window. The Visual Basic or Delphi system then takes the graphical description and generates the required language instructions needed to implement the interface. The program developer need never know what the actual language instructions look like.

Event handling

A GUI program does not only need to create an interface, it must also specify the event handling code that is to be executed when a user interacts with a graphical component. That requires some mechanism whereby event handling code can be associated with each graphical component.

When we are developing a Visual Basic or Delphi program and wish to attach event handling code to a graphical component in a form, we open the **code window** for that component. The code to be executed when an event generated by that component occurs is then entered into this window. A menu allows us to choose from the different kinds of event supported by that graphical component. Behind the scenes, the Visual Basic or Delphi system provides an event loop, but that is hidden from the programmer. The system will, for example, pick up an event such as a mouse click, determine where it occurred on the computer screen, determine which graphical component is positioned there and cause the associated code (the event handler) to be executed.

To show what is involved, let us consider the creation of a Delphi program that has two buttons and a text box. We can press either of the buttons and the text box will inform us which button was pressed most recently.

The Delphi graphical development system contains several parts, including a **form designer window**, a **toolbox** of built-in components and an **Object Inspector** window containing the properties of the components and through which they can be changed. Using the mouse, we can select the button component from the toolbox and place it in the chosen position in the form designer window. To put the label Left on the button, we edit its caption property in the Object Inspector. Similarly, a second button can be added to the form designer window and labelled Right. We then select the edit box (i.e. a text box) component from the toolbox and place it in the window. The default internal names for these components are respectively Button1, Button2 and Edit1.

Now that we have designed our interface, we want to write the code to be executed when a button is pressed. In the Object Inspector, we select the Events for Button1 and choose the OnClick event. A window is opened with the skeleton code for a Pascal procedure called Button1Click and we insert the code:

```
Edit1.text := 'Left pressed';
```

In a similar way, we enter the code associated with the other button. We now save our work and compile and run the program. A window with two buttons and a text box appears. When, for example, we press the Left button, the string Left pressed is assigned to the text attribute of the Edit1 text box and that causes it to be displayed. Note that we have only typed in two lines of code, all our other actions have been interactions with the development system. Although the development of more complex Delphi programs will require the addition of a much higher proportion of handwritten code, the Delphi approach is that programmers should do much of their work by interacting with the Delphi visual development system.

Visual Basic works in essentially the same way, except that the inserted code is in an extended Basic rather than Object Pascal. As Basic programs are interpreted rather than being compiled, Delphi programs run much faster than their Visual Basic counterparts.

As with Visual Basic and Delphi, the event loop in Java is hidden behind the scenes. Development tools exist to allow Java programmers to create interfaces in a similar way to that just described for Delphi. However, Java programmers normally write the code that associates event handlers with the graphical components and it is instructive to trace how this is carried out as the Java approach follows a standard pattern used in several languages. To be able to handle events, an object must be declared to be an **event listener** and must register itself with the graphical objects that can generate the events in which it is interested. An event listener object contains the definition of an appropriate event handler. There are different kinds of event listeners and events, but we will only consider ActionListener and ActionEvent which together deal with button events. The principle behind the others is the same.

Most of the processing that takes place is hidden from the applications programmer. For example, when a user performs an event such as clicking on a button, the Java Virtual Machine, behind the scenes, informs the relevant Button object by calling its processActionEvent method. Execution of processActionEvent causes the Button object to inform the ActionListener objects that have registered with it that an ActionEvent has occurred by calling their action event handler (a method called actionPerformed). All a programmer has to do is register their ActionListener object with the appropriate Button objects and provide a suitable implementation for the actionPerformed method. A UML class diagram showing the associations involving the Button and WhichButton classes and the ActionListener interface is given in Figure 13.1. The diagram shows that

WhichButton implements the ActionListener interface.

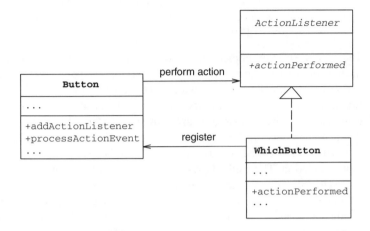

Figure 13.1   Associations in an event listener.

The UML diagram is implemented in the following applet which gives a Java solution to the problem of having two buttons and a text box (a TextField in Java) with the text box reporting which button was pressed most recently.

```java
import java.applet.Applet;
import java.awt.*;
import java.awt.event.*;

public class WhichButton extends
      Applet implements ActionListener {
  private Button first, second;
  private TextField result;

  public void init() {
    // FlowLayout is the default layout manager
    first = new Button("Left");
    add(first);
    first.addActionListener(this);
    second = new Button("Right");
    add(second);
    second.addActionListener(this);
    result = new TextField(11);
    add(result);
  } // init

  public void actionPerformed(ActionEvent ev) {
    if (ev.getSource() == first)
      result.setText("Left pressed");
```

```
    if (ev.getSource() == second)
      result.setText("Right pressed");
  } // actionPerformed
} // WhichButton
```

The WhichButton applet imports the graphical and the event handling classes from the awt library and declares two Button variables and one TextField variable. Execution automatically begins with execution of the init method where the Button and TextField objects are instantiated and added to the applet window using add. We have made the applet an event listener by stating in its class heading that it implements the ActionListener interface. This interface contains a single abstract method called actionPerformed for which the applet must provide an implementation. The method actionPerformed is the event handler.

WhichButton registers itself with the Button objects first and second by calling their addActionListener method. Now, whenever one of these two buttons is clicked, it causes the applet's actionPerformed method to be called with an ActionEvent parameter. During execution of actionPerformed we can find out which button has been pressed (i.e. the source of the event) by calling the getSource method of its ActionEvent parameter. Execution of actionPerformed carries out the processing that we require in response to the button click, in this case updating the TextField.

An applet implementing an event listener therefore listens for an event and when it occurs, its appropriate event handler is executed and that will typically initiate some processing. The applet will then wait for the next event. All the difficult programming is done behind the scenes. We are able to consider the execution of programs in terms of high-level events such as a button being pressed and have abstracted away from all the low-level implementation details. However, it can often be difficult to see the overall flow of control as the interface consists of a set of disjoint event handlers.

Event handling using the Java Swing components occurs in exactly the same way as with the AWT components. The Swing classes provide many extra facilities, but converting a program using the AWT to Swing is straightforward. In our example WhichButton, we must add the statement:

```
import javax.swing.*;
```

and replace the classes Applet, Button and TextField by JApplet, JButton and JTextField. Instead of adding a GUI component directly to an Applet, we add it to the ContentPane of a JApplet and so the calls of add must be replaced by calls such as:

```
getContentPane().add(first);
```

The fact that, at the time of writing, Java has alternative ways of defining graphical components demonstrates both the strengths and weaknesses of defining GUI facilities in class libraries that are not part of the core language. It makes it straightforward to define a new improved approach to GUI design, but has its downside it that it is perhaps too easy to make changes. Programmers and system developers want stability so that they do not have to be continually making changes to working programs.

The WhichButton example showed how a text box can be used to output information in Delphi and Java. A text box is also the usual way in which textual or numeric information is entered into a system through a graphical user interface. However, the information obtained from a text box is a character string and so, when numerical input is required, the string must be explicitly converted into a number. Built-in conversion routines are therefore required. The following calls will convert the string input from the text box inTxt into an integer i:

```
i = Integer.parseInt(inTxt.getText()); // Java
i := StrToInt(inTxt.Text); { Delphi }
```

There is, of course, the possibility that the string does not represent an integer and so conversions like this should always be done within a **try** block so that we can handle the exception thrown when the conversion does not work.

13.4 Binary and direct access files

Binary files

Up till now, the discussion on I/O has concentrated on text files. However, when a file is created by one program, so that it can be read by another, there is no need for conversion between some internal representation and a human readable external form. We therefore have the notion of a **binary file**.

In Pascal, for example, instead of declaring a file to be of type Text, it can be declared to be a file of, for example, Integer:

```
var old : file of Integer;
```

The exact way in which the integers are represented in the file is implementation dependent, although the probability is that they will be in binary; that is, in the same form as their internal representation. All that can be guaranteed here is that a file written by a Pascal program on a particular system as a file of Integer can be read as a file of Integer by another Pascal program on the same system.

A file can be considered to consist of a series of records where each record consists of a series of fields. This structure can be represented in Pascal by declaring a record type with the appropriate field structure. Assuming a record type RecordItem, file variables can then be declared as:

```
var oldFile, newFile : file of RecordItem;
```

If the variable thisRecord has been declared to be of type RecordItem, the following loop will cause the contents of file oldFile to be copied to file newFile:

```
reset(oldFile); rewrite(newFile);
while not eof(oldFile) do
begin
  read(oldFile, thisrecord);
  write(newFile, thisrecord);
end;
```

Each call of read reads the contents of the next complete record in file oldFile into the record variable thisRecord, while each call of write outputs the contents of a complete record. In a similar way, object-oriented languages allow us to have files of objects.

In Ada, the generic package Sequential_Io contains the definition of I/O for sequential files. To deal with a sequential file of items of the record type RecordItem, this package has to be instantiated as:

```
package Seq_Int_Io is new  Sequential_Io(RecordItem);
```

The package contains definitions of file management procedures such as open, create and delete similar to those declared in Text_Io. One difference is that reading and writing is done by calls to read and write instead of get and put.

Direct access files

As well as having sequential files, many languages support direct access files where items may be read or written in any order. Thus, there must be some means of indicating which position in the file is being referred to. Such facilities are available in Fortran, C, C++ and Ada, but not in standard Pascal.

To illustrate how direct access is handled, consider the facilities available in the Ada generic package Direct_Io. It is very similar to Sequential_Io except that, as well as having procedures read and write with the specification:

```
procedure read(file : in File_Type;
    item : out Element_Type);
procedure write(file : in File_Type;
    item : in Element_Type);
```

which transfer an item to or from the current position in a file, it also has:

```
procedure read(file : in File_Type;
    item out Element_Type; from : Positive_Count);
procedure write(file : in File_Type;
    item in Element_Type; to : Positive_Count);
```

in which the position of the item can be specified. The subtype Positive_Count is an implementation-defined integer subrange.

This package also has a file of mode inout_file as well as in_file and out_file, which allows the contents of a file to be updated while it is still open for reading.

13.5 Multimedia

The representation of graphical, video and audio information has become increasingly important and file formats have been designed to represent such information. The GIF (Graphics Interchange Format) and JPEG (Joint Photographic Experts Group) formats are commonly used for graphics. Most users do not need to know the internal details of such formats as these files are created and manipulated through packages or by special library routines. The Java standard library, for example, contains classes to support both these formats. Similarly, audio clips can be represented and played in several different audio file formats using Java library classes. Delphi also provides full support in its library so that applications can play video and audio clips. Most modern computers have special hardware to deal with audio and so the only language support needed is to initiate and stop the playing of the clip.

The ability to manipulate and display graphics and play audio information has meant that computers have become **multimedia machines**. The distinction between television, telecommunications and computing has almost disappeared. This area of programming is therefore becoming increasingly important and will have an increasing impact on the facilities that will be expected from general-purpose languages.

Summary

1. Graphical user interfaces are the usual way in which users interact with application programs.

2. Programs using graphical user interfaces are event driven; they wait for some user interaction, handle the interaction, carry out some processing in response and then wait for further user interaction.

3. There is general agreement in languages and systems as to the graphical components that should be provided and standard frameworks have been developed for the handling of user events.

4. Input and output is complex and languages abstract away from the physical details.

5. Most languages provide support for input and output through a set of predefined or library routines rather than by special statements in the language.

6. After information in human readable form has been input into a computer, it must be converted into a suitable internal representation. Conversion in the opposite direction is required on output.

7. In Pascal, all I/O, including interactive I/O, is considered to be to or from a sequential file. A Pascal text file is a file of lines. This approach has been followed in many later languages.

8. A graphical user interface is created in Visual Basic or Delphi using a visual development environment.

9. In Java, an event listener registers itself with the graphical objects in which it is interested. The event listener contains the definitions of appropriate event handlers.

10. In standard Pascal, the association between logical file names and particular physical files cannot be changed during program execution. This is in contrast to many other languages which have explicit open and close instructions.

11. In direct access files items may be read or written in any order.

13.1 Compare the relative ease of presenting the results of executing a program as a table in Pascal and in Fortran.

13.2 Languages like Fortran have special I/O instructions while later languages use predefined procedures and functions to handle I/O. Which approach is to be preferred and why?

13.3 Many languages treat all I/O as if it were to or from a sequential file. What difficulties does this cause with interactive I/O?

13.4 Java provides a system-independent graphical user interface while Visual Basic and Delphi are closely tied to a particular operating system. Discuss the advantages and disadvantages of these two approaches.

13.5 In what way are programs that provide a GUI event driven? How does this affect the structure of the resulting program?

13.6 To what extent is the provision of facilities for graphical user facilities a language feature and to what extent is it part of the operating system?

13.7 In Java, a graphical user interface can be created using visual development tools or it can be programmed explicitly. Compare the advantages and disadvantages of these two approaches.

Bibliography

Input and output in the various languages is described in the language texts listed at the end of this book. The Java `Swing` classes are described by Walrath and Campione (1999).

Walrath, K. and Campione, M. (1999). *The JFC Swing Tutorial*. Addison-Wesley.

Chapter 14

The future

The first part of this chapter looks at how computer use has changed during the 1990s and at the expected developments in programming languages in the first few years of the twenty-first century. Speculation beyond this point is too unreliable to be useful to current computer users. The second part of the chapter then looks at language design in general and examines how it is likely to develop. As the use of computers in safety critical systems continues to increase, particular attention is paid to those features that support the production of reliable programs, such as data abstraction and the need for language structures that make it easier to reason about a program's effect.

14.1 Introduction

The increase in computer use throughout the 1990s has been spectacular. It has been driven by several factors:

- The speed and capacity of computers has increased significantly while they have continued to decrease in price. Home PCs are now more powerful than the expensive workstations used in research laboratories a decade ago.

- The cheapness and reliability of digital technology has led to:

  (a) its widespread use in control systems,

(b) the amalgamation of telecommunications and the technology supporting the entertainment industry (e.g. digital television and CDs) with the computer industry.

● The World Wide Web has revolutionised how the Internet is used. Electronic commerce has become a practical proposition.

This has led to new ways in which computers are being used and the need either for new languages or for extensions to existing ones.

14.2 Procedural and object-oriented languages

Given the far-reaching changes that have occurred in both hardware and software design, it is surprising to find that 40 years on, the old war horses, Fortran and COBOL, still hold a sizeable share of the scientific and business programming markets, respectively. Other long-lasting languages are Pascal, BASIC and C which were developed in the late 1960s and early 1970s, although a major part of their current use is within newer systems or languages: Pascal within Delphi, Basic within Visual Basic and C within C++.

As was stated at the beginning of this book, there is a great deal of inertia in the computing world. Once a language has been accepted, has a large user community and a large body of algorithms, systems and programs have been developed, it is difficult (if not impossible) to replace it. Certainly, despite the wishes of their critics, Fortran and COBOL will continue to be used in the foreseeable future, with new versions continuing to emerge. However, it is far from certain that all programmers will use the facilities provided by a new version. Hence, many people supposedly programming in C++ are really still programming in C and it would be interesting to determine the proportion of Fortran programmers who restrict themselves to the features of Fortran 77.

It is therefore clear that the main development in language design, at least as far as it impacts on widely used languages, has been evolutionary rather than revolutionary. Ideas in software development such as ADTs, modularity and object-orientation emerge and lead to a large number of new experimental languages. These ideas then impact on the next versions of the most widely used languages and it is these new versions that become dominant rather than one of the completely new languages. As an example, the 1980s and 1990s saw object-oriented features being added to virtually all widely used procedural languages.

It could be argued that Ada and Java are exceptions to this rule, but Ada required the massive backing of the US Department of Defense and it has not become the dominant language that its supporters in the 1980s expected. The design of Ada was also very influenced by Pascal. Ada is no longer a new language and it provides another example of the evolution of languages, as Ada 95 has incorporated object-oriented constructs. Java is a new language which has made a major impact. However its designers were very careful to base the core language on C++ so that it would be attractive to C++ programmers. It can be argued that a much better Java could have been developed by not following C++ syntax so closely, but it is then likely that it would not have been so successful.

Cost is another reason why new experimental languages have not supplanted revised versions of existing languages. A language such as Java is described as being small, but that is not the whole story. A central reason for the success of Java is its large library which not only provides support for standard abstract data types, but also for graphical user interfaces and networking. The resulting Java system is very large and required the resources of a large company (Sun Microsystems) in its development. The days when a small research group can produce a successful general-purpose language such as Pascal or C seem to be over.

A major reason is that there is now no clear dividing line between a language and its support environment. The problem is not in designing a good, clean and useful core language, for it is the provision of the support environment that requires major effort and therefore is very expensive. As the importance of large standard libraries and integrated support environments is likely to continue to grow for the foreseeable future, this problem is not going to disappear.

New languages aimed at a particular application domain can continue to be developed and become widely used, an example being scripting languages such as Perl. If a new language clearly fills a gap then it can build up an enthusiastic user base even though its library is very small. Enthusiasts in the user group can then work together to enhance the support environment. This is the way that many scripting languages are being enhanced.

Scripting languages are not new, but the latter half of the 1990s has seen a great upsurge in interest about them. As computer systems, including networks of systems, become more sophisticated, the need for their different parts to communicate with each other becomes of increasing importance. This leads to the need for 'glue languages' to integrate components written in different languages. Scripting languages such as Perl are ideal for this. Of course, one of the reasons that Perl was readily adopted, initially by the Unix community, is that its syntax is based on C.

The fact that most widely used languages are enhancements of earlier versions does not mean that there have not been exciting developments. The visual development environments of Visual Basic and Delphi, for example, make radical changes to the way that people develop programs. Graphical user interfaces have become ubiquitous, both within development environments and in the software being developed. Describing what you want your GUI to look like by drawing it on the screen and letting the development system generate the required code is an obvious way of easing a programmer's workload. As PCs and workstations become ever more powerful, it is likely that the power and sophistication of visual development environments will continue to increase.

The challenge for language designers is then to ensure that there is a straightforward connection between the code automatically generated for the graphical interface and the event handling code to be written by the programmer. Not only should the connection be simple for the programmer to use, there should be a simple conceptual model so that the programmer can understand what is happening even if this understanding is at a very high level of abstraction. Although visual development environments exist for Java, it is common for the Java programmer to write the code for the graphical user interface rather than to have the code generated automatically. However, the event-handling model is at a sufficiently high level of abstraction that complex GUIs can be written by novice programmers. Being able to program GUIs in this way is one of the main attractions of Java.

One of the reasons for the widespread adoption of object-oriented languages is that they provide the basis for the necessary abstraction. An object-oriented program can be considered to be a set of components which interact with one another through strictly defined interfaces. An automatically generated graphical interface can be regarded as one of these components.

The changes in the way that languages are being used to create programs do have a downside. If software development becomes largely concerned with interacting with a visual development environment and programs consist largely of calls of routines from predefined libraries then traditional skills such as algorithm design become less important. For the majority of programmers, the very nature of programming may be changing to something more like component engineering, with only a small percentage of programmers implementing the methods which others will use.

Of course, the majority of computer users have never needed or wanted to learn how to program in a general-purpose language such as Fortran, COBOL or C++. Their interest is in using spreadsheets, accessing databases or using languages whose use is restricted to a particular user domain. The interface to such systems is of course a language, but users do not usually consider their actions as programming. A user-friendly graphical interface is a central feature of these systems and we can only expect that the power and flexibility of such systems will continue to increase and make inroads into problem domains which have traditionally been tackled by conventional programming languages.

Systems and languages for creating and defining documents are also becoming more powerful. For example, HTML is the language used to define the content of a web page. A web page is an example of an active document with which its users can interact. HTML scripts are interpreted and can include active elements such as hypertext links, forms, Java applets and JavaScript code. Extensions to this concept such as XML (eXtensible Markup Language) can embed information about their own structure. In this book, we have not regarded HTML and XML as programming languages, but as more information is encoded in documents, the distinction between programs and documents is likely to become blurred.

14.3 Declarative languages

The main declarative languages are the functional subset of Lisp, together with the newer functional languages such as ML and Haskell and the logic language Prolog. The 1980s and early 1990s saw great interest in declarative languages and experimental hardware was developed for their efficient implementation. However, although research interest in them remains high, they have made little impact outside academic circles. The programming world seems to be divided into two camps. There are those who believe that their simplicity and elegance, combined with the fact that they are amenable to mathematical reasoning, make it self-evident that declarative languages are the obvious way to express algorithms and there are those who do not. The two groups face each other with mutual incomprehension.

When discussing procedural and object-oriented languages, we dealt with the importance of a development environment including the provision of extensive libraries.

Wadler (1998) suggests that one of the main reasons for the lack of penetration of functional languages into the wider programming community is the lack of such application support. This lack is surprising because one of the reasons for the success of Lisp in the 1960s and 1970s was that it provided a development environment at a time when they were unusual. It remains to be seen if the functional programming community will follow Wadler's advice.

Their high level of abstraction and lack of side-effects mean that declarative languages are more amenable to mathematical reasoning than imperative languages and so they are well suited to the development of safety critical systems. Also, because of their lack of side-effects, it is relatively straightforward to implement functional languages on parallel hardware. Although interest in parallel hardware seems to have declined during the 1990s, there is no reason why interest will not revive, especially when we reach the limits of what is possible with a single processor. If hardware meant that functional languages could be implemented more efficiently than imperative languages then everything would change.

(14.4) Language design

The aim of this section is to look at language design in general to see if any conclusions can be made about the features that are central to the design of a modern language. To some extent, this will of course depend on what the language is to be used for, but it should be possible to identify common goals.

A principal aim of a programming language should be to support the development of reliable programs. This means that it should help the designer or programmer during the development process and should lead to programs that are straightforward to read and understand. It is, of course, possible to write obscure programs in any language, but there can be no doubt that the development of techniques such as programming by stepwise refinement, coupled with the introduction of languages such as Pascal that support the systematic development of programs, led to an improvement in programming standards.

What then are the features that support the production of reliable programs? Among the language features that help support programming by stepwise refinement are the structured control statements introduced in Algol 60 and refined in later languages. Each structured statement has only one entry and one exit point. A program constructed from such statements consists of a linear sequence of program components and the flow of control closely follows the program text. The reason for the unpopularity of the `goto` statement is that the arbitrary transfer of control that is then possible makes reasoning about programs much more difficult.

Apart from the `goto`, two other language constructs have been identified as villains in the programmer's repertoire: global variables and the assignment statement. The ability to modify global variables means that one program component can have an unforeseen effect on another and is an obstacle to the decomposition of large programs into self-contained units that can be reasoned about independently. This is especially so when aliasing is involved. Without the assignment statement, it is not possible to have aliases. Although pure functional languages manage without assignment, it is central to imperative languages and so curbing its abuses seems more appropriate than total abolition.

There has been a general trend in language design to raise the level of abstraction as short high-level programs are generally easier to read, write and understand than long low-level programs. One way of doing this is to use high-level constructs where the programmer states 'what' is to be done rather than giving the details of 'how' it is to be achieved. By removing such details, the opportunity for error is reduced. That is the approach adopted in functional and logic languages. An alternative approach, used in object-oriented languages, is to have large libraries of standard classes which act as the implementations of abstract data types. We are then able to reason about a program in terms of these ADTs and a program consists largely of calls to ADT operations.

Reliable programs should be straightforward to read and understand. Ideally, a language should contain a minimum number of independent concepts which can be combined according to simple rules. As there will then be few, if any, special cases to be considered, such a language should be simple. Unfortunately, the combination of independent concepts in all possible ways usually leads to certain features which are of dubious value and which are difficult and expensive to implement, as was found with Algol 68. In certain cases, the introduction of restrictions on how features may be combined can actually increase the simplicity of a language. After all, a feature of high-level languages is that they do restrict usage, examples being strong typing, restrictions on the arbitrary transfers of control and on performing arithmetic on addresses.

A programming language's design must, therefore, exhibit a proper sense of balance. On the one hand, it is important to have a small set of concepts that can be combined, since this leads to a set of regular rules that can be learned and used much more easily than a set of *ad hoc* rules. On the other hand, it is important to have a small set of restrictions that outlaw those constructs which few, if any, people would ever want to use.

Another important feature of a language design is that there should be no surprises. Features which are similar should look similar; for example, procedure and function declarations should have the same structure. Conversely, features that are different should look different so that similarities are not sought where none exist; for example, the notation used in Pascal to indicate a file buffer variable (filename↑)is the same as that used with pointers and students are often misled into pushing the analogy further than is useful.

Reliability is greatly enhanced if most errors can be detected by a static scan of the program text rather than having to wait till program execution. This suggests the need for static strong typing so that certain logical errors, which would otherwise lie dormant until run time, show up during program translation.

Static typing has been criticised for its lack of flexibility. For example, to sort an array of reals and an array of integers in Pascal, two separate sort procedures are required. In Ada and C++, on the other hand, this can be achieved by generic subprograms and packages and it is no longer necessary to write two separate sort procedures. Instead, there are two instantiations of a generic sort procedure: one for integers and one for reals. This means, however, that two separate sort procedures still exist. In a language like ML, a single polymorphic sort procedure can be used and there is no need to create special purpose forms.

There has been a long debate about the need for types in programming languages. The balance seems to have swung decisively towards the static typing school on the grounds that the need for reliability is more important than flexibility. The functional language ML makes an interesting contribution to this debate. It has types, but the types of objects do not have to be declared. The ML system deduces what the type of objects must be from their use and can report on inconsistent use.

It is also important that a simple typing mistake should cause a syntax error rather than leading to a program which, although logically wrong, is syntactically correct. The classic example of this is the Fortran statement:

```
DO 20 I = 1.6
```

where a decimal point has mistakenly been typed instead of a comma. Thus, the statement, instead of describing the beginning of a loop, represents an assignment statement where 1.6 is assigned to the variable DO20I. Errors of this nature cannot occur when spaces are significant in the program text and when all identifiers are declared before being used, rather than being implicitly declared by their first use.

Security is also enhanced by the introduction of redundant reserved words so that errors can be detected as soon as they occur. For example, in the Pascal statement:

```
if a > 2 then b : = 47
```

the reserved word **then** is not strictly necessary. In a statement such as:

```
if a > 2 b : = 47
```

it is always possible to tell when the end of the Boolean expression has been reached. The appearance of **then** not only helps readability in correct programs, it helps the compiler provide good error diagnostics for wrong programs.

If a language is to be used in the development of reliable large programs, it is essential that it contains some mechanism to support modular decomposition. There is general agreement that this should be achieved by organising programs as a collection of modules. Each module has two parts: a visible part that defines its interface with other modules and an implementation part that is hidden. If a user of a module cannot see, and therefore cannot use, the information in the implementation part then, provided that it has no effect on the module interface, a change in the implementation part cannot have an effect outside the module. The consequences of change are therefore localised and this is essential if reliability is to be maintained when a large system is modified. In object-oriented languages the module (class) is a type. This gives many advantages in the construction of abstract data types.

For large programs, a class is really too small a unit to be the only structuring mechanism. Hence, in Java for example, classes are collected into packages which provide a larger program structuring unit.

14.5 Implementation considerations

The syntax of modern programming languages are formally and unambiguously defined by meta-languages such as Backus–Naur Form (BNF), or graphically by means of syntax diagrams. Having a language syntax defined in this way leads to a regular language structure. Modern compilers directly use a language's syntax rules to translate a source program into machine code. It is therefore important that the syntax can be defined in such a way that it can be easily handled using conventional compiler techniques. This really means that the language should be defined by either an LL(1) or an LR(1) grammar. Such languages are always unambiguous and can be parsed by efficient standard techniques.

The needs of the compiler and the human user as regards the definition of a language's syntax appear to coincide exactly, since language constructs that can be easily translated also seem to be simple for humans to understand, whereas constructs that are difficult to translate are also difficult for humans to comprehend. Indeed, Wirth suggests that the process of language design and language implementation should go together for this very reason, and he has followed this approach in the design of Pascal, Modula and Modula-2. Given the success of these languages, Wirth's views must be taken seriously, although concern with implementation issues can be taken too far.

Often, when a language is being designed, a lot of pressure is placed on the designer to include additional features because they might be useful. Such pressures can be balanced by requests to keep things simple if the language implementation team are in day-to-day contact with the design team.

The importance of language size should not be underestimated. The size and complexity of a language affects the speed at which it can be translated, the size of machine required to host the translation, the complexity of the required compiler and the amount the programmer has to learn in order to be able to use the language. The relative ease with which Pascal could be implemented, coupled with the existence of a portable compiler, greatly enhanced its acceptance while the size of PL/I and the complexity of Algol 68 led to their relative lack of success. Similarly, the widespread adoption of Ada was hampered by the size, cost and lack of speed of its compilers compared with C, C++ and Modula-2. Java perhaps shows the way of the future. It is a small language with much of its power coming from its extensive standard class libraries. Beginning programmers only have to learn the core language plus how to use a small number of the libraries. The other libraries can be ignored until an application that requires them is tackled.

14.6 Development methods

Object-oriented software development supports an integrated approach to the analysis, design and implementation phases of the software life-cycle. In object-oriented analysis, a problem-oriented model is created with real-world entities being modelled as objects which provide services to, and require services of, other objects. This model acts as a specification of the required system. In object-oriented design, the problem-oriented model is transformed into a form which is oriented towards computer implementation. Ideally, there will be a simple mapping from objects in the problem-oriented model to objects in the design model. In the implementation phase, the objects in the design phase are implemented in either an object-based or an object-oriented programming language.

This approach to software development leads naturally to modular systems and, as it supports the goals of data abstraction, encapsulation and information hiding, the resulting systems can be easily maintained or enhanced. The modelling of real-world entities as objects leads to implementations which resemble the original problem. This can be a major help in the understanding of large software systems.

The creation of UML as a standard set of graphical notations for representing object-oriented specifications and designs is a major step forward. When different object-oriented development methods all use the same notation, they can be examined and judged on their real differences and not on presentational issues. Also, now that there is a standard language, it can be expected that a significant proportion of programmers will become familiar with it. Although UML notation is centred on diagrams, these diagrams do have a standard meaning and can form a focus for work on formal development methods.

Once a program has been produced, it is important to ensure that it satisfies its specification. The usual way of doing this is to run the program with suitably chosen data. Although testing is an important stage of the software development process, it does suffer from one major drawback; it can show the presence of errors, but it cannot prove that no errors remain. The ideal approach is therefore to verify a program; that is, to **prove** that the program conforms to its specification. A specification is often written in an informal notation although the trend is increasingly towards using a formal (mathematical) notation, which has led to the development of special specification languages.

A lot of research has gone into proving that programs meet their specification and into how specifications can be automatically transformed into executable programs. Although progress has been made, this research is still a long way from either being able to prove the correctness of large programming systems or automatically generating them from their specification. However, it is at present possible to reason about the effect of programs and thereby to increase one's confidence that the specification is met. To reason about the effect of a large program, it is important that it has been constructed in such a way that it can be decomposed into separate components. It is then possible to reason about these components independently and so use the separate results when reasoning about the program as a whole.

14.7 Conclusions

A major advantage of object-oriented languages is that they are extensible. They provide a small number of built-in types together with the class facility that enables new types to be defined. A standard library can provide a large number of type definitions and the programmer can add more. When a vital new application emerges, support for it can easily be added to the language by defining new library classes. Object-oriented languages are therefore well suited to coping with a rapidly changing world. This suggests that we are not likely to see major changes in the core of the current widely used languages. The additions to their capabilities are more likely to be through changes in their support environment and in additions to their libraries.

One major growth area could be in special purpose languages. By concentrating on a particular problem domain, they can be at a higher level of abstraction and be much smaller and easier to learn than traditional languages. It will, for example, be interesting to see if networking applications will be written using the library facilities of languages such as C++, Java or Delphi, or whether small special-purpose languages will emerge.

The definition of what we mean by a programming language is changing. It is difficult in systems like Delphi and Visual Basic to make a clear distinction between the language and its development environment. It can be argued that this is not a new phenomenon, as development environments were always integral to Lisp, Smalltalk and Basic systems, but it seems clear that this blurring of boundaries is going to increase.

The main change to languages is likely to come as a result of technological change. As hardware continues to increase in power while decreasing in cost, the range of application areas will increase. For example, Java was initially developed to control small household appliances. In this, it was ahead of its time and was re-invented as a language for the Internet. It could well be that it will find increasing use for its original intention.

Summary

1. Languages such as Fortran, COBOL and Lisp, although developed in the 1950s and early 1960s, are still in widespread use.

2. Declarative languages may require the development of new architectures if they are to become widely used.

3. The object-oriented approach has become increasingly important in the requirements analysis, specification and design phases of software development as well as in programming language design.

4. The principal aim of a programming language should be to support the development of reliable programs.

5. There is a correlation between language constructs that are simple for a human to understand and those which are easy for a compiler to translate.

6. There is still much research to be done before it will be possible to prove the correctness of large programs or to generate them automatically from their specification. Reasoning about the effect of a program can, however, increase one's confidence that it meets its specification.

7. As computers become more powerful, the importance of the development environment in which a language is used will increase.

Bibliography

A good description of the formal approach to software development has been given by Partsch (1990).

Partsch, H.A. (1990). *Specification and Transformation of Programs*. Springer-Verlag.

Wadler, P. (1998). 'Why No One Uses Functional Languages'. *ACM Sigplan*, 33(8), 23–27.

Language summaries

This appendix summarises the features of the principal languages dealt with in the text. The languages are given in alphabetical order and are Ada, Algol 60, Algol 68, C, C++, COBOL, Delphi, Fortran, Java, Lisp, ML, Modula-2, Pascal, Perl, PL/I, Prolog and Smalltalk. References to these and all the other languages referred to in the text are given in Appendix 2.

Ada

Ada is a large and powerful language based on Pascal. It includes features to support data abstraction, concurrency and the production and maintenance of large systems.

Program structure and visibility

An Ada program is a collection of modules (subprograms or packages) whose inter-dependency is given by context clauses. One of the modules is the main program and it must be a procedure. A module is compiled in the context of those modules from which it imports information. A package is in two parts: a specification which gives its interface with the rest of the program, and a hidden implementation part. This allows separate compilation.

Data types

The predefined types are `Integer`, `Float`, `Character`, `Boolean` and `String`. Scalar user-defined types are the derived subrange types and the enumeration types. Structured types can be defined using arrays, records and pointers. Abstract data types can be implemented using packages and parameterised abstract data types using generic packages. Ada 95 supports inheritance and dynamic binding.

Type checking

Ada is strongly typed.

Manipulation of structured data

Arrays and records can be passed as parameters and returned as function values. Fixing the size of an array can be delayed until block entry. Dynamic data structures are created using records that have one or more fields of a pointer type. Strings are arrays of `Character`.

Control structures

Structured control statements have explicit terminators. The conditional statements are **if** and **case**. The iterative statements are **while**, **for** and a **loop ... end loop** construct which may be left using an **exit** statement. Exception handling is also supported.

Concurrency

Parallel processing is achieved using tasks. Message passing is used both to pass information and to achieve synchronisation.

Input/output

I/O is supported by a hierarchy of packages whose specifications are given in the Ada Reference Manual. At the highest level, text I/O is supported while the lowest level supports direct access to peripheral devices.

Algol 60

Algol 60 was the original block-structured language and is the direct ancestor of Pascal and many modern imperative languages. It was the first language to have its syntax defined formally using BNF.

Program structure and visibility

It is block structured with blocks inheriting declarations made in enclosing blocks. Procedures may be recursive in Algol 60 and all its descendants. There are no facilities for dealing with very large programs or for separate or independent compilation.

Data types

The predefined types are `Real`, `Integer` and `Boolean`. The only structured type is the array. User-defined types are not available.

Type checking

Implicit conversions are allowed between numeric types.

Manipulation of structured data

Arrays may be passed as parameters, but may not be returned as the value of a function. The bounds of an array do not have to be fixed until block entry.

Control structures

The **if** statement has been copied in most later languages. Iteration is performed by the **for** statement which has several forms, one of which includes a **while** variant.

Concurrency

Not supported.

Input/output

Not defined in the language. Each implementation introduced its own statements.

Algol 68

Algol 68 was designed as the sophisticated and elegant successor to Algol 60, but although it proved popular with theoreticians it was far less popular with programmers. Its definition was difficult to follow and no concessions were made to ease the implementation – a compiler writer's nightmare.

Program structure and visibility

It is a block-structured language. There are no facilities for dealing with very large programs or for separate or independent compilation.

Data types

Predefined types are Int, Real, Char, Bool and String. Array, pointer and structure (record) types can be defined.

Type checking

It is strongly typed.

Manipulation of structured data

There are good facilities for the manipulation of structured objects. The size of a (flexible) array can be changed during program execution. Strings are implemented as flexible character arrays. Subprograms can have subprograms as parameters and functions can return subprograms as values.

Control structures

Unlike Algol 60, control statements in Algol 68 have explicit terminators. The conditional statements are **if** and **case**, but as all statements have values, they are also conditional expressions. As in Algol 60, loops are constructed from the many variants of the **for** statement, which include a **while** statement.

Concurrency

Parallel processing is supported with semaphores being used for synchronisation.

Input/output

I/O (called transput) is by a set of predefined routines. Files may be opened and closed at run time and formatted, unformatted and binary transput are supported.

C

C is a systems programming language and is at a lower level than the other languages dealt with in this book. It has the control and data structures found in modern high-level languages and, as its wide range of operators mirror the machine code instructions found in many computers, C programs are comparable in efficiency to assembly language programs. C is closely identified with the Unix operating system.

Program structure and visibility

The source text of a C program can be distributed among several files, each of which can be compiled independently. Full type checking is not possible, however, across these boundaries. Although it has some features of a block-structured language, subprograms may not be nested.

Data types

The predefined data types are `int`, `char` and `float` together with `short` and `long` (for integers) and `double` (for floating point). User-defined types are enumeration types, arrays and structs (records). Dynamic data structures can be created using pointers.

Type checking

As it is a relatively low-level systems programming language, strict type checking is not imposed although this situation has been greatly improved in ANSI C.

Manipulation of structured data

This is largely achieved by manipulating pointers to structured objects. Strings are implemented as arrays of character.

Control structures

It has structured control statements. The conditional statements are **if** and **switch** and the iterative statements are **while** and **for** together with a **do ... while** construct which tests at the end of a loop.

Concurrency

Not supported directly, but new processes can be created through calls to Unix system routines.

Input/output

I/O is not directly defined in the language, but is implemented by means of a standard library.

C++

C++ was designed to add data abstraction and object-oriented features to C.

Program structure and visibility

Classes support the decomposition of large programs into self-contained units.

Data types

The types are as in C with the addition of classes. This gives information hiding and allows the definition of abstract data types. Class templates support parametrised abstract data types. Derived classes inherit the properties of a base class which they can extend through the definition of new data and function members, or the redefinition of existing function members. Dynamic binding is supported.

Type checking

The type checking of C has been tightened up significantly.

Manipulation of structured data

As in C, this is largely done using pointers. Objects can be allocated space dynamically.

Control structures

As in C.

Concurrency

As in C.

Input/output

A library of predefined routines is available.

COBOL

COBOL is the most extensively used programming language in data processing and is oriented to dealing with large files of data. It has been revised several times and the latest revision includes object-oriented features.

Program structure and visibility

A COBOL program is divided into four divisions. The IDENTIFICATION DIVISION provides commentary and is essentially program documentation; the ENVIRONMENT DIVISION contains machine-dependent program specifications relating logical and physical entities; the DATA DIVISION describes the data and its structure; and, finally, the PROCEDURE DIVISION gives the algorithms. Subprograms do not exist as such, although it is possible to use labelled sequences of statements. There is no recursion.

Data types

The basic types are character strings and numbers whose precision is defined by the programmer in the DATA DIVISION. Arrays exist, but the main structured variables are records, which can be combined together to make files. Dynamic data structures are not supported.

Type checking

Since implicit type conversions are an integral part of COBOL, little type checking is possible.

Manipulation of structured objects

The REDEFINES clause allows more than one data structure to be mapped to the same piece of storage. Array bounds are fixed.

Control structures

There is a restricted IF ... THEN ... ELSE statement, but most control is exercised by the PERFORM statement, which can be used as an iterative statement or as a primitive form of subprogram call. There are labels and GOTO statements.

Concurrency

Not supported.

Input/output

Extensive read and write facilities are provided for both sequential and random access to the records of a file.

Delphi

Delphi is a rapid application development environment that provides support for graphical user interfaces, database access and Internet programming. Its underlying language is Object Pascal.

Program structure and visibility

In addition to Pascal's block structure, Delphi has units (modules) and classes.

Data types

In addition to Pascal's data types, users can use classes to define new types and there is a large library of standard class definitions.

Type checking

Dynamic binding means that the variant record feature of Pascal is not needed.

Manipulation of structured data

Good support for abstract data types.

Control structures

As in Pascal.

Concurrency

Delphi supports active objects through a TThread class and has good library support for distributed systems.

Input/output

It provides excellent support for graphical user interfaces.

Fortran

Fortran is still widely used for numerical applications by scientists and engineers and has been revised to take account of the ideas of structured programming. Fortran 90 supports features such as modules.

Program structure and visibility

A Fortran program consists of a set of independently compiled subprograms. There is no block structure and subprograms communicate through parameter lists and COMMON lists. Recursion was not supported until Fortran 90.

Data types

The predefined data types are INTEGER, REAL, DOUBLE PRECISION, LOGICAL, CHARACTER and COMPLEX. Originally, the only structured types were fixed-size arrays, but Fortran 90 supports arrays whose size can be fixed on subroutine entry, records and pointers.

Type checking

In early versions of Fortran, type checking of actual and formal parameters could not take place due to the requirements of independent compilation, but Fortran 90 provides support for this through module interfaces. There is implicit conversion between integer and real in assignment statements.

Manipulation of structured data

Arrays can be passed as parameters, but may not be returned as the value of a function. Strings are character arrays.

Control structures

Early versions of Fortran did not have structured control statements. This was remedied in Fortran 77 with the block IF statement. Iteration is provided by the DO loop.

Concurrency

Not supported.

Input/output

Special read and write statements with channel numbers to indicate the device and optional FORMAT statements are provided.

Java

Java was developed from C++, but its core language is much simpler. Unlike C++, it is a purely object-oriented language. It is interpreted, allowing a program compiled on one machine to be run on any machine that has an implementation of the Java Virtual Machine. Much of its power comes from a large standard library. As well as ordinary programs, Java has applets which can be used to animate web pages.

Program structure and visibility

Classes support the decomposition of programs into self-contained units and provide support for information hiding. It also has packages which enable classes to be grouped into larger units.

Data types

It has int, char, float, double and boolean as primitive types. All other types are defined using classes. The large standard class library provides built-in types and new classes can be defined by users.

Type checking

It is statically typed although it has casts which require run-time checks.

Manipulation of structured data

Good support for abstract data types. Objects are always accessed by reference and Java has automatic garbage collection. Arithmetic on pointers is not allowed.

Control structures

Similar to C++.

Concurrency

Java supports active objects through a Thread class and has good library support for distributed systems.

Input/output

Extensive library facilities make it simple to implement graphical user interfaces.

Lisp

Lisp is primarily used in artificial intelligence applications and, although it is not a purely functional language, it has all the features needed for functional programming. Its syntax is simple although it is rather offputting to the beginner.

Program structure and visibility

A program consists of function definitions and expressions in which the functions are applied. There is no support for dealing with very large programs.

Data types

The objects manipulated in the language are S-expressions, which can be lists, atoms or functions. Atoms may be symbolic or numerical.

Type checking

Lisp is dynamically typed.

Manipulation of structured data

Lists are first-class objects and so they can be manipulated as easily as scalar objects in imperative languages. Functions may be higher order. Automatic garbage collection is supported by Lisp systems.

Control structures

Recursion is used instead of iteration.

Concurrency

Not dealt with explicitly although, as pure functions have no side-effects, they may be executed in parallel.

Input/output

A set of predefined functions are used to read and write S-expressions.

ML

ML is a modern functional language which, unlike Lisp, is statically typed. Pattern matching is used, as an alternative to conditional expressions, in function definitions.

Program structure and visibility

A program consists of a set of function definitions. Standard ML includes modules as originally defined in the language Hope.

Data types

It supports the implementation of abstract data types.

Type checking

It is strongly typed, but has a type inference system. The user does not have to specify all types as the system can work out what they must be and report on any incompatibilities. Polymorphic functions are supported.

Manipulation of structured data

Lists, functions and instances of abstract data types are first-class objects and so they can be manipulated as easily as scalars in imperative languages. Functions may be higher order and automatic garbage collection is supported.

Control structures

Recursion is used instead of iteration.

Concurrency

It is a sequential language.

Input/output

This is done in a non-functional way.

Modula-2

Modula-2 can be regarded as Pascal extended with modules and with low-level features to support systems programming.

Program structure and visibility

Modules, which can be divided into a definition and an implementation part, support information hiding, data abstraction and separate compilation. Procedure declarations may be nested within modules.

Data types

The predefined types are INTEGER, CARDINAL, REAL, CHAR and BOOLEAN together with LONGINT, LONGCARD and LONGREAL. Scalar user-defined types are subrange and enumeration types. Structured types are arrays, records and sets. Dynamic data structures can be constructed using pointers. Abstract data types can be implemented using modules.

Type checking

The language is strongly typed with the exception of variant records.

Manipulation of structured data

As in Pascal, except that string comparisons are not allowed.

Control structures

Structured control statements have explicit terminators and so compound statements are not required. There are **if** and **case** conditional statements. As well as the Pascal-like iterative statements, **while**, **repeat** and **for** there is a **loop ... end** statement, which may be left by execution of an **exit** statement.

Concurrency

Processes communicate through shared variables with monitors being used to guarantee mutual exclusion. Signals are used to synchronise processes.

Input/output

I/O is provided by a set of library modules.

Pascal

Pascal was designed as a vehicle for the teaching of good programming style. Its emphasis on the importance of types and data structures has been very influential and most recent imperative languages can be classified as Pascal derivatives. It is relatively small and, partly as a consequence of it being designed so that it would be easy to implement, it is available on most computers.

Program structure and visibility

It is a block-structured language, but as there is a single outermost block, neither independent nor separate compilation is supported in the ISO standard language. The only inner blocks are procedures and functions. Inner blocks inherit all declarations made in enclosing blocks. Most implementations of Pascal have added a module facility.

Data types

The predefined data types are Integer, Real, Boolean and Char. Array, record, set, pointer, subrange and enumeration types can be defined.

Type checking

It is strongly typed, apart from variant records.

Manipulation of structured data

Arrays and records may be parameters, but may not be returned as function values. Dynamic data structures are created using records, which have one or more fields of a pointer type. The size of arrays is fixed at compile time, although arrays of different sizes may be passed as parameters. Strings are packed arrays of Char.

Control structures

It has structured control statements. The conditional statements are **if** and **case**; the iterative statements are **while**, **repeat** and **for**. The compound statement is used to group statements together.

Concurrency

Not dealt with.

Input/output

Handled by a set of predefined procedures and functions that do not follow the usual language rules. The association of internal file names with physical external files is not handled in the language. Interactive I/O is dealt with in the same way as I/O to a sequential file.

Perl

Perl is a scripting language with good string manipulation facilities. It is often used to support communication between programs written in other languages and for CGI programming.

Program structure and visibility

It is a language for getting things done simply and quickly rather than for writing large software systems.

Data types

Strings are primitive types. It has associative arrays in addition to ordinary arrays.

Type checking

Variables do not have a type, but are classified as scalar (numbers and strings), array or hash. Hash variables are associative arrays.

Manipulation of structured data

Excellent facilities for string manipulation.

Control structures

Based on C. In addition it has good pattern matching facilities.

Concurrency

It is a sequential language.

Input/output

Good simple file handling facilities.

PL/I

PL/I is a large general-purpose language that was designed to be suitable for both scientific and data processing work. It brought together ideas from Fortran, Algol and COBOL but turned out to be large and unwieldy.

Program structure and visibility

A program consists of a set of external procedures, which may be compiled independently. External procedures may communicate with one another by passing parameters or through EXTERNAL variables. Within an external procedure, the declarations of internal procedures may be nested. Internal procedures inherit declarations from their enclosing blocks.

Data types

Types may be defined in great detail. For example, numeric types can have a mode (REAL or COMPLEX), a scale (FIXED or FLOAT), a base (DECIMAL or BINARY) and a precision. However, the default options are heavily used in defining types. Structured types are arrays and structures (records). Dynamic data structures can be created using pointers. Character strings can be defined to have either a fixed size or to be variable up to a fixed maximum size.

Type checking

When types do not match, implicit conversion rules are applied.

Manipulation of structured data

Structured values can be parameters of procedures, but they may not be returned as values of user-defined functions. There is an extensive set of operators and built-in functions for string handling.

Control structures

A structured **IF** statement is available and the **DO** loop can include a **WHILE** variant. Exception handling is also available.

Concurrency

Primitive tasking facilities are defined, but seldom used.

Input/output

Extensive facilities are available to support data processing work as well as the simpler requirements of scientific programmers.

Prolog

Prolog is a logic programming language in which the programmer states what is to be done rather than how it is to be carried out. The Prolog approach is goal oriented and along with Lisp dominates the artificial intelligence scene.

Program structure and visibility

A Prolog program consists of a database of facts and a series of rules. Although programs can easily be extended by adding new facts and rules, there is no support for the creation of very large programs.

Data types

Prolog has (symbolic) atoms, numbers and structures.

Type checking

It is dynamically typed.

Manipulation of structured data

Structures (which are similar to records in Pascal) can be manipulated as easily in Prolog as can lists in Lisp. Structures are mainly used to represent lists, trees and graphs.

Control structures

To achieve a goal, subgoals are generated and achieved. Tree searching and associated backtracking are built into the interpreter and are not explicitly programmed.

Concurrency

Not dealt with.

Input/output

All data values in Prolog programs can be directly read or written. The standard input and output streams can be redirected to give access to disk files.

Smalltalk 80

Smalltalk is the archetypal object-oriented language. It is not just a language, but is a complete programming environment. Everything in a Smalltalk system is an object, which means that the number of separate concepts are kept to a minimum.

Program structure and visibility

Objects support information hiding. Data local to an object may only be accessed by sending a message to the object. An object responds to a message by selecting a method to carry out the requested task. Objects give a hierarchical structure to large programs.

Data types

The only type is the object. Objects belong to a class, which is itself an object. New classes (subclasses) can be defined which inherit the properties of an existing class (their superclass) which they extend through the definition of new methods. There is automatic garbage collection of inaccessible objects.

Type checking

When messages are sent to an object, the required method is selected dynamically at run time. The nearest thing to a type error is when an object is unable to respond to a message.

Manipulation of structured data

As the Smalltalk approach is centred on the manipulation of objects, its facilities are excellent in this area.

Control structures

Control structures are implemented as messages involving objects of class `block`. A `block` object represents a sequence of instructions which are to be executed when a suitable message is received.

Concurrency

A concurrent system can be built as a collection of concurrent objects that communicate with one another by sending messages.

Input/output

The Smalltalk environment introduced windows, icons and the mouse and so was one of the first languages to support GUIs.

Language texts

Ada

The original Ada reference manual was published in 1983. The revised version of the language is known as Ada 95. There are a large number of books on Ada, three of which are given below.

Barnes, J.G.P. (1998). *Programming in Ada 95* (Second Edition). Addison-Wesley.

Booch, G. and Bryan, D. (1994). *Software Engineering with Ada* (Third Edition). Benjamin/Cummings.

Ichbiah, J.D. *et al.* (1983). *Reference Manual for the Ada Programming Language.* ANSI MIL-STD-1815A-1983.

ISO (1995). *Reference Manual for the Ada 95 Programming Language.* ANSI/ISO/IEC 8652:1995.

Smith, M.A. (1996). *Object-Oriented Software in Ada 95.* Thomson.

Algol 60

Two of the early books on Algol 60 are given below as well as the classic paper edited by Peter Naur which gives the language definition.

Dijkstra, E.W. (1962). *A Primer of ALGOL 60 Programming.* Academic Press.

Ekman, T. and Froberg, C-E. (1967). *Introduction to ALGOL Programming.* Oxford University Press.

Naur, P. *et al.* (eds) (1963). 'Revised Report on the Algorithmic Language Algol 60'. *Comm. ACM*, **6**, 1–17.

Algol 68

The defining document is not easy to read. The description by Lindsey and van der Meulen is more accessible.

Lindsey, C.H. and van der Meulen, S.G. (1977). *Informal Introduction to Algol 68* (Revised Edition). North-Holland.

Van Wijngaarden, A., Mailloux, B.J., Peck, J.E.L., Koster, C.H.A., Sintzoff, M., Lindsey, C.H., Meertens, L.G.L.T. and Fisker, R.G. (1975). 'Revised Report on the Algorithmic Language Algol 68'. *Acta Informatica*, **5**, 1–236.

Algol W

This language is described in the following paper.

Wirth, N. and Hoare, C.A.R. (1966). 'A Contribution to the Development of ALGOL'. *Comm. ACM*, **9**, 413–431.

Alphard

There is only one text.

Shaw, M. (1981). *Alphard: Form and Content*. Springer-Verlag.

APL

The designer Kenneth Iverson wrote the original book on the language before a computer implementation was considered. The implemented version is somewhat different.

Falkoff, A. and Iverson, K.E. (1973). 'The Design of APL', *IBM Journal of Research and Development*. **17**, 324–334.

Iverson, K.E. (1962). *A Programming Language*. John Wiley & Sons.

Polivka, R.P. and Pakin, S. (1975). *APL: The Language and its Usage*. Prentice-Hall.

BASIC

The designers John Kemeny and Thomas Kurtz wrote the first book about the language. Since then the market has been flooded.

Kemeny, J.G. and Kurtz, T.E. (1967). *BASIC Programming*. John Wiley & Sons.

C

A large number of C books have been published, but for a long time the only text was by Kernighan and Ritchie. Their second edition deals with ANSI C. A simpler introduction is given in the book by Kelley and Pohl.

Kelley, A. and Pohl, I. (1998). *A Book on C* (Fourth Edition). Addison-Wesley.

Kernighan, B.W. and Ritchie, D.M. (1988). *The C Programming Language* (Second Edition). Prentice-Hall.

C++

Stroustrup, the designer of C++, has described its design and evolution. The book by Dale *et al.* gives a good undergraduate introduction.

Dale, N., Weems, C. and Headington, M. (1996). *Programming and Problem Solving with C++*. Heath.

Ellis, M.A. and Stroustrup, B. (1990). *The Annotated C++ Reference Manual*. Addison-Wesley.

Stroustrup, B. (1994). *The Design and Evolution of C++*. Addison-Wesley.

Stroustrup, B. (1997). *The C++ Programming Language* (Third Edition). Addison-Wesley.

CLU

The most accessible reference is given below.

Liskov, B., Snyder, A., Atkinson, R. and Schaffert, C. (1977). 'Abstraction Mechanism in CLU'. *Comm ACM*, **20**, 564–576.

COBOL

There are many textbooks to choose from, two of which are listed below.

Doke, E.R. (1997). *Introduction to Object-Oriented COBOL*. John Wiley & Sons.

Parkin, A. and Yorke, R. (1996). *COBOL for Students* (Fourth Edition). Edward Arnold.

Delphi

The text by Williams and Walmsley gives an introduction to Delphi suitable for an undergraduate course.

Williams, S. and Walmsley, S. (1999). *Discover Delphi*. Addison-Wesley.

Eiffel

The two books by Meyer describe, respectively, the language definition and the use of the language.

Meyer, B. (1992). *Eiffel: The Language*. Prentice-Hall.

Meyer, B. (1997). *Object-oriented Software Construction* (Second Edition). Prentice-Hall.

Euclid

A complete issue of Sigplan Notices was devoted to the language.

Lampson, B.W., Horning, J.J., London, R.L., Mitchell, J.G. and Popek, G.J. (1977). 'Report on the Programming Language Euclid'. *ACM Sigplan Notices*, **12**(2).

Fortran

There are textbooks on Fortran to suit all tastes. The following text adopts a structured approach.

Ellis, T.M.R. (1990). *Fortran 77 Programming: With an Introduction to the Fortran 90 Standard*. Addison-Wesley.

GPSS

O'Donovan, T.M. (1979). *GPSS Simulation Made Simple*. John Wiley & Sons.

Haskell

The following text gives an introduction to functional programming as well as describing the Haskell language.

Thompson, S. (1999). *Haskell: The Craft of Functional Programming* (Second Edition). Addison-Wesley.

Java

The official definition of Java is given in the text by Arnold and Gosling. A good introduction that concentrates on the GUI rather than OO aspects of the language is by Bell and Parr.

Arnold, K. and Gosling, J. (1998). *The Java Programming Language* (Second Edition). Addison-Wesley.

Bell, D. and Parr, M. (1999). *Java for Students* (Second Edition). Prentice-Hall.

JavaScript

Flanagan, D. (1998). *JavaScript: The Definitive Guide* (Third Edition). O'Reilly.

Lisp

The classic text is written by John McCarthy *et al*. Since then, many texts have been written. The book by Winston and Horn is oriented towards Common Lisp and the book by Steele gives a full definition of Common Lisp.

McCarthy, J., Abrahams, P.W., Edwards, D.J., Hart, T.P. and Levin, M.I. (1965). *LISP 1.5 Programmer's Manual*. MIT Press.

Steele, G.L. (1984). *Common Lisp: The Language*. Digital Press.

Winston, P.H. and Horn, B.K.P. (1988). *LISP* (Third Edition). Addison-Wesley.

ML

The definition of Standard ML is given by Milner *et al*. The book by Reade uses ML as the main language.

Reade, C. (1989). *Elements of Functional Programming*. Addison-Wesley.

Milner, R., Tofte, M., Harper, R. and MacQueen, D. (1997). *The Definition of Standard ML – Revised*. MIT Press.

Modula-2

The original text is by Wirth and, like most books on Modula-2, assumes prior knowledge of a language like Pascal. The book by Terry is suitable for a first course on programming.

Terry, P.D. (1987). *An Introduction to Programming with Modula-2*. Addison-Wesley.

Wirth, N. (1985). *Programming in Modula-2* (Third Edition). Springer-Verlag.

Pascal

The original book is by Jensen and Wirth, but many more readable books are available, such as the one by Dale and Weems. The third edition of Jensen and Wirth describes the language defined in the ISO Pascal Standard.

Dale, N. and Weems, C. (1987). *Pascal* (Second Edition). D.C. Heath.

Jensen, K. and Wirth, N. (1974). *Pascal User Manual and Report*. Springer-Verlag.

Jensen, K. and Wirth, N. (1985). *Pascal User Manual and Report* (Third Edition). Springer-Verlag.

Perl

The text by Wall (the creator of Perl), Christiansen and Schwartz gives a full definition of Perl while a more introductory text is by Schwartz and Christiansen.

Schwartz, R.L. and Christiansen, T. (1997). *Learning Perl* (Second Edition). O'Reilly.

Wall, L., Christiansen, T. and Schwartz, R.L. (1996). *Programming Perl* (Second Edition). O'Reilly.

PL/I

There are many textbooks available. Conway and Gries is worth noting as it contains a well known and useful subset called PL/C.

Conway, R. and Gries, D. (1979). *An Introduction to Programming – A Structured Approach Using PL/I and PL/C* (Third Edition). Winthrop.

Prolog

The first book available was by Clocksin and Mellish. The text by Bratko deals with its use in artificial intelligence.

Bratko, I. (1999). *Prolog Programming for Artificial Intelligence* (Third Edition). Addison-Wesley.

Clocksin, W.F. and Mellish, C.S. (1984). *Programming in Prolog* (Second Edition). Springer-Verlag.

RPG

Essick, E.L. (1981). *RPG II Programming*. SRA.

Scheme

There have been several revisions of the definition of Scheme. The book by Abelson on the teaching of programming using Scheme was very influential.

Abelson, H. and Sussman, G.J. (1985). *Structure and Interpretation of Computer Programs*. MIT Press.

Kelsey, R., Clinger, W. and Rees, J. (1998). 'Revised Report on the Algorithmic Language Scheme'. *ACM Sigplan*, **33**(9), 26–76.

Simula 67

The main text is as follows.

Birtwistle, G.M., Dahl, O-J., Myhrhaug, B. and Nygaard, K. (1975). *Simula begin*. Auerbach.

Smalltalk

Smalltalk is not just a language, but is a complete programming environment. The main text is given below.

Goldberg, A. (1989). *Smalltalk-80: The Language*. Addison-Wesley.

SNOBOL

The original designers have written the standard textbook.

Griswold, R.E., Poage, J.F. and Polonsky, I.P. (1971). *The SNOBOL 4 Programming Language*. Prentice-Hall.

Solutions to selected exercises

Chapter 3

3.9 Floating-point values are only held approximately and so the equality operator does not always give the expected result.

3.10 **type** Month **is** (January, February, March, April, May, June, July, August, September, October, November, December);

Operations: nextMonth, lastMonth, monthNumber

3.11 Pascal: Array index, case label, in a subrange, element of a set, value of a loop control variable. Java: Array index, switch label.

3.13 A local variable in a procedure or method is only allocated space during the execution of the procedure or method. If, using the & operator, the *address* of the local variable is assigned to a non-local variable or is returned from the procedure or method then we can have a reference to a variable that no longer has storage allocated to it, i.e. a dangling reference.

Chapter 4

4.2 In either of the expressions:

A **or** B where A is true
A **and** B where A is false

and B contains an expression that cannot be correctly evaluated or whose evaluation has a side-effect.

4.5 Ada leads to the more reliable programs as the programmer has to make a positive decision when writing a program about all possible cases. This allows some errors to be picked up at compile time, which in Pascal would lead to run-time errors.

4.7 The Pascal solution requires n and a half loops because, as Pascal does not have an **exit** statement, the statement to read a number has to appear twice.

```
sum := 0;
read(number);
while number >= 0 do
begin
    sum := sum + number;
    read(number)
end
```

Chapter 5

5.4 An implementation in Ada is:

```
function nextMonth(mo : Month) return Month is
begin
   if mo = December then
       return January;
   else
       return Month'succ(mo);
   end if;
end nextMonth;
function lastMonth(mo : Month) return Month is
begin
   if mo = January then
       return December;
   else
       return Month'pred(mo);
   end if;
end lastMonth;
function monthNumber(mo : Month) return Integer is
begin
    return Month'pos(mo) + 1;
end monthNumber;
```

The Pascal implementation is essentially the same. A Java implementation is given in the answer to question 5.12.

5.12 An Ada package is:

```ada
package months is
   type Month is (January, February, March, April,
      May, June, July, August, September, October,
      November, December);
   function nextMonth(mo : Month) return Month;
   function lastMonth(mo : Month) return Month;
   function monthNumber(mo : Month) return Integer;
end months;
package body months is
   --function definitions as in 5.4
end months;
```

A Java class is:

```java
public class Month {
   public static final Month
      January = new Month(1),
      February = new Month(2), March = new Month(3),
      April = new Month(4), May = new Month(5),
      June = new Month(6), July = new Month(7),
      August = new Month(8),
      September = new Month(9),
      October = new Month(10),
      November = new Month(11),
      December = new Month(12);
   private final int m;
   private static final Month[] conv = {null,
      January, February, March, April, May, June,
      July, August, September, October, November,
      December};

   private Month(int val) {
      m = val;
   } // constructor

   public Month nextMonth() {
      if (m == 12)
         return January;
      else
         return conv[m + 1];
   } // nextMonth

   public Month lastMonth() {
      if (m == 1)
         return December;
      else
```

```
                    return conv[m - 1];
            } // lastMonth

            public int monthNumber() {
                return m;
            } // monthNumber
        } // Month
```

As Java does not have enumeration types, twelve public constant values for Month have been defined. A Month value cannot be changed, but a reference to a Month can be given an initial value and then be given a new value as follows:

```
    Month m = Month.February;
    m = m.nextMonth();
```

Chapter 6

6.2 The result $j = 2$, $a[1] = 1$, $a[2] = 3$ is obtained except with call by name which gives $j = 2, a[1] = 2, a[2] = 1$ when the call is swap(j, $a[j]$) and the same result as the others when the call is swap($a[j]$, j).
    As long as the addresses of all the actual parameters are computed on subprogram exit before any of the actual parameters are updated, call by value-result (Algol W) gives the same answer as call by value-result. If this is not the case, it gives the same result as call by name.

6.4 It is a reference to an object that is passed by value.

Chapter 7

7.2 Assume BA, the base address, is where the first element of the array is stored and each element occupies s locations.

```
    Mapping function for x[i] = BA + s * (i - 2)
    Mapping function for a[i, j] = BA + s * (6 * (i - 1) + j)
```

Hence:

```
    x[7] is in BA + 5 * s
    a[3, 2] is in BA + 14 * s
```

7.8 A Java class is:

```java
public class Queue {
   private int maxSize;
   private int front, back, qSize;
   private double[] theQueue;

   public Queue(int size) {
      maxSize = size;
      theQueue = new double[maxSize];
      front = 0;
      back = -1;
      qSize = 0;
   } // constructor

   public boolean empty() {
      return qSize == 0;
   } // empty

   public boolean full() {
      return qSize == maxSize;
   } // full

   public double remove() throws QueueException {
      if (empty())
         throw new QueueException("Queue empty");
      else {
         double x = theQueue[front];
         if (front == maxSize - 1)
            front = 0;
         else
            front++;
         qSize--;
         return x;
      }
   } // remove

   public void add(double val)
      throws QueueException {
      if (full())
         throw new QueueException("Queue full");
      else {
         if (back == maxSize - 1)
            back = 0;
         else
            back++;
         theQueue[back] = val;
         qSize++;
```

```
                    }
                } // add
            } // Queue
```

It is assumed that the queue is represented by a circular list.

7.10   **procedure** polish(p : Ptr);
     begin
        if p <> **nil then**
        begin
           write(p↑.data);
           polish(p↑.left);
           polish(p↑.right)
        end
     end {polish};

7.12 CORRECT

Chapter 8

8.7 Student is a subclass of Person and we can use a reference to a subclass anywhere a reference to the superclass is expected. In the call pList[i].getInfo() we have dynamic binding and the version of getInfo that is called depends on the type of the object to which pList[i] is currently pointing. The call of pList[i].getRegNum() will result in a syntax error as the type of pList[i] is 'reference to Person' and that class does not have a getRegNum method.

Chapter 9

9.4   (ISMEMBER 24 '(17 24 59))
    => (COND ((NULL '(17 24 59)) NIL)
       ((EQ 24 (CAR '(17 24 59))) T)
       (T (ISMEMBER 24 (CDR '(17 24 59)))))
       => (COND (NIL NIL)
       ((EQ 24 (CAR '(17 24 59))) T)
       (T (ISMEMBER 24 (CDR '(17 24 59)))))
    => (COND ((EQ 24 (CAR '(17 24 59))) T)
       (T (ISMEMBER 24 (CDR '(17 24 59)))))
    => (COND ((EQ 24 17) T)
       (T (ISMEMBER 24 (CDR '(17 24 59)))))
    => (COND (NIL T)
       (T (ISMEMBER 24 (CDR '(17 24 59)))))
    => (COND (T (ISMEMBER 24 (CDR '(17 24 59)))))
    => (ISMEMBER 24 (CDR '(17 24 59)))

```
=> (ISMEMBER 24 '(24 59))
=> (COND ((NULL '(24 59)) NIL)
   ((EQ 24 (CAR '(24 59))) T)
   (T (ISMEMBER 24 (CDR '(24 59)))))
=> (COND ((EQ 24 (CAR '(24 59))) T)
   (T (ISMEMBER 24 (CDR '(24 59)))))
=> (COND (T T)
   (T (ISMEMBER 24 (CDR '(24 59)))))
=> T
```

```
IsMember(24, [17, 24, 59])
=> if 24 = 17 then true
   else IsMember(24, [24, 59])
=> if false then true
   else IsMember(24, [24, 59])
=> IsMember(24, [24, 59])
=> if 24 = 24 then true
   else IsMember(24, [59])
=> if true then true
   else IsMember(24, [59])
=> true
```

9.9 (a)   **fun** Sum(nil) = 0
      | Sum(first :: rest) = first + Sum(rest);

Its functionality is:

    val Sum = fn : (int list) → int

(b)   **fun** Length(nil) = 0
      | Length(first :: rest) = 1 + Length(rest);

Its functionality is:

    val Length = fn : ('a list) → int

(c)   **fun** RemoveNeg(nil) = nil
      | RemoveNeg(first :: rest) =
        if first < 0 **then** RemoveNeg(rest)
          else first :: RemoveNeg(rest);

Its functionality is:

    val RemoveNeg = fn : (int list) → (int list)

9.10   **fun** filter f nil = nil
      | filter f (first :: rest) =
        if f first **then** first :: filter f rest
        else filter f rest;

Its functionality is:

```
val filter = fn : ('a -> bool) ->
    (('a list) -> ('a list))
```

9.13   ```
        fun generate10(m) =
            if m <= 10 then m :: generate10(m + 1)
            else nil;
        ```

Reduction without lazy evaluation:

```
lowsquares(generate10 1)
=> lowsquares(1 :: generate10(2))
=> lowsquares(1 :: 2 :: generate10(3))
...
=> lowsquares(1 :: 2 :: 3 :: 4 :: 5 :: 6 :: 7 :: 8
    :: 9 :: 10 :: nil)
=> 1 * 1 :: lowsquares(2 :: 3 :: 4 :: 5 :: 6 :: 7
    :: 8 :: 9 :: 10 :: nil)
=> 1 :: 2 * 2 :: lowsquares(3 :: 4 :: 5 :: 6 :: 7
    :: 8 :: 9 :: 10 :: nil)
...
=> 1 :: 4 :: 9 :: 16 :: 25 :: lowsquares(6 :: 7 ::
    8 :: 9 :: 10 :: nil)
=> 1 :: 4 :: 9 :: 16 :: 25 :: nil
```

Reduction with lazy evaluation:

```
lowsquares(generate10 1)
=> lowsquares(1 :: generate10(2))
=> 1 * 1 :: lowsquares(generate10(2))
=> 1 :: lowsquares(2 :: generate10(3))
=> 1 :: 2 * 2 :: lowsquares(generate10(3))
=> 1 :: 4 :: lowsquares(3 :: generate10(4))
=> 1 :: 4 :: 3 * 3 :: lowsquares(generate10(4))
=> 1 :: 4 :: 9 ::
    lowsquares(4 :: generate10(5))
=> 1 :: 4 :: 9 :: 4 * 4 ::
    lowsquares(generate10(5))
=> 1 :: 4 :: 9 :: 16 ::
    lowsquares(5 :: generate10(6))
=> 1 :: 4 :: 9 :: 16 :: 5 * 5 ::
    lowsquares(generate10(6))
=> 1 :: 4 :: 9 :: 16 :: 25 ::
    lowsquares(6 :: generate10(7))
=> 1 :: 4 :: 9 :: 16 :: 25 :: nil
```
```

Chapter 10

10.2 The question:

```
?- goodmatch(A, B).
```

requires the subgoals:

```
loves(A, B), loves (B, A)
```

to be satisfied. The substitutions **A** ← **john** and **B** ← **jane** allow the first subgoal to be matched with the first fact, but the second subgoal then fails. The system backtracks to the first subgoal and tries **A** ← **bill** and **B** ← **jane** so that the second fact is matched. The second subgoal again fails. The system again backtracks and tries **A** ← **james** and **B** ← **jane** which satisfies both subgoals.

10.3
```
within(X, Y) :- district(X, Y).
within(X, Y) :- region(X, Y).
...
within(X, Y) :- district(Z, Y), region(X, Z).
within(X, Y) :- region(Z, Y), country(X, Z).
...
within(X, Y) :- district(A, Y), region(B, A),
country(C, B), continent(X, C).
```

Better to define:

```
inside(X, Y) :- district(X, Y).
inside(X, Y) :- region(X, Y).
inside(X, Y) :- country(X, Y).
inside(X, Y) :- continent(X, Y).
```

and then to define:

```
within(X, Y) :- inside(X, Y).
within(X, Y) :- inside(X, Z), within(Z, Y).
```

Chapter 11

11.4(b) The **try/catch** block in method give is no longer required. The call of notify in method take can also be removed.

11.9   Assuming the type declaration:

```
type Ready_State is (off, snooze);
```

the two task bodies are:

```
task body Person is
   state : Ready_State;
begin
   loop
      accept alarm_call(response : out
                           Ready_State) do
         ... determine value for state ...
         response := state;
      end alarm_call;
      exit when state = off;
      ... go back to sleep ...
   end loop;
   ... get up ...
end Person;
task body Alarm is
   continue : Ready_State;
begin
   loop
      Person.alarm_call(continue);
      exit when continue = off;
      delay 2.0;
   end loop;
end Alarm;
```

Chapter 12

12.1(a) `<digit> ::= 0 | 1 | 2 | 3 | 4 | 5 | 6 | 7 | 8 | 9`
`<digitsequence> ::= <digit>`
`  | <digit> <digitsequence>`

12.1(b) `<realnumber> ::= <digitsequence>.<digitsequence>`

12.2 `<exp>`
`<exp> + <term>`
`<term> + <term>`
`<term> * <factor> + <term>`
`<factor> * <factor> + <term>`
`<identifier> * <factor> + <term>`
`a * <factor> + <term>`
`a * <identifier> + <term>`
`a * b + <term>`
`a * b + <factor>`
`a * b + <identifier>`

```
a * b + c
```

12.5 The sentences are A AB AC AD ABB ABC ABD ACB ACC ACD. The equivalent BNF grammar is:

```
<sequence> ::= A | A <bcdpart>
<bcdpart> ::= <borc> | <borc> <bcdpart> | D
<borc> ::= B | C
```

12.7
```
<sentence>
a <first>
a b <first>
a b <third> g
a b a g

<sentence>
<second> g
<third> <second> g
a <second> g
a <third> b g
a a b g
```

12.8
```
<sentence>
p <char> <continue>
p a <continue>
p a , <char> <continue>
p a , b <continue>
p a , b , <char> <continue>
p a , b , a <continue>
p a , b , a ;
```

The derivation was straightforward because, at each stage, the right part to be used could be determined by scanning one symbol ahead.

Index